Mister Pulitzer and the Spider

THE HISTORY OF COMMUNICATION

Robert W. McChesney and John C. Nerone, editors

A list of books in the series appears at the end of this book.

to press with a grant, fairplay
Figure Foundation

Mister Pulitzer and the Spider

Modern News from Realism to the Digital

KEVIN G. BARNHURST

UNIVERSITY OF ILLINOIS PRESS

Urbana, Chicago, and Springfield

The quote from Ray Bradbury's *Fahrenheit 451* on page 1 is reprinted by
permission of Don Congdon Associates, Inc. © 1953, renewed 1981
by Ray Bradbury.

Library of Congress Control Number: 2016937571
ISBN 978-0-252-04018-4 (hardcover)
ISBN 978-0-252-09840-6 (e-book)

For Alina and a future of good news

Contents

Preface

A current commonplace is that the world has changed in the digital era, but how to understand what happened? To answer, technologists and scientists focus on the technical, sociologists on the cultural, political scientists on government, parties, and voters, and communication experts on media and interpersonal channels, while historians and philosophers wait for the dust to settle. Journalists have taken the earliest and riskiest look at the changes, reassessing the spider-web-like digital networks even as colleagues lost jobs in the roiling shifts underway. In news coverage the keyword *media* entered flux; "the media" became "legacy media," and personal interactions mutated to add "social media." New terms place communication at the center of whirling change, with news in its eye, but not because of the usual explanations. New technologies alone do not account for the move of "scavengers from the press," in the words of sociologist Max Weber more than a century ago, into "the salons of the powerful on this earth."[1] Neither economic competition nor rivalry among news outlets can fully explain the move, nor can the occupational ambitions of news practitioners.

The bold claim here is that texts as conveyors of ideas produced the modern world of the twentieth century. First, ideas in the end of the nineteenth century and beginning of the next formed "the journalist" through two strains of modernism. Realism of the nineteenth century and American modernism of the twentieth century found full expression in news of a particular kind. "News" settled into cultural imagination and remained fairly stable as a way to see the world, even though the content, technologies, practices, and cultural conditions continued changing. But beliefs about what news *is* began to contradict what news *became*, so that by century's end practitioners misrecognized what they were producing and audiences grew dissatisfied with what they were receiving. News occupations, audiences, and businesses finally reached crisis in the new century, despite a concerted industry effort to adapt. The crisis mystified observers and policymakers who, unaware of the internal contradictions, focused on competition from the web.

Of course "the world" has not changed everywhere or in concert, but even areas largely disconnected from the outside have altered some ways of living. Through new technologies, "communication" has morphed into activities unthinkable a few decades ago. In parts of Africa, mobile phones now operate as a local scrip used in small exchanges, usurping national currency and credit.[2] One might see the big picture through many such small instances, a massive task to encompass the deep and uneven alterations across human societies. Or one might instead look at the always-peculiar USA, where widespread changes have emerged and seem to concentrate without the oversight or control attempts found in places like China or the European Union.

To understand digital transformations, the United States provides a key setting, and news is a central case. Societies have viewed their communication systems through the lens of news at least since the eighteenth century, when several writers about the British Parliament called the gallery of reporters the "fourth estate."[3] Understanding recent changes requires going back to the great social transformation underway by the 1880s, when Mister Pulitzer began to imagine modern news, one bookend here. The other bookend is the twenty-first-century web of networked communication, where "man bites dog" sits equally alongside "dog bites man," opening new possibilities while upending modern news.[4] But historians will find the history here a mere sketch. Other areas of scholarship receive their similar share of abuse. Political scientists, sociologists, and economists will want more focus on the data, technology scholars more on technics, especially recent social media, and cultural studies theorists more critique.

My project proposes that from a baseline in long-term content analysis, one can read out the sociological conditions of the journalist occupation and explore cultural studies of the context. But the main work to understand recent change is historical and philosophical. History can sketch out how surrounding groups view the content of news media and explore competing ways to explain contradictions between what news contains and what practitioners and audiences believe about and expect from it. Philosophy can dissect how modern news sets up, reproduces, and changes the terms and conditions of knowledge. The main themes for understanding the changes—nineteenth-century realism and twentieth-century modernism—come from the arts and humanities, with their interest in peculiar cases that illuminate the general, and so require patience from scientists. And the main insights, with due apologies, come from a duffer's bag of philosophy.

Here the parts on "who," "what," and "where" present a kind of ontology, the persons, places, and events that modern communication creates and sustains. One example is the "public," which philosopher John Dewey identified as the product of interactive communication (not of earlier kinds of public opinion or later polling techniques). The initial parts here examine aspects of knowledge such as how best to containerize information, the status of the persons involved, the type of occurrences deserving attention, and the locations worth including. Two further parts elaborate a rough-and-ready epistemology. A part on "when" examines the periods appropriate for knowledge, outlining some aspects from the philosophy of time. And a part on "why" explores the level and aims of explanation on offer, summarizing how modern communication makes knowledge from the raw materials of occurrences.

For a shortcut through the text, review the logic of the argument outlined in the table of contents and read the introductory chapter before jumping to the conclusion. Specialists might concentrate on one part, such as historians on the "when." Each part moves more or less in chronology from print to broadcast and then digital news, and so another path could lead through each part's chapter on a particular medium. The digital chapter ends each part with a discussion of the main philosophical viewpoints that help make sense of recent transformations, an avenue through the book for anyone interested mainly in theory and ideas.

News turns out to be a knowledge system, its content expressing practitioner ideas about what is knowable and its audiences interacting in the production of a particular kind of knowledge in culture. Viewed through the amalgam of these ideas, the journalist, which began as an occupation, appears to have moved into creating knowledge over the past century, producing the perspective on knowledge called journal*ism*. During the American century known for specialist knowledge, journalism has made one of the most central if tacit claims of producing general knowledge.

But its practitioners will no doubt dislike the idea. Research on news is about as useful to journalists "as ornithology is to birds," in the words usually attributed to physicist Richard Feynman.[5] Academics have little to offer the practitioner of digital or legacy news. One I interviewed objected to my studying without ever having worked in news. I may not be a musician, goes the old saw, but I play the radio, and I have tried to listen, watch, and read with empathy. Mine is the perspective of an audience member, but one equipped with data. After inspecting the graphs of the results, another practitioner I interviewed dismissed them as "just statistics." News insiders are smart to resist mere data, especially charts that give only a quick picture of the overall trends. For further detail on the methods and data behind the illustrations, the original peer-reviewed studies are available online.

Brief versions of the main parts of the book have appeared elsewhere: part 1 as "When Faster Takes Longer: Length, Authority, and the Fate of U.S. News," in *Leonardo Almanac*; part 2 as "Ideology and the Changing Representations of Persons in U.S. Journalism," in *Form and Style in Journalism*; and part 3 as "The Problem of Realist Events in American Journalism," in *Media and Communication*. Part 4 is forthcoming as "The Problem of Modern Locations in U.S. News," in *Journal of Media and Cultural Politics*. Part 5 appeared as "The Problem of Modern Time in American Journalism," in *KronoScope*; and part 6 as "The Interpretive Turn in News," in *Journalism and Technological Change*. A longer version of chapter 20 appeared as "Paradoxes in News Epistemology" in *Media, Culture, and Society*.[6]

In a project that lasted three decades, reading more than a hundred years of news biased me toward storytelling over other kinds of information. Recent news stories can be deadly dull to read or hear, despite the splashy packaging. Every assistant involved in the coding complained of boredom, even those enjoying the luxury of print or audio editions. The complexity of recent reports makes them difficult to recount. Turning to the older content, coders dreaded the prospect of scrolling through transcripts or microfilm. But the stories were riveting. Coders retold favorites and made copies to pass around. Consider one about an 1894 fire in Milwaukee in which nine firefighters died:

> It was a few minutes after 5 and the firemen were pouring great streams of water on the burning roof and the water was beginning to trickle through into the theater below, when the entire roof over the theater part of the building suddenly began to sink and in an instant dropped to the floor, fifty feet below. The ill-fated firemen had not a moment's time to think of the possibilities of escape. A cry of horror went up from the firemen who saw the awful catastrophe. The people from the hotel, who had left their rooms, knew nothing of the frightful tragedy that was taking place in the theater. The crowd of onlookers who saw it knew nothing of the disaster until the firemen who had escaped with blanched faces ran to the street and tremulously told of the sad fate which had befallen their brave brothers, who were buried beneath the burning girders, roof, and floors in the theater.[7]

Politicians and civic leaders no doubt talked about Chicago's fire problem, and local history buffs might have known its background, but readers in 1894 learned none of that. Instead the story tumbles out without a pause. Reading passages like this, we researchers shook our heads in disbelief—could the story be true? Modern journalism would call the story poorly attributed, the details fabricated, and the context lacking. Reporters today use slices of life to introduce their longer reports, vignettes that rarely stand alone. Small stories like the one about boys hiking together, which a reporter describes in an interview here, can leave the reader to ponder timeless themes. They settle on the mind and lead to an understanding of others. But news has become something else, bigger stories that convey an abstract, predictable meaning. Simple stories demand active listening, but news, supposedly all about stories, has turned away. "The art of storytelling is coming to an end," wrote the philosopher and cultural critic Walter Benjamin in the 1930s. "It is as if something that seemed inalienable to us, the securest among our possessions, were taken from us: the ability to exchange experiences."[8]

My preference for stories aligns with older, realist news. But that era of storytelling gave U.S. Americans a sad parade of stereotypes, bad for women and former slaves, and unhealthy even for the advantaged few.[9] My hope for stories told fairly and with care may be just the pipedream of an audience member. For audiences the story presents a concrete way of thinking that has value in everyday life. Hearing of my project, a colleague in Italy shared an apocryphal story: In an encounter with a famous journalist, a pedantic critic said, "Please excuse me, but the phrase 'an aching void' does not seem very apt." "Why?" asked the reporter. "Because an empty thing cannot be painful," replied the critic. "Oh, that depends," said the journalist. "You never had a headache, did you?" The story uses down-to-earth language, but the joke is a complex play of categories (the critic's head as one of the empty things, the critic as one of the reporter's headaches). Modern news uses concrete images to present abstract patterns that have more value for insider one-upmanship or policy debates than for everyday life.

Being a member of the audience helped me spot the interpretive news trend in the 1980s, an idea I first presented as a fellow at the Columbia University Media Studies Center. But my essay in a literary journal missed researchers' attention.[10] After I shared my observations at Columbia, political scientist Diana Mutz mentioned the trend in a convention talk in 1991. It generated so much argument and questioning that she returned to our shared office to ask, "Where's the data?" She suggested we test my hunch together. Our article became a cause célèbre when the *Journal of Communication* accepted it but then delayed publication over objections to its first line, "Shit happens, but that is not necessarily news."[11] People considered two assistant professors crazy to insist that Oxford University Press publish the phrase, but it fit our argument and the earthy stuff of news.

That study grew only slowly into a larger project. The list of colleagues and students who helped out grew from study to study and appears in each one. I thank them all. Communication historian John Nerone has been an inspiring figure whose insights weave throughout my and others' work. I owe him a debt of gratitude and friendship. Articles with other colleagues also helped me understand the "long news" hypothesis, its forms in different media, its misapprehension among those working in news, and its part in the transforming the past century. A 2001

Shorenstein fellowship at Harvard supported the first studies of the trend online. A 2009 sabbatical from the University of Illinois at Chicago opened perspectives from abroad, including feedback from hosts at the universities of Copenhagen and Tampere, Finland, and questions from colleagues in France, Holland, Italy, Norway, and Switzerland after my talks.

A 2015 study leave from the University of Leeds supported manuscript completion, and half of that time, spent at the University of Munich, helped me reconceive the book in light of detailed and thoughtful feedback that publishers solicited from eight anonymous reviewers. At the University of Illinois Press, acquiring editor Danny Nasset gave steady support. Series editor John Nerone read the entire manuscript. At Leeds, Stephen Coleman did the same, and so did Jay Blumler. I appreciate their suggestions, which led to big changes. Expert copyediting, design, and production at the press added further improvements.

But I could not address all the criticisms. Instead of amassing more data, I supplemented the widely spaced measurements by looking at crucial historical periods, especially at the beginning of Mister Pulitzer's modern dream that news can be enlightening instead of debasing or a thing to resist, and at the ending with modern news ensnared in a digital web, its troubled state providing insight into the current century. For more periods and countries, other scholars have begun testing the interpretive trends.[12] Practitioners objected that the argument hits when the journalism occupation is down, eroding its ability to supply public information. The complaint first came in 2001, when an acquisitions editor objected that the long-news hypothesis was "too far out" and inimical to then-embattled National Public Radio (NPR). While working in a journalism department, I thought students might benefit more from outsider questions than from the settled answers that industry insiders supplied, a possibility that seems firmer today. Doubt about what journalists do is good for their product: news.

A final note regards the Five Ws, which title the parts and are a tribute to the realism and enthusiasm for broad learning of the late nineteenth century. The Chautauqua movement and Sunday-school teaching of practical wisdom helped shape the emerging occupation of the journalist. The Five Ws drew from classical rhetoric, especially Aristotle's Four Causes, and retain a faint echo of his attention to oratory as an act of public information and persuasion. As a heuristic device, the Five Ws took more elaborated form in Burke's five keys of dramatism, and they tackle fundamental philosophical questions including ontology, epistemology, and ethics. The status of persons and places, the existence of things, the dimension of time, and possibility of explanation are fundamental questions with a history of fruitful discovery in the social sciences.[13]

Rudyard Kipling memorialized the Five Ws in "The Elephant's Child," from *Just So Stories*, calling them "honest serving-men / (They taught me all I knew)." The young Kipling had worked as a journalist in India, and his story is an allegory for news. In the long ago before elephants got their trunks, an Elephant's Child full of curiosity begins asking too many questions. Ostrich, Giraffe, Hippopotamus, and Baboon each spanks him for his impertinence. When he dares to ask aloud what the Crocodile eats for dinner, everyone gasps and then spanks him "for a long time." Instead of sating his curiosity, their reaction sends him on a journey to find answers. The inevitable happens when he meets the Crocodile and survives only with the help of the Bi-Colored-Python-Rock-Snake, who coils around the elephant's legs as an anchor to the shore. Afterward the Elephant's Child sits dejected on the bank, waiting for his nose to shrink back, and the snake helps him adjust by pointing out all the "'vantages" of a long trunk. Returning across Africa, the elephant uses his trunk to whisk flies, pick fruit, and trumpet in song, arriving rambunctious: "Then that bad Elephant's Child spanked all his dear families for a long time. . . ." The other elephants make a pilgrimage "to borrow new noses from the Crocodile."[14]

News springs from the same "'satiable curiosity," the shortened form suggesting fulfillment as well as deferred satisfaction. The accepted response to questioning is rebuke, because breaking with taboo is inherent in reporting news. The hero's companion, a loquacious and dangerous snake, saves the day and then signals a way back home by suggesting the broader view central to modernism. A growing nose alludes to Pinocchio, born twenty years earlier to tell stories with a complex relation to truth. But the journey yields a peculiar tool useful for handling everyday demands, for issuing calls heard far and wide, and for subduing troublemakers. All those tropes and the families' continuing astonishment track with the course of two modern literary achievements, the novel and the news.

Kipling was a product of imperialism and its values, not a figure easy to admire, but the Bi-Colored-Python-Rock-Snake is the model for this troublesome academic companion to news practitioners and their publics as we journey into a life with mobile social media. Kipling's story ends with everyone else getting that same tool the Elephant's Child first acquired, a condition that foreshadows the practice of news today, which has spread across and so illuminates the current state of technological society.

Stoddard, New Hampshire, USA
November 2015

PART 1

News Pursued Modernism from Machine to Digital Times

Picture it. Nineteenth-century man with his horses, dogs, carts,
slow motion. Then in the twentieth century, speed up your camera.
Books cut shorter. Condensations. Digests, Tabloids. . . .

Speed up the film. . . . *Click, Pic, Look, Eye, Now, Flick, Here,
There, Swift, Pace, Up, Down, In, Out, Why, How, Who, What,
Where, Eh? Uh! Bang! Smack! Wallop, Bing, Bong, Boom!*
Digest-digests, digest-digest-digests. Politics? One column,
two sentences, a headline. Then, in mid-air, all vanishes! Whirl
man's mind around about so fast under the pumping hands
of publishers, exploiters, broadcasters that the centrifuge
flings off all unnecessary, time-wasting thought!

—Ray Bradbury, *Fahrenheit 451* (1953)

CHAPTER 1

Industrial News Became Modern

The nineteenth century began with the slow-motion technologies Ray Bradbury lists in *Fahrenheit 451*, but by 1900 the industrial era had reached its height, and concepts of time, place, and society had transformed. Avant-garde artists adopted many-sided views of persons, natural and social scientists saw machine-like progress in events, and trains and steamers were making remote places seem like neighbors. Philosophers found a multitude of perspectives on time, and the closing of the American frontier and the success of worldwide exploration made it seem possible to explain everything. An older way of crafting stable personages, places, and performances gave way to a new factory metaphor for imagining the changing social and physical world.[1]

U.S. news is largely a product of that era of change, when a new journalism emerged to embrace a machine understanding of the world. It adopted the latest techniques and shared a kind of realism with science and the arts of the time, marking the shift to the industrial news era. Newspapers pioneered the sensational, some as a way to activate reform, preparing the ground for progressive news of the twentieth century. The rhythm of machine printing pumped out a flow of multiple editions that reached the street with breaking stories about real occurrences. News offered a cornucopia of tales hawked in the streets for avid buyers, and those stories went "viral" through the government-supported system of press exchanges and story reprints around the country.[2]

So many stories manufactured like widgets required a new occupation, the journalist—part collector of flotsam from the flow of urban life and part worldly naturalist sorting actions and their actors into categories and types.[3] The occupation fused mental work and mechanical labor, aligned with the ideas of individual minds from newly invented psychology as well as with the machine age. Occurrences stamped into news stories drew from all kinds of people located at street addresses, but the high-speed production involved a rough kind of brainwork that divided the miscellany of life into departments, such as another invention: pages for sports, society, radio, and the like. In an explosion of innovation, the press created entertainments like comics and crosswords but at the same time imagined a reader also capable of interpreting the contents of an entire daily edition. U.S. news took on a particular character, famous for being brief but aimed at telling the truth. The amalgam of industrial facts with individual intelligence promised to inform a wider public and foster progress.

Modern news was a masterful creation of its era, bridging between ideas and practical inventions. Two examples can illustrate its global and virtual ambitions. Timely updates from the telegraph connected humanity in a global network, and breathless stories from the wire added a kind of commotion to news pages, which expressed urban jostling and the hubbub of mass production. The factory metaphor could connect places through systems like mass transit and could organize the processing of people, such as the "masses yearning to breathe free," from the sonnet gracing the Statue of Liberty. Immersive experiences also arose, ranging from tourism of world expositions and big-game hunting to patronizing nearby popular destinations like amusement parks and movie houses. The invention of grand department stores promised a kind of virtual reality, an experience of great wealth made available in print by perusing display advertisements. The physical technology of cast-iron construction allowed emporiums like the Marble Palace in New York, Wanamaker's in Philadelphia, or Marshall Field's in Chicago to display goods behind enormous plate-glass windows. The invention of window-shopping had its parallel in newspaper ads, and the vast array of daily news matched the abundance available in stores for consumers.[4]

By the first decade of the twentieth century, the press had added to its physical roots in American realism of the nineteenth century by deepening its intellectual dimension, absorbed from the emerging movement called American modernism. Technical change also anticipated the shift. The electric dynamo fired the imagination of Henry Adams and others in the era. Street lighting and electrified transportation seemed to ease the process of urbanization. Industrialization moved into electric technologies that let industry reimagine factories from scratch. At newspapers the telephone was giving reporters faster access to new content, and rotogravure images made Sunday supplements startling. But electrified life held hidden complexities that required new ideas to sustain the hope for progress. One was corporate organization for the growing mass media, designed top-down to supply authoritative content to tame the modern world. News became a product best served fresh for the widest consumption, spreading even wider as consumers adapted to the idea of technologies from radio sets to airplanes.[5]

The new kind of news disseminated as an icon in popular culture. Earlier newspaper covers were full with small ads, so that readers started in the center pages and read the newest news from the inside moving out, and advertising was a kind of wrapper left for reading last. The modern paper distilled its form in something new, called the front page, which used the cover to announce events in priority, top to bottom, mapping the social, political, and economic landscape. *The Front Page* became the title of a play that made news flesh in the idealistic young reporter, the acerbic editor, the corrupt cop or politician, the innocent bystander, and a cast of other stereotypes. That iconic picture of news permeated media culture of the twentieth century, illustrated in comic books, movies, and television series, and had its real-world parallels. From progressive muckrakers to the Watergate investigators, the popular and romantic picture of the journalist settled into the public and practitioner mind.[6]

The content of modern news was, well, newsy. The stories were short and punchy, a quality that influenced all the other aspects of the content. Persons were the main attraction, including ordinary and working folk as well as the rich and powerful. Experts and commentators were rare, organized groups hardly appeared, and politicians stuck mostly to politics. What happened to persons mattered most, and a multitude of items told their stories. Names alone could identify them, but they lived at particular street addresses, often at or near the scene of the action. The main geography was local, but events from afar lent urgent and exotic appeal. The *now* of news stories was current, the latest update available at press time, mere hours before an edition hit the streets. There was little time for or patience with a history lesson or future prediction, except in the newfangled horoscope. But all the small bits of news added up to more than the sum of the parts, so that a whole edition in a succession of days made sense of the city, the nation, and the globe. The news relied on the distributed native intelligence of its readers.[7]

Fast-forward a hundred years, half a century after Bradbury imagined the future. By the year 2000, the spider's web of digital connectivity was reaching its span, and concepts of time, space, and society had again entered flux. Persons adapted to an unstable system of privatized and mobile life, and audiences fragmented into malleable "users" able to disrupt politics and business as "flash" or "smart" mobs. Artists made works that viewers could change or carry away, undoing the art object. Place warped into digital space, collapsing positions into video chat windows containing both there and here. Quarks and strange or charmed matter challenged Newtonian notions of time, and multitasking melded private into public moments and play into work, in a digital web that imposed tighter temporal coordination.

Chaos and the butterfly effect in mathematics undermined the concept of linear change or progress, as what philosophers had called "irrealism" overturned older ways of explaining daily life.[8]

Observers considered the changes a paradigm shift on the magnitude of what had occurred a century before. It caused upheavals throughout society. Flextime and telecommuting arose, rearranging work patterns, and e-commerce caught and ate up brick-and-mortar operations. Bookselling and reading went digital, remaking the circulation of ideas. On social media, politicians arose outside party structures and business kept clients under closer surveillance. Once-stable purposes for large industrial sectors fell into doubt. The spider of digital media sent images on paper into retreat, leaving printing in disarray. Paper manufacturing went into a decades-long decline, buffeted by "winds of global, social economic and political change" that pushed beyond "the mass production paradigm to another, as yet uncertain, one."[9]

How did it look for news? At first the prosperous media businesses embraced change, fielding centers and projects for "mediamorphosis." Captains of industry pointed to the failure of U.S. railways to recognize they were in the transportation business, and news executives proclaimed they were in the information—not the news—business. But digital competition contributed to a growing crisis. Craigslist absorbed swaths of classified advertising, once a mainstay of newspaper profitability. Display advertising and commercials moved online, where the prices that advertisers would pay per viewer were closer to the levels of junk-mail flyers. Critics called the old outlets "mediasaurus" and predicted the quick demise of "legacy media." Print and broadcast news organizations pushed forward online in a mix of aggressive competition and passive reservation as their incomes fluctuated and declined.[10]

News headlines have always moved through other channels, for free on bulletin boards of the early 1900s or later on lighted ticker displays outside press offices, systems under press control and pushing viewers to the newspaper or newscast. There the consumer paid little but lent more eyeballs to the circulation or ratings for news, sold in turn to advertisers. Page views and clicks on free strands of web platforms escaped press control, and so news websites added the logos and links for social media, making matters worse. Later, in the first decade of the twenty-first century, business models that had placed news among the most profitable of industries broke down, and investors panicked, driving down the market value of media properties. Some news operations closed their doors and others cut back, leaving thousands of workers out of a job. Once-comfortable outlets had to streamline, including the *New York Times*. After the venerable *Times-Picayune* of New Orleans reduced its paper edition from seven to three days a week in 2012, its online, tablet, and mobile editions generated "softer, less-well-sourced, poorer quality news."

The solution, news leaders proposed, was a return to quality content to attract followers.[11]

The mass media system knew something about what audiences did with news but professed to shield the news side of its operations from circulation and ratings data that the business side held. Eye-tracking research in the 1990s, which showed readers are active and selective in skimming information, got pigeonholed as merely about design. Online, reporters and editors could see for themselves the traffic for their stories, and the measurable clicks revealed how little attention audiences paid to most news content. Instead of intelligent agents in search of facts to sustain political engagement, citizens seemed to require prodding to eat the bitter spinach of public information from legacy media. Editors who had long known of the problem could no longer ignore it when reporters could see audience activity online.[12]

Searching to explain the crisis, observers noticed that news was no longer newsy. For one thing, it seemed much longer, and the observations turned out to be measurable.[13] From the 1880s through the 1990s, newspaper stories did grow longer. The change occurred in small city papers as well as regional and national outlets across the country. The items in the late nineteenth century were so short that more than fifty would fit on the typical front page. By the second half of the twentieth century, only a handful would fit, and they had to jump onto inside pages. After television began broadcasting the first report of events, stories on national network news grew longer through the quarter century beginning in 1968. Commercial competition was increasing and visual images becoming more prominent in print and TV, but the same trends occurred without commercials or visuals on National Public Radio (NPR) from the 1980s to the early years of the 2000s. The trend ran deep, affecting the coverage of persons ranging from U.S. presidents, the ultimate insiders, to outsider groups such as gays and lesbians. And although the internet brought expectations for change, online news reversed course only briefly before returning to the growth in length, even as news organizations struggled financially. Research confirmed the surprising discovery that news stories grew longer from the 1880s to the 2010s.

What occupied the added words in longer stories? Across the coverage of natural, human, and social topics, the content and its visual presentation changed how news presented people, events, and places (the "who," "what," and "where"). The treatment of time ("when") and processes and explanations offered ("how" and "why") changed even more dramatically.[14] The impact of longer news on content was also counterintuitive. Instead of "human interest" growing, ordinary and working-class people disappeared from news, replaced by groups, officials, and experts. Stories had fewer—not more—events. Although audiences presumably preferred local stories, locations moved away from the street address, as references to faraway places expanded. Communications speeded up, but the time dimension of news added to the *now* by expanding to the past, the future, and trends over time. And news no longer aimed to report events-as-they-happened for the public to process. It explained larger problems or tried to make sense of issues, aiming to interpret events.

What can explain so dramatic a change? In trade publications going back to the nineteenth century, industry insiders point to technology as a force.[15] They also report experiencing greater rivalry with others producing news, and industry managers had to adjust to markets crowding with news and entertainment outlets. In interviews, practitioners with experience going back to the 1950s described adjusting their routines through waves of change. The competition from insider rivalry and newer technology and for greater profitability deserves attention. But a strange contradiction remains: most industry sources have tended to see market, technical, and practical influences having little impact on the core substance of quality mainstream news.

The difference between what news practitioners say and what the research shows about news content suggests another explanation. When social actors overlook documented results or hold counterfactual views about their activities, ideological processes may be at work. Under one definition, ideology is any set of beliefs that obscures the power relations of social groups, which well-meaning elites may unwittingly encourage with the effect that other groups stay under elite domination. A kind of false consciousness leads the poor and disenfranchised, for instance, to participate in keeping themselves under hegemonic control. But in other cases, ideology may serve particular sectors by expanding the power of some occupations. Beliefs in the stability of news could be part of a social process that serves unrecognized occupational ambitions. That ideological dimension of news practice also matters and deserves attention.[16]

But practitioners are not alone in believing that U.S. news is a relatively stable and easily identifiable thing, and so the ideological explanation may go beyond occupations. *Reification* is the way cultures turn abstractions into social facts, with consequences for concrete lived experience.[17] Studies show that audiences expect old media to remain as they always were, and the reliable newsboy hawking in the street, paper whopping on the front stoop, and voices of newscasters droning in the background seem like certainties. The wide acceptance of the idea of short, people-filled, event-centered, and local U.S. news suggests that the abstraction "news" solidified in the culture. Continual critiques about the lack of the background that publics need and the insufficient explanations in news do the same. Other studies show that ordinary U.S. Americans think of news in much the same way and see similar rewards and challenges as do career news practitioners. The misrecognition of what news has become seems to extend widely.[18]

Broader historical work can look at the characteristics of cultural products to discover what preceded them, when they emerged and evolved, and how the ideas surrounding them changed. Insider and critical explanations require some exploring, but the main subject here is a current in U.S. culture when news emerged: modernism. News is a record of and a case study in the history of the modern idea, how it expanded and then seemed to falter. News makes an ideal case because the relation of news to modernism seems inadvertent, remaining unobserved in much of news practice and the industry. Unlike art or literature, where modernism is central, news is an emblem if low culture, cousin to word of mouth and the object of ridicule. Its unlikely success in the past century is a rags-to-riches story. That it seems to have fallen victim to the spider's web of digital times can illuminate the paradigm shift underway and the fate of the modern today.

What is modernism? Its ideas have a long history but tend to focus on the possibility of human progress, especially through technical invention, extension, and adaptation, including new ways of building an ordered society.[19] Some philosophers say that modernism first emerged in Greece, with the invention of concepts to replace older habits and fantasies about the world. Instead of basing writing on pictograms to show objects, for instance, the Greeks took up a Phoenician invention, letters abstracted to stand for sounds of speech. Greek ideas ranged from cartography to map the inhabited world and democracy to organize it and extended to philosophy to make thought systematic and several of the sciences to make it effective in practice. Human progress may have inspired later works, such as the Columns of Trajan and Marcus Aurelius, with friezes spiraling up to convey the history of Rome in the monumental medium of the age.

Communication has played a central role in the modern idea and its relation to knowledge. The invention of new kinds of media seems to give modernism its spark. Although feats of stonework served to bring Neolithic people together at Stonehenge for feasting rituals that disseminated ideas throughout the British Isles, the early modern era began later, when printing burst upon Europe of the fifteenth century.[20] The printing revolution made it possible for scientists to compare each others' work and for religious reform to spread. It also shifted the terms of power, overtaking the potentates' ceremonies that once established accepted meanings for events. Newspapers, the first manufactured medium to circulate widely, were also a product of modern ideas in Europe and a principal organ sustaining early forms of public life.

In the course of the modern, tension has emerged between idealism and realism. Idealist philosophy, which may have ancient roots but became prominent in the eighteenth century, asserts that the most important aspect of human reality is *mental* experience. Realist philosophy, which emerged in the ancient world and advanced in Scotland and America of the eighteenth and nineteenth centuries, asserts the existence of reality in the external world, accessible to humans through *physical* experience. Modernism has nineteenth-century roots in realist works such as the writing of Émile Zola and the paintings of Gustave Courbet, as well as the grand architecture that made Paris modern in the mid-nineteenth century.[21] In realist movements, words, images, and things (such as newspapers) assert the theory that honest depictions of details from lived experience expand knowledge and can open a deep understanding of the world. But realism in U.S. news also turned reader-citizens into reader-purchasers, making the commercial even more central to the general circulation of ideas.

American modernism as it emerged in the first decade of the twentieth century was idealist, seeking precision and brevity in literature and an escape from slavish realism into the beauty of the abstract in art. It took inspiration from artists such as Paul Gauguin, who offered, "Some advice: do not paint too much after nature. Art is an abstraction; . . . think more of the creation which will result than of nature."[22] The modern conception for words imagined a spare and clean language to contrast with Victorian excess, presented in a typographic object as understated as a simple "crystal goblet" designed to let the content shine. Of course every container influences the reception of its content in some way. Abstraction, simplicity, and clarity turned out to be friendly to the belief in business efficiency and endured in corporate architecture throughout the century. Modern news fused those qualities with the excitement for the new in a product replenished daily and remodeled periodically, one of the first things of modern culture to introduce rapid style obsolescence, a precursor to the throwaway society.

The real and abstract continually interact in the modern. Both aspects rejected the romantic and historical arts of the previous century, which had responded to industrialization and urbanization by seeking escape into fantasy or the past. Realism sides with common sense in philosophy and with everyday life in the arts. Its bottom-up representations stand opposite the top-down deductive forms in the strain of modernism that followed. But in words, images, and things, both strains jostled side by side. In the early twentieth century, the Ash Can School of art asserted realism even as modern idealism advanced. Most of the Ash Can artists had worked on the staff of Philadelphia newspapers, and so the realist attitude of the press fed back into art.[23] Both strains also embraced communication, commerce, and contraptions, often in conflicting ways but to pursue positive change. A vital instance was photography, which could capture the modern "big picture" while recording exact details of "the real thing," fusing the sharing of ideas with a saleable product. And photos seemed to have clarity and simplicity, in contrast to the decorated and posed drawings of the Victorian press.

The historical process of modernism is visible in news content, which is continuous and comparable over time, where other artifacts are lumpy and incommensurate. For instance, new technologies that seem capable of changing the world may instead become trivial or precious. The poet, tinkerer, and Harvard medical professor Oliver Wendell Holmes Sr. in 1859 foresaw stereographic photography ushering in a "new epoch in the history of human progress" that would be apparent "before another generation has passed away."[24] By divorcing the form of things from their material substance, photographs made "matter as a visible object . . . of no great use any longer." Images reproduced on paper and viewed in stereo seemed poised to make seeing the original unnecessary. One could simply travel no farther than the nearest stereographic library. But by the 1960s the stereoscope lived on mainly in the View-Master, which the company Fisher-Price continues producing for toymaker Mattel. Unlike news technologies, news content is perennial.

In hindsight Holmes was wrong in focusing on the detail of tools but right about the general transformation in his era. Machine-age inventions eased the burden of labor and promised a better world.[25] The Linotype, for instance, removed typesetting from human hands, automating the painstaking process of setting each metal letter in place for printing. Mass production of words on paper seemed capable of widening engagement in democracy. But the ensuing century saw entire occupations such as Linotype operators vanish in the face of photographic alternatives. Hand typesetting and letterpress printing managed to live on as fine-art graphics. The original object fell out of everyday use when first photo reproduction and then digital type generation of took its place. But the ideal of setting the news into type, a practical activity with a civic purpose, lives on in news content.

To understand the transformations underway in the digital era, media content can provide a jumping-off point. As devices and their operations change, words and images endure. What happened to content over the twentieth century provides continuous traces of social and technical upheaval because words and images are comparable across platforms. Close attention to content reveals how news producers presented the world to their audiences, which in turn allowed my interviews with producers to explore how generations of media makers envisioned their own practices. Understanding the dialogue among practitioners next required looking beyond the texts to the conditions that produced them. The contents and practitioner experience, the context of history, and some attention to audience responses together can shed light on the history of the surrounding society in broad strokes and help illuminate the era of spidery connective webs.

What makes the text, praxis, and context most interesting is the view of knowledge they propose. Academic research and business R&D speak to specialists. Governments, schools, and churches speak more broadly but mostly codify and inculcate existing ideas. News is a prime space for making and disseminating knowledge for all. In an era of identity politics and mobile private society, general meaning is a territory under siege. But beliefs about news have resisted cultural change, even as its contents and practices have transformed over more than a century. A contradiction so weird—and maybe worrisome—is worth probing, even though the importance of journalism has tended to go unrecognized alongside the usual suspects: capitalism, socialism, and other "-isms." But the case of U.S. news encapsulates the American century and illuminates the current state of general knowledge.

Its state of crisis appears to emerge from modernism and the tensions between its principal strains, which New York street photographer Robert Englebright captured in his worm's-eye perspective on the Rockefeller Center.[26] One grand tower looms above, its windows obscuring any sign of human activity in a pattern of rectilinear facets—a monument to the purity, precepts, and power of American modernism. The pale stone converges in one-point perspective at a mast extending from the building below. Its surface, by contrast, looks compressed, its one clear facet marking a pathway to a dark, rectangular base. There, a fragment of bas relief sculpture suggests a roiling mass cast in metal, where human forms confront the weight of institutions and manage to survive and resist—a monument to the heroism, humanity, and fidelity of downtrodden realism. As modern news grew to influence the powerful at the top, what it became may not matter because U.S. Americans managed to steer a course despite its flaws.[27] But in another sense what happened to news matters a great deal because its realism made the frailties at the political and social pinnacles knowable from below. Both strains of modernism endure and have continual consequences for knowledge in the digital era.

Views of what and how one can know—or epistemology—are also what distinguish the captains of older media from the young Turks of newer media. They squabble over every conceivable terrain, as things ranging from refrigerators to paper—even the physician's touching of the human body—become connected in digital networks. Modern news allowed practitioners to ride the crests of technical change, but realism is what could rivet readers of print yesterday and blogs and social media feeds today. Has the spider of digital networks entrapped legacy media and their workers? The answer, which can shed light on recent social and technical upheavals, starts from a question of form: How long should a news story run?

CHAPTER 2

Stories Only Seemed Shorter

Realist news was mainly short when the occupation of journalist first emerged in the nineteenth century, and everything in the modern world has seemed to go only faster for more than a century. First radio picked up the pace and then television followed, requiring shorter attention spans. Along came faxes, then electronic mail, and now video messaging. MTV made images move faster, television commercials got shorter, and online ads shrank to a few seconds. Critics call it sound-bite society or McDonaldization, reducing information to nuggets. Over the past century, has daily news gone along with what seems like the modern trend?

Some insiders say yes and point back to the impact of *USA Today*. Science writer James Gleick, in his book *Faster: The Acceleration of Just About Everything*, summarized the view: "*USA Today* caters to your more modern reading habits by keeping copy short. Other newspapers have catered to them by going out of business."[1] Observers point to the shrinking of sound bites on television newscasts by the end of the twentieth century and to the rise of images everywhere. Critics say these two trends are related: as pictures became more prominent, they squeezed out words. In magazines, according to the *New York Times*, "the 4,000-word article has become a relic, first replaced by the 800-word quick take and then further boiled to a 400-word blurb that is little more than a long caption." Following the trend in magazines, insiders say, daily news has become shorter.

Others are less sure. Jon Franklin, in an article for the *Columbia Journalism Review*, says that long-form writing has waxed and waned in news. He began working as a journalist in 1959 for the Navy magazine, *All Hands*, and then spent a couple of years at the *Prince George's Post*, in the Maryland suburb of Washington, D.C., before joining the Baltimore *Evening Sun*. He remembers being "constrained by the hoary old rules of 'real' journalism" in the 1960s. "If we ran longer than 20 inches, our endings were subject to arbitrary amputation."[2] He then describes a scene in the early 1970s, when managing editor Phil Heisler changed the rules at the *Sun*: "I will never forget the day Phil came out, plopped down on the edge of the city editor's desk and announced in a voice loud enough to carry halfway across the newsroom that all important stories would henceforth be at least 50 inches long. He sat there for a few moments, listening to the silence crackle, and then he got up, marched back into his glassed-in office and closed the door. . . . Similar scenes were being played out across America."

Franklin became something of a specialist in long-form news. He won a Pulitzer Prize for feature writing—the first ever given—for his 1978 article "Mrs. Kelly's Monster," an extended close-up of how a neurosurgical operating room works. He later won the first Pulitzer Prize for explanatory writing. At the *Sun* he remembers "taking two to three months to do a story," a long time for a newspaper reporter. Explanation serves the modern urge to make sense of and give order to information, along with the quick clarity or gestalt that overarching structures supply. The pendulum swung back to brevity in the 1980s, Franklin says, when long stories fell out of fashion. Industry research showed at the time that readers would rarely stick with a story once it jumped to an inside page, and so the era "ended by thousands of managing editors popping out of their offices and announcing that, henceforth, no story would jump off the front page."

Trends in news recur about every twelve to fifteen years, Franklin quips, "calculated by the periodic rediscovery of the killer bees story."[3] The cycle began again in the mid-1990s, he says, when the American Society of Newspaper Editors published a new study showing the value of longer stories to readers. Five years later, the Nieman Foundation at Harvard University began sponsoring an annual conference on narrative journalism. The grand scale of modernism that lent importance to art and design seemed to apply to news. But then *American Editor* magazine, in a theme issue on "Writing Long," began to question the "mistaken belief that the more important a story, the longer it must be." By then, long stories had reached another peak.

Andy Glass remembers it another way. His career as a reporter, editor, and columnist began in the mid-twentieth century. At his first job with the New Haven (Conn.) *Journal Courier* in the 1950s, news came into the newspaper office on a teleprinter hooked to a teletype machine that set the type and justified it in columns. "It was virtually impossible to edit," except by snipping from the bottom, he said in our interview: "I remember once there was an execution that occurred in California at two in the morning our time, which was eleven o'clock at night in California. It was a sensational execution in 1957. So I had to change the tense of the story because the prisoner died literally on—not on deadline, but on press start in New Haven. So I had to go into the copy and actually edit the copy. And I remember that because it was so rare that we changed things."[4] Glass invokes a common explanation about news, that technology is in control, and concludes that "stories tended to be longer" back then. "You couldn't go in and cut a paragraph, other than to go to the stone and physically throw the type away after it had been set." Reporters wrote about two stories a day, he recalls, and the general rule they followed was, "Tell the story in as much length as you need to tell it properly and then stop."

He joined the *New York Herald-Tribune* in 1959 and landed an assignment with the Washington bureau in the early 1960s. During that time, he says, "I cannot remember any prolonged or any sustained discussions about story length. It literally never came up." In the late 1960s he moved to the *Washington Post*, then under the editorship of Ben Bradlee. Glass says his work began to have an impact when he broke the story in the mainstream press about CIA connections to the student movement. A few years later he left the *Post*, and after a stint on Capitol Hill as a press secretary for Sen. Jacob Javitts (R-N.Y.) and executive assistant for Sen. Charles "Chuck" Percy (R-Ill.), he returned to news at the *National Journal*, a magazine publishing pieces as long as twenty-five thousand words.

In 1974 he joined the Cox newspaper chain, where he became the Washington, D.C., bureau chief and a columnist, moving away from the kind of reporting that he remembers for its length. He recalls "editors generally pressuring the bureau to keep it short: 'You're writing too long.'" During the 1990s the Cox newspapers went through major redesigns, with more graphics and new layouts and type that introduced more white space, what editors call *air*. The formats of the papers changed, *re-webbed* in the jargon, so that "their physical size went down by 15 to 20 percent." Glass invokes another explanation common among practitioners, the influence of visuals and design, and says that conditions created "a direct—not implied, but a direct—demand," passed from the top editors through the news editors, "to keep the story short." In sum, Glass remembers technical limitations keeping stories long in the 1950s and 1960s, and then: "What I have felt as a manager is strong pressure for shorter stories, consistently since the nineties." Technologies and then publishing decisions from the top seemed to push change.

Others I interviewed or talked to casually tell similar stories. What they see depends at least partly on their job titles. Editors and producers, who have to manage the demands for space in the newspaper or for time on the air, pressure reporters to be concise. If editors are succeeding, news is getting shorter, and they remember their success. Reporters may sense that the demand for briefer stories has been waxing and waning. The best articles—writing that attracts the attention of colleagues, has a political impact, changes things, and wins Pulitzers—tend to be long, but reporters see long pieces as the exception. They think of their writing as short, and that makes sense. Realist practice of the late nineteenth century defined news as brief, and the idea stuck despite a century of modern influences. Everyday experience pushes reporters to write and editors to edit shorter. It should come as no surprise that they see the trends the way they do. If they had to place a bet, insiders would likely put their money on the idea that daily news—on the whole—has been getting shorter along with everything else.

But they would lose the wager. Editor and commentator Michael Kinsley, a notable figure in magazine (*The New Republic*), television (*Crossfire*), and online (Slate.com) circles, was onto something when he surmised that "newspaper articles are too long" and so "seekers of news are abandoning print."[5] A series of studies shows that news has been getting longer, moving away from brief realist descriptions of stand-alone events and aligning with modern impulses toward big-picture explanation. The trend occurred across legacy news media: newspaper reporters writing longer, television reporters speaking more, and even reporters on public radio, the home of extended news, talking more in longer stories. First consider newspapers. In three different papers with different circulations geographically dispersed in U.S. cities of different sizes, news articles grew longer. The growth is clear (figure 2.1).

At the *New York Times* and the Portland *Oregonian*, the length of stories doubled over a century. The *Chicago Tribune* stories ran longer, too, although growing not as much. Stories about three different topics—accidents, crime, and employment—all went up, which reveals a general climate for news at work, instead of the particularities of different content. The changes are substantial, overall and also for each newspaper and for each topic. That is, stories grew longer, at different newspapers, for different topics, and in different places across the United States.

Compared to a one-paragraph *New York Times* story that sticks to the realist facts of factory jobs in 1894, a 1994 story on employment on Staten Island runs twenty-seven paragraphs of modern context and structure, elaborating on a theme, the revival of the port. A typical crime story from the *Chicago Tribune* of 1894 ran one paragraph: "James McCune of 319 South Green street, a packer, is at the County hospital with a fractured skull. He was knocked down by William Warrington of 528 South Halstead [*sic*] street, a teamster. The men quarreled at West Congress and South Halstead streets. The police held Warrington without booking him." The realist reporting leaves the reader to make sense of the conflict between packers and teamsters. The *Tribune* no longer runs short local crime stories that lack a modern rationale to explain the broader significance.

After the 1960s, accident stories showed a steep increase in length. Two examples illustrate how they grew longer. Shortly before the turn of the century, the

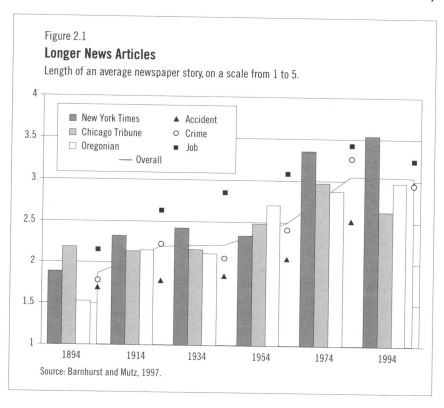

Figure 2.1
Longer News Articles
Length of an average newspaper story, on a scale from 1 to 5.

Source: Barnhurst and Mutz, 1997.

Times contained a two-paragraph item that begins this way: "Four-year-old Dora Cohen was run over before her father's eyes by a horse and wagon in front of her home, at 87 Hester Street, at 7:30 o'clock last evening. The child's ribs were crushed in and she died an hour later in her father's arms." The story conveys the drama and pathos of an occurrence worthy of attention. The second paragraph reports a chronology of the accident, describing the street, express wagon, and driver in realist detail. Short items disappeared over the century, so that by 1994 the *Times* covered only much bigger accidents that revealed the abstractions of trends and patterns or the complexity of major, underlying problems. For instance, a report on a flooding incident in Fort Fairfield, Maine, on April 19 that year runs much longer by adding information on previous floods, state emergency measures, and the damage, as well as what triggered the flooding. It illustrates the modern penchant for providing an interpretation, which takes first more research and then more space.

Another way to look at the length of stories in newspapers is by counting the number of items (whether typography or image) on the front page (figure 2.2).[6] In three newspapers—the metro daily San Francisco *Chronicle*, the small daily Springfield, Illinois, *State Journal-Register*, and the small-town weekly *Peterborough* (formerly *Contoocook*) *Transcript* of New Hampshire—items declined. News is more than a jumble of items but groups any related headlines, texts, and images into a story. For every story, one other item, such as a stand-alone illustration or an ad, also ran on average. The one-to-one pattern did not change in a century, but what did change was how many stories could fit. The length increased. As modern news advanced, main stories acquired a grander scale, so that dramatically fewer stories would fit on the front page.

A typical page in 1885 had room for almost twenty-five stories, but by 1985 the number dropped to about five. Other things happened, of course. The pages themselves got smaller to match modern notions of efficiency, usually justified for their economy. The text type grew larger under the influence of modern design and legibility science, and ads disappeared into inside pages as modern ideas of content organization advanced. Much of the descriptive labor of realist reporting moved out of stories, and more photos and illustrations took its place. Modernism

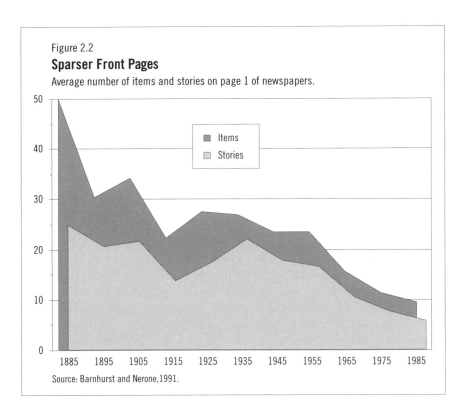

Figure 2.2
Sparser Front Pages
Average number of items and stories on page 1 of newspapers.

Source: Barnhurst and Nerone, 1991.

found expression in all aspects of form and content, as well as in story length. The text of stories grew longer to provide a modern perspective on events. A century ago most stories that began on the front page ended on the front page. Only the biggest stories continued onto another page. By the late twentieth century, the few stories that would fit on a typical front page ran long enough to jump to another page inside the paper. The segment inside grew longer than an entire story from a front page of the late 1800s. Modern sense-making needs room.

U.S. newspaper reporting by the early 1900s had gained fame for its brevity, especially compared with the European press. The "new" journalism of that era was brief and denotative, the expression of the machine age and a kind of factual realism that defined the emerging occupation and became fixed in the public mind. News by that definition is brief and realistic, but news in practice has come to produce something else. Despite the pressure they feel to be brief, U.S. reporters write longer news stories than their colleagues did a century ago. Their beliefs misalign with their actions, and that misrecognition, shared with academics and the general public,[7] is a central, unacknowledged aspect of news as it enters the digital twenty-first century. American news is short and snappy, and that realist picture of news stuck, but modernist news came to defy that expectation, at least in the case of newspapers. What about in other media?

The picture on U.S. television evening news is a bit more complex, but news reports have grown longer overall in line with modernism. Some studies have extrapolated from the declining number of news stories and the static length of newscasts to calculate how much longer.[8] Two studies took direct measures of story length, showing that the average news report grew from just over a minute and a half (in the first period, 1982 to 1984) to more than two minutes a decade later on the big three broadcast networks of the era, ABC, CBS, and NBC. There is no indication of what elements ran longer, such as the descriptive material from images or the explanatory material in speech, but the images tend to run in the background in any case.

In some ways speech—the contents of text—moved faster. Election reports on the broadcast networks shrank by about a fifth, from about three minutes in 1968 to two and a half in 1988.[9] The reports were always short, the equivalent of about twelve inches in a column of newspaper text. As election reports got shorter, newscasters cut down on pauses by the end of the 1980s, but most of the change resulted from the shrinking sound bite. The realist representations from sources, speaking in audio and film or video clips, declined, falling to less than a quarter in length from 1968 to 1988 (from 43.1 to 8.9 seconds). The drop was so dramatic that "sound bite" became a household term, fueled debates among media critics and practitioners, and spawned a cottage industry of books and articles. The realist stuff of news was shrinking, causing alarm.

But newscasters themselves were talking more, substituting modern structure and sense for realist actualities. Researchers can measure length several ways: how long reporters went on each time they talked, how often they talked in a story package, and what share of the total time they were speaking in a report. By the three measures combined, newscasters gained time to use for explaining what happened.[10] They ran slightly shorter each time they talked, giving the experience of increasing speed to the hearer, but they spoke more than twice as often, and their share of the average election report grew in a clear trend (figure 2.3).

The anchors and correspondents spoke much more often, and correspondents spoke much longer as a share of each report, leaving sources, an element of realism, with a much smaller share. Consider what a typical election report sounded like in 1968:

CRONKITE: The presidential campaign today featured a long-range debate over presidential debates. From Portland, Oregon, Vice-president Humphrey issued another challenge to Richard Nixon.

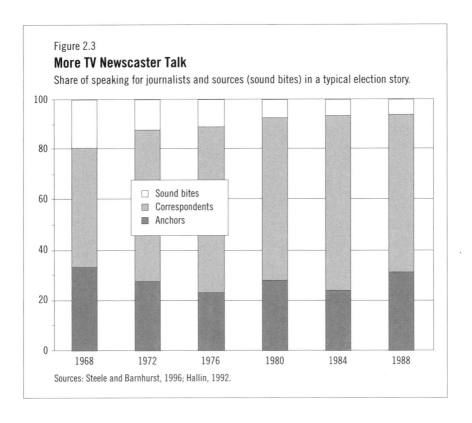

Figure 2.3
More TV Newscaster Talk
Share of speaking for journalists and sources (sound bites) in a typical election story.

Sources: Steele and Barnhurst, 1996; Hallin, 1992.

HUMPHREY: Yeah, I've been trying to get Mr. Nixon to come on a platform like this. I think you ought to ask him; I've been asking him. Why can't we have national debates along the style of the Lincoln-Douglas debates? Why shouldn't the American people hear from Mr. Nixon, Mr. Wallace and myself at the same time? Why shouldn't we be able to come to Portland? You've got a fine auditorium here, you have television, and the national networks, they wouldn't miss it, you know. It'd be just too much fun, and besides that, it would be free, it would be on them, instead of on some of us having to go around and ask you to contribute to our campaign coffers. In all candor, I think the time has arrived in a city, in a country of over 200 million people, where we have the media that we are privileged to have today. Where candidates quit acting like they're running around playing games with each other, talking to partisan audiences. I think we ought to have the candidates side by side, sitting up here, just as these men are here, and we take our turn on a subject like this, present our case, answer your questions, and you go out of here like the jury, and make your own decision.

(*1-second pause*)

DEAN: Humphrey has been all fired up over this debate issue for weeks now and is especially miffed today. In a talk prepared for tonight, he scornfully labels Nixon as the Shadow and Brand X. "Where is he?" Humphrey taunts, "Where is the Shadow? When will you meet with me somewhere that the American people can look at both of us?" Hubert Humphrey on the attack—it's been just about that way at almost every campaign stop. Morton Dean, CBS News, with the Humphrey campaign in Portland, Oregon.

CBS aired the report on September 27 that year, followed by a second report on Nixon's response, including the anchor's introduction and wrap up, correspondent John Hart's introduction, description, and sign-off, and four sound bites of Nixon rejecting any debates (including the quip, "It's one thing to 'Give 'em hell,' but it's something else to give 'em Humphrey, believe me!"). The central element in the reports is the realist actuality of a politician talking. The newscasters do a lot of talking, too, but they use some of that time to quote directly or paraphrase what the candidates said.

Now compare that pattern against coverage from 1988. An ABC newscast on September 28 also includes two political reports. In the first, anchor Peter Jennings introduces candidate Lloyd Bentsen's "strong words" critical of his opponent Dan Quayle: "I would pray for the good health of George Bush every night." Then, to describe "the new post-debate rock 'em, sock 'em Michael Dukakis," correspondent Sam Donaldson speaks six times and weaves in five sound bites, four by Dukakis and one by the Soviet foreign minister. The example is less extreme than the average but shows how newscasters speak more than the politicians and when conveying politicians' ideas tend to provide interpretations in the modern mode. Coverage continues with a second report:

JENNINGS: Well, it was a shirt-sleeved George Bush who added a bit of country flavor to his campaign today. ABC's Brit Hume was with him.

HUME: The Bush campaign rolled up the spine of Illinois today in a bus caravan intended to portray the vice-president as a man in tune with rural America. Indeed, the tunes were supplied by country music stars Loretta Lynn, Crystal Gayle, and Peggy Sue.

(The three stars inside the tour bus sing "Stand by George Bush" to the tune of "Stand by Your Man.")

HUME: Bush's bus, by the way, had a microwave oven, a fancy restroom, and, best of all, no reporters. They now travel with Bush, but not near him. At a series of small-town rallies, a shirt-sleeved Bush was introduced by Loretta Lynn. He told folks he was with them, unlike the other guy who wants to tighten tax collection to cut the deficit 35 billion dollars, something Bush said would require doubling the Internal Revenue force.

BUSH: No, I do not want to create an auditor army of IRS agents, and I believe that everyone should pay his or her fair share, no question, but I'm not for a program that is going to increase IRS seizures and give the IRS more power. *(Video from a street rally)*

HUME: Earlier Bush also worked the IRS into an attack on Dukakis's college loan plan, which would be financed by continuing payments much like Social Security.

BUSH: We do not need to put the IRS on your tail for the rest of your life as a reward for a college education.

HUME: Polls show Bush behind in Illinois and he apparently thought getting out among the people would be just the thing. Did that also mean he would answer reporters' questions? Not today. After all, you can carry this accessibility stuff too far. Brit Hume, ABC News, Ottawa, Illinois.

In the latter reports, newscasters talk more often and speak longer overall, unlike the politicians, whose sound bites average about ten seconds. The reporters again use some of their time to paraphrase and quote each candidate, but they also do something new: they talk about themselves and how politicians are treating them. Modern ideas tend to serve elites, and the controversy over politician sound bites exposes the tension between traditional political elites and the emerging voices of news practitioners taking control in media coverage.

Visual images supply realism to television, and another way to look at the change in the news is by counting the number of times newscasters appear on screen. A study of election reports on the big three evening news shows reveals that the rate more than doubled (figure 2.4).[11] In the late 1960s the anchor appeared once and read the typical report; a correspondent appeared in only half the stories. By the mid 1980s the anchor would appear twice during an election story, usually at the beginning and end, and the campaign reporter would appear twice in the middle. Correspondents were appearing four times as often as they did twenty years earlier, and anchors were providing the big picture leading into and out of the report. Both roles became more central to making sense of events.

In 1988 the number of shots with news people dropped along with visual elements such as graphics, captions, and video clips. By that election, candidates had learned the lessons of the image-conscious Reagan era. Bush and Dukakis postured for cameras in media events designed to convey a message through images. Political handlers set up scenes for the media and distributed video press releases. As politicians asserted control, newscasters seem to have backed off at first. But the networks reacted to candidate visuals with skepticism, scoffing, for example, at the image of Dukakis on a tank, his helmet perched awkwardly on his head.

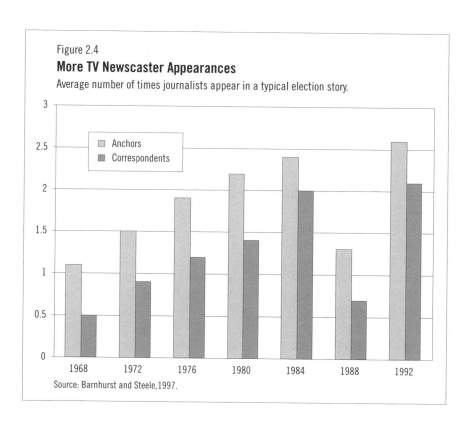

Figure 2.4

More TV Newscaster Appearances

Average number of times journalists appear in a typical election story.

Source: Barnhurst and Steele, 1997.

For the 1992 campaign, the networks began to pool their resources, buying more stock video footage and funding a joint exit poll. The cost-saving measures made them look more alike, and so they again added more visual elements. They used modern explanatory graphics, impressive sets, and a cast of news personalities to differentiate themselves from the competition. Visual techniques also insulated networks from the growing influence of spin doctors and from the flow of ready-made images that the Clinton, Bush, and Perot campaigns distributed. The number of newscaster appearances climbed to a new high that year.

What happened on the small screen relates to what happened in print. News-papers were the place where the first U.S. newscasters got their training and where they looked for standards and inspiration. In newspapers the length of articles jumped between the 1950s and 1970s, during the time when TV network newscasts moved from fifteen to thirty minutes and became more than headline-reading services. Newscasters did try unsuccessfully to expand the evening news to an hour, and they followed the lead of newspaper reporters by doing a bigger share of the talking on air and appearing on screen much more often. Modern news clearly advanced on television. But is there an exception to the pattern of news practitioners writing and speaking more in print and on TV?

One place to look is National Public Radio (NPR), the home of long audio reports. *All Things Considered* started out in 1970 to provide alternative content during the early evening, when the television networks were broadcasting conventional news.[12] It built its reputation on lengthy, sound-based features unlike anything on commercial radio. Historians say that by the time *Morning Edition* joined the program schedule late in the 1970s, NPR news was already becoming less an alternative outlet. But did reports get shorter as NPR news evolved away from feature style? A study of election-year content from 1980 to 2000 found that instead they did the opposite (figure 2.5). What aired on serious radio defied the definition of realist news.

The typical report on NPR grew almost a third longer.[13] Longer reports meant less room—fewer stories in each broadcast, fewer chances for listeners to encounter the real, and more encounters with modern explanations. In 1980 the programs would air about eight segments in thirty minutes, but the number fell to 7 seven in 1984 and six in 1988. By 2000 only four segments aired during a typical half hour. The number had fallen by half over the two decades. Initially the two programs followed different patterns. *Morning Edition* ran short features designed to fit the needs of commuters, and *All Things Considered* was looser, with more variety and some lengthy reports. Slowly the programs began to resemble each other. In 1992 *Morning Edition* went from ninety to 120 minutes, matching its afternoon counterpart—another expansion.

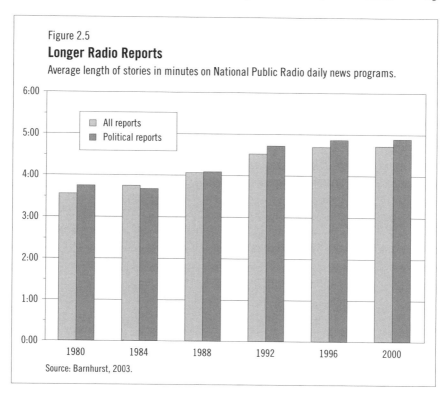

Figure 2.5

Longer Radio Reports

Average length of stories in minutes on National Public Radio daily news programs.

Source: Barnhurst, 2003.

One factor making the news longer was politics. Political reports run longer than other topics on NPR news. A typical day's coverage of the U.S. presidential campaign includes two reports from the trail, but on average the coverage ran more than a minute shorter for candidates Jimmy Carter and Ronald Reagan in 1980 than for George W. Bush and Al Gore twenty years later. A minute is a long time in the world of broadcasting, where ads that length command a premium. In news the largest jump of some forty seconds occurred in 1992, when Bill Clinton first ran for election. Other stories covered politics besides U.S. national elections, such as federal and state policies, court-decision skirmishes, and foreign-government actions. NPR reported on more politics of all sorts, and the share of political reports doubled between 1992 and 1996 alone. In 1980 only one out of six stories covered politics. In 2000 the share had grown to one out of three. In other words, all sorts of stories grew long, the broadcasts extended in length, and one of the longest topics took a bigger share of airtime. Politics is the premier beat in news, and so the growth relates to the modern, elite status of the work.

Were radio newscasters talking longer as their TV colleagues did? Yes, they were, but again in complex ways. Although sound bites (the recordings of sources) shrank on NPR, the average speech of newscasters stayed about the same. In a 1980 *All Things Considered* story on a speech where he faced hecklers, Ronald Reagan has three sound bites (averaging more than half a minute) and takes up more than half of the time (in a report of almost three and a half minutes). The reporter provides transitions between the excerpts:

CRAVEN: And in response to anti-ERA chants, he defended his position on women's rights.

REAGAN: I don't believe that there is anyone in this crowd who does not support equal rights for everyone in this country. [*long applause and cheers*] Now, it just so happens that I do not believe that simple sounding amendment is the answer to securing those rights. [*cheers and applause*] It will remove from elected representatives, and put in the hands of unelected judges, that entire matter.

CRAVEN: Most of the speech, however, was on education . . ."

Sound bites grew longer on NPR over the next two election cycles but then began to shrink. In a 1996 healthcare discussion during the presidential debate, Bill Clinton and Bob Dole speak five times (averaging two seconds) for less than a sixth of a report that runs more than six minutes. The newscasters, in contrast, speak eleven times (averaging almost half a minute). The shrinking reached a low point in 2000 but was worse for politicians' sound bites. During a routine campaign update from Michigan on *All Things Considered*, October 5, two of Al Gore's sound bites amount to a greeting, "Hi guys," followed by the sound of laughter in a daycare center, then his departing "Bye-bye." The newscasters speak seven times, always at length to provide modern structure and order to tame the seeming chaos of politics.

Longer reports and expanded programs made room for everyone to talk more often. Newscasters spoke more often too, but their speech did not shorten when the NPR sound bite began shrinking, and they also began interviewing each other as sources, a further expression of their status as modern explainers. One way to see the overall result is by adding up all the talk of newscasters and comparing it to the total for other speakers during the programs (figure 2.6). Although it bounces around from year to year, the trend is up almost 10 percent on average every four years. Newscasters always did the lion's share of the talking during NPR reports, but they talked even more, increasing their time by more than half. The total increase for all others was smaller, about one-third. Did others' speech expand because the reports grew longer? No, after controlling for the length of reports, we found the difference between newscasters and others is still strong.

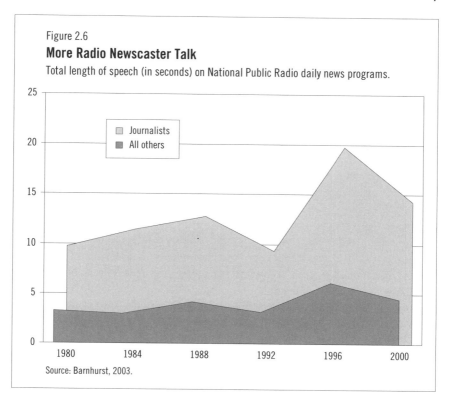

Figure 2.6
More Radio Newscaster Talk
Total length of speech (in seconds) on National Public Radio daily news programs.

Source: Barnhurst, 2003.

Their portion changed the most, enlarging as an element of the longer reports and the longer broadcasts. The modern way of reporting clearly advanced on NPR.

Newspapers, television, and radio are "legacy" media, older industries but with well-known, influential outlets. Whenever newer venues for news have appeared, they have tended to rely on established patterns of media practice and content. Young U.S. newspapers of the colonial era published clippings from the established European press, television newscasts of the 1950s drew their standards and a picture of the day's news from newspapers, and radio even before NPR followed the same pattern. Print and broadcast news are "legacy" media in another sense, because they accept an older view of news that relies on twentieth-century modernism. Its realist events have been losing ground to modern issues and problems, but practitioners and observers misperceive the change that puts actual news content at odds with expectation. It is long, not short, for one thing.

Modern news, like modernism in literature and the arts, reacted against traditional handicraft and sided with the orderly ways of industry and mass production.

Mass communication harnessed new technologies for high-speed manufacturing and delivery, building economies of scale on the model of few senders connected to many receivers. Like other expressions of the modern urge, modern news is elite. A model with elites holding resources at the center and receivers holding less at the periphery contains its own justifications. It supplies order, efficiency, and authority, and it promises public service, consumer choice, and progress. Mass communication emerged along with the growth of urban areas, which required organization and infrastructure. The modern aim to be progressive imagines fairer distribution of goods and information. It embraces the consumer, who can opt for the delights of novelty, chosen as a kind of progress. But a story of growth is a simplification that masks the complicated course of change with simple amassing quantity. News modernism prefers that kind of abstraction, which seems rational but moves news away from concrete realism and toward modern explanation.

In the digital era, modern ideas may seem quaint when legacy media fail to excite the imagination as newer technology does. Despite the financial woes of print news operations and huge losses in the reporting jobs they once fielded, newspapers continue to provide most original reporting in the United States. Although that pattern may be changing, newer media now distribute the bulk of news, especially through online aggregators and search engines. They deliver events in snippets that make the news seem short and realist. But what about the online presence of outlets that do the reporting? Is their content shorter, or do those presenting news in digital venues follow legacy patterns that misrecognize how news practices have moved away from realism?

CHAPTER 3

Longer News Turned Elite

What happens to news seems to hinge on the spidery webs of emerging digital technologies. The early years of the internet in the 1990s saw high expectations for new media and harsh criticism for legacy news. Tom Koch, a former daily news reporter and editor who worked for UPI, predicted in 1991 that new technologies would "eventually redefine" news, perhaps making stories longer and more involved.[1] A decade later a majority of U.S. newspapers had an online presence, and reporters and editors said that technology was changing what they do. But it remained unclear how news stories might change online. Instant electronic distribution could focus news on brief items, but websites have ample space for reporters to write longer accounts. The new generation of web interactivity emerging in the new century and the growth of mobile devices put further pressure on news organizations. By 2009 respondents to an insider survey for *The Atlantic* magazine could not "see anything on the internet that produces news—that is, detailed responsible empirical journalism" and concluded: "The internet trains readers to consume news in ever-smaller bites."[2]

Shorter news might accompany a return to a kind of realism, where longer news would imply a continued commitment to modernism. Did reports get shorter as mainstream news outlets focused on web editions? Three studies tracked the content changes as newspapers moved online.[3] To compare the changes long term meant using the same outlets in the hundred-year newspaper study: the *New York Times*, *Chicago Tribune*, and Portland *Oregonian*. By 1994, news stories in the study had grown in length (to 3.0 on the 10-point scale). Online the stories were even longer by 2001 (jumping above 3.5 on the scale), fell back in 2005, and then rebounded in 2010 (figure 3.1), following a sawtooth pattern common in content over similar periods. By the second decade of the new century, the news sites, like their print editions, had returned to the upward trend in length seen during the previous century.

The biggest change occurred in the *Oregonian*, often the briefest of the three newspapers. By 2010 it approached the average. The *New York Times* continued running the longest stories, but the three websites became more alike in story length. After an initial flirtation with other options, the online sites returned to modern ways. The trend ran deep in content, so that all the topics reflected the return to longer stories. Accident stories were the shortest, followed by crime, employment, and politics, consistently the longest topic since 2001. The return to the older trend in length is surprising because in other ways the sites adapted online. At first they posted mostly identical stories to the print and electronic editions, and by 2010 most staff-written stories were still similar online and in print, but a growing

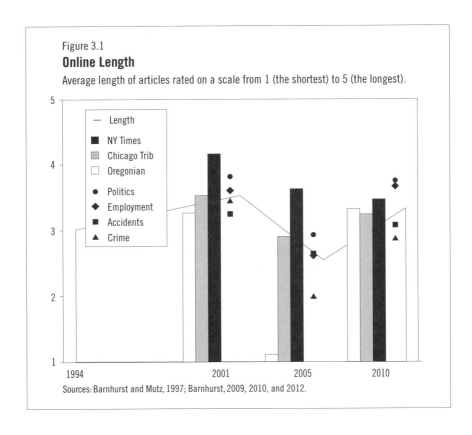

Figure 3.1
Online Length
Average length of articles rated on a scale from 1 (the shortest) to 5 (the longest).

— Length
■ NY Times
▨ Chicago Trib
□ Oregonian
● Politics
◆ Employment
■ Accidents
▲ Crime

Sources: Barnhurst and Mutz, 1997; Barnhurst, 2009, 2010, and 2012.

share on the websites (especially stories from wire services) differed from what appeared in print editions.

The data probably understate the longer trend because the related texts that form a "story" were also growing. For instance, even when short reports appeared only online, the string of reader comments could add many more words. In 2008 the Fort Myers, Florida, *News-Press* published a five-sentence, seventy-five-word accident report that generated three web pages of reader comments.[4] Most of them shared opinions, ranging from compassionate to cruel; few contained any new information. Only the most interested of readers read stories in their entirety, and reader comments expanded the bodies of text for them to scan, equally contradicting and reinforcing the image of shorter U.S. news.

Instead of returning to realism or reinventing news in the digital era, mainstream U.S. news organizations advanced modernism by moving to longer news texts and more newscaster speech across the board. Even the weekly newsmagazine, famed for pithy summations on everything, found ways to go on longer about each topic by breaking up a report into sections, sidebars, and smaller bits, much like television news. Newsweeklies, once Goliaths of news, have been in decline for years and have tried moving away from print. The U.S. newspaper industry ran into trouble and television evening news seemed to lose its way in a climate where audiences were using something else, mainly online and mobile news accessible through the news briefs that aggregators or social media supply. So why has U.S. news followed, even continuing in digital venues, the century-spanning trend of growing longer?

Some insiders say news changed because of competition. The classic example is the advent of television. In their history of TV news, Robert J. Donovan, former Washington bureau chief for the *New York Herald-Tribune* and the *Los Angeles Times*, and Ray Scherer, former NBC White House correspondent, say that television pushed the press away from its classic brevity. They quote sources from the *Atlanta Constitution*, *Philadelphia Inquirer*, *Wall Street Journal*, and *Washington Post*, among others who witnessed the change. Before the 1960s, newspapers thrived on telling the story first. Eugene J. Roberts, who reported for the *New York Times*, says, "Papers were event oriented" in the 1950s.[5] A focus on events is central to the realist idea of news. But television began to scoop print reporters every day, outstripping even the fastest presses.

Newspapers responded by publishing longer stories. The change began in major papers and spread through the wire services. The Associated Press (AP) distributed a forty-thousand-word report—a previously unheard-of length—after North Koreans seized the USS *Pueblo* in January 1968. Long stories seemed like an antidote to TV news. Afternoon papers faced the most direct competition, losing readers to the evening newscast. The p.m. press fought back. In Minneapolis, for example, the *Star* went though a redesign in 1978. "Small insignificant stories were replaced by long" ones, and the increased white space and larger photos meant the paper "contained a smaller volume of news."[6] The dramatic experiment failed; in 1982 the *Star* merged with the morning *Tribune*. Even so, Ben Bradlee of the *Washington Post* concluded in 1988, "We no longer write as if our stories were breaking the news for the first time."[7] Once they could no longer beat the competition with a first-day story, newspapers instead published what practitioners call a "second-day" story, a form that reports at greater length.

But news articles got longer well before television arrived on the scene (see figure 2.1). They grew in the early decades of the century. Newspapers dominated the media landscape through the period, with many millions in combined U.S. circulation. But before television they confronted a different challenger that delivered news through the air: radio. "Since the early 1920s, newspaper executives had been disgruntled" by "radio delivering headline news and selling advertising."[8] Beaming a bulletin by radio required less equipment than by television and took the first bite out of newspaper advertising revenues. In response newspapers started publishing longer stories during the radio era.

The same thing occurred as news magazines emerged. They started publishing much longer accounts of each week's events in the 1930s. Magazines could do extended pieces looking back over several days, besting what newspapers could manage in a second-day story. But the daily press responded by making stories longer in the golden era of magazines, too. Newspapers then used weekly news magazines as a model when television emerged as a competitor in the 1950s. The former editor of *Newsweek*, John Denson, took over the reins of the *New York Herald-Tribune* in 1957, promising to do every day what news magazines took a week to do. His period as editor of the *Tribune* "had a lasting influence on other papers." As newspapers again made their stories longer, magazines in the 1960s "turned from summarizing news of the week" to writing longer, "thoroughgoing articles."[9]

After television, digital media came next in the line of competitors. In the 1990s a variety of existing and start-up providers began to carry news on the web, which lacks the limitations on time in television or space in print. Digital mobile media can be the king of length, but how did newspapers respond? They were publishing longer stories by 2001 and after some experimenting mid-decade resumed publishing longer stories by 2010. The return to longer articles included all three newspapers and four story topics in the studies and applied equally to print and internet editions.[10] News practitioners may experience competition as a game of thrusts and parries, but regardless of the competitor that emerged—shorter radio and television news, longer magazines and internet news—their output responded the same way, with longer reports. On the air, newscasters talked relatively longer, not only in the highly competitive evening news on television but also on NPR.

Competition presents a paradox. Practitioners remember differentiating their own output, but the trends toward modernism as expressed in longer news stories occurred across the mainstream outlets.

Newspapers, television, and NPR saw each other as competition. All were producing the same thing: the news. Each outlet might get its scoops and pride itself in telling the whole story, but everyone had to cover the most important stories. When products compete in the market, they tend to become more fundamentally alike. The differences that distinguish one from another become more superficial, although the claims made about them become more exaggerated. For example, entertainment programming on television began with a wide variety of forms in the 1950s but within a decade settled into a limited menu, with all sitcoms, to take a common genre, very much alike in structure and substance. The same thing happens in consumer products, such as those designed to clean teeth: the nineteenth-century powders are gone, and toothbrush makers now claim big advantages for what are cosmetic differences that supply the modern shock of novelty.

The clearest example is the length of newspaper and television coverage. For years TV stood accused of being a lightweight. When Walter Cronkite started out as anchor for CBS News in the 1950s, he wanted to end each program by advising viewers: "For more information, read your local newspaper." After network executives nixed the idea, he instead chose the phrase, "And that's the way it is . . . ." He thought that reports on television or radio could not "deliver all that a citizenry needed to be well informed."[11] Almost forty years later, at his urging, the Media Studies Center at Columbia University compared newspapers with television. Cronkite reported the results during a 1995 special for the Discovery Channel. The ABC, CBS, and NBC evening news had room for about four thousand words a day and were similar in other ways. They covered mainly the same stories and spent about the same amount of time on each one. Only a fifth of their time went to unique stories. A viewer who tired of the O. J. Simpson story on one network could change channels, but the three newscasts, then as now, had almost identical content within their differing decor.

Network news also resembled the most-read kinds of newspapers at the time. Mid-sized dailies like the *Atlanta Constitution* and the *Des Moines Register* had room for more words, what editors call a larger "news hole." The papers dedicated about 7,750 words a day to all national and international news stories, but almost three-quarters of the coverage overlapped with the evening network news. The stories newspapers covered exclusively were short, averaging only 175 words apiece, the equivalent of less than a minute of network airtime. The important stories overlapped with television news. The study also found that "network news coverage of several top stories was either comparable to or in some cases superior to coverage in the midsize daily papers." The newscasts dedicated more words to major national stories such as California flooding and welfare reform. The assumption that newspapers always provide more extensive coverage than the evening network news "is not true," the study concludes.

The main news outlets have become more alike, which may seem paradoxical in the market but fits with the larger course of modernism. The news is the news, at least in the major U.S. media, and it is modern. The main stories get similar coverage in newspapers, on television, on NPR, and in high-traffic sites online. Unique or original coverage is minimal in any mainstream medium. NPR *Weekend Edition Sunday* has run an audio puzzle segment for years, but playing a different game—reading the *New York Times* while listening to the news program—has fewer surprises. Doing both at once is no marvel because on major stories and even on features the two outlets are similar. Reading a story first in the *Times* leaves no need to listen closely to the NPR coverage. Hearing a story first on *Weekend Edition* leaves little to skim in the *Times* report. Economics do matter, but the market did not force news organizations to differentiate. Practitioners remember the push and pull of everyday competition in the short term, and on television they feel especially constrained. But along with other forces, the market did what it has done with everything from shampoo to hamburgers: it made competing products more alike. Mainstream daily news has been going longer for a century, but not mainly because of economic conditions.

Words are one of those things that come in an almost unlimited supply. Talk is cheap. Economics has a hard time explaining anything that defies the iron law of scarcity. Oversupply has resulted in disaster ever since the fairy tale pot made boundless porridge on demand: porridge soon fills the town, driving everybody out, and no one can return without eating a pathway back. Where to put the endless supply of words? In any news medium, the answer is a problem of containers. In newspapers, each page imposes a constraint, but publishers can make the pages bigger. Or they can add more pages. Within those limits, they can also make each story longer, and story length is flexible—perhaps the easiest thing to change. That means length has two external dimensions: the number of containers (page count) and the size of container (page format). Page count and format are somewhat rigid because of physical constraints; story length is not. Looking at the page count over a long period may help make sense of the format. How have the physical containers for news changed through history? A study of U.S. newspapers tracked all three dimensions from the eighteenth through twentieth centuries (figure 3.2).[12]

Newspaper operators decide how many pages to print. The decision in essence sets the number of containers—how big should a newspaper be? Early on, custom controlled the decision almost entirely; the number of pages started out as a rigid given. Newspapers were four pages during the colonial era and stayed that way for a century, continuing through the federal period of the early republic. Even

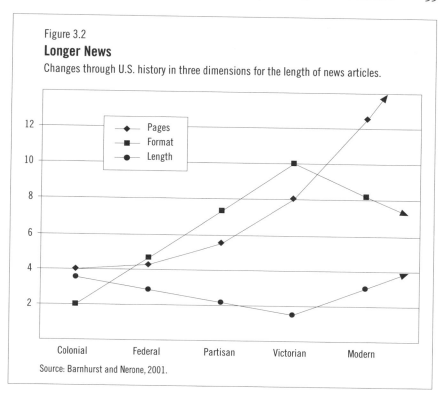

Figure 3.2
Longer News
Changes through U.S. history in three dimensions for the length of news articles.

Source: Barnhurst and Nerone, 2001.

when they came under the control of political parties during the partisan era, most newspapers printed the two sides of a single sheet and folded it in half to make four pages. A news periodical was called a newssheet because it was just that, a single sheet, and the singular term news*paper* also derives from the extended period when custom developed a vocabulary about news, printed on just one piece of paper.

Publishers had no need to increase the number of pages as long as they could increase the size of the sheet they already published. The format—the size of the container—responded initially to the political climate. Newspaper pages in the colonial era were the size of book pages, but the American Revolution changed that. Under pressure to present more news during the conflict, printer-editors increased the page size. During the early years of the republic, newspaper pages were about the size of now-familiar magazine pages. In the partisan era, more readers and more content from a growing market that traded (and advertised) more goods added an economic push on the limited page size. Technical changes also allowed the format to grow consistently larger. U.S. newspapers reached the size of standard broadsheets and then surpassed them in the nineteenth century.

At their largest, Victorian newspapers used sheets of paper as big as today's baby blankets and called, appropriately enough, blanket broadsheets.

Newspaper publishers considered the huge pages and huge capacity for news a technical achievement of imperial proportions, and the nineteenth century esteemed imperialism the way the twentieth century honored modernism. Imperial pages wedded the politics of empire with technology. First the telegraph and then the telephone helped increase not only the speed of transmitting information but also the quantity of news material available. Newsgathering became industrial, requiring more reporters and correspondents to generate a reliable supply of news to papers and news agencies. During high imperialism in the arts and culture, realism emerged to push against established forms such as historical paintings, religious icons, and elite portraiture. Realism presented labor and laborers instead of saints and monarchs, a populism that accompanied the invention of the occupation of journalist and continued to inform its practice.

The blanket broadsheet pushed things to their limit. Presses had grown larger and might grow larger still, but paper itself was expensive. The format then bumped into a human boundary: how big a page any user could physically handle. For newspapers to expand, publishers had to find another direction. Slowly the custom of printing and folding a single sheet gave way. The change began in the larger cities, where some papers went to eight pages in the latter half of the nineteenth century. Not coincidentally, "politics lost its old prominence as papers grew longer,"[13] and so articles on other topics came to fill the extra room.

At first, custom controlled the number of pages, but politics began influencing the format. Later, economics pressured the page count and format. Technology and practical limitations had an effect on politics and economics, but publishing profitability eventually became the biggest factor for both. In the 1870s James E. Scripps founded the *Detroit Evening News*, expanding newspaper circulation into the underserved working-class market through slashing the price by more than half, to two cents a copy. To cut costs Scripps reduced the size of the printed page, reducing paper costs. His *News* "was approximately one sixth the size of other papers."[14] The same economic logic spawned another competitor by the turn of the century: the tabloid press. The smaller format required less folding and assembly and was cheaper to produce. Working-class readers found it easier to handle on crowded subways and streetcars. Led by Scripps and the tabloids, the formats of all newspapers began to shrink after more than a century of growth.

By the 1920s, newspapers had begun to modernize. Modern newspapers strove for further efficiency. Each time the cost of newsprint increased over the course of the century, broadsheets again reduced their page format. As other competitors emerged and newspapers began to lose circulation, installing more efficient presses that produced smaller formats became a favorite cost-saving investment.

Little by little the grand broadsheet of the late nineteenth century contracted, until it has now become not much larger than a tabloid once was.

The high cost for presses makes the page format inflexible from day to day, but the number of pages in any edition is more tractable. As the format for news pages got smaller, the page count became more variable. Initially the Scripps newspapers were all four pages long, but by the 1890s newspaper publishing had changed. Retail moguls founded department stores that placed large advertisements, newsprint prices fell, and newspapers began to publish more pages. Pulitzer's *New York World* reached sixteen pages and added new sports, comics, and women's pages, and other newspapers followed suit.[15] As their management became more modern, newspapers might publish only a dozen pages on a day when advertising sales were slow but then put out a mammoth Sunday edition running into dozens of pages during a busy advertising season. Big stories—during wartime, for instance—could have the same effect, within the limits of profitability. In the background, emerging ideas about modern efficiency had a growing influence.

How did the length of stories track with the changes in format and page count? Most of the time, it moved in the opposite direction. The colonial newspaper could carry long articles, written as letters from distant correspondents or transcribed from the actions of governments nearby, and it borrowed much of its content from other newspapers. The unit of writing was the essay. During the nineteenth century, all the factors that pushed up the format also pushed down the length of articles. The discussion among elite gentlemen during the colonial era gave way to a partisan debate by the mid-nineteenth century. The partisan press still published plenty of sermons and essays, but writing grew shorter with the emergence of cheap newspapers in the 1870s. "Even editorials . . . partook of this more condensed but lively style."[16] The unit of writing became the paragraph, a form better suited to working-class readers without leisure time, as well as to the give and take in a courtroom of public opinion. Realism had emerged. By the end of the century the number of lists and tables increased dramatically; debate had yielded to something more like a shopper's catalog. Entire columns filled with items called *sparks* made the newspaper a compendium for all sorts of lists, the height of modern classification.

The direction changed as modernism advanced. While economic efficiency came to rule the other dimensions, story length somehow escaped. Throughout the twentieth century, news stories grew longer. The economic constraints on newspapers increased, curbing page counts and shrinking formats, but news stories defied those pressures. Something fascinating has been going on under the surface of news and out of sight of its publics, something the usual explanations fail to explain. Taking close measures of the text reveals a surprising contradiction, which the advance of modernism might clarify. Beyond newspapers, the same pattern emerged in other organs of daily news, under their own technical and financial conditions.

For television news, the container capacity is the number of news programs. Custom at first required only a few programs for any broadcaster, enough to satisfy the Federal Communications Commission when the time came to renew a local license. The number of news programs remained stable early in television history, coinciding with network (but not news division) profitability. Meanwhile the format of news programs grew from fifteen minutes to half an hour in the 1960s. The networks made several attempts to expand the evening news to a full hour, but local affiliates resisted losing control over another half hour leading into prime time. Other types of news programs in other time slots did adopt the one-hour format as standard.

Once the program length (format) reached a peak, the space available to report realist stories during news shows began to decline. In the 1980s networks became less profitable, and the number of news programs (containers) grew in response to the market, generating softer content with less original reporting. Modern analytical talk is cheaper to produce than realist news packages on television. On the network evening news, formats became a marketing tool as well. Advertising minutes increased along with the time spent in audiovisual introductions, teasers, closing sequences, and the like, but the format had less room left for the news reports themselves (and, not coincidentally, less time for politics). Even so, newscasters expanded their relative share of talking. They went longer in parallel to what the writers of newspaper articles had been doing for some time.

A brief account of how newspapers and television developed cannot approach the nuance the original studies describe, but the broad strokes seem clear. Market competition can help explain changes in the containers and formats of news in the twentieth century. The length of news stories is another matter. Perhaps economic forces and the pressure of big events, political change, and more information made news stories shorter in the nineteenth century. In the twentieth century the rise of modern news was not just an economic phenomenon. It came more from some other quarter.

Longer news of course has more words per story, and all those additional words must be doing something more. What do those words do? One possibility is that adding words made news more coherent or rational, that is, modern—something words do well. Each period in news history has presented a different view of the world.[17] The colonial era and early republic in America organized news according to a scheme of global history, moving from the important events at world capitals such as London through regional to local events in, say, Boston. Realist news is organized the other way around. Editors and reporters begin from what they project as concerns for the audience and cover only the more-distant affairs they consider important enough to have an impact at home. The idea of news expanding out from the here and now is especially strong among local and regional outlets and has spread widely among U.S. news audiences.

Each succeeding period of the nineteenth century added another view of news. In the era of partisan politics, editors organized news as a national stage for political partisanship. Later, as economic life became more focused on manufacturing, publishers of the Victorian era organized news as an abundant marketplace overflowing with facts, including plenty of information about industrial goods, sold on the strength of realist events. Since then news organizations have retained some elements from previous periods—the partisan newspaper is holed up on the editorial page, for example. But on other pages, news followed a different order, becoming a modern map of the social world. One reason that sections such as Entertainment, Business, and Women developed was to assemble the right readers together for the right advertisers. Critics say that the modern way of treating information as a commodity and treating readers as consumers (and then selling those readers in turn to advertisers) will be the end of journalism.[18]

The end of one kind of news and its view of the world has always given birth to another news. Each worldview was coherent and sensible in its time. The length of news stories may have expressed each view in turn. The crowded partisan newspaper, its front page filled to the brim with scores of unrelated ads, would make little sense to modern readers, but it made sense in the partisan era. The longer news of the twentieth century might have bewildered the Victorians but explained a sensible worldview to modern audiences in their time.[19] The point is that, over history, longer news has not automatically made better—or worse—sense of the world.

Longer stories track with the writer's status. The authors of the epistles that ran in colonial newspapers were the elite, from the class of landed gentry who sat in government councils and eventually formed the United States. Writing and then seeing one's words published in journals of the era went hand in hand with political status. Gentlemen like John Adams and James Madison wrote not so much for newspapers as for a public at first made entirely of their peers among the ruling elite, which, once imagined, emerged more broadly around the issues they raised. But each succeeding generation of news-authors through the nineteenth century was less autonomous.

Partisan editors had considerable power, but unlike colonial gentlemen, they worked within overt constraints from the party. Partisan newspapers contained a record of political life and documented its speeches, political manifestos, and the like. The editors of the partisan press had a good chance of advancing in politics. More than fifty printers, editors, and publishers of political journals won election to national office from 1789 to 1861.[20] Perhaps the most famous was Horace

Greeley, a printer who worked almost forty years in journals of the Whig Party. He founded the *New York Tribune* in 1841 and won a seat in the House of Representatives in 1848, where he served one term. The prominent publisher ran unsuccessfully as the Liberal Republican candidate for president in 1872, shortly before his death.[21] His polar opposite was Missouri Democrat Thomas Hart Benton, a lawyer who served thirty years in the Senate, followed in 1853 by one term in the House. Before returning to Congress as a member of the House in 1821, he spent three years working at the *St. Louis Enquirer*, which supported the Republican party of the time. In the partisan era, a revolving door developed between politics and the press. More than twenty-five former members of the first thirty U.S. Congresses took up newspapering after leaving office.

By the end of the nineteenth century, the new journalism that emerged relied less on the partisan model that transcribed the documents of public life and instead manufactured items of its own, built on the realist idea that readers would make sense of them. The concise, compact, and easily digestible items contained facts, something shocking at first. At the time they appeared, "the bald assertion of fact outside the conventions of public speech was a violation of good behavior."[22] Reporters who transcribed news of public discourse and added commentary lost their place to something new: journalists. A journalist was partly a pieceworker, paid by the line for the labor of factual news production. Although their bosses, publishers like Joseph Pulitzer, continued to have political aspirations, the new journalists did not.[23] The journalist Lincoln Steffens likened them to machines stamping out facts in New York of the 1880s. The sociologist Max Weber, in a lecture in 1918, remarked, "The journalist belongs to a sort of pariah caste," with very little chance "to attain a position of political leadership," and noted that "the salons of the powerful on this earth" called them the "scavengers from the press."[24]

The newfound occupation set out to change the status of the journalist and, by the early twentieth century, joined the managers of emerging corporate newspapers around the modern idea of nonpartisan fact. News reports began to grow longer again. As the century marched on, more news practitioners held a college education and staked a claim to professional status.[25] The piece-laborers still abound—part-time stringers and unpaid interns who crank out facts—but full-time workers can lead a middle-class life. Some do much better than that. Elites at major news organizations, especially television, wield political influence. Walter Cronkite, at his height as an anchor, was mentioned as a viable vice-presidential candidate. Although their status as neutral experts usually prevents them from aspiring to elective office, elite workers may accept appointed positions in government. Examples abound.[26]

Long stories are a sign of status in line with the elitism of American modernism. Elite writers appear to write the longest and elite readers to read the longest daily news. Our research shows that elite news outlets put out the longest news reports on a given topic. There is something to be said for keeping the elite well informed. They are the most likely to vote and the most likely to have leisure time to spend on politics. It takes time and a good education to write persuasively to representatives and bureaucrats. Although elites may be too comfortable to join in civil protest, they are the most likely to contribute to political parties and to run for political office. Longer news may serve them well.

But a press primarily benefiting elites narrows its base. Short, realist news articles match the predilections as well as limited time and resources of the non-elite: the wage laborer, the working parent, the immigrant learning the language, the less educated, the young, the poor. Through history, longer news accompanied the rising status of the occupation, but shorter news accompanied the rising popularity of news media. In newspapers, long news of the colonial era gave way to popular politics and wider newspaper circulation. The paragraph is a much more accessible unit than the essay for most readers. The number and variety of people who appeared in the newspaper grew large in the Victorian press, when readership was burgeoning as well, especially among the working classes. News was at its shortest then, at a time when realism flourished.

Modernists of the early twentieth century objected to shorter news. They considered the old news nasty and brutish, as well as short. It was noxious to readers because it gave them only events. Longer news could tie those events together.[27] It was brutal to reporters because it doomed its producers to menial labor. Longer news could free them from the assembly line. As modern newspapers adopted longer news, they became more exclusive on the whole and their popularity declined.

The quandary of long, modernist news brings into stark relief the interlocking fates of news practitioners and their audiences. Long essays made the colonial newspaper a nation talking to itself, in the phrase of Arthur Miller, but left out most Americans of the era. It would be too simple to conclude that length, by itself, is either good or bad. It depends on contexts and consequences. In the seventeenth century, the mathematician and philosopher Blaise Pascal apologized, "The present letter is a very long one, simply because I had no leisure to make it shorter."[28] On television, shorter voice-overs and other speech by newscasters were most common when their programs were most widely viewed in the decade beginning in the late 1960s. But modern lengthiness has consequences when it becomes, for ordinary readers and listeners, "the news that maybe isn't news," in Robert Frost's poetic phrase.[29] The erosion of the network news audience coincided with the period of lengthier talk by newscasters after the 1970s.

Even when the capacity for words shrinks in any news format, the status associated with length encourages news practitioners to say a little more. In hundreds of small moments, all sorts of news producers in all sorts of markets covering all sorts of topics are making a choice. They are defying the editorial pressures to "Keep it short!" and the economic pressures that limit the available space and time. They are going long, their stories taking more space and time to cover what happens.[30]

But long-term trends grow only partly from each worker's free agency. Political institutions, social structures, and cultural expectations affected by ideas like modernism leave their tracks in those day-to-day decisions. And so the question remains: what has news writing done with those extra words? Perhaps the longer news of the twentieth century really did serve well the core of dedicated, active citizens. Perhaps news abandoned the realist interests and concerns of common audiences because they abandoned news. Or perhaps something else entirely was going on. In the past each new kind of news may not have made more (or less) sense of the world, but it made *different* sense. To discover how the sense of the world changed as news grew longer requires looking closely at news content, beginning with people, the "who" in newspapers, on television, over public radio, and via the internet.

SWEET PROSE

A [reporter] went into the forest, where an old [editor] presented her with a little pot, which when she said, "Little pot, [write]," would [write] good, sweet [prose], and when she said, "Little pot, stop," it stopped [writing]. The [reporter] took the pot to her [editor], and now they could have as much [prose] as they chose. One time when the [reporter] had gone out, her [editor] said, "Little pot, [write]." And it did [write], but when she wanted the little pot to stop [writing], she did not know the word. So it went on [writing] until the [place] was full, and then the whole street, just as if it wanted to satisfy the hunger of the whole world. It was terrible, and no one knew how to stop it. At last the [reporter] came back and just said, "Little pot, stop," and it stopped [writing], and anyone who wished to return to the town had to eat his way back.

—Adapted from Grimms' Fairy Tales, no. 103, 1884

PART 2

"Who"—People Disappeared as News Expanded

Well, now can I make any Joan a lady.
"Good den, sir Richard!"—"God-a-mercy, fellow!"—
And if his name be George, I'll call him Peter;
For new-made honour doth forget men's names . . . .

—William Shakespeare, *King John* (1887)

CHAPTER 4

Groups Supplanted Persons

A growing element in the media landscape for several decades has been people news. The *New York Times* was running the Notes on People column by the early 1970s. PBS aired *The American Family*, showing raw life in a California home in 1973. Time Inc. founded *People Weekly* in March 1974, and the Family Circle group brought out its first edition of *Us* magazine in late 1976. Other media outlets followed suit, increasing the number of people features and human-interest coverage. By the 1990s a growth area for U.S. television networks was the prime-time news magazine, a genre oriented to people stories. Reality shows, always an element of American TV, grew into a dominant genre by the early twenty-first century and made supposed "real" people the center of attention. News cannot happen without the people basic to realism. It would be no surprise if daily news increased attention to people in news as well as features, going along with the rest of the media.[1]

But the opposite happened. By the end of the twentieth century, studies first noted that people were disappearing from the front page. When feminists took measurements to see how women were faring, they expected to find female references increasing modestly while males continued to dominate front pages. The *New York Times* and the *Los Angeles Times* did refer more often to men than to women, but references to both genders had been declining. A follow-up analysis added other terms related to the human element in the newspapers, such as *wife, father, child,* or *in-law*. It confirmed that words referring to gender, such as *he* and *she*, had dropped, and the broader measure of human relationships had also been declining for decades. References to persons fell by a third from 1900 to 1960 (from more than 750 to fewer than 500 references per 10,000 words), with little recovery since then. The newspapers were presenting society "not from the point of view of single persons but from the point of view of groups." The newspapers also increased their use of quantitative words (from 140 in 1900 to just under 260 by the 1970s), leading the researchers to wonder whether the trends reveal that "people as individuals are becoming less important and numbers more important." The pattern reversed briefly in the early twenty-first century, during the height of online experimentation, but the trend had returned by 2010.[2]

The depopulation of front pages has many causes. One is that news stories are getting longer. Even if the average news report included a stable number of persons, they would populate the news more thinly as the typical story grew longer—fewer of them would appear on any page. Modern long news spreads out the references to persons over more column inches, pushing most of them off the front page (where previous studies looked). Beyond that simple observation, the studies are onto something deeper, something about the "who" in news. Persons were at the core of realist news of the late nineteenth century and remained a focus for workers I interviewed.

Did individuals become less important? To find out, we started by counting every individual and group mentioned in any way (whether named or identified otherwise), not just on the front page but also per story in content throughout the study newspapers. The results suggest three observations (figure 4.1). Individuals identified by name only became a minor element. Just about everybody named in the newspaper is also described, usually by a group affiliation. And the number of groups in an average news article went up more than half by the end of the century. My follow-up studies looking at a decade of internet editions of the same newspapers found that the trends went further. Identifying individuals by name alone all but vanished, describing individuals became more common, and references to groups peaked by the end of the century.[3]

For example, on April 16, 1894, the *New York Times* reported a railroad accident in Hazelton, Pennsylvania. A front-page story lists every casualty by name, hometown, and medical condition. The format emphasizes individuals, some of them rail workers: "The man killed was DAILEY, PATRICK, of Milton, Penn. He was riding on the freight train. The injured are: ARTHUR—Sunbury, Penn., conductor of freight train; back injured. BIDDLE—brakeman of express train; body bruised and back wounded. . . ." A similar front-page story from the April 10, 1894, *Chicago Tribune* about an accident at a school lists each injured child's home address, age, and medical condition in a separate paragraph. In 1914, individuals' names still ran in the lead paragraph in a *Chicago Tribune* article (on p. 11) describing an April 20 accident: "Four men were seriously injured when their automobile rolled down an embankment near Gary, Ind., today. One of the injured men is F. W. Kurtz of Chicago. The others are Fred Hass, Thomas Murrey, and Frank Whitson of Knox, Ind."

By 1954 the reports placed more emphasis on groups than individuals. Here is a typical lead, from the April 21 edition of the Portland *Oregonian*: "A veteran

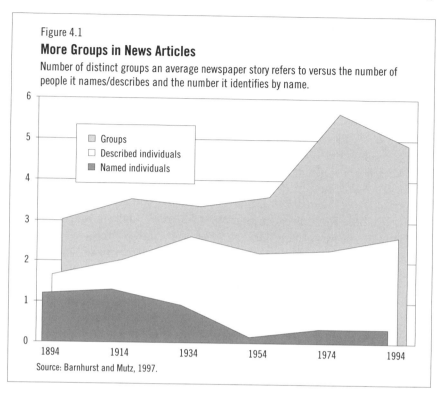

Figure 4.1

More Groups in News Articles

Number of distinct groups an average newspaper story refers to versus the number of people it names/describes and the number it identifies by name.

- ☐ Groups
- ☐ Described individuals
- ■ Named individuals

Source: Barnhurst and Mutz, 1997.

West Seattle high school teacher who refused to say whether she ever belonged to the Communist party will be dropped from the Seattle school system, the school board announced Tuesday." The job-related story has four groups—a high school, the Communist Party, the school system, and the school board—surrounding a person identified only by a job title that connects her to other groups: teachers and women.

Compare the train and school accident stories to a typical report from 1994, about a jetliner crash, where the September 28 *New York Times* focuses on the national origins of those involved and lists no names. In news stories most persons no longer stand as individuals in themselves. Identifying ordinary individuals by name alone does exist in monuments, the Vietnam Memorial being the most prominent, where group connection tends to overpower the individual name. In U.S. news, persons serve as exemplars of human categories—Russians, transgender persons, or Latinos, say—or of types: workers, athletes, or small-business owners. Citing someone's group affiliation is a balancing act. In a well-known letter to the Friars Club in Hollywood, Groucho Marx wrote, "Please accept my resignation. I don't care to belong to any club that will have me as a member."[4] Although his words seem self-deprecating, they also assert his own fame. A person who matters need not depend on group affiliation.

The push and pull between naming and grouping has played out in the news throughout U.S. history. The colonial-era press introduced government officials with their full names and titles. An edition of the *Pennsylvania Journal* in 1757 identified the New Jersey governor as "his Excellency Jonathan Belcher" when introducing his address to the General Assembly. Naming a less potent figure would not be so thorough. The paper's report about a storm at sea in 1767 says, "Capt. Greenway . . . informs us . . . that one of his people was washed overboard and drowned, and himself narrowly escaped." The title and surname separate the captain from the unnamed sailor. The *Connecticut Courant* that year contained this item about a fire: "A few Days ago, a Dwelling-House, belonging to one Waterous of Marlboro' was consumed by Fire, together with a great Part of the Furniture." The property owner has a surname, but the text introduces him as "one Waterous" from Marlborough, to indicate his limited claim on public attention. Another item from the same issue identifies a woman who lost quadruplets after delivery only as "the Wife of one Flint of Windham." The examples illustrate the power of naming.[5]

Naming separated out a class of historical actors. They had names connected to property deeds in public records, and they held the right to vote as citizens interested in public life. The historical classes were capable not just of taking action but also of saying what it meant. As verbal actors, they could stand on their own words.[6] No one had to speak for them, and so their group affiliation could go unstated. Ordinary persons were mere physical actors, who left no mark on ideas or history. Colonial news stories about "a farmer's wife" or "a laborer" or "a Negro servant" clearly showed who did not matter as an individual. The class of everyday folk engaged in labor, which followed regular cycles that reproduced conditions of the material world without controlling it consciously. Instead they were subject to control, like any other property. The newspaper, then as now, reduced them to social categories. Group identity has continually put them in their place.

One analysis of who appeared in news coverage looked at an event that occurred with surprising regularity for a century after Lincoln: the death of U.S. presidents in office. We found important people named and more often pictured in the elite *New York Times* than in the popular *Chicago Daily News*. Ordinary individuals appeared as an undifferentiated mass of mourners along the routes of trains moving the deceased president to his grave. When William McKinley died in 1901, the *Times* depicted the category of laborers as an elemental flow from nature: "A little later and the great down-town buildings began to empty their hordes of workers for the day, and then City Hall Square became a great sea of upturned faces, shifting and eddying in a struggle to get nearer the bulletin boards. . . ." Reports of John F. Kennedy's assassination described the people as ants, as if seen from the perspective of television or perhaps from Air Force One, the presidential jet returning the body to Washington, D.C.[7]

In the time from McKinley to Kennedy, news began sorting the people into demographic categories. With the death of Franklin D. Roosevelt, the *Times* showed groups that stood for regional and neighborhood geographies: South (Warm Springs, Georgia) and North (Hyde Park, New York), as well as Uptown, Downtown, East Side, and West Side in New York City. The Kennedy coverage divided citizens by place (not neighborhood) of residence and also by race, class, age, and religion. The *Times* showed unnamed students weeping on campus, black children, commuters, and Catholic nuns—none singled out, interviewed, or identified beyond their group affiliation. The *Daily News* followed a similar pattern, writing about ordinary mourners as groups: "At a crowded bar–lunch room at State and Kinzie Streets, laborers from a nearby construction project gasped as the announcement of the death came over a radio. A husky Negro workman knocked a glass of whiskey from the bar, said 'for God's sake,' and rushed out the door. Women at a table burst into tears. All was silent except for the radio announcer's voice." The realism of the story masks the subtle long-term shift. News that collapses individuals into groups is an act of power that puts people in their (subordinate) place.[8]

As ever more subdivided groups appeared, stand-alone individuals began to vanish. In 1894 nearly half of all individuals in the news went by name alone. The front page of the *New York Times* contains a crime story about two Long Island residents who "were speeding their trotters on the Oyster Bay Turnpike Saturday evening. As they tried to pass, their vehicles became locked together." The drivers jump out, argue, throw punches and begin a "tussel." On the calm landscape with a gristmill and pond nearby, the fight suddenly splashes into the canal. As the loser is about to drown, a passer-by intervenes. The case goes "this morning" before a justice, who fines the aggressor fifty dollars. Each person goes simply by name—not a tag representing particular subgroups—because the realist story's the thing. Narratives like this one (which ran about four column inches) packed front pages with the people. The practice all but disappeared over the course of the century.[9]

Reporters at first adopted one standard way to identify individuals, by name and domicile. In the late 1930s a daily column called City Locals in the *Beverly Evening Times* in Massachusetts contained items like these: "Edgar Main, of 2 Bay Street, Alfred H. Massary of 13 Cherry Street, Salem, and Nathan Davidson of 43 Bow Street, three local merchants, launched their newly acquired boat this morning. Mrs. Charles Callahan of 22 Mathies Street is visiting her brother in Nova Scotia for a week."[10] The reporter, a kid on summer vacation whose dad knew the publisher, would walk along the main commercial street of Beverly, a small town outside of Boston, "stopping in one store after another and asking the employees what was new in their lives. Any birthdays, new arrivals, deaths? Illnesses? Any visitors at home? Any vacations planned? Home alterations? Parties, retirements, confirmations?

College acceptances? Dean's lists?" Name-and-address format became the norm for identifying ordinary folks, rooting them in a neighborhood connected to all the tacit knowledge about what kinds of people lived there (which varied more in the era before zoning laws). Only notables and celebrities escaped the binds of social locations. A reporter could identify them by name alone. The sociologist C. Wright Mills called them "the Names that need no further identification."[11]

As groups rose in importance, two things happened to ordinary individuals. Their street addresses dropped out of the news. (In the frightening world of the twenty-first century, who would want a home address published in an item about a pending trip that will leave it vacant?) The new standard identification used group affiliation. And another thing happened: fewer ordinary folks made it into the news at all. Papers publish no small items about ordinary goings-on anymore. Instead news focused more on the well connected and well to do. In the 1950s, sociologists found that newspapers named the elite far more often than anyone else, while also mentioning hundreds of voluntary associations.[12] The heyday of naming ordinary folks in news had passed.

Maybe the shift from individuals to groups, which first peaked in the 1970s, reflected a social reality that the people themselves were taking their identity more from groups. By that decade, Vietnam War protests, the women's movement, gay liberation, and racial and ethnic rights had taken center stage in American social and political life. In jurisprudence, courts had shifted from guaranteeing the common good of the people to protecting the interests of groups competing in pluralist democracy. In popular culture, Alex Haley's book *Roots* came out in 1976, followed the next year by the mini-series, a phenomenon on television. Maybe the shift to groups also reflected the way news practitioners viewed the world. Instead of rousing stories of individual action, reporters and editors responded to the larger shifts in the social landscape by trying to show the complex interplay of social forces. That required groups, part of the shift to modernism.[13]

By the end of the twentieth century, individuals acted as stand-ins for groups. The August 4, 2002, front page of the Sunday *New York Times* featured two individuals: "Joshua Hastert, 27," was "the eldest son of J. Dennis Hastert, the speaker of the House," and one of "numerous relatives of Congressional and administration officials . . . employed in lobbying shops around Washington." In a foreign report, "Adrian Wilkinson, 50," was like "most of Zimbabwe's white farmers." Both appeared in pictures, giving the impression that the news focused on them. But groups outnumbered individuals on the front page by more than two to one and dominated the top half of page 1. In the first column, the one individual named and described in the lead paragraph appeared in a sea of groups arrayed for a legal battle: "The main combatants are the attorney general and federal prosecutors on one side and a network of public defenders, immigration and criminal defense lawyers, civil libertarians and some constitutional scholars on the other, with federal judges in between." The reader encounters no specific group from the list—and no individual speaks for them—until after the story jumps from page 1 to fill an interior page.

As the new century began, more groups stood alone as the actors in news, and ordinary named individuals almost never did. Newspapers had left behind one of their most powerful attractions to readers: "'Tis pleasant, sure, to see one's name in print," Lord Byron wrote in a couplet, "A book's a book, although there's nothing in 't."[14] The substance of news was always secondary to its power to name the people (and get them involved that way). But a person's name has given way because in the late modern world individuals can no longer stand alone. They act primarily through groups.

Groups have been growing more central to everyday life for a long time. Before the Middle Ages in Europe, each person belonged to a fixed social order. Although they acted in concert at times, orders became covenant parts of the body politic in Renaissance thinking, when the head of the collective body took corporeal form in the body of the monarch. Among the first collectivities to act as a group were medieval cities, where citizens gained chartered freedoms to take action together as a single entity. The creation of cities and other corporate persons, including craft guilds and trading combines, led to modern capitalism and gave groups power. They gained the rights of natural persons, but unlike mere mortals, corporate persons could survive forever. Even so, group actors did not take center stage in the popular imagination for some time. In the nineteenth century, public opinion still held individuals responsible for the actions of businesses, sometimes using violence to make the point. It was not unusual in the case of newspapers for an editor who published offensive material to be tarred and feathered and then run out of town on a rail.[15] All that has changed. Public discussion rarely holds individual company officers responsible for routine corporate actions, even when they devastate towns at home by transferring jobs to low-wage laborers abroad. The worst possible cases of corporate malfeasance lead to no local vengeance against individual executives because accountability has diffused into institutions.

News is something of a throwback to an earlier time. Standing up for individuals is part of the spirit of realist news. It acts as an advocate, bridging the gap between individuals seen as weak and groups seen as strong. In some cases reporters exert leverage on an individual's behalf in a modernist way by identifying the groups involved and assessing their responsibility. To press for justice, reporters use the power of naming. A reporter for the *Courier Journal* in the late 1970s, Michel Marriott—one of very few black reporters in Louisville—would get calls from folks "who never called the newspaper before," asking for his help, he said in our interview. Often there was little he could do other than listening and taking the caller seriously. But sometimes he managed to help someone hold an institution to account. He tells the story this way:

A poor, really poor, teenage mother had a first child out of wedlock. She's all by herself—lived at home with her mom . . . —and the child was born prematurely but lingered long enough to have . . . a name, and [the] teenage mother is devastated. So she goes home. Then . . . the hospital calls and says, "How are you planning to dispose of the body? . . ." And the mother got on the line and said, "No, we're gonna have a funeral. . . ." So they contact the funeral home.

A day or so later the funeral director's people go out there, and . . . they can't find the body. The hospital has lost the baby's body, and they . . . just brush them off. . . . So the mother calls me [because] someone told her that "there's this guy—maybe call the newspaper. . . ." I listened to the story, and I thought this was the very thing that a newspaper is supposed to do—give a voice to the voiceless, give them some . . . institutional muscle . . . to right a wrong. So now I'm "Michel Marriott of the *Courier Journal*" talking to the hospital. They're not going to brush me off quite as easily, but . . . they didn't have any answers.

It happened that . . . twin nurses in the maternity ward . . . are my next-door neighbors, and so I take them to lunch and say, "You've got to know something about this." . . . . they start telling me things. . . . At one point . . . they said, "Guess what? . . . They buried the body by mistake, and they actually had somebody go in the middle of the night with a back hoe and dig it up." . . . The next day the hospital called me and said [they've] found the baby, but they're not offering any apology, any explanation. . . .

I went to the pauper's field. There's a black guy just sitting around, smoking a cigarette, . . . the guy they asked to do it. . . . He was upset, and so he tells the whole story. I never thought about this, but there's so much human waste from hospitals. You get your appendix taken out and where does it go? They freeze it in this big chest, and when the chest gets filled, then it's buried in a pauper's field. So I'm standing in the pauper's field, and he's showing me where they dug the hole. . . . I then approached the hospital spokesman and said, ". . . . If . . . there is something the hospital needs to tell me, let me know, because this is what's going to be in the paper tomorrow." And they called a meeting that night.

I put my tape recorder in the middle of the table, and they put their tape recorders on the table, and they told the whole story. It confirmed everything. . . . But . . . they were going to apologize, . . . pay for treatment for . . . a therapist, and . . . do all these things that . . . she was never going to get otherwise . . . and it hit exactly what made me want to get into this work in the first place. . . . It made a tremendous difference in her life.

In the story Marriott tells about how the news unfolded, the key moments are all institutional: when the hospital asks for instructions about the body, how another corporate entity, the newspaper, gets involved, and especially when the newspaper calls the hospital. The newspaper acting through a reporter effects change. The story pivots on one group's actions to help the helpless individual defend herself against another group's power. That logic makes the story possible and makes news practice satisfying—the exercise of power making a difference.

What does the story say about individuals? Perhaps it depends on who reads it. Those with power, the verbal actors who have a say in what groups do, may see it as an object lesson, teaching them to make decisions with care, and as a warning about their use of power: other groups are watching. Those without power, the physical actors who nurse the sick and dig the graves, are all at one remove. Their words become the reporter's tool, and the nurses and cemetery sexton themselves vanish from the narrative: "This is what I know," he says, shielding his sources, whose livelihood depends on a group they have exposed. And they also clearly share a racial identity, collaborating to extract the justice their group has repeatedly been denied.

Michel Marriott is unusual. African Americans are scarcer at newspapers than they are in the U.S. population. At the *Courier Journal* he was one of the reporters on a series for Black History Month, "A Dream Deferred: Growing up Black in Louisville," for which he won an Outstanding Achievement Award from the National Association of Black Journalists in 1981. After that he was in demand. The *Washington Post* hired him, and he stayed for four years although other job interviews came his way. He took an offer from the *Daily News* in Philadelphia, spending two years with the popular tabloid while being wooed by the *Los Angeles Times*, by his old employer in Washington, and by his next employer, the *New York Times*.

He also has what he calls "a reputation for going into difficult places." Instead of doing the typical Black History Month feature by interviewing a few prominent African Americans, he and his collaborators went out into the community. At other newspapers he did the same. He covered riots in Los Angeles and Miami, becoming what he calls an "urban disintegration specialist." When working on drug coverage, he went into crack houses and shooting galleries, hung out in a Methadone clinic or with heroin addicts, and brought back "some amazing stories." His reporting involves what he calls unsavory places and some danger. His kind of news is Robin Hood all over again. The rich are no longer nobles (or usurpers who claim their good name) because wealth and power seem now to reside in collectivities. News producers play unlikely heroes, the Friar Tucks and Little Johns who come to the rescue of individuals held captive by groups. But the romantic story is not the usual news.

One perhaps small reason that news grew longer through the twentieth century might be that groups came to dominate the coverage. Where realist news talked about persons in action through stories, modern news shifted to the less concrete terrain of groups. Unlike the physical bodies of individual actors, groups form and un-form and get blurry around the edges of who belongs and who remains outside. Groups are harder to explain because they exist in abstract relations with institutions, part of the monumental expression typical of modernism. Until recently groups tended to have leaders, a clear figure at the head of the collectivity. What happened to leaders then?

CHAPTER 5

Authorities Replaced Others

I f more groups dominate the news, more group leaders may play roles, and modern news is about officials. Research in the 1970s showed how news organizations cast their net to gather stories. An ordinary person slips through the holes in the net built to pick up stories about bigger fish. Sociologists say the share of official voices has not changed for decades. In newspapers an early study of sources found more than half were from government. In the *New York Times* and the *Washington Post*, American and foreign officials populated the front pages of the 1950s and 1960s because reporters wanted to speak with someone in charge for any news event. A similar study ten years later showed that not much had changed. Studies that count words per page document a persistent growth in terms relating to officials on the front page, with steep increases since the 1960s. Regulatory terms referring to the federal bureaucracy have also increased, as have terms associated with the national government in general. A related study found that terms used to attribute information to officials have increased. Although new technology intervened and the news industry reorganized, officials remained at the forefront in newspaper stories, reinforcing the existing system of power and legitimacy.[1]

For television the sociologist Herbert Gans divided people on the evening news into two categories, finding that *knowns* appeared about three times more often than *unknowns*.[2] Among the widely known in 1967, presidents and presidential candidates, members of Congress, and federal, state, and local officials accounted for about 45 percent of all persons in the national news. Gans concluded that reporters relied on knowns because they were accessible but also suitable. Accessible means ready and willing (or seeking) to act as sources, as well as physically nearby and socially proximate. They were suitable because of their connections to the centers of power, their access to information, and their reliably articulate speech. A study conducted in the early 1980s found no change.[3] About the same shares of knowns and political sources populated network evening newscasts then, in the early 1990s, and in the first decade of the 2000s. Each of the studies examined sources over the short run, but taken together, the research looks at newspapers for about fifty years and network newscasts for almost twenty years. In print and broadcast news, the focus on official sources stayed about the same, sociologists say.

Over a much longer period, our research shows some strong shifts in the roles persons play in the news (figure 5.1).[4] The number of individuals who take action in a news event or become the victims of those actions in the press dropped at midcentury to fewer than three in the average crime, accident, or job story. Others took their places. A century ago, an official would appear in only one of four stories. Officials involved in or having direct responsibility over activities in the news increased fairly consistently until at least one official appeared in almost

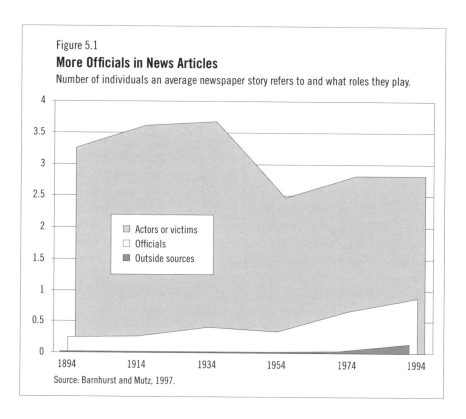

Figure 5.1
More Officials in News Articles
Number of individuals an average newspaper story refers to and what roles they play.

Source: Barnhurst and Mutz, 1997.

every news story. My studies of internet editions for the same newspapers found that the number of officials continued to be large through 2010. With political stories added to the other topics, more than two officials appeared in the average story by 2001.[5]

Ordinary citizens and unaffiliated individuals did of course continue appearing in stories, but as news grew longer, it replaced more of them. Political stories from the newspapers and their internet editions are the most pronounced example: officials and others have come to outnumber individual actors. A peculiar relationship emerged between actors in the news and the officials in charge. A typical article from the New York Times on the Web, "Calls for Change in Ancient Job of Sheepherding [sic]," begins its coverage of a guest-worker program with a passage about a shepherd in the Mojave Desert, a model of realist storytelling. To close the anecdote, the writer says, "The man, who would not let his name be used for fear of angering his employer, is typical of shepherds in the United States, about 800 of whom toil in California." The article then moves on to groups, officials, and their affiliations: the unchanging shepherd's *trade*, their *geographic origins*, the broader *labor pool*, the *regulatory bodies* policing wages, the California *legislature* and its proposed program, and so on through lobby groups, industry groups, labor-advocacy groups, and legal-aid groups. Leaders of all sorts speak for half of the ten groups in the story; the other groups stand alone. Individual actors without an institutional role do not appear again until the end of the long article. After a general paragraph that describes shepherds laboring in Fresno and Kern Counties in California, the story closes with the man from the opening anecdote. "I get depressed here very often," he says. The story concludes: "And while he has never seen a movie, eaten at a restaurant, attended a church service or even spent a free hour walking around the one city in the United States he has glimpsed, Bakersfield, he said he would renew his contract and do the work for another three years. 'My sons are 11 and 12 and I want the best for them,' he said. 'That's what I keep remembering all the time while I'm here.'"[6]

The powerful realist story turns the individual into a modern rhetorical device. Herbert Gans noted how television news reports most often used individuals as epitomizing cases. Reporters call the technique the *anecdotal lead*. Exemplars have become common in print stories and came to appear in about half of television news stories.[7] Audiences may have a strong response to exemplars, which may then sway opinion if the anecdote is powerful. But the audience may reject the exemplar as merely one case rather than accepting the reporter's proposition that the case is typical. Exemplars can be misleading when reporters choose the most dramatic case. Even when they explain that the exemplar is unusual and give details about the low frequency of similar cases, members of the audience remember the anecdote and forget the statistical rate. If a story says two-thirds of small family farms operate at a profit, but then tells stories about failing farmers and bank fore-closures, the reader may remember the failures, not the success rate. The pattern is testament to the power of realism.

Using exemplars is common in trend stories, especially if the trend involves something threatening.[8] In the story about shepherding, the vignettes describing an individual use realism to open and close the main act that covers something else, the modern exercise of official power. A news report, like biography, "assumes the value of an individual," says novelist A. S. Byatt, whose writing blends realism with fantasy: "Whether you see that individual as unique or as a type depends on your view of the world."[9] News practitioners may imagine a version of realism by aiming to respect each person as unique, but the everyday content of news treats the individual as a type. In the modern worldview, types stand for problems that group leadership can solve.

Besides playing the populist outlaw, news practitioners take on an elite role as a watchdog. In popular myth, the press watches over the public estates (the government) and alerts its master (the voters) of any disturbance. A reporter I interviewed got a tip while working on one of the zoned editions of the *Pittsburgh Press* and filed a story about a suburban town that forgot to pay withholding taxes for employees. Citizens complained at the next town meeting about the oversight, but the town council expressed outrage when the newspaper published the story. Citizens replied, "No, then we wouldn't have found out." The town had to raise taxes, but the consequences spread to council members: voters cleaned house in the next election. The reporter found it gratifying to see the people rally around the newspaper and to see the newspaper make lives better by correcting errors in government. "It's a small story," said the reporter (who prefers to remain anony-mous), "but it's important to the people involved."

The Pittsburgh story depended on the leaders of groups. The event itself was institutional, involving federal accounting and tax departments, the town council and administration, and the newspaper. The people watched from the sidelines, as spectators who took collective action at formal moments: the town meeting and the ballot box. The reporter could have spent time with some of the town employ-ees or residents, to witness the consequences for them as they filed or paid their taxes, but those would have been different stories appearing much later. Instead, the newspaper played the pivotal role as the recipient of the initial tip and the focus of the council members' resentment. Modern news is about groups in contest, about blocs of voters, not individual persons.

Officials and those who cover them play the leading roles in the drama of news. Michel Marriott, soon after starting at the *Louisville Courier Journal*, got an assign-ment nobody else wanted, to go to a dinner the school superintendent hosted every year for the press. As the night wore on, the superintendent drank too much and said too much, describing his vision of splitting the district in two, with one for poor kids, most of them from minority neighborhoods. The event was on the record, Marriott had a recorder, and he taped it. He called in the story to the paper at ten o'clock that night. It ran the next day on page 1 of the Metro section, setting off a firestorm among black educators and the black churches in Louisville. Television coverage followed, and the superintendent claimed he was misquoted. That Sunday the paper ran a full transcript, and the superintendent eventually resigned.

Work that costs officials their jobs can also burn a reporter's bridges.[10] Too much of it would put a newspaper out of business. After news coverage ends up ousting officials, new ones soon replace them, but leaders become wary, making it more difficult for news media to cover routine actions of the town council or the school system. If news practitioners want to get the story, they have to make peace with official power.

Another kind of leadership exerts influence through expertise. Like others in the working classes a century ago, journalists had little use for experts. Realist news was a commonplace written by an everyday observer and speaking to an ordinary reader. Reporters continued to be generalists well past midcentury. Joseph Lelyveld, who covered South Africa in the 1960s before his rise to editorial positions at the *New York Times*, said that he lived by the reporter's maxim, "Every person is an expert on the circumstances of his life."[11] The other kind of expert, an observer who watched events from a distance and had no direct stake in them, was the object of scorn in news memoirs for much of the century. Sociologists noted the same attitude as late as the 1970s when they studied the occupation by spending time with reporters and editors in the newsroom. The news practitioners viewed sociologists with suspicion as academics.[12]

Somehow despite the disdain of previous decades, experts have become a fixture in the news. In the 1980s researchers began to notice the large numbers of expert sources. Some turned up in obvious places, such as the medical specialists in health news.[13] Others turned up in stories focused on private tragedy, such as the coverage of victims caught up in a 1985 hijacking of a TWA flight. On the three national television networks, experts from aeronautics engineers to trauma psychologists, former government officials, and others were the most frequent sources, after hostages and their relatives.[14] On a wider range of news stories, expert academics, professionals, and former officials commenting on their specialties accounted for around 20 percent of all TV network news sources.[15] The population of experts has been growing for some time in U.S. Census data as in the news.[16] Since the 1880s the frequency of expert and professional words appearing on the front pages of the *New York Times* and *Los Angeles Times* roughly doubled.[17]

In the late nineteenth century, those not directly involved, so-called "outside" sources, were rare. The number in the average story grew gradually until around

1974 and then more rapidly into the 1990s (see figure 5.1).[18] Experts on television also multiplied. Newscasters identify them as analysts, consultants, academics, former officials, and the like, but they are also *news shapers*.[19] In the decade from the late 1970s to the late 1980s their number almost tripled on the three major broadcast networks. By 1988 there were three in the average newscast. A few dozen shapers accounted for nearly half of all appearances in network news, and two of them appeared as many as ten times. Some of the most widely used experts in the news had little expertise beyond an ability to deliver dramatic, quotable sound bites. Appearing on national television enhanced their expertise. Through what sociologists call *status conferral*, experts acquire an aura of knowing—just by appearing in the media. Correspondents intensify that aura by relying on the same experts repeatedly. The rule in news is the more you get cited in news, the more the news will cite you, and modern news is about authority.

During conflicts in the Gulf region, the large number of experts has created an illusion of depth for decades. In the early 1990s, rather than understanding the region profoundly through its language, history, or culture, shapers supplied a different kind of expertise through knowing the *players*, having an inside scoop on *policies*, and being willing to make *predictions*. TV experts deliver the three *p*'s using a fourth, *patter*, the ability to talk in snippets for television.[20] The same notion of expertise was at work in major U.S. newspapers during the next decade.[21] A 2008 *New York Times* investigation documented how the government was deploying generals and others under contract to appear as neutral experts deployed to shape public opinion about its wars.[22]

As modern news embraced experts, people paid attention. Experts and others who comment on network news do shift positions on major issues, and when they do, a parallel shift can occur in U.S. public opinion.[23] During Senate consideration of the second Strategic Arms Limitation Treaty (SALT II), each network put retired generals and arms experts on the air. They argued against the treaty because it had verification difficulties and would tip the balance of forces away from the United States. Public support for the treaty then dropped by almost a quarter. Because similar changes have occurred for other policy issues, TV newscasters conclude that expert sources do influence public opinion. In a complex world, modern society grows more dependent on expertise.[24]

As the cult of expertise grew, reporters themselves began joining the ranks of news shapers, acting as expert sources on topics they cover. In newspapers they tend to turn up as unnamed sources. A reporter from a major newspaper, speaking (not for attribution) at the Media Studies Center at Columbia University where I was a fellow in 1992, described using himself as a source when covering a country in Asia. When he first began as a correspondent there, more than a decade earlier, he relied on Asia-watchers. After he had been in the country for a few years, he thought he understood what was happening better than most of the Asia-watchers. From that conclusion, he took the next step: at times he explained events by attributing his own ideas to an unidentified observer.

The practice was part of the growing use of what are called veiled sources, which the American Newspaper Publishers Association began examining in the 1970s.[25] In other news media, reporters appear openly as expert sources. Newspaper reporters go on television and radio to talk about events they are covering, and it became common practice for news anchors and hosts to treat reporters from their own networks as experts by conducting interviews with them on the air. The pattern has grown in the past quarter century.[26] The well-known study of television sound bites from 1968 to 1988 observed a large growth in *wrap comments*, the concluding words that summarize the correspondent's expert conclusions.[27]

On National Public Radio (NPR) more newscasters began speaking on the air as experts (figure 5.2).[28] Their share of speech on daily news programs grew in the two decades after 1980, the first presidential election year when *Morning Edition* and *All Things Considered* were both on the air. Their appearances as expert sources dropped

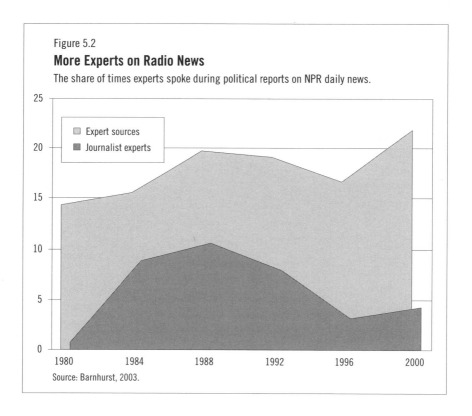

Figure 5.2
More Experts on Radio News
The share of times experts spoke during political reports on NPR daily news.

Expert sources
Journalist experts

Source: Barnhurst, 2003.

off during the 1996 election year, perhaps because Senator Bob Dole mounted such a lackluster challenge to the incumbent Bill Clinton. Although the share of reporter appearances as expert sources was small at first, it grew swiftly. After declining in 1992 and 1996, the share rebounded, ending up four times higher than it had been twenty years earlier.

To NPR listeners the pattern became familiar. Hosts routinely interviewed correspondents. In the following segment from 1996, host Bob Edwards gives a typical introduction for his two sources on *Morning Edition*:

EDWARDS: . . . . Joining me now is NPR's Cokie Roberts and Kevin Phillips of *American Political Report*. Good morning.

ROBERTS: Good morning, Bob.

PHILLIPS: Good morning.

EDWARDS: So, did last night's debate really change anything?

ROBERTS: I don't think so. I think that—that the polls coming out of it looked pretty much like the polls going into it. Now, they're highly partisan. . . .

The series of exchanges that follow repeats the pattern more than a dozen times. Edwards asks, "So, do you think—was Dole's move into the ethics area too tepid? Should he have been—you know, should he have turned the heat up?" And Roberts responds, "I don't know how he could have," before describing examples from the debate. The questions and answers throughout the report place newscasters in the role of authoritative source. The number of cases involving reporters as experts grew over the period. They became the best judge of modern news events.

Besides the share, the length of speech for newscaster-experts grew. All the voices on the NPR reports saw an initial jump in average speaking length between 1980 and 1984, but the voices of news practitioners as experts increased the most of any group. Other sound bites then grew shorter in subsequent years, but reporter-expert speech, after an initial decline, grew again, reaching almost a minute on average by 1996. Although it then dropped in 2000, the pattern in length was also clear: newscasters as expert sources spoke longer on average than all other newscasters (and all other speakers) every year after 1980.

We found a similar trend on television news. In 1968 correspondents asked questions of sources. Anchors asked no questions at all. Twenty years later the opposite became more common. Anchors asked more questions and correspondents gave more answers. The anchors had begun treating correspondents as expert sources. In a 1988 ABC News broadcast, for instance, Peter Jennings gave this lead-in to a report: "Well, with both candidates claiming the high ground on defense and painting each other as unrealistic on the issue, we've asked our national security correspondent John McWethy to look at what each candidate is saying and at the realistic choices which the next president will actually face."[29]

In his revised role, Jennings presents the correspondent as a source in better touch with the big picture. An earlier sound-bite study accounted for part of the shift by noting an increase in "truth-squad" stories, in which newscasters played the part of experts who corrected the claims of candidates and their advertising.[30] Being answer-providers gave correspondents higher status by recasting them as modern specialists. McWethy was no longer just any reporter but an authority in national security. In the interest of its public, modern news mounts a forthright-seeming effort to offset the calculating self-interest of candidates.

It might be tempting to think that reporters rely on expert and official voices and even use themselves as sources out of convenience, because of time pressures. In our interview, Michel Marriott described the following example. Each year a local scout troop would earn its stripes by walking from Marion, Indiana, through a state park to a nearby town—an ordeal that lasted into the night during the cold of February. Usually, the Marion *Chronicle-Tribune* would send a reporter the night before to do some interviews and take pictures at the scoutmaster's house, where the group would sleep over before their early start. On the day of the trek, the reporter would return to get more pictures and interviews at the outset, then drive late that evening to the endpoint, watch the kids coming, and do some final interviews. The reporting would typically depend more on interviews with the scoutmaster and some of the troop leaders—the obvious choices for a reporter with little time—than on profiles of the scouts.

When the paper assigned Marriott to cover the event, he thought, "Man, the real story is the journey." He asked his editors to let him make the entire walk, and because he was a young reporter on his first full-time job, they said yes. He did the trip, from spending the night in a sleeping bag at the scoutmaster's house to the end of the hike. "It was tough," he told me, but he got to know the kids well and became a buddy, not just an outsider. He filled four reporter's notebooks, front and back, with stories about the hikers who faltered and the ones who helped them. He had so much stuff when he got back that, besides writing the usual story, he wrote a cover article for the Sunday magazine. "It was a big deal," he said in our interview. His story gave ordinary individuals a greater voice although they lacked any status in the official hierarchy of the troop and were no experts. But his reporting took more time.

The two main uses of time in content production are reporting (research, groundwork, interviews) and writing. Longer stories take longer to write, no matter what sources reporters interview. Because stories in general have been getting longer for more than a century, the writing itself did not change the choice of sources for a story. What about the time spent doing the reporting? When news had more individual actors and fewer experts and officials, someone was spending time with the main actors or victims who had no official title or expertise. Reporters are still talking to the people—their anecdotal leads come from that labor. In the example from the New York Times on the Web, the reporter traveled around the Mojave Desert, meeting and interviewing more shepherds than the one in the published story. The cost of doing that sort of reporting did not shift attention to officials and experts. Reporters were writing fewer stories than they did a century before and spending more time on reporting and writing.

Comparing sources to staff bylines shows that individual reporters have some latitude when deciding whom to interview and include.[31] They slowly adopted the practice of focusing attention on official and expert sources for other reasons, not to save money. Cultural critic Stuart Hall called it over-accessing the powerful and privileged. There is no inherent reason that news could not have kept the same ratio of individual actors to authoritative sources as it grew longer, but modern news chose the authorities. At the same time, Marriott's story shows how reporters imagine and carry out their tasks early in their careers, how editors justify the labor for the young only, and how their making sense of events takes more space. Even though people become exemplars, the realism that remains in news still seems to serve its populist aims. But modern news overall has become more elite by focusing on leaders and experts. What price does the occupation then pay for its content choices?

CHAPTER 6

News Gained Status but Lost Touch

After Ben Bradlee joined the *Washington Post* management in 1965 he went on a hiring spree and shook up the existing staff. One of them, Gerald Grant, recalls: "After the first wave [of hiring] one of the editors invited a dozen young city staff reporters to lunch. As he sipped his Dubonnet on the rocks, we nervously wondered about our fate. Most of what he said now escapes me. But I have a vivid recollection of his curiosity about the social circles we traveled in. Whom did we see? What parties did we go to? Whom did we know?" Bradlee made a practical point: the best place to learn Washington goings-on is at dinner parties. After-hours social relationships give a reporter the inside track for stories on the job. "Some of the best journalists in Washington had grown in reputation as their sources had grown in responsibility," Grant says. "At the time his message struck me as mildly offensive," he continues. "As I look back, however, his inquiry no longer strikes me as saying so much about upward mobility of journalists as about patterns of thought in journalism."[1] Before tackling their patterns of thought, one might consider the question Grant rejects: Have news practitioners been upwardly mobile?

Once upon a time the scion of an old Boston family grew up and went to Harvard, but then the United States entered World War II. He left school and joined the Navy, becoming an ensign and serving in the Pacific. When the war was over, he moved to Washington, D.C., where he eventually became prominent and powerful. Does his career sound familiar? It describes not only John F. Kennedy but also Ben Bradlee himself,[2] and is more than a coincidence. Not long after starting out in news practice, Bradlee and his wife were taking a walk pushing a baby carriage when they met a Georgetown neighbor, the junior senator from Massachusetts and his wife Jacqueline, also pushing a baby carriage. The two families became fast friends, eventually vacationing together. Bradlee was not upwardly mobile in the sense of moving from one social class to another, as his trust fund attested (he was fifty-second in the line of Bradlees who went to Harvard), but his reputation grew as John F. Kennedy became more powerful.

An occupation moves up as its members make social connections in high places, but its status also grows by attracting higher-class members. The stature of news practitioners, as documented in Washington beginning in the 1930s, has risen since the end of World War II. Writing in 1971, Daniel Patrick Moynihan said that "twenty years and more ago the preponderance of 'the working press' (as it liked to call itself) was surprisingly close in origins and attitudes to working people generally. They were not Ivy Leaguers."[3] In the 1930s about half of Washington reporters held a college degree, but that figure grew to more than 80 percent by the 1960s. At the end of the 1970s more than 90 percent of Washington reporters were college educated, compared with about 17 percent of the general public. About 35 percent of the reporters had highly selective alma maters: Ivy League schools, small private colleges like Swarthmore and Carleton, and prestigious universities like Stanford and the University of Chicago.[4]

Reporters outside of Washington also became more educated. The share of college graduates entering news practice nationwide grew from 60 percent in 1971 to 75 percent in 1982, 82 percent in 1992, 89 percent in 2002, and more than 90 percent in 2007. The share holding graduate degrees also increased to nearly a quarter by 2007, and the share of white (93.2 percent) and male workers also increased. Women account for less than one quarter of them (23.6 percent). Nonwhites are also underrepresented. Reporters from racial and ethnic minorities grew from 4 percent to 8 percent between 1982 and 1992, and inched up to 9.5 percent in 2002, lagging far behind the job growth of the same groups in other sectors, but then dropped back (to 6.8 percent) by 2007. In the Washington press corps, the shares of minorities and women are even smaller.[5]

Especially at elite news outlets, reporters are mostly well educated, mostly whites, and a majority male. As a group, they match the description of what sociologist C. Wright Mills called the power elite: professionally employed, urban, and products of comfortable families. As members of a key institution—the media, where "serious public figures too, must now compete for attention and acclaim"—they share the origins, education, and styles of life that make it easy to intermingle with others from the power elite. Research on the press and corporations, trade associations, policy groups, civic groups, and social clubs reveals "a web of affiliations" linking newspaper-owning companies "to the nation's power structure."[6] Similar connections exist with the local powers that be. Does that intermingling matter?

Those with the education, connections, or good fortune to get jobs in mainstream news outlets have seen their collective fortunes rising. But many of them still put in long hours for low pay with little chance of advancement, especially at small-town newspapers and within chain-owned operations.[7] The same is typical of other professional groups, such as attorneys in one-person practices or doctors in the largest HMO clinics. Those within wealthy independent organizations can afford to adopt high ideals, compared with those laboring in smaller concerns at the mercy of market forces, especially under private or factory-like chain ownership.[8] News practice has come late to professionalism, and while other groups have moved away from their early aristocratic noblesse oblige and now base their authority on expert knowledge, news practitioners have only recently moved in that direction.

As soon as the journalist emerged and acquired modern aspirations, the occupation began to face charges of elitism and the lack of diversity among its members.[9] The American Society of Newspaper Editors (ASNE), from its founding in 1922, carved out an exception. News could expose the racism of other institutions, but editors treated themselves as super-citizens whose particular strengths might (without noticing) discriminate in staffing news operations. The ASNE was an exclusive club for white males, barring other races until the 1960s and limiting their access even later. Becoming a member first required rising to the upper echelons in one of the major newsrooms, places with implicit racial and sexist practices when promoting reporters into editorial positions. The club did not give full voting rights to women who became editors through their marriage or family inheritance. The National Press Club also barred women during the first half of the twentieth century.[10] A similar pattern emerged in the accrediting of journalism schools, with rules that preferred elite universities and excluded historically black colleges. The structure of elitism made diversifying newsrooms impossible even late in the century, and interest within the mainstream tailed off in the new century as the industry shed jobs.[11]

The rising status and lack of diversity in rank-and-file news matters to outsiders, the audiences of readers, viewers, and listeners, and also to elites—the officials of government and other institutions. Whoever makes daily news decisions influences who appears in the media, who has a face, who has a say, and who counts, raising again Gerald Grant's question about "patterns of thought in journalism." By the late 1960s and mid-1970s the evidence mounted that reporters "learn from peers and personal contacts, notably relatives and friends." So they "move within a relatively small and narrow aggregate of sources," "dominated by the people they contact or who contact them regularly."[12] Reporters consider their families, neighbors, and co-workers—or others they meet at parties—credible representatives of the audience. They also use themselves as implicit sources, relying on their own lives and experiences for story ideas.

Within newspapers and newscasts, reporters come up with ideas for stories from others like themselves, rely on the same sources when interviewing, and treat a circle of contacts as a stand-in for the audience while writing about and choosing how to present them in print, on air, or online.[13] The variety of contacts tends to contract as reporters move up the hierarchy of news organizations. Reporters on the job get to know more varied sources than do editors working in the newsroom. Reporters and editors imagine their audience being much like them or like what ethnographers call the *proximate audience* made up of persons they know.[14]

U.S. American news has always been personal. In the colonial era, editors relied on personal contact with gentlemen and other editors, a pattern that has hardly changed despite two centuries of technological transformation in gathering and distributing news. By the late 1900s the journalist's occupation was as much "an information system based on personal contacts"[15] as it is now. Personal patronage was once the norm for government. A new president, governor, or mayor in the 1800s could fill official jobs by appointing friends, acquaintances, friends of friends, and perhaps even family members. The patronage system was one of the chief targets of the Progressive movement, which helped pass laws establishing a corps of civil servants who win their jobs through merit and hold them even when administrations change. Only the upper echelons of managers are now appointees dependent on political bosses.

A similar movement away from dependence on charismatic leaders and toward rationalized modern systems has occurred throughout U.S. society.[16] Large corporations and even religious groups, although not obligated by law, now customarily hire and fire workers at the lower levels based on something like a merit system. In the study of politics and organizational behavior, systems based on personal patronage appear unjust or worse—corrupt. They rely on something called *personalism*, focusing power on a leader in a position to pass out favors. The other face of personalistic systems is called *clientelism*, the dependency of any group or individual who owes personal fealty or is in the leader's debt. Clientelism is more complex than its definition suggests because the agencies of power also become the captives of their dependent clients. A basic feature in business and political life in parts of southern Europe and Latin America, clientelism also characterizes media organizations.[17] Even in the United States an interlocking system of direct personal influence still drives news businesses, newsgathering, and practitioners' concepts of the audience.

Newsroom ethnographers find the relationship of practitioners with the audience oddly paradoxical. Reporters and especially editors have a hunger to know who is reading and viewing the news, but resist knowing the answer. They reject almost all of the available information, except what they can gather from a few proximate stand-ins they know. Reporters "have trouble crossing social barriers that separate them from strangers."[18] Outsiders from other classes, ethnicities, or gender identities or with less education have difficulty reaching reporters as well. A case study of who gained access to and attention in a Boston newspaper found that non-elites had a hard time unless they speak standard English. Reporters want quotable speech—dramatic, articulate, and concise. Modern news requires the language of elites, which poor people, immigrants, and outsiders may not know how to produce.[19] To get beyond the usual sources, one newspaper assigned reporters once a month to eat lunch with someone they did not know and had not used as a source and then report on their conversation to the metro editor.[20]

Editors have tended to resist formal feedback from the audience.[21] They may reject audience statistics, the television ratings and circulation audits that characterize viewers and readers as large aggregates. Reporters may also distrust statistics. If their training is in the liberal arts, they may feel uncomfortable with numbers. They say in interviews that most statistical evidence is either obvious or irrelevant and changes too little over time to be a useful guide. Following what statistics dictates would require them to surrender their own news judgment, especially because advertising and business managers, who gather the statistics, may not subscribe to the civic justifications for modern news.

Editors and reporters may also be uneasy with the massive numbers of their audiences. People in aggregate seem to make poor choices by preferring gossip to real news. Social science research has tended to confirm that view. Techniques for large-scale surveys of public opinion began emerging in the twentieth century, and the results seemed to leave little doubt about the low levels of information that most Americans possessed.[22] The average U.S. citizen could not identify important political leaders and did not understand the processes of government or the workings of other institutions and corporations. Ignorance on survey questions has remained static. Pew Research Center surveys show little change since 1989.[23] If news realists of the nineteenth century considered their public attentive and astute, the evidence from social research did not sustain that same respect among modernists of the next century.

The other form of feedback available to news practitioners comes unsolicited from individual readers, viewers, or listeners. Reporters and editors consider audience mail idiosyncratic. They treat the letters, phone calls, and electronic messages they receive just the way anyone treats mail or calls from strangers: with suspicion. And reporters are right. An examination of letters to NBC News found they came from an entirely unrepresentative subset of viewers.[24] When call-in radio programs became popular in the 1990s, some editors began listening in, trying to learn more about the people out there. They gave it up after discovering what they already knew from their earlier experiences with letter writers, who are also older, more conservative, and mostly disgruntled, just like those now commenting on digital news sites.[25] The exceptions are fans who want an autographed picture from news personalities on network programs.[26] Television reporters who received calls from viewers routinely threw their notes in the trash, except during unusual events, such as the verdicts that set off rioting and protests after the Rodney King beating in Los Angeles, when they received large numbers of unexpected calls from people like themselves.[27] When selecting what to publish in the letters-to-the-editor column, newspapers followed the same patterns set for other sources, preferring officials, experts, and other "authorized knowers."[28]

A typical white, male, middle-class reporter is stuck with those he knows and can rely on: others like him socially, psychologically, economically, and so on, sources he talks to often enough to trust that what they say will pan out. When those sources are unavailable, he goes first to others whose job titles and reputations make them seem most reliable. Studies have shown that getting into the news depends on having close connections to the news organization.[29] The press in Indiana and Kentucky published more stories with a greater number and wider variety of sources when news staff members had a direct involvement in the community they were covering. The diversity of sources is also greater for *enterprise reporting* that explores or investigates new stories.[30] But routine daily news produces a narrower range of sources—reporters and authorities talking among themselves in so-called *horizontal communication.*[31]

The personalism and clientelism of everyday news practice and the narrow range of views those contacts express have consequences: audiences see the news media as biased and unrepresentative.[32] To move out of the lowest ranks, reporters have to uproot themselves and move from smaller markets to larger markets. As outsiders in their new communities, reporters turn to officials and to others like themselves. Diverse audiences recognize that distance and lose confidence in news as their own direct connections to the press grow weaker along with their store of experiences shared with reporters. Confidence in the press has shown steep declines over the period when the status of news practice among elites has risen.[33] In the 1970s around 25 percent in public opinion polls expressed a "great deal of confidence" in the press, but by the 1990s the share had fallen to around 10 percent.[34] Pew surveys show that public assessments of press accuracy reached a two-decade low in 2009. Newspapers and television newscasts provide the greatest exposure most U.S. citizens get to views unlike their own. They encounter little divergent opinion at work and almost none in private activities within voluntary associations or at home.[35]

The attentive public is stuck. The press is one place to find out easily about others nearby, important elites, yes, but also non-elites with experiences and views unlike one's own. Alternative U.S. outlets producing oppositional news do exist. Pacifica Radio, the network of community broadcasting that emerged from California in the 1940s, later opened grassroots stations in several major cities.[36] The Independent Media Center network (IMC or Indymedia) that partisan activists began during the 1999 World Trade Organization protests in Seattle grew to more than 150 outlets within five years, despite government efforts that shut down some. Local Indymedia sites eventually allowed users to post their own news in two-dozen U.S. cities as well as the San Francisco Bay Area and statewide in Vermont.[37] But independent news collectives involve mostly elites—well educated, white, and so forth—and remain the exception.

Digital media seem to promise a wider array of perspectives on news, but comparing citizen journalism to mainstream media websites has shown more diversity of sources in legacy media.[38] Blogs tend to provide no original reporting, instead responding to and commenting on the officials and experts that mainstream news covers. Blogs offer a minor share of factual news traffic online.[39] Digital news shows a growing concentration of traffic at just a few sites or apps, usually those owned by large old-media corporations. Newspapers in some markets have moved aggressively to close down or buy up online competitors, reinforcing their monopoly control of their markets, with consequences for who appears in the news. As people vanished from news, their dwindling numbers focused on the rhetorical poster-child, the group leader, and the elite stand-in—sources known to reporters. But mainly group identity absorbed stand-alone individuals, contradicting a central tenet of realist news.[40]

U.S. news practice still holds to an American ideal of defending individuals in the face of institutions, a view that echoes Emerson's "Self-reliance" essay: "Society everywhere is in conspiracy against . . . every one of its members. Society is a joint-stock company, in which the members agree . . . to surrender [their] liberty."[41] Defending "the little guy"—the individual facing society—was a central, realist storyline emerging with the journalist's occupation more than a century ago. But as modern news advanced, reports abandoned individuals in favor of groups, and news practice fell into a position at odds with its roots in realism.

News about sexual minorities can illustrate how groups fared in the press. In the 1992 presidential campaign, Bill Clinton began to give speeches and hold fundraising events among gay men and lesbians. No national politician had ever courted them so openly before. Gay men had begun to people the news regularly in the 1980s in health stories, but political leaders during the Reagan and Bush administrations preferred not to mention sexual minorities at all. Clinton's action suddenly brought the queer vote into mainstream politics. In the decade from 1992 to 2002 news organizations inadvertently ran something rare, a natural experiment in what happens when an ignored segment of voters becomes a regular element in news. In the case of NPR, changes occurred in who spoke on the air as queers moved out from the margins. From 1992 to 2000, reporters shifted away from quoting gays and lesbians involved directly in events.[42]

In a 1992 story on the anti-gay-rights amendment in Colorado, *Morning Edition* correspondent Mark Roberts included two sound bites from involved citizens, both of them participants in a rally on Capitol Hill in Denver. Unidentified Man No. 1, in a talk at the rally, described the expressions of fear and support pouring in from queer communities around the country after the amendment passed. Unidentified Man No. 2, who participated in the rally, gave a reaction sound bite: "It is a terrible feeling to be hated by other people for something that you had no choice in." Reporters referred to speakers like this one as activists, and the gay men (most often unidentified) generally contributed coherent, fully formed thoughts in complete sentences. NPR allowed individual citizens to take courage, step forward, and speak out for themselves. But ordinary people do not have office hours or job titles, they are hard to find on deadline, and they cannot always give good sound bites. They may not necessarily move in the same social circles as reporters. Their comments add a little spice and realism to reporting, but they lack modern authority.[43]

Over the course of the next two elections, the NPR coverage replaced active citizens as sources. Two types of speakers took their place. Uninvolved citizens almost quadrupled in number. The average report allowed one or perhaps two onlookers to speak in 1992, but included more than twice as many in 2000. The typical quote from non-elites became brief, such as the repeated shouts of "That's right!" at a 2000 rally against the civil unions law in Vermont heard on *All Things Considered*. The other type of speaker grew even more common. Leaders of interest groups, associations, policy think tanks, and lobbyists acted as sources almost ten times more often. The elite voices included spokespersons for organizations such as the American Civil Liberties Union and the major U.S. political parties, as well as for gay groups like the Human Rights Campaign and Lambda Legal Defense Fund. The Christian Coalition figured most prominently among anti-gay groups, along with the organizers of initiatives against political rights for sexual minorities. The representatives from all the groups were typically the most like elite reporters and the least likely to offend the ears of dominant groups: well-spoken, professional, upper-middle class, and probably white.

A habitual NPR listener heard the following sources in a typical week of gay coverage during the 1992 campaign: two citizens and one onlooker, one official and no spokespersons for groups. Two decades after gays and lesbians first appeared in AIDS news and a decade after mainstream political news began paying attention, the habitual NPR listener might hear two officials and as many as three group leaders along with an expert, but only one active citizen spoke, along with several bystanders who uttered short phrases. The voices of experts and officials replaced the citizenry, and ordinary voices diminished to mere fragments. After that, media coverage of gays and lesbians continued to rely on official sources.[44]

When ignored communities come into mainstream politics, reporters at first may do the job they dream about: giving voice to the voiceless. But then the topic gets folded into news routines. Reporters start relying on sources like themselves, on authorities and experts, and on organized groups. The pattern emerged as news practice became more upwardly mobile, but did the changes reflect the larger "patterns of thought" former *Washington Post* staffer Gerald Grant identified?[45] Over the same period, U.S. society and jurisprudence came to treat the individual with nostalgia, redefining something central to human experience: the relation of self to others in all their variety. Group came to trump individual identity in the twentieth century across U.S. society, its laws and news.[46] The "who" of news is something like a modern romance. The people or citizenry should play a leading role, but instead the central character is the reporter, and the central relationship—between reporters and their audience—seems to develop offstage, in the imaginations of news practitioners.

Reporters and editors hunger to know the people, but audiences remain elusive, just beyond reach. Despite wanting to know their public, news practitioners cannot surmount two obstacles. One is perceptual. When any bit of information or insight comes their way, either general or specific, they find themselves rejecting it. They want to understand their public at close quarters. General measurements leave the audience vague and disembodied, tainted by the measurer. Editors cannot rely on statistics or online hits, because any collective is abstract, not directly knowable. Specific responses, when individuals reach out through letters, calls, or other messages, are personal but also too real and visceral, strangers speaking often in anger. The available responses from audience members seem insufficient and inadequate or irrational to reporters and editors.

The other obstacle is conceptual. Knowing their public would dilute occupational control over the news craft. Accepting the available information would involve ceding to others at least some news judgment, a central skill of news and its expert status.[47] News judgment—the nose for news—is an attribute that gives them pride of place, acquired not from books or courses but through tough experience, failure, watching seasoned correspondents, and hearing the stories of veteran editors.[48] Obeying the statistics about what readers read would abdicate control to sales persons, marketers and advertisers, the business office, or the web traffic counter, all of them lacking an understanding of news. Obeying what comes over the transom would abandon control to disgruntled cranks. But little else comes from audiences. The unknowable public plays a tragic role in the romance of modern news.

Sources play another role in the story. Politicians and leaders from every sort of group press themselves forward, wanting the reporter's attention to gain the hard currency of news: public attention (the people again, imagined but out of reach). Journalists may satisfy their occupational needs through their relations with officialdom, but they treat their sources lightly, cutting their sound bites shorter and disdaining their efforts to get attention.[49] Officials speak for groups who seem to stand in for the audience, but groups themselves represent only vaguely the definable segments or attributes of the citizenry. The general public has some concern for the environment, for instance, but environmentalists who let that concern take over cannot represent the people. When using individuals to typify groups, modern news practice once again rejects the specifics. The downtrodden shepherds are not readers, the report implies. The disconsolate mother of the infant lost in childbirth belongs to an unlikely demographic for news in print or online. As soon as a private individual comes under the bright lights of news, she no longer represents the people and becomes either exceptional or deviant. And experts by definition distance themselves from the mass of readers and viewers who claim no expertise. The kind of expertise suitable for news combines fast talk and insider access not found among the audience. The specialists at media-talk stand outside the general run of the people.

Unable to reach the elusive audience, reporters turn inward. They cover the beat of their own lives, find quotations for their own ideas, and interview each other, becoming speaker, source, and listener. Journalists, unlike other professionals, lack access to the full range of everyday people. Doctors, lawyers, and professors have routine contact with the sick, errant, and unlearned but still claim a public mission. All professionals may carry an ingrained and unthinking picture of their public, an *internalized* image.[50] When I asked Umberto Eco, a professor who wrote for newspapers, about how he conceived of his audiences, he said they are like a ghost, but much smarter than editors and publishers think.[51] Modern news practitioners serve not a collective (known-from-instances) but an imagined people. The distinction matters. Modern news seems to speak from two minds, but is of only one. When reporters and editors argue, they may seize the high ground by claiming to serve the reader, listener, or viewer. As the sociologist Pierre Bourdieu observed, *the people* is often what is at stake when elites struggle among themselves.[52]

The result? In modern news more groups, officials, and experts have replaced freestanding individuals or unexceptional citizens in the news. More reporters turn inward to themselves and their peers as sources. And more members of the audience reject modern news, shift to digital headline services, or never join the news audience at all. The reading public seems to have moved on, into another era, one enamored of crowdsourcing, distributed labor networks, smart mobs, and multitasking social lives. Modern news seems a throwback to another age, out of touch with the digital era. The "who" of news is fundamental—how persons appear in news reports across mainstream media—and illustrates the gap between the ideals and practice within news. But the people or the leaders and groups replacing them must be doing something, taking actions that can turn into stories, and so to understand the recent transformations in society, the next important element of news is the "what."

ECHO AND NARCISSUS

Echo was an imaginary being, given to talking and would have the last word. One day the goddess passed sentence in these words: "You shall still have the last word, but no power to speak first."

One day Narcissus shouted aloud, "Who's here?" Echo replied, "Here." Narcissus looked around, but seeing no one called out, "Come." Echo answered, "Come." "Let us join one another," said Narcissus. Echo answered with all her heart in the same words, and hastened to the spot. Narcissus started back, exclaiming, "Hands off! I would rather die than you should have me!' "Have me," said Echo; but it was all in vain.

There was a clear fountain, with water like silver. Narcissus stooped down to drink and saw his own image in the water. He could not tear himself away. He pined away and died; Echo mourned for him.

—Thomas Bulfinch, *The Age of Fable*, 1855

PART 3

"What"—Events, the Basic Stuff of News, Declined

All things are full of labour; man cannot utter it: the eye is not satisfied with seeing, nor the ear filled with hearing.

The thing that hath been, it is that which shall be; and that which is done is that which shall be done: and there is no new thing under the sun.

Is there any thing whereof it may be said, See, this is new? It hath been already of old time, which was before us.

—Ecclesiastes 1: 8–10 (King James Version)

CHAPTER 7

Events Dwindled in Print Stories

When Will Irwin, the famed muckraker for the *San Francisco Chronicle* and the *New York Sun*, wrote an assessment of American news a century ago, huge numbers of events entered the flow of news. "Every night there happen in New York, Philadelphia, and Chicago a thousand events which fit the definition of news," he says and then adds with great confidence, "information on most of them reaches the newspaper offices."[1] Fifty years later, the wire editor of the morning *Peoria Star* in Illinois reported receiving twelve thousand inches of wire copy during the week. A well-known study of news described his work as *gatekeeping*, a metaphor for what editors do to manage the flow of occurrences.[2] Where realists assumed readers could manage, modernists saw a problem requiring intervention.

Since the early twentieth century, the reach of news organizations has grown. Wire services built networks that circled the planet by the mid-twentieth century. Although some newspaper and television network bureaus began to shrink later on, the modes of communication continued multiplying beyond radio and television to cable, satellite, and digital signals. Research suggests that television news has become more focused on events.[3] The conveyances for news expanded as well, from telegraph, telephone trunk cables, air couriers, and fax and teletype machines to computer and wireless devices. The rise of the internet and cellular telecommunications gave reporters access to ever more events. The expanding ways and means—the growing reach—of newsgathering suggest a commonsense assumption: that more news events reach audiences than ever before.

News insiders call the deluge of occurrences a "glut" they must govern. A veteran reporter who worked for the *Sacramento Bee* and *Baltimore Sun* says that "a beat reporter" has "too many stories, too little time."[4] Veteran correspondent Mort Rosenblum writes that what was once a lack of content became "a flood of dispatches, broadcasts, tapes, films, and photographs."[5] Outside observers also noted the flood,[6] and Rosenblum a dozen years later found "no shortage of news" when he updated his assessment.[7] "We are all flooded with too much information," he says. "People are intellectually and emotionally capable of absorbing only so much."[8]

Belief in the flood of news has spread. During crises, such as the financial meltdown that began in 2008, U.S. media quoted audience members unable to "keep up anymore with all of the news and current events."[9] Public opinion polls have reported consistently that about a third of U.S. Americans—those who most attend to news—feel overloaded, and despite rises and falls, the glut of events continues to cause stress as crises come and go.[10] Almost two-thirds of U.S. white-collar workers in 2008 and 2010 said that having too much information slows them down, and almost all reported not finding what they need to know when they need it and losing time searching. There seems to be too much for those who work with information, members of the news audience, and especially the young.[11] The growth in events seems to follow from the "relentless rise in the number of news outlets, the frequency of news reports, and the media's clamor for every scrap of new information." As a result, "society is immersed . . . in a flood," an accelerating surge that "has created a kind of widespread attention deficit disorder."[12] The consequences follow because, whether or not an information overload exists, the belief in it leads reporters and editors to order and explain the news even more.

How did news practitioners handle all the occurrences? The form and content of the news changed, leaving room for fewer stories.[13] But fewer articles and items per page would not imply that fewer events get reported because those remaining grew notably longer, and longer stories might include more events. Instead of running three reports on three different fires in the city, as newspapers did a century ago, an editor now might manage the information by combining all three events into one package, or a reporter might write one story built around a similarity or a theme the three events share. Did either happen? No, news stories included fewer events through the twentieth century (figure 7.1).

The number per article declined markedly across newspapers, especially early in the period with the advent of twentieth-century modernism.[14] Two large papers, the *New York Times* and *Chicago Tribune*, moved strongly away from multiple events, and the trend was solid at the smaller Portland *Oregonian*. Different news topics also followed the trend. Events in crime stories changed the least, but accident stories included fewer events, and the number in employment stories declined even more. The general consistency for newspapers and topics indicates something

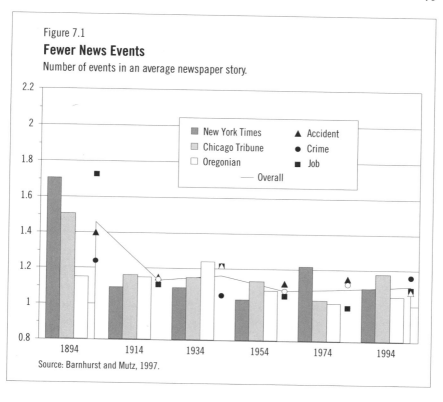

Figure 7.1
Fewer News Events
Number of events in an average newspaper story.

Source: Barnhurst and Mutz, 1997.

fundamental, not just a regrouping of events the press covers. Instead of chasing after every fire engine, modern news became more selective. Once a reporter covered half a dozen stories in a day, but that number dwindled to a few or even less. And editors, instead of running a roundup of several fires that day or week, would publish only the biggest (if they included any at all). One of the fires might become an example, representing all the fires of that sort, and the longer story might then focus on fire-related issues, but not on individual fires as events. The production of news had become modern, in search of the bigger picture.

The largest downturn in event coverage, between 1894 and the beginning of World War I, occurred during a period of turmoil in Europe that produced large numbers of news events. After the Dreyfus Affair in 1896, other scandals, diplomatic intrigues, and territorial annexations continued among the major European powers. Anarchists carried out a series of assassinations that reached beyond Europe with the death of U.S. President William McKinley. War flared up repeatedly: the Italian army entered in Ethiopia, the British fought in the Boer War, and the Spanish-American, Russo-Japanese, and Balkan conflicts broke out. Unrest and revolt in Russia and a revolution in Mexico took place. The seeming verge of chaos was an impetus toward modern ideas seeking order and explanation.

In the same period, practitioners began to have at their disposal much wider means for gathering news. Telegraph lines expanded their reach, radio emerged, air flight made airmail possible, and newly laid transoceanic cables allowed the first transcontinental telephone calls. Technical change opened the modern hope for progress through industry. There were all sorts of events to cover: the Panama Canal excavation, the San Francisco earthquake, Halley's Comet, expeditions to the North and South Poles, and the loss of the *Titanic*, each contributing to the modern shock of the new. The range of outlets for news also expanded, introducing consumer choice, and the number of newspapers published in the United States reached a peak. New York City, according to the U.S. Census, had twenty-nine papers by 1900.

Conditions of the era seem to point to more events in news, but as the pressure of occurrences increased and the means for transmitting them expanded, the number of events included in stories dropped. Rather than merely conveying occurrences, news practitioners began selecting actively what to include, and then writing and publishing lengthier stories. The tools of news practice also changed. In the late nineteenth century, newspapers began to do interviews,[15] which were at first a shocking departure from straight reporting. Conducting an interview created an event at the behest of editors and under the control of reporters. The new pseudo-events soon entered widespread practice. The press was no longer just selecting among available occurrences; it had begun manufacturing even more events by the early twentieth century. The new occupation of the journalist was taking charge of the "what" of news.

Such a large redefinition of news did not go unnoticed. In the wake of the change, an important and widely circulated critique of the press took place. The first salvo discharged when Irwin published his fifteen-part series on American news in *Collier's*, the weekly magazine that had taken a leading role in progressive reforms. Theodore Roosevelt had called its brand of coverage *muckraking*, but it helped clear slums, outlaw child labor, allow direct election of senators, and give women the right to vote. Irwin's 1911 series of articles sought to extend progressive thinking by returning news to its roots. The problem at the time, he argues, was the slant of interpretation. "Newspapers, good and bad, honest and venal, have come more and more to put their views into their news columns," he writes. "It looks simple at first sight" to report "just what occurs in the world," but the path toward a real account is strewn with obstacles: pressures from advertisers, corporate buyouts, and the tendency among newspaper conductors to become cronies of the country club set. "Most news" is no longer facts, he says, quoting a popular quip: "It is gossip about facts." In the last installment of the series, he proposed a solution: event-centered news, stripped of opinion.[16]

World War I and the 1918 Sedition Act made the need for realist news even more urgent.[17] In 1920, *The Brass Check*, Upton Sinclair's bestselling attack on the press, called the newspaper a mental "munitions factory" that was building the "bombs and gas-shells" used to impose ideas on and instill fear among the people. His solution was to call for a newspaper that was not "a journal of opinion, but a record of events pure and simple."[18] The following year Walter Lippmann, a founding dean among intellectual columnists, and Charles Merz, a reporter who left the *New York World* to become editorial page editor of the *New York Times*, published "A Test of News" in the *New Republic*. Their article examined three years of the *Times*—more than a thousand newspapers—for coverage of the Russian Revolution. The two writers call the paper's coverage "nothing short of a disaster." In news columns, the *Times* had reported events that never happened. And stories and accompanying headlines and captions also emphasized unsupported (and, as it turned out, unsupportable) interpretations. How, the authors ask, did such systematic misrepresentations occur in the *Times*? Driven by the wish for an outcome favorable to the Allies in World War I, the paper published not news of real occurrences but "semi-editorial news dispatches" based on "what men wanted to see," write Lippmann and Merz. They conclude that "a great people in a supreme crisis could not secure the minimum of necessary information on a supremely important event."[19]

Other critics agreed. In a January 1922 article for the *Atlantic Monthly*, magazine writer Frederick Lewis Allen, having witnessed censorship, propaganda, and "controlling or doctoring the news" during World War I, writes: "It is immensely important that the press shall give us the facts straight; and not merely the facts relating to department stores and other large business concerns, but the entire mass of facts about the world in which we live—political, economic, religious, scientific, social, and industrial."[20] The need was urgent after World War I as a wider public became aware that besides the Germans and the British, even the U.S. government had mounted propaganda efforts within the United States.

The U.S. Committee on Public Information went beyond circulating handouts, pamphlets, posters, films, advertisements, and exhibits to creating a system of speakers and committees, blanketing the country with messages designed to whip up and solidify public opinion in favor of an idealistic war portrayed as a battle between democracy and evil.[21] After the war, scholars led the reaction against propaganda. Historians, political scientists, psychologists, and sociologists developed a new approach called *propaganda analysis* to study the systems of social influence and control in modern societies. Their view spread widely in magazine articles and popular books. It reached into secondary schools, colleges, and adult education programs through study materials that an Institute for Propaganda Analysis distributed from Columbia University. Propaganda analysts aimed in part to arm the citizenry against future efforts, either covert or overt, to slant the news. It aimed to give the people enough knowledge to judge an event for itself.

In the decades following their critiques, the number of events covered in the average report appearing in the *New York Times* and other newspapers increased slightly. Realist, event-centered reporting advanced alongside and in tension with the growing influence of American modernism on the design of newspapers and management of news companies. But the average number of events in reports then fell again after 1934, a second downturn that occurred as fear of propaganda gave way to another urgent concern: that giving bare bones information about occurrences could itself become misleading. The notion grew in reaction to the Great Depression and World War II, pioneered oddly enough by the wire services, first United Press and then the Associated Press.[22] The "what" of news would again decline, not because of how much was happening or how many occurrences technology made accessible, but because of the assumption that people felt swamped and needed modern news to tame the flood of events.

Midcentury news personalities started discussing the weaknesses of event-centered news, prompted by political crisis and the rise of television. Beginning in 1947, the Newspaper Guild hosted a series of talks at the University of Minnesota where key speakers issued warnings about reporting events alone. The first three, by James Reston of the *New York Times*, Marquis Childs of the *St. Louis Post-Dispatch*, and Thomas L. Stokes of the *New York World-Telegram*, had a common thesis: "The press was not truly communicative in the early postwar years. It put before the reader a confusing welter of facts from the varied life of the nation and the world."[23] But "vital issues were not interrelated and interpreted in understandable form for the reader."

One way to understand the changes in news events is by considering the model of science. According to Thomas Kuhn's *The Structure of Scientific Revolutions*, scientists learn their craft less through abstract concepts in the classroom than through action in the laboratory. Craft-based knowledge forms a paradigm, a lens that reveals a particular view, a way to see the world. Kuhn calls that lens the "prerequisite to perception itself."[24] Only when the controlling paradigm faces a crisis do scientists begin a conscious effort at making new rules. The process then sometimes produces a new paradigm to replace the old—in what Kuhn calls a scientific revolution. Like scientists, reporters learn their craft through action. Their laboratory is found in places like the police department, the White House, or the street, along with the newsroom. Craft-based knowledge forms a paradigm in news, and although theory gets little traction, reporters and editors engage in rulemaking when the controlling paradigm enters a crisis. News practitioners in the nineteenth century drew from a partisan and literary paradigm, but when news became industrial, another paradigm emerged. As a new occupation, "journalists" resembled naturalists, gathering specimens that, they assumed, would allow a reader to understand the world. They considered chronicling occurrences their job, and so the paradigm supplied a realist lens for viewing the world.

In any practical activity, the means can overtake the ends,[25] and occurrences in the multifarious world soon seemed to overwhelm understanding. At the height of the new machine age, twentieth-century modernism emerged and in the next crisis shifted the paradigm toward sorting occurrences into categories. Reporters were still realists, accepting the need to focus on what happens, but modern editors were finding ways to select and organize events. The tension between modernism and realism is central to the paradigm that replaced partisan, literary news. It valued facts but struggled to balance objectivity with making sense. The strains of modernism emerged through news routines, in the ebb and flow of efforts to police the boundaries of news practice, such as the demarcation line between "news" and "opinion."

Other categories for sorting content also arose within practical processes— covering beats or editorial desks while competing with other news organizations, adapting to newer technologies, and adjusting to market pressures. The processes produced a set of mental tools called rubrics, such as relying on social types.[26] Rubrics grow out of necessity when writers or other cultural producers must work on a tight schedule. In news a *type* is a fiction necessary to the high-speed, high-volume action of reporting, editing, and producing content. Many types are familiar: the individual (as audience member or source), for example, versus a group, or a person-on-the-street versus someone in an official role, or a generic U.S. American versus someone defined by a local identity (New Yorker, Texan, Parisian). Some rubrics are simple stereotypes, such as the shorthand that invokes jobs or vocations (a bricklayer, a professor, a priest) or relies on stand-ins (the president for the U.S. federal government, or the Dow Jones Industrial Average invented in 1896 for indexing large and inscrutable markets). Others invoke grander notions: democracy, the public good, or freedom.

As news practice absorbed modern ideas, the classifying of events began to rely heavily on rubrics such as typecasting. Although rubrics began as conveniences, their use contained a seed that would move news away from realism centered on events. Practitioners know the types to be mere constructs, and they know them to fit only loosely—useful in general but untrue in specific instances. Editors in interviews describe making ethical choices based on a mental picture of the audience consuming news while sitting together as a family at breakfast. Faced with deciding whether to run a grisly wire story, editors call up their audience picture to counterbalance other pressures—from their peers, the market, and so forth. Does anyone really believe in that audience picture? The U.S. family is itself difficult enough to describe, most often not a father and mother with one- or two-point-something children, and they may no longer sit down for breakfast, or at least not be seated, together, or using the same device for news. The picture is inaccurate or false, but editors find it a useful shortcut.

In balancing realism with modernism, news practitioners employ the philosophy of *as if*, acknowledging a concrete world out there but relying on abstract types not because of their truth but because of their helpfulness.[27] As reporters and editors make the news through everyday actions, they produce a reality through their labor, rather than actively considering their relationship with the real. In a classic description of the process, a reporter encounters a plethora of *occurrences*, natural to the world out there and a potential resource. The reporter's job is to find occurrences and elevate them, through news procedures, to the status of *events*. Events are occurrences that are useful, and practitioners become skilled at identifying usefulness. Realism helps generate resources from the world out there, and modernism helps put them to functional use in sense making. Politicians hold a news conference or parties organize conventions for their own uses, and news producers view the occurrences with skepticism. Informers also have their own use in mind for any scandal that grows out of occurrences they reveal. Politicians, informers, and others pursue their own ends, but news practice finds most useful anything that occurs unintentionally. Kudos goes to the reporter or photographer who ferrets out the accidental or serendipitous. Free of the uses and intentions of others, chance occurrences lend themselves most to the uses of news. The reporters' use matters most. A need to appear rational, competent, original, and so forth may motivate them, and the news industry has organized itself to support and reward those motivations. Usefulness is a product of modern thinking that pursues functionalism.

Manufacturing news useful to its practitioners makes a difference because information about events "does not merely go to publics, it creates them."[28] The philosopher John Dewey described the idea that a public takes shape in the process of forming events from the raw information about occurrences. Under tensions within the new paradigm in news, the focus on events or analysis waxed and waned, but both imply something broader about conditions in society. When reporting tends to stick to events only, that coverage may mean consensus exists, or it may signal only the suppression of disagreement. In either case the predominance of event-centered reporting can sustain itself because it describes a society in consensus, however reinforced. The shifts toward event coverage in the first part of the twentieth century may have reflected a growing consensus in U.S. society, which reached a high point around midcentury, along with a tendency to downplay opposition.

Sometimes the groups promoting a particular occurrence as worthy of becoming a news event come into conflict. They disagree about what type of event it should become—that is, about what the occurrence means or should mean. The contentions define an event as something else: an *issue*.[29] For news, issues have ready-made usefulness, because the sides develop arguments for reporters to convey. An added payoff is that the news organization itself can take the middle ground, occupying the rational and competent space between the contenders. Although issues are convenient and useful, in the process of identifying and covering them news media may unintentionally sow disharmony or stir up strife. The opposing sides appear less than reasonable, while reporters (but not columnists and commentators—an important distinction in the craft) may appear not to be tendentious themselves. The problem solidifies in the most intractable issues of U.S. society.

After midcentury another crisis helped move news away from event-centered coverage. The paradigm for news evolved but still held realism fundamental (a tenet that scientific paradigms share): reality is still out there for reporters to observe and describe. The transition in news accompanied a general shift in the technologies of everyday life, especially the emergence of television. What happened in broadcast news?

CHAPTER 8

The "What" Waned in Broadcast News

The crisis that finally solidified thinking against the value of realist, event-centered news was the McCarthy hearings. When Sen. Joseph R. McCarthy mounted his virulent attacks in early 1950, accusing the Truman administration of harboring Communists in the State Department, the press simply reported who said what. The Republican Party won the 1952 election and took control of the Senate, and McCarthy became committee chair and expanded his attacks, going after defense industries, universities, and the broadcasters themselves. ABC Television came into national prominence by airing the hearings about supposed Communist infiltration of the U.S. Army, riveting national attention with the live proceedings.

But the events could not really speak for themselves, a discovery that seemed to expose a weakness in realism. Every name named exacted a human cost, as McCarthy dragged innocent individuals into the public eye, and his baseless accusations harmed their relationships and destroyed their livelihoods. The consequences, although not lost on the press, were not in themselves news events as then defined. Elmer Davis pointed out the contradiction. He had left reporting for the *New York Times* to become a commentator on CBS Radio, where he recommended that the U.S. government centralize information during World War II. President Franklin D. Roosevelt later named him to head the new Office of War Information.[1] When Davis returned to broadcasting after the war, he challenged McCarthy and other congressional committees and questioned the conventions of event-centered reporting.

In a speech titled "Must We Mislead the Public?" Davis cited example after example when "the best papers in the country gave their readers . . . a seriously mistaken impression." The "practice of reporting what everybody said" about an occurrence "and letting the reader make up his own mind" imposed "a considerable burden on the reader," Davis said. It also gave a lot of attention to "proven liars": "Consider Senator McCarthy; not a single one of his charges has ever been proved, most of them have been pretty conclusively disproved in public hearings—yet he can repeat those same charges and still get space in the papers, sometimes on the front page." Davis revealed that "editors may know that this is old stuff," but "if a United States Senator keeps on saying it," the norms of event-centered news require they print it. "This kind of dead-pan reporting—So-and-so said it, and if he is lying in his teeth it is not my business to say so—may salve the conscience of the reporter (or of the editor, who has the ultimate responsibility)," Davis said. "But what about his loyalty to the reader?" In other words, realist event coverage clearly missed the truth, but the newer, modern component of the news paradigm could help. Davis proposed that radio news commentary like his own provided "a mixture of news and interpretation" and could "admirably illuminate and explain the news for the customer." Well aware of the dangers in the course he suggested, Davis said, "I believe the present tendency is toward more interpretation. But just how it can effectively be done . . . on the front page—that is something that must still be worked out."[2]

Under the realist definition of news, reporters could cover a rebuttal to Sen. McCarthy only when another usable occurrence took place. It happened in front of a television camera on June 9, 1954, when Special Counsel for the Army Joseph N. Welch, in his now-famous testimony before the committee, challenged McCarthy's needless defamation of a young lawyer. "Until this moment, Senator, I think I never really gauged your cruelty or your recklessness," he said and then after further exchanges concluded, "Let us not assassinate this lad further, Senator. You have done enough. Have you no sense of decency sir, at long last? Have you left no sense of decency?"[3]

Other prominent broadcasters took up Davis's critique. Eric Sevareid had started at CBS News as one of the so-called Murrow's boys working under news chief Edward R. Murrow to cover World War II. In a Newspaper Guild speech called "The Big Truth," Sevareid observed "the enormous flood of facts" and noted "we are not really getting it across, not really preparing the American mind." After recounting specific episodes of McCarthy's demagoguery, Sevareid said, "The warp and woof of what the papers print and the broadcasters voice—our flat, one-dimensional handling of the news, have given the lie the same prominence and impact that truth is given; they have elevated the influence of fools to that of wise men; the ignorant to the level of the learned; the evil to the level of the good." He then waxed philosophical: "For every age, there is one unpardonable sin," he said, quoting an ambassador in Washington. "Do you know what is the unpardonable sin of the present age? It is superficiality, lack of depth, absence of perspective—a happy skimming over the surface of things." From start to finish, Sevareid implicitly condemned realist news centered on events: "We have not really moved into the era of three-D journalism, although some are trying; we are not providing the depth, not illuminating the background, making it a living part of the picture with the third dimension, which is Meaning."[4]

Press historian Frank Luther Mott also argued that processes "looming up as background" are "far more significantly important than most of the thousand little happenings . . . that fill so many newspaper columns."[5] Along with other researchers, he considered attending to obvious events the greatest failure of midcentury U.S. news. Historians analyzing the Army-McCarthy hearings cited newspaper reporters but called the press an "unwilling instrument" that did not play a central role beyond acquiescing in McCarthy's campaign or the "tacit compact to ignore him" after the Senate censured him.[6] The press did raise objections on the editorial page, most notably the *Washington Post*, but could not justify doing the same in news columns. In realist terms, the sensation from McCarthy's unexpected accusations about Communists infiltrating the centers of power outweighed their questionable basis. In a climate of consensus about the dangers of Communism, his announcements at press conferences were without doubt *news events*.

Broadcast news came on the scene as attitudes toward event coverage began to change, and on-air coverage in its early decades continued the trends found in print. The press further reduced event coverage in the second half of the century. One way to measure broadcast events is by counting the number of stories in the average show. A thirty-year analysis of ABC, CBS, and NBC evening news found a consistent trend on all three networks toward fewer and fewer items per show each year. *World News Tonight* on ABC included a dozen stories on average in 1970 but three decades later had fewer than eight. The negative trends were strong, indicating that "network news was covering less."[7] A later study suggested a rebound, but the number of stories might not give a complete picture of how many events the programs included.[8]

Another way to examine event coverage is by looking inside each story to take stock of the "what" of news reporting.[9] How often were television newscasters giving information about current events? In their voice-overs, stand-ups, and other speech, they shifted away from saying merely what happened (figure 8.1). In 1968 they stuck to giving information about occurrences at least a third of the times they spoke on the air, but that share of event focus declined over the next two decades. The data followed a sawtooth pattern, going up and down in the four-year

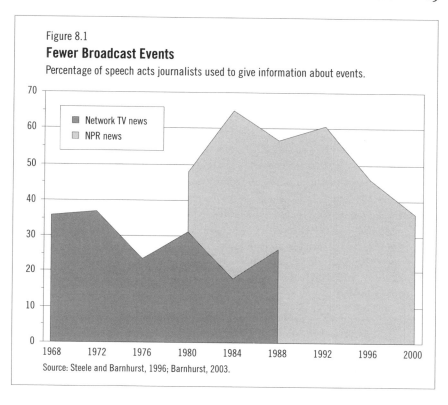

Figure 8.1
Fewer Broadcast Events
Percentage of speech acts journalists used to give information about events.

Source: Steele and Barnhurst, 1996; Barnhurst, 2003.

intervals between national elections, but overall the downward trend continued for event-centered news. Newscasters became less involved in the realist task of giving information, spending a greater share of their activity on other things, such as offering opinions, showing agreement, and voicing reactions, the stuff of making modern meaning.

Unlike the television networks, National Public Radio (NPR) did not face the full brunt of market competition and the constant squeeze for more advertising time,[10] but NPR news followed the same trend. The 1980 election was the first when *Morning Edition* and its afternoon counterpart *All Things Considered* were both on the air. Over the next few elections, NPR newscasters managed to stick to informing the audience about events nearly half—or even more—of the times they spoke. But then a steep decline began, dropping that share of their speech to nearly a third. The change becomes most clear by comparing excerpts from two reports, one early and the other late in the period.

On October 13, 1980, Correspondent Linda Wertheimer began her campaign story this way:

> **WERTHEIMER**: President Carter went to the Forest Hills Jewish Community Center to, as he said in his speech, "let the people of Queens know exactly where I stand," but when the president began to speak, demonstrations began as well.
>
> **CARTER**: Let there be no doubt where I stand. The United States opposes [*heckling interrupts Carter*] . . . The United States opposes and I oppose any PLO state.
>
> **WERTHEIMER**: President Carter said he wished to confront without mincing words a question that has been raised in the Jewish community about the president's support of Israel after the election, especially if large numbers of Jewish voters defect the Democratic Party.
>
> **CARTER**: I want each of you, even including the demonstrators, to go back to the people in your communities and neighborhoods and tell them this: The president will never turn his back on Israel. I never have and I never will. [*applause*] And this president will never use economic and military aid to Israel as a lever against Israel. Not in the last four years. Not now, and not in the next four years. [*applause*]

Wertheimer opens her story by focusing on what happened with Carter, the community center, and the hecklers. Any terms implying a judgment, such as "mincing" and "defect," come as she paraphrases the candidate. The rest of the package is straight event coverage.

By 1996, event-centered reporting on NPR had begun to fall. On October 17 Joanne Silberner reported on a healthcare discussion during the presidential debate:

> **SILBERNER**: What a difference four years makes. In the last presidential campaign, then-candidate Bill Clinton drew plenty of support for his promise of universal health care.
>
> **CLINTON (1992 PRESIDENTIAL CANDIDATE)**: I have pledged that within the first 100 days of a Clinton administration, I would submit a comprehensive healthcare plan for real change that deals with cost and coverage and access, with quality and the maintenance of consumer choice.
>
> **SILBERNER**: In the 1996 campaign, both Republicans and Democrats are offering vaguer, less ambitious plans for changes in the nation's healthcare system. [*Goes on to introduce an expert source.*]

The first noticeable change is in sound bites. Wertheimer used much more of the speech from Carter than Silberner used from Clinton, whose sound bites also run shorter. The trends away from giving realist information and toward modern highlighting of the reporter's interpretations of what happens are just as clear.

Silberner opens her story with a personal exclamation, and she then expresses her judgment about the Clinton's then-current (and by implication, past) healthcare proposals.

Although the share of event coverage went up and down from election to election, the overall trend was again a sturdy one. The archetypal activity for newscasters—reporting what was happening—declined during the NPR political coverage. In the decades before the rise of NPR as a major news outlet, network TV news saw similar declines. But practitioners and historians tell a different story, that event-centered television news grabbed the breaking news from newspapers, forcing them to abandon the many one-off items retelling small events and switch to a few longer reports explaining big events.[11] Intense time limits and the pressures of live reporting seem to make broadcasting more episodic, but contrary to expectation, national television and serious radio news followed the trends of the mainstream press, covering fewer events.

How do newscasters explain the shift? Rick Kaplan started out as a copy boy in Chicago and rose to become president of CNN News. Along the way he produced national programs with Walter Cronkite, Ted Koppel, and Peter Jennings, among others. His views illustrate how insiders think about covering the "what" of news. In our interview, he suggested three points about the shift from realist news. First, reporters have a valuable resource to offer. Long experience allows a reporter to "know the players, what to expect from them, and how they've gotten where they've gotten." Kaplan suggests imagining a summit where world leaders first meet: often the newscasters have been in place longer than either head of state and bring more to the table than just a description of what is happening. "Ted Koppel is one of the smartest people I've ever met," says Kaplan. "I want his knowledge. This is a respected, trusted colleague, and he knows what he's talking about." The press also has depth in numbers, Kaplan says, and they back each other up, making the press corps stronger.

Kaplan was working for ABC News on the night the Berlin Wall fell, producing a new program called *Prime Time Live,* which led the evening's edition with live pictures two hours after the wall came down. The program had yet to establish a track record of covering serious stories to build viewer loyalty, he says. "People did not remember or were not reminded about the history," and the event itself lacked any looming danger. Without that modernist big picture or future impact, the coverage failed to attract a big audience. Kaplan says it "was a huge shock to me and to everybody else" when it received low ratings. He sees in the experience the need for a pattern of (modern) authoritative insight.

Second, reporting who-said-what only can do harm by ignoring context. Kaplan cites the case of global warming: "You'd always go out and find the two sides of the story. So never mind there were nine hundred environmentalists—experts—who believed in global warming, to every two who didn't. In a story of four minutes, it almost looked like it was fifty-fifty: 'There's a debate over whether there's global warming.' But reporters, in an attempt not to come down on one side, would portray to the audience: 'There's this raging battle over global warming.'" He calls climate change "a great example of stories where the 'unbiased' media did an enormous disservice to the public." A supposedly balanced report, he says, can be as misleading as it would be to quote experts on "both sides" of the Holocaust. Good reporting should include what he calls *learned sources*, and "learned sourcing might even include themselves"—the reporters. "If they know," says Kaplan, they "ought to communicate that to people."

Modern practitioners in print and broadcast alike now agree that news requires more than just reporting of events or relying on quotations that reduce issues to two sides. The call for more context is not new. In his book on Detroit, reporter Ze'ev Chafets says the local newspapers "relentlessly chronicle the events in America's most violent city." And, he says, "What you read in the papers . . . is not inviting. . . . Average murders get reported on the inside pages under laconic headings like IN THIS WEEKEND'S SHOOTINGS. Partly this is a simple variation on the old journalistic rule that a dog biting a man is not news; every year, upwards of three hundred kids are shot in the city."[12] That kind of event coverage reflects but also reinforces stereotypes, leaving the news media open to charges of racism. The problem of uninviting news is perennial and extends beyond big cities. The editor of the *Kent Reporter*, located in a small city outside Seattle, Washington, says in an Editor's Note, "I don't relish putting bleeding headlines on my front page," but the coverage reflects the context, "the truth about" Kent.[13] Like Kaplan, others warn practitioners of the dangers in focusing narrowly on event coverage.

Finally, Kaplan argues, event coverage ignores the growing complexity of the world. What was acceptable when the Soviet Union was intact no longer makes sense since the USSR broke into independent countries. The region presents a greater reporting challenge, he says: "That's why *Nightline* was such a satisfying program to work on. We just did one story. We took the lead story every day and spent thirty minutes on it—spent the entire evening newscast on it. And we still sometimes didn't tell you enough, in our view." The complexity of events requires longer, modern news. Others agree that a more complex world is a main reason for going beyond events. Rosenblum says the news system "responds inadequately when suddenly called upon to explain something so complex and menacing as a dollar collapse—or a war in Asia."[14] When complicated processes get covered as a series of reports, with reversals and changes day after day, readers become "snow-blind," says Doug Clifton, executive editor of the *Miami Herald*. "We report on so many snowflakes that they can hardly see."[15] The 2008 meltdown in the U.S. housing market followed a yearlong flurry of news reports on the dangers of questionable loans, but people "weren't paying attention."[16]

Recent observations echo insiders from the mid-twentieth century. Back then Elmer Davis said newspapers fall short "because of the vast and continually increasing complexity of modern life with which the news must deal," and Eric Sevareid decried the tendency "toward oversimplification at a time when the substance, the truth, has become more and more complex and must be understood in all its complexity."[17] Even a century ago Will Irwin waxed eloquent on what the Progressives saw as a need for news, in "the complex organism of modern society."[18]

Some critics agree that reporters should do more than cover only events.[19] They say the lack of context is especially acute on television, and research suggests the preponderance of TV network news is *episodic* rather than *thematic*, focused narrowly on specific events rather than on the broad social, economic, and political circumstances behind an event.[20] Episodic news leaves viewers struggling to attribute political responsibility when important issues arise, and "the same pattern" has held for decades.[21] The critiques and research push news toward modern explanations. Kaplan's position—that event-centered news wastes correspondents' and anchors' knowledge, does damage by lacking context, and remains blind to social processes in their complexity—occupies the mainstream among news producers and researchers. As he moved into more prominent positions in broadcast news, other critics objected. Conservatives have taken up the opposition toward modernism, arguing for event-centered news.[22] A prominent political scientist, writing under the aegis of the American Enterprise Institute, says, "The news is not a reporter's perception or explanation of what happens, it is simply what happens."[23] Anything else, says a former CBS News correspondent, is "junk journalism." What practitioners call *substance* is just "an editorial masquerading as real news," an excuse to introduce *unnecessary* complexity, when everything from tax law to news itself needs simplifying.[24]

A century ago Progressives with a realist faith in citizens proposed that straightforward reporting of what happens will change the world. A century later traditionalists with many "facts" of their own making resist change by arguing for just-the-facts news. The political reversal is dramatic. But mainstream and conservative viewpoints are not at opposite poles. Beneath the two positions is a shared belief in a concrete reality open to observation and description, even if little honored. Both sides at least start from a realist perspective. The Right has developed a *rusé* realism, the cunning opposite of naïve, to oppose the news media. Modern news practice, which emerged from literary activity in the nineteenth century along with the modern novel,[25] shares with the novel a continued reliance on mainstream realism. For realists, all writers and their audiences have access to the concrete world, but journalists, unlike novelists and readers, have a privileged vantage point (disdained on the right). They focus on documenting reality full time and have routine contacts with sources who themselves observe reality. The efforts of news practitioners day after day build a comprehensive picture of reality, so that knowledge of the world accumulates, following Kaplan's argument.

But how then did the news end up moving away from event coverage? If the mainstream view were correct, news would still center on events, but it no longer does. If the conservative view were correct, then audiences would detect bias and cant on MSNBC and find on the Fox network a kind of fair and balanced news distinct in reporting events alone. But plainly event-centered U.S. news remains absent, and audiences know MSNBC and Fox by their political reputations and partisan alignment at the center and far right. Neither the mainstream nor conservative view can account for the changes in news content. An explanation for why news centers less on events than ever before will not come from news practitioners and their critics. But perhaps the assumptions underlying news can shed light on the change. The realism beneath the surface of partisan debate survives because U.S. Americans across the political spectrum share ideas of how knowledge grows. Even those who recognize modern assumptions at work employ the rhetoric of realism when trying to sway news media, critics, and the general public. Realism seems the default in politics, economics, and society and hangs on in the arts.

After the advent of broadcasting, the paradigm of news entered a new phase, where making meaning added value to event coverage and news practitioners found ways that events indicated broader issues. News practice began to require making sense of events, an improved lens for viewing what happens. Modern news practitioners came to consider mere facts potentially misleading, and a primary standard for quality news became how well it could make events understandable and expose trends and problems. In contrast to the consensus society of event coverage, issue coverage describes a society in conflict. Both types of coverage are representations typifying society through general patterns, in contrast to what individuals experience. Issue-centered reporting may mean honest disagreement exists, or it may signal something less hopeful, a basic contentiousness of society. Either way implicates news practice in the creation of those meanings. Modern news reached its high point, for instance, in the dispute over the meaning of a burglary—with the investigative reporting during Watergate.

Internal debates about straight reporting then emerged as dissenting voices returned to prominence. Those left out of the consensus through the 1950s began speaking out, including minority groups at the margins of economic life, peace activists opposed to military expansion, and others. The shift in news toward making sense and identifying difficulties then grew throughout the second half of the century, as conflict erupted over racism and war, sexism and abortion, and homophobia and AIDS. The long period of disputation polarized U.S. politics, and news media participated in the trend by increasing first issue coverage and then partisan reporting. Issue coverage gave solid form to and helped make intractable the issues of U.S. society.

Issue stories have a distinct life from the time they enter the news until they run their course. Take the example of female genital cutting, which the New York Times first reported in 1980.[26] Initial stories described the practice as a realist drama of human concern, covered because feminists and activists, who spoke out at international conferences, disagreed with those who performed it about its meaning (what kind of event it should be). Was it a ritual akin to male circumcision, as its adherents believed, or a mutilation and debasement of women? After a decade of infrequent reports, coverage expanded in the 1990s, when a novel and a documentary film came out against the practice. CNN then filmed the operation on a ten-year-old girl in Egypt, and other media joined in covering another case, of a Togo native seeking asylum to escape cutting. The shocking coverage gave way to legal and medical information, and then to the policy realm, as the U.S. government finally took action. It banned the custom and made support for international institutions contingent on whether nations receiving loans also conducted educational campaigns against it. Once the policy debate ended, female circumcision coverage declined after 1998.

The entire life cycle of the issue took two decades, as the coverage moved from human interest to scientific information, shifted to policy debates, and finally dwindled to the occasional report on enforcement. Along the way, activists brought their complaints into view, and the discussion widened to include scientists and government leaders. Editors fashioned news—especially in the case of CNN—with a growing public looking on and engaging, until U.S. action resolved the issue at least symbolically. In what was probably a foregone conclusion, the activist definition of genital cutting won the debate within the U.S. media, pushing aside competing definitions.

The growth and decay of news coverage does not spring from the issue itself. The parallel debate about male genital mutilation, which has become an issue in some European countries, exists in most cases outside mainstream news or in reports about outsiders in the United States. In U.S. news, the removal of a large share of the sensing tissue of male sexual organs in infants goes by the bloodless name "circumcision," despite the absence of scientific support for the practice and the presence of an angry movement called intactivism. The neutral, harmless-seeming term "cut" applies to men in the U.S. context, not unlike the words applied to women in countries that practice its parallel.[27]

News operates to reflect and to focus, shining the light "out there" but focusing it with potential hazard. In a sense, reporters and editors cannot win—their output comes off as either dim or too bright. If they stick to events alone, they face censure for ignoring the complex context and their own common sense. Realist, event news cannot see the nose on its face. But the more news practitioners try to make sense of events, the more they face censure for claiming too much say over what matters or for taking sides in a contest best left to the politicos. Modernist, sense-making news is a know-it-all.

But oddly the occupation has gained ground either way, adding economic and social status through each phase of the news paradigm. The turn to realist fact at the end of the nineteenth century made the journalist into a stronger observer, generating neutral descriptions that publishers found desirable for expanding market share. And the turn to investigation and explanation lifted news institutions even higher in public esteem as modernism reached its zenith in news around the 1970s. But a solid grounding in realism helped modern news prosper through the twentieth century. In each era a version of news practice emerged to reflect and captivate a public caught up in new kinds of realism and modernism: mapping the complex social world early in the century and shifting to ways of indexing the social landscape later in the century.

When practitioners justify their work, they employ not *realism* but other terms for their aims: *facts* and *truth*. They have practical definitions for both terms. First, the facts: although in ordinary settings practitioners talk about events and facts almost interchangeably, facts are the larger item.[28] Reporting facts carries a heavier burden than reporting events because factual coverage requires a reporter to say how the world is, and not just what happened in it. The first challenge when selecting and arraying events is to reveal facts. Editors judge event reporting by whether it sticks to facts, and that means they try to align new occurrences with the accumulated experience of previous reporting.

Sometimes reporters simply cannot get access to the facts of how things are but must convey events anyway. In a period of stock market declines, the Dow Jones Industrial Average in August 2001 fell below 10,000, and brokerage firms announced a series of layoffs. The Charles Schwab Corporation "sent a pre-Labor Day ripple of tension" through the market, according to a two-paragraph item in the *New York Times*.[29] "Additional Cuts at Schwab Add to Troubles on Wall St." ran its headline at the top of the Business Digest. Glen Mathison, a spokesman for Schwab, was doing damage control. The layoffs went well beyond U.S. market conditions, which meant closing down foreign offices, Mathison told me in an interview that week, but Schwab did not want that fact revealed yet. The *Times* ran a twenty-inch story inside the Business section, "Schwab to Eliminate 2,400 Jobs in New Round of Cuts," predicting similar moves by Credit Suisse and other firms. The story quoted a Schwab official saying, "To make up for the shortfall in trading commissions," the company would be "consolidating offices in cities around the country and merging some branches," but the story did not report the larger move, despite pointing out the unusually high cost of the layoffs. In August 31 coverage on NPR, another reporter used a sound bite from Mathison staying on message by pointing to investor decisions, not the foreign office closings.

The event report did not encompass the defining facts. In the world of news, reporters gave meaning to the event at Schwab. It marked a U.S. economic downturn, expressed in job cuts within a sector closely connected to the stock market. In the world of Schwab, a fundamental shift in its business, away from foreign offices and more focused on the U.S. market, was also taking place. Schwab was becoming a different kind of company, and the transformation would have been a much bigger story. But that change in the facts about how the world was becoming (in one company and its connections) was not the event reported. Before reporters could go deeper, the September 2001 attacks interrupted the routines of news outlets.

While reporting what happens, news stories convey small, working conjectures about what the world is like. Think of those guesses as facts-in-waiting. If they succeed, they become facts, but otherwise they sink into oblivion. To decide what amounts to fact, reporters compare their own against their colleagues' output. "From my own experience," Michele McLellan, then special projects editor for the Portland *Oregonian*, said in our 2001 interview, "there's sort of a self-reinforcing quality about the culture of a newsroom" whether in newspapers or television. Not that all reporters set out to tell "the same story," she says, "but that's all we're talking about": "I can imagine a news meeting, at 10 o'clock in the morning. Thirty people go in there to talk about what's happening for the day. The managing editor probably walks in every morning and says, 'So what's going on with the war today,' and it all kind of flows from there. It's self-reinforcing."

Change in news occurs because reporters are always trying to come up with new angles (which contain new conjectures about the world), and sometimes they succeed. McLellan describes the creative process: "A story appears—somebody may have just come up with it." A smart reporter does an unusual story and "creates a model. And . . . in the newsroom they talk about it. They like it . . . and it catches on." A reporter demonstrates competence by going along with the consensus but showing occasional flashes of originality.

Uniformity and creativity both receive reinforcement. Reporters check each other by repetition, reporting on or ignoring similar occurrences and aligning them with the facts. Normal reporting tends to be fairly uniform. Besides watching each other and watching the world, reporters and editors are noticing who gets recognition and awards. When innovations occur, news practitioners seem to move together, doing what others have found success at doing.

Practical success with facts drives reporting toward a larger goal: the truth. Truth is the highest aim and justification of journalism, as Eric Sevareid's speech indicated in the mid-twentieth century. Modern news practice continues to pursue the ideal. A long-time police reporter for the *Miami Herald* writes, "There is something noble about venturing out every day to seek the truth."[30] What works is realist, the finding of events that match the facts, but what works best is modern, the producing of events that align those facts with understanding the wider world. As practitioners critique each other—and as they join in the process of individual and then group innovation—they define truth by what has worked or failed as a way to view the world. Realist news gleans that worldview from the concrete expressions of the culture, but a worldview that works, at least until recently, has tended to be modern, producing more facts, especially reliable and useful ones, that reveal a bigger picture.

News practitioners also judge others by the same standard of truth. Competing political parties make conflicting assertions about what an occurrence means, and they take out advertisements with dramatically different claims that use "facts" to show what their candidates stand for. Reporters then do "truth-squad" stories, asking whether the statements and the images in the advertisements report the facts. Truth, by their definition in practice, is a larger judgment about whether a statement squares with how the world is or what it is like. A claim about or an image of an event is true if it corresponds to the facts.

Sometimes the reports of events misfire, as they did during the U.S. stock market bubble of the late 1990s.[31] When *Fortune* magazine writer Bethany McLean questioned what the energy firm Enron did for its money, only TheStreet.com followed up. Within a year Enron had gone belly-up, but a picture of what happened finally emerged many months later. The *New York Times* then covered the ignored story in its multi-page "Enron's Many Strands." McLean's initial report proposed facts that did not square with conventional knowledge about the firm, which insiders recognized in hindsight.[32] A similar process occurred for reporting on weapons of mass destruction (WMD) a decade later. Leading up to the Iraq War, the news reported national intelligence confirming WMD activity. But when the military discovered none, the *New York Times* and *Washington Post* reviewed their coverage and issued apologies.[33]

The job of reporting events generates a conjecture about the world, giving occurrences their initial meaning. Then through repeated event coverage—and through the resolution of issues—the guesses about things settle into established facts, with implications for policy and society about problems such as genital cutting. Slowly, knowledge of the world accumulates, a realist would say, in the form of a truth, the supreme achievement of journalism, which amounts to a way of knowing based on broader statements that correspond to the array of facts. When new occurrences fail to fit into the meanings available for events, news practice adjusts through discussion, sparks of creativity, and trial and error. So reporters confronting the propaganda of World War I had to refocus on events, and the McCarthy hearings refocused news on the need to stand apart from occurrences and instead to emphasize issues. Both moves attempted to realign news with facts and truth. Through the ebbs of realism and flows of modernism, the paradigm grew stronger from small changes. They emerged out of new angles combined with practical necessity to transform the news. Realism and modernism operated in tandem, with realism shrinking at the base and modernism expanding overall.

First-hand accounts of the shifts in the "what" of news add detail to what the larger perspective of realism explains. Scientists also generate conjectures about the world, which they call hypotheses, and they repeat their experiments in a process they call replication. They seek to resolve issues in scientific theory, and their efforts confirm or unsettle a larger picture or paradigm of the world. They judge paradigms by "their heuristic power: how many new facts did they produce?"[34] Although the vocabulary differs for scientists and journalists, the processes are parallel. Both occupations attend to occurrences out there, formulating guesses that become either "events" or "hypotheses," both resolve issues to arrive at either "facts" or "concepts," and both seek to establish a larger reality, either "truth" or "theory."

The accounts from rank-and-file scientists and reporters hew to realism, but their objects of attention differ. Both position themselves as observers and describers of the world, and the insights from each occupation enhance the rationality, competence, and originality of the observers. *Social* scientists who study news have even more in common with its practitioners. A researcher's account of news makes its own claim to establish facts and truth of a sociological sort. The pictures of news that journalists and sociologists paint are not incompatible. They begin with occurrences at the foot, build a main body of events and issues, and add a head full of facts and a crown of truth. Or so it worked through most of the twentieth century. But by the twenty-first, things had changed. Modernism came under doubt as audiences fragmented and U.S. intellectual life entered ferment. What worked in the 1970s no longer worked in the changing spider-web world since the 1990s. To understand what was happening to U.S. society in the digital era requires looking at the news paradigm at century's end and its realist and modernist stock in trade as news moved onto digital media.

CHAPTER 9

Modern Events Resumed Online

Alex Jones, a Pulitzer Prize winner who directed a Harvard think tank, says that U.S. news practice got itself "in trouble" because new technologies produce not facts but irreality in the new century.[1] He and others tended to place legacy news in opposition to digital, mobile media, but in response Jill Abramson, working at the *New York Times*, argues against putting "the guardians of print journalism" on one side and digital media on the other. She says the industry should focus on "championing serious, quality" news that subjects the "human craving for trustworthy information" to skilled analysis and judgment.[2] The call for credibility returns modern news to its longstanding public service mission.[3] The move seems urgent because on newer venues, "the line has blurred between real reporting and faking it," a former political reporter says. "The risk is that readers and viewers—voters—won't be able to separate reported fact from fabricated fiction in what they see and hear."[4] In the Wild West of internet news, how did the "what" of news fare?

Online versions of major news outlets went through a period of experimentation but then returned to "serious, quality" news (figure 9.1). The "what" in accident, crime, employment, and political stories in the first decade of the 2000s at first began reporting more events in stories, reversing decades of declines. Accident stories in 2001 referred the most to related events, and employment stories the least, as reporters tended to draw connections among current accidents but treated employment stories as isolated events.[5] By 2005 they again were adding events to stories, and the news sites diverged; the larger sites were already stepping back to focus on fewer events in stories.[6] Surveys found the number and depth of news reports decreasing as more online outlets emerged.[7] U.S. news was in state of ferment, but why?

Industry insiders at the time tended to blame new technology, but digital media did not have the competitive edge.[8] Allowing the web edition to scoop the print edition—letting a free product compete with a profitable one—lost money for publishers. Some invested as little in web editions as necessary to block rival sites and used little of the technological potential of the internet, such as interactive links or multimedia features.[9] Along with some news staffers, publishers proposed technical options that failed to get traction, and so they became late adopters of technologies that succeeded, such as social media. Although the availability of ways to publish news online did not itself change the content of news stories, reporters and editors did respond to the *idea* of a powerful technology. Increases in events included in stories resemble the sudden rediscovery of the link. As digital mobile media came into popular use, reporters could link events together and gained access to networked information.[10] Michele McLellan of the *Oregonian* said that web editions did not make news change but that networks and their reach were in the background. In other interviews, those producing for print or digital venues said they were thinking of the other platform. In our interviews, Michel Marriott of the *New York Times* said print reporters and editors began to think of posting

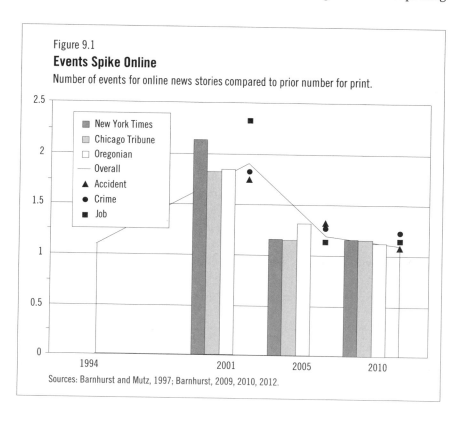

Figure 9.1
Events Spike Online
Number of events for online news stories compared to prior number for print.

Sources: Barnhurst and Mutz, 1997; Barnhurst, 2009, 2010, 2012.

online, and former Women.com editor-in-chief Lisa Stone said those creating stories online began to influence print reporters.

But by 2010 the references to current events within stories had declined to the levels of the 1990s, with political stories concentrating even more than other topics on a single current event.[11] The changes in the "what" echo earlier patterns of modern news, when practitioners responded to then-new technologies by reverting to established ways. Online, the news outlets again moved together, a pattern that suggests a missed opportunity. News practice might have escaped from conventional constraints, pushing to a linked perspective on what happens. The general public was using interconnectivity to cope with the flow of information in the new century, a third of them sharing news stories on social media, half relying on word of mouth, and more than three-quarters using email links.[12] Instead of finding ways to stay in tune with public habits, news practitioners pushed back, closing ranks around modern truth.

Practitioners and researchers lamented the downsizing, financial turmoil, and competitive pressures the industry faced in the new era. But few questioned the modern assumptions behind the pursuit of news facts and truth. The reading public began shifting to a new regime of "what-ness," not abandoning news but finding it through aggregators, blogs, and other go-between venues for brief recycled news content. Their move questioned once-common beliefs in the attributes of "quality" news: the authority, context, and pattern recognition that modernism offered in a complex world. News organs reasserted meaning-centered news, even as event-centered thinking advanced in other spheres. The face-to-face and media experiences of some audience members merged so that "friending" and "informing" crossed almost seamlessly between online and embodied modes of contact. Audiences and users concentrated on small moments—illustrated in videos going viral—and on grassroots phenomena such as flash or smart mobs, which renewed realist lenses for viewing the world. News practitioners at first experimented and then returned to the familiar ground of facts and truth to justify what they do, reasserting modernist values. News organs may have helped usher in a new realist consensus by reasserting meaning-centered news and rejecting the event-centered thinking even as it grew more prominent elsewhere.

Professional claims to factual truth have come into question in the twenty-first century. In the prevalent view, facts have two qualities: they are independent of what individuals may think about them, and they are stable in meaning over time. Together the qualities establish a view that philosophers call *naïve realism* (or *naïve empiricism*). Naïve realism assumes the existence of "events out there to be observed and appropriately described."[13] But there are two problems with the standard of realism, and they reside, not surprisingly, in the processes of observing and describing.

What does it mean to observe? Reporters sometimes go out on the streets to witness occurrences, but they can see only what happens within their range of vision. Other occurrences—some of them preceding, others simultaneous but separated by space—are outside what the reporter can observe. Interviews make the idea of observing even less concrete. Reporters select among many sources, make the interview take place, and choose the questions. When it happens by telephone, without any other occurrence and without the physical cues of face-to-face contact, does that count as observing? The stories *New York Times* reporter Jayson Blair invented, which led to his dismissal and to the resignation of senior editors in 2003, had some basis in occurrences;[14] he made up his stories by starting from other news stories. What about the press or wire reports that become fodder for a story with a local angle? When reclassifying distant events as cues for local occurrences, is the re-write person observing?

Here modernism enters in. "Observation involves the application of categories to sense impressions."[15] Classifying things (or persons and their states of being and doing) is an act of interpretation, and interpretations generate expectations. A trivial case is a widely held belief about wine glasses. After news reports said that the shape of the drinking glass affects the taste and even the chemistry of wine, the story circulated widely in the daily press, in food and science magazines, and on the radio through commentators such as Paul Harvey. But the original report got it wrong. Kari Russell's senior thesis at the University of Tennessee discovered just the opposite. But observers tend to find what they are looking for. Other interests came into play in the wine story, including marketing efforts of a wine glass manufacturer, but so did the reporter's hunt for something new and unusual.[16]

What news researchers and practitioners *want* to see can color their perceptions and reporting, and so observing has an important limitation. As in the 1920s case of Russian Revolution coverage, in the 2000s the *New York Times* reported not observations about the buildup for U.S. invasion of Iraq but what officials providing information wanted to be true, and the pro-war stories got more dramatic play, just as did stories leading up to World War I. Unlike the earlier case, the *Times* editors a century later recanted, citing the "strong desire" of sources, the eagerness of Bush administration officials, and reporters "too intent on rushing scoops into the paper."[17] The large errors of judgment underline a limitation of reporting. Even if news covered only what reporters themselves witnessed, the limits to observation would remain. New technology further complicates direct observation because occurrences such as online securities fraud and social-media mobbing happen in digital zones. Observing involves some interpreting and depends on the observer's perspective and assumptions.

What does it mean to describe? To say what happened, reporters have to draw on the language resources at hand. They tend to rely on standard wording, and some newspapers publish columns and news radio programs air commentaries that reinforce the standard. The working press rarely makes up new words but does pick up on newly popular terms and phrases. From crime waves throughout press history to so-called metrosexuals of the 1990s, the mistaken prevalence of "sexting" among teens of the subsequent decade, and "lumbersexuals" of the 2010s, emerging trends need exist only in sources' imagination before they can enter the vocabulary of news and then into commonsense reality.[18] Philosophers and historians of science have debated inconclusively how much the limits of available language narrow or constrain what scientists can conceive.[19] Journalism as a system of knowledge trades less at the cutting edges than at the center of shared beliefs, adopting the language that sources and audience members readily understand.[20]

The way novices learn the news craft imposes a more serious limitation. An untrained reporter might describe (or fail to describe) just about anything while covering, say, an accident or a labor strike. Through a process of responding to the reporter's output, demanding revisions, and cutting out all or part of a story, editors communicate to the reporter the acceptable limits of description. The process, called *literary reason*, permeates what reporters do to translate their daily labor into stories, through composition for an imagined audience, peer and editorial review, and revision for publication.[21] The craft imposes other kinds of reasoning. Reporters must follow the routine tasks and processes of their jobs, using *practical reason*. They look for clues, tips, and opportunities (such as breaks, scoops, and editors' quirks) to stand out on the job, using something called *indexical reason* (because the clues mark and sort experiences, providing an index to what matters). They emulate models of successful reporting, using *analogical reason* to seek familiar parallels when covering unfamiliar occurrences. They operate within systems of economic rewards, interpersonal relationships, and external resources and public demands, relying on their socially *situated reason*. And they must do all four while defending what they do as distinctive from what ordinary folks do, but also as separate from and equivalent to the public-service missions of other professionals—a process called *symbolic reason*. The five kinds of reasoning behind news description may lead practitioners away from how their audiences reason, and so reporters and editors end up misrecognizing their own output as short, realist, and so forth.

The shift leads to something called *constructionism*, because what practitioners are doing is constructing news. In a fundamental difference from naïve realism, constructionism assumes that the social-world-out-there does not exist as a stable object. Because it is changing, objective knowledge about it cannot accumulate. Instead of merely adding to the stock of existing knowledge, practitioners like social researchers and news reporters construct facts connected to objects in the world but following social processes. News practice has a productive quality that sociologists recognize, and social constructionists bring the process of building facts into stronger relief. Their view returns to an older meaning of the word *fact*, which comes from the Latin *facere*, to make.

A concrete example of that construction in action is the recent (in historical terms) and surprising notion that statistics "makes" people.[22] Two centuries ago, Europeans considered chance little more than a vulgar superstition. Well-informed society thought that events grew out of a set of previous conditions as a result of particular causes. Through the course of the nineteenth century, the informed account changed. Enumeration of just about everything expanded, and governments as well as scholars and amateurs discovered patterns in occurrences like crimes and suicides. The science of statistics emerged to find that human behavior (as first measured among workers taking astronomical measurements) happens along a bell-shaped curve, which swells in the middle and peters out at both ends. The normal distribution indicates that, far from being a superstition, chance reveals a picture of the aberrant (at the extremes) but also the normal person (at the center). *Normal* can mean desirable, right, and good, but may also mean ordinary and mediocre, or worse. In the revised picture of chance, governments found a new source to control deviancy. By defining the outliers, governments and institutions can take measurements of those at the extreme edges of society, plan ways to intervene in their lives, and track the changes that result (pursuing a system of knowledge called *positivism*). No matter the source, statistics feeds back into society, defining what people are, and so statistics makes people.

The same applies to news. Although reporters and editors avoid thinking of themselves as agents of social control, their work furthers institutional power over those at the social margins. News tends to emphasize occurrences at the far reaches of society, among those who strayed into crime or rose to heroism, became or stood up against employers, came to accidental calamity or triumph, or rose to or fell from political leadership. The outliers can define and reiterate the center of things, without actually pointing to the norms, through a process called *simultaneous contrast*. The idea is that one cannot say one thing without implying its opposite: saying black, for instance, brings to mind its antithesis (not black).[23] News practitioners may consider their coverage of marginal groups a sort of progressive activism, intervening on behalf of the weak and downtrodden, but in the process of social construction it may tend to have the opposite outcome. Pointing to the fringes reinforces the center. The structure of news, from the organization of a newspaper or newscast to the layout of a news website, creates models of personal identity and models of society, and so news makes people. When people learn from news how others like them behave and how still others respond—how their society works—and then act on that learning, the news has helped make them into who they are.[24]

Social constructionism has faced a strong reaction. Historian of science Ian Hacking says that "a great fear of relativism" is one thing at work. "What are we afraid of?" he asks. Well, if everything is constructed through social interaction, then nothing remains solid or secure, and "any opinion is as good as any other." But no one has seriously proposed that everything is constructed. Societies create three types of constructions: objects (including persons, such as women refugees), ideas (including time periods or qualities such as kindness), and something else called *elevator words*. Words like *facts* and *truth* occupy a higher (elevator) level because they try to say something about what the world is like, not what is in the world. Elevator words have two peculiar qualities: "First, they tend to be circularly defined," deriving their meaning from each other (as in the relation of facts to truth). And second, they "have undergone substantial mutations of sense and value." The angry responses to social constructionism rely heavily on elevator words.[25]

Beginning in the 1970s, academics began to apply constructionist views to news. Historian Robert Darnton, who had a brief career in the press, described the reporter's working reality, the complex relations between reporters and sources, and the pressures to standardize coverage, concluding that workers "bring more to the events they cover than they take away from them."[26] About the same time, Stuart Hall and his co-authors from cultural studies examined British news and found that the "media define for the majority of the population *what* significant events are taking place."[27] The next two decades of critical scholarship sustained their views. In practice, constructionism finds easy evidence in the news.[28] In a 1920s scandal in newspapers, prominent New York socialite Leonard Rhinelander tried to annul his marriage to Alice Beatrice Jones, a working-class girl from New Rochelle. The case turned on whether Leonard knew Alice's race:

> Throughout the trial, reporters carefully scrutinized Alice's deportment, clothing, and appearance. They searched for any detail that might explain who she was and give a fuller hint of her race. They also looked to see if she betrayed any lingering affection for Leonard. The reporters characterized her as "fair" or "slightly tanned" or "dusky" or even "ebony," her skin tone waxing and waning with the tides of evidence and scandal. At perhaps the most memorable point of the trial, Alice, at the request of her lawyer, partially disrobed before the court, baring her breasts, back, and legs. Although no reporters were actually in the judge's chambers when she exposed her body, all were sure she had proven her attorney's point: that Leonard must have known from viewing her body prior to marriage that she was not white.[29]

Reporters and editors constructed Alice's race to fit the ideas behind the reporting, so that she looked darker the more the outcome of the trial seemed likely to go against her. She became "colored" whenever the proceedings seemed to prove she was what passed for "colored." Constructionists do not doubt that Alice herself existed but instead reveal how her existence takes on differences according to the reporters' expectations. They do not construct Alice in a concrete sense, but that sense is trivial. To say "Alice existed" has little meaning without referring to her skin color and the debate over racial identity that surrounded her body. The question was, which Alice existed, a white or a "colored" one?[30]

Some in the working press do acknowledge the role of news organizations and workers in the construction of news. Nora Ephron told the story of standing outside, waiting and waiting for things to start, back when she was a young reporter for the *New York Post*. When the *New York Times* reporters arrived, the activity would begin, and she would stand there wondering, "How do they always know when an event will really start?"[31] Ephron went on from the *Post* to become an editor and columnist for *Esquire* and *New York* magazines and published two bestselling collections of essays, removing herself from the ranks of workaday news. But ordinary reporters do tell of similar experiences, if not for attribution.

One I interviewed remembers working as a clerk in the *New York Times* Washington bureau during the presidency of the first George Bush and witnessing reporters in the office receive advance warning that the Gulf conflict was going to begin in a few hours. Instead of saying whether or when the war would start, the tipster just suggested the *Times* reporters put off going to dinner for a couple of hours. While reporters from lesser news organizations went to eat as usual, the *Times* team stayed put. Sure enough, they led in covering the big story. The process reiterated another constructed dimension of news by reinforcing the preeminent position of the *Times* in defining U.S. events and their meaning.

Constructionism cannot replace the close analysis of news processes that sociologists offer, but it does take some of the gleam off the paradigm driving news. It also deepens the explanation for changes in the "what" of news during the twentieth century. After succumbing to propaganda in World War I and after conceding to McCarthyism at midcentury, those producing news did not take opposite tacks. Despite the superficial contradiction—toward realist events in the former case, toward modern explanation in the latter—both responses to the crises produced similar results for the paradigm. The occupation responded by reasserting power over constructing news itself. It took a central position in public discussion, playing the role of moderator and facilitator for correcting the ills of political life. As doctors of the public sphere, content producers prescribed something different in each case, but the remedies left them in charge of news and more influential in the construction of general knowledge.

Instead of being victims of their economic conditions and training, modern news practitioners participate in social power, because by building useful knowledge they engage in practices that define what *is*, what is known (or knowable), and what matters. Every member of a society does the same, but those working in news have a greater reach than many others. And their definitions confer status on the view they promote about the world, while also reinforcing the standing of news practice. They advance journalism as a way of knowing. The cultural position of the journalist, enhanced by the responses of the occupation to previous crises, puts its practitioners on par with those who occupy posts in the formal structures of government and business.

But reporters take a humble, realist stance when asked. They present themselves as mere laborers in the mines of occurrences, transcribers of events, and seekers of facts and truth. Sociology reveals the connection of that labor to news economics and to modern occupational status. Cultural scholarship dismantles the basic supports for realist observation and description, showing that in some ways the distinctions between event-centered and explanatory news collapse. All the processes in deciding what becomes news involve interpretation, an activity that empowers the producers of news content.

Whatever view one finds persuasive, a dramatic change has occurred in the "what" of news. News practitioners and audiences feel inundated by information, but news reports include fewer events, no matter how one measures them. The incongruity between beliefs in the glut of news events and the evidence of their decline exposes a misapprehension among news practitioners about what they do. Once online media emerged, audiences seemed able to adapt, riding on the waves of change in receiving news, but news practice pushed back, reasserting modern facts and truth. The reversion to modern definitions of "quality" distanced the news paradigm from emerging habits in the digital era.

Of course news practice extends beyond individual reporters and editors to the occupation of the journalist, the publishing and broadcasting industries that trade in news, and the systems of regulation surrounding public information and intellectual property. The individual practitioner lives enmeshed in a surrounding society that *expects* news to be realist. That is one reason that modern news ran into trouble in the United States in the new century. Events declined in content as the reading public gained access to more sources of news, eroding the credibility of modern news. The social world shifted at the century's end, trapping news in modernist expectations just when practitioners needed another perspective.

IMAGINARY NEWS

Your typical [reporter]. . . . sees nothing obscure in [news], nothing doubtful, nothing difficult * * * When a [journalist] speaks to us . . . he repeats the romance of [news]. But when you test the truth of what he has told to you, you find that it all ends in nothing; it is like those . . . dreams which only leave you in the morning the regret of having believed in them. * * * Every one at their own risk and peril may believe what he likes. * * * But only strong and robust constitutions can bear [news] in addition to life. . . .

—Adapted from Molière, *Le Malade Imaginaire* (1674)

PART 4

"Where"—Locations for News Grew More Remote

"The world is big enough."

"It was once," said Phileas Fogg, in a low tone.

Stuart took up [the] thread. "What do you mean by 'once'? Has the world grown smaller?"

"Certainly," returned Ralph. "I agree with Mr. Fogg. The world has grown smaller, since a man can now go round it ten times more quickly than a hundred years ago."

But the incredulous Stuart was not convinced . . . : "You have a strange way, Ralph, of proving that the world has grown smaller. So, because you can go round it in three months—"

"In eighty days," interrupted Phileas Fogg.

—Jules Verne, *Around the World in 80 Days* (1872)

CHAPTER 10

Local Lost Ground to Distant News

In the first half of the twentieth century, informed opinion held that the "world has become . . . close-knit," and scholars set out to explain "how the world grew smaller."[1] The modern world developed closer connections through faster communication and transportation and tighter coordination among nations, which required a public-spirited effort to catch citizens up on their new neighbors.[2] Modernism assumed an expert elite ready to supply a bird's-eye perspective for an uninformed public. About half a century later, an editor at the *La Crosse Tribune* in Wisconsin wrote on the editorial page, "The notion of a shrinking world has become a cliché. It remains true nonetheless." News organs were striving to inform their audiences about faraway locations because "as a nation and as a community," the editor wrote, "we can run but we can't hide from the impact of world events on our daily lives."[3] That motivation still inspires news practice.

But the U.S. general public, when it comes to knowledge of the world, seems trapped. Prominent figures for a century have been describing the citizenry as ill informed, especially about geography, and not merely inattentive but lazy or too stubborn to change. Former Sunday *New York Times* Editor Lester Markel, after a year of studying what he called the global challenge to the United States in the mid 1970s, concluded that "the public has scant information" and "makes little effort to understand."[4] After leading panel discussions with press, academic, and government experts and conducting interviews and surveys, he reported that prominent figures ranging from pollster George Gallup to *Times* editor C. L. Sulzberger were in consensus: people knew little about distant places. Not much has changed in the ensuing years. At the end of the century, the editor of *Foreign Affairs* magazine pointed to "post–Cold-War provincialism" and the lack of public knowledge about foreign news.[5] And as online access to information grew in the next decade, the *Columbia Journalism Review* noted that "the American public is no better informed."[6]

Despite a shrinking world and public ignorance, one assumption about locations is that news from outside the United States has been declining. In the 1920s, Walter Lippmann called "carrying distant news to the private citizen" a *burden* for newspapers needing to build circulation.[7] A decade later the volume of foreign news was "too often pitifully small," a political scientist wrote.[8] By the 1970s U.S. news organizations closing overseas bureaus said they had to cut back on foreign newsgathering because of economic factors and because innovations such as jet travel could replace a permanent presence abroad.[9] And industry analysts said a dwindling corps of foreign correspondents made views and perspectives from abroad less diverse.[10] Observers wrote of the *starvation* and *plight* of foreign news and noted that cuts in correspondents continued in the 1980s because "the costs are beyond the scope of all but a few news organizations."[11] By the late 1990s the Associated Press reported that "interest in overseas news has flagged" and quoted the chairman of CNN News on the "need for more international coverage."[12] Over the next decade news industry publications reported that "U.S. news organizations" were still backing "away from foreign news" and lamented the "massive slicing" in staff and bureaus, curtailing international coverage it seemed.[13]

Another assumption about the "where" is that news is growing more local, a trend that would align with realism. Locations are never one-dimensional because defining anyplace depends on someplace else. "Here" and "there" work in tandem. The closing of bureaus outside the United States even among wealthy news organizations, observers say, "reflects another trend: emphasis on local news."[14] A prime example is the Gannett media group, which began with "no full-time foreign correspondents of its own" and relied instead on wire service reports, a dependence that observers say has spread. The Gannett flagship *USA Today* distributes nationally but "assiduously hones local angles," notably in its weather page covering every state and major city. To enhance local coverage, regional papers subdivided at least part of their content along with advertising and supplements into zoned editions. The *Los Angeles Times* at its height as the largest metropolitan daily in the country published multiple editions to cover surrounding areas.[15] "Being very local," writes the editor of the *American Journalism Review*, "is the key to survival."[16] If the decline of foreign and growth of local news have occurred, news content will reflect both assumptions.

Has the amount of news from afar really shrunk? U.S. industry analysis usually inferred any declines from the number of foreign correspondents, but researchers found the number growing at times.[17] Going further back in history might help. News "in early American newspapers was almost exclusively European," writes media scholar James W. Carey, because editors relied on correspondence and on clipping the contents of other newspapers that arrived by ship from abroad.[18] In the nineteenth century, publishers' enthusiasm for news from faraway grew along with faster means of transport and transmission, but the share of foreign news in the press was already high.

When the broad change in spatial understanding occurred between 1880 and 1920, the U.S. Census revealed the closing of the American frontier, and systems of railroads and canals were knitting the planet together, making it conceivable to go *Around the World in Eighty Days*, as Jules Verne's 1873 novel imagined. The spread of bicycles and the automobile along with urban transport systems changed the sense of the local, giving rise to studies of urban crowds. The great powers finished taking control of the last un-colonized spaces of the world, triggering the study of geopolitics.[19] Travel to foreign places became accessible and tourism more common. By the end of the period, American modernism had emerged. Historian Stephen Kern writes that "new ideas about the nature of space in this period challenged the popular notion" of space as "continuous and uniform." Biologists and sociologists began to explore how different species and human cultures perceive and organize space. In modern art, cubists and others rejected uniform perspective and depicted objects from more than one angle. Novels and the new movies employed multiple standpoints, and in philosophy, Nietzsche and Ortega y Gasset developed *perspectivism*, the existence of "as many different spaces as there are points of view."[20]

Kern suggests that information about foreign events became everywhere present during the period, and readers could learn about conditions throughout the world. Whatever the trend might have been in magazines and books of the era, the share of newspaper content would not have increased from the large proportion of foreign reports the U.S. press relied on early in the 1800s. But news did participate in the general shift in public sensibility about place at the turn of the century.[21] One irony of news content is its interaction with popular topics: the press rides the wave of growing interest until topics become commonplace, and then its attention subsides. When building home radio sets, which allowed tinkerers to reach across long distances, emerged early in the twentieth century, for example, newspapers started radio pages, which waned as the practice became a mere hobby. When an interest is no longer new or unusual but becomes the norm, it loses its newsworthiness and turns into a background element in news.

But reports from hard-to-reach places remain appealing. In the nineteenth century, location was the main obstacle to gathering news. Publishers trumpeted their feats of getting news from anywhere distant and organized their news pages geographically, by where dispatches originated (not necessarily where events occurred). Once the telegraph along with new modes of transport had made long distances more bridgeable and the telephone made local distances even smaller, places lost some of their importance.[22] For instance, in the *Cincinnati Enquirer*, the number of items and diversity of places dropped off after the end of the nineteenth century.[23] As access to other locations increased, newspapers could pay less attention. And as they abandoned the illustrated news of the nineteenth century and moved to modern photojournalism in the twentieth century, news lost a repertoire of decidedly local reporting techniques, such as *walking description*, a way of recounting events as an observer moving through the immediate scene.[24]

The changes in news accompanied the broader decline in spatial interest.[25] Two large streams of social thought at the turn of that century shared a conception of geography. Marxism treated place as an incidental constraint, and social science treated place as an external constraint, but the competing movements shared an ambition to make sense of events and interpret social life. They tended to set aside geography by rejecting how places may influence what happens (in science) or by defining patriotic loyalty to place as false consciousness (in Marxism).[26] In the changing intellectual climate accompanying the growth of realist news, the long decline in foreign coverage during the nineteenth century should come as no surprise.

But through the twentieth century did news from abroad continue to wane? Yes, according to international comparisons of *news flow* across national borders since the 1930s. One way to understand how news flows across national borders is through the metaphor of transportation. In the transport of news, editors are "gatekeepers" who decide whether to let foreign reports in, and their decisions produce content that reveals the structure of news flows. Distance turns out to be a poor predictor of how news moves between countries for several reasons. Countries with elite status (so-called *news centers*) fill a larger share of other countries' news holes, and neighbors within the same region (*news neighbors*) get more coverage. Major stories influence news anywhere (*news topicality*), but some countries always remain remote (*news periphery*). The transport metaphor predicts that media in the United States will run a limited amount of foreign news compared to, say, the media in European nations, because it is an elite country with few immediate neighbors and takes action and sets policies that tend to drive major topics.[27]

News flow studies try to track a function over the long term, but they start by assuming a long-term decline and then usually examine a limited period. They also use inconsistent measures, such as identifying foreign stories by dateline, which indicates place of origin. Foreign datelines exclude U.S. visits of dignitaries from abroad, United Nations events, activities of foreign embassies, and the like. News-flow rationales treat nations as comparable, but the U.S. press has no parallel. Its outlets are more local and regional than those in European and other countries, and the greater distances on the North American continent make comparison difficult. One editor says, "After all, if you're in Omaha, you're a lot farther from Chicago than you are from Paris if you're in London." The transport metaphor sets out to explain minimal or declining foreign coverage and not surprisingly ends up finding some evidence.[28]

Another way to understand news flows is through a critical view, which shows institutions and industries constructing the news across national boundaries.[29] International organizations dominate the flows, producing global uniformity in news while mapping reality onto ideologies such as capitalism or imperialism. The resulting news uses emotion to push products in the service of business interests and conveys Western ideals to serve that region's expansionist aims. Demands for the free flow of information provide high-sounding justifications for big media to gain access to other national markets and sell information commodities. Demands for free trade require those same markets to export the raw materials needed to manufacture cultural goods. U.S. companies expect Canada first to export—under free trade—the supply of paper they need at a low, bulk price and then—as part of the free flow of information—to import at a premium price the U.S. American cultural products manufactured from that paper. Economic benefits redound to the United States through both types of transactions. The containerized exchange of raw materials and industrial information products creates serious trade imbalances.[30]

But the critical view also has contradictions that arise from assumptions that the United States is comparable to other countries and has less foreign news. Even before the euro became a common currency, the European press paid more attention to Europe than the U.S. press paid to North America, and the U.S. wire services focused less on North America than the European services did on Europe.[31] A confederation of independent nations in Europe is unlike the North American region. But the critique helps account for *beliefs* that foreign coverage is in decline. Where the transport metaphor seems too narrow, the critical view may be too broad. Both start from and end at the same assumptions and imply that U.S. news does not supply what its public needs. But capturing long-range trends might provide a corrective. Longer-term research has found increases in foreign news, and one of the longest studies (two decades) with the most careful definitions found a "small but steady increase in the amount of attention given to the rest of the world" on evening newscasts of three major U.S. networks.[32]

Measuring content consistently over a much longer time period—we counted each location mentioned within each story over a century—shows a meaningful increase in foreign places in U.S. newspapers (figure 10.1). Two types of locations moved in diametrically opposed directions, illustrating another surprising way that realism lost ground and modernism advanced. The number of the most specific locations, street addresses, decreased the most, while the broadest locations, news about other countries, increased even more strongly. Both changes run just the opposite of expectation.[33]

Two crime stories illustrate the changes. The first envisions an 1894 robbery in the realist mode, by focusing on its location: "The Post Office is in a small building a short distance from the Long Island Railroad station. There is a very little room outside of the partition. In one end of the latter is a door, and inside, near the door, stands a small safe." The second from a century later reports a murder, but in the modern mode that elevates it to broader importance. Two maps with the article show the Caribbean and the island of St. Thomas next to the caption, "The slaying of a tourist in Charlotte Amalie has become a symbol of crime in the Virgin

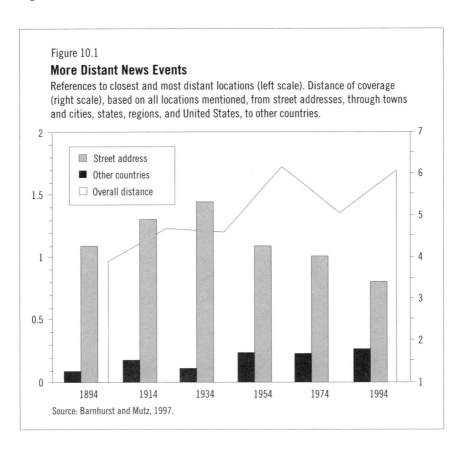

Figure 10.1

More Distant News Events

References to closest and most distant locations (left scale). Distance of coverage (right scale), based on all locations mentioned, from street addresses, through towns and cities, states, regions, and United States, to other countries.

Source: Barnhurst and Mutz, 1997.

Islands." The story begins: "According to the license plates on the cars and buses that hail tourists around this bustling port, the Virgin Islands are still an 'American Paradise.' But a surge in violent crime over the last year, including the slaying of a San Diego swimming instructor this week, has put that in jeopardy." The report takes the entire island as its location and reaches the U.S. mainland. A subhead reads: "Island officials say mainland values are leading the young astray." Unlike the 1894 article, which tells a fairly universal story but at a particular address, the 1994 article elaborates a geographic thesis based on national origin. It shows both long-term trends: the local dimension of news shrinking and the distant dimension expanding.

What does news location look like at the level of the practitioner? Before joining the *New York Times* and later Yahoo News to cover politics, Matt Bai had been a national correspondent for *Newsweek*, but he started out in a college internship for the *Providence Journal Bulletin*. There he worked with middle-aged staffers "in these far-flung rural bureaus," he said in our 2001 interview, although most reporters "wanted to be downtown—the competition when the slots came open was intense. But you went to work in a shopping mall, a strip plaza (that's where most of the bureaus were), . . . you had one page that was just your region, and your job mostly was to fill the page. So even though the *Providence Journal* was covering a large media market, you were going to the town council meetings at night or examining the water sewage management issues or the local police blotter because you were essentially doing a local paper inside the paper every day."

It was fine experience for a beginner, but he imagined himself doing a different job by the time he reached forty. "It just wasn't me," he said, although he considered covering local news "a genuine public service." Of the dozens of stories he wrote for the *Journal*, one stood out:

> I was alone in the bureau one weekend. And you had to man the police scanner—this was in the main regional bureau. . . . There came a car chase over the scanner. I heard an officer say, "We've had a gun shot." And I called the desk in Providence, and I said, "There's a gun shot report." And they said, "Well, check it out."
>
> I called back, and the police said that that didn't happen. . . . But somebody wrote a letter to the paper and said, "I saw that chase, and some cop fired a gun at the car. What were they thinking? Are they crazy? They're on a main street, and they fired a gun—we can't have this! And how could your paper fall down on the job and not tell us what had happened?"

The head of the bureau "just erupted at me," Bai said. The *Providence Journal* was pushing local coverage so that readers near the bureau would buy the paper. "There was a little paper called the *Westerly Sun*. It was one of the smallest dailies in the country—we were competing with them." The *Journal* zoned editions targeted small newspapers by attracting readers, adding pressure on reporters. Bai left and migrated to the *Boston Globe*, a large metropolitan daily.

His story describes a common experience in news practice: humdrum local reporting with evening shifts at local meetings. Others I interviewed told similar stories, with the old-timer as a stock character. Reporters rarely see dramatic events on the street but may hear about them by phone. And the story that reporters do witness can then come into conflict with local authority or trap them between the demands of authorities and editors. Despite the mantra to focus on the local, reporters who want advancement, freedom, and amenities tend to migrate to urban centers, where they can cover more than a suburb or small town. After they move away from local news jobs, they continue to enliven their reporting about larger domains by highlighting a local angle. An opening vignette describing places on the ground gives realism to news focused on broader horizons.

Foreign correspondents begin from distant locations. In the early 1990s, Tim Sullivan started full-time reporting at the *Ft. Worth Star-Telegram*, where he covered the standoff at Waco, Texas. After a year, ready for bigger things, he left for New York City and landed work with the Associated Press (AP), which posted him to West Africa. His beat included twenty countries. In mid-1999 he flew into Sierra Leone, where rebels had ended a campaign of terror. He and a photographer spent several weeks generating half a dozen stories, including one he was particularly proud of, "a feature about life in the city that was half destroyed by the offensives," he said in our interview.

The story begins this way: "Nearly every day, the gray clouds that hang low over Freetown burst into a downpour, and thousands of umbrellas blossom across the seaside city."[34] The article traces the course of the "small rivers of muddy brown water" past several landmarks: the burned-out City Hall, "a refugee camp on the edge of town," a place where heavy fighting occurred called Kissy Road, and finally "the once-ornate Holy Trinity Church." Sullivan then characterizes the entire capital: "Freetown, a city long accustomed to war, is also a city that refuses to be broken." Shoppers and street vendors have returned, reconstruction begun, and "bored soldiers sleepily wave drivers through many roadblocks." What makes the feature good, Sullivan said, is its geographic sweep: "It wasn't simply a story about these people" but also "a story about this country," a place "so stuck it had to sign a deal with this evil rebel movement."

Six more of his articles from inside Sierra Leone appeared through October that year. One gives an account of the country's elites by profiling a place where they "have congregated for more than 80 years," a watering hole called "the Hill Station Club, a whitewashed colonial compound crumbling under the weight of recent history."[35] The story Sullivan remembered most vividly also has a realist focus. After signing a peace accord, rebels, who six months earlier would enter a town "executing children, suddenly were part of the government."[36] The story—long by AP standards—conveys the entire country's quandary through the experience of Ishmael Dramane, an aging "itinerant miner and truck driver," struggling "to find the words to describe" what the rebels did to him. "Instead, he kneels in the dirt of the Freetown camp for war victims where he now lives" to show "how the rebels tied his wrists behind his back" and then "one picked up a machete and chopped off both his hands." They left him bleeding and in agony, twelve hours' journey from a hospital. "'How can I live with these people?' Dramane demands angrily, waving his stumps in a visitor's face. 'I lost everything.'" Sullivan called the story "difficult to read because it was so explicit," but in response he received a rare thing for an AP reporter: letters from readers "expressing sympathy for these people." The article drew the audience into the specific and detailed location of events in an unfamiliar place. Sullivan hoped it also made readers "care a little, because Americans don't care about West Africa."

His last two stories with a Sierra Leone dateline that year contain other profiles, one about "Tamba, a jug-eared sixteen-year-old with a broad smile and two years as a rebel soldier behind him." Through him the story profiles the camp: "In Lakka, in a blue, two-story clapboard building that used to be a beach resort, they are allowed to be children again." The article differs from what Sullivan published before his stay in the country. One story from January with the bureau dateline in the Ivory Coast relies on quotations from other countries and has no place descriptions. Beyond mentioning Freetown and Washington, D.C., the only locations are broad: "across the war-weary West African nation" and "across the country."[37] From the abstract story about the entire country, Sullivan's stories progress from the September profile of the entire capital city to the intimate and moving reports of October. His reporting drew authority from being "on the ground" but in tension with the need to explain entire countries. News draws strength from using the realist particulars to reveal modern vistas about faraway places.[38]

The assumptions about foreign and local news intertwine in complicated ways. Both reflect widespread beliefs about the U.S. public and present news practice as thankless service in the face of geographic ignorance or indifference. The assumptions show how realism and modernism push and pull on each other. If local news is advancing, news practice is staying true to its roots, grounded in realist description. And if foreign news is declining, news practice needs to take up wider modern perspectives to serve the people. Local news and local angles on other news may pander to a kind of self-centered provincialism among audiences, and the modern corrective would give them the geographic knowledge they need but resist. News became more distant in the twentieth century, but the faraway reports that capture audience attention seem the exceptions that prove the rule. As nearby places were waning, a growing reliance on small, memorable vignettes seems to prove the opposite. The aspirations of news practitioners are more faithful to modern trends, the escape from small-town life into a broader horizon, but their hard-won direct experiences and poignant storytelling sustain the realist illusion that news is hardly distant at all. In news practice on the ground, the complex strains of modernism come clear.

In print news the malleability of words allows both strains to operate in tandem, but does the same hold for broadcast news? Broadcasting relies on realist materials, the moving pictures and audio actualities from immediate locations. Did realism lose ground and modernism make gains in the "where" of broadcast news? As TV became the go-to source for news, its treatment of the local and the far away might suggest how general knowledge about locations evolved.

CHAPTER 11

Newscasters Appeared Closer

The idea of "mass" distribution of information emerged along with a similar understanding of change by the end of the nineteenth century. Urbanization was gathering masses of people in cities, industrialization had concentrated jobs for them in mass-production factories, and mass-transit systems emerged to move them between work, home, shopping, and entertainment. New mass-distribution systems joined mail-order catalogs to move industrial products to buyers. Department stores had invented an early version of mass marketing through newspaper display advertisements and were early to adopt the emerging system of radio transmissions, some of them built atop the store to beam music for an enhanced shopping experience inside and for luring in others nearby. The emerging mass-media system showed promise of building a knowledgeable modern citizenry. As local papers improved and radio programs became "more numerous and more available," the number of those attending to "foreign matters . . . increased continuously" through the first half of the twentieth century.[1] Unseen supply webs connected goods, services, and information to the mass society of the modern era at its center: the individual at a mailing address and with a radio set.

Realistic images brought the world into the home, and mass-circulation magazines, especially *Life* and *Look*, made distant places present through pictures. The photograph as a trace of real life seemed to trump its potential as art, and the documentary pictures of photojournalism renewed the emphasis on realism in news. But the transformation embodied a contradiction between modern and realist perspectives. The photograph of a distant place knit the world together for modern coordination but presented it as faraway and nearby at the same time, shifting the experience of "there" to "here" through its form and through the conditions where viewers received it. Pictures in magazines and the press create "a pseudo-world, a picture out of focus which readers sometimes confused with the real thing."[2] The contradiction between "here" and "there" seemed to repeat itself as each new medium for news emerged.

Local coverage remains close to the heart of U.S. news, where audiences experience a romance with small places, according to long-time PBS host and commentator Ben Wattenberg.[3] News practitioners place covering nearby events at the heart of the occupation. An editor from Missouri says, "The farther it is from Kansas City, the less it is news."[4] At an industry roundtable, an editor from Florida said the news business drums the local focus into the heads of interns and reporters, and an editor from Alabama said only local reporting has an *emotional* tug.[5] An editorial in a trade magazine calls "content that is 'local, local, local'—always repeated three times"—a mantra for news.[6] To supply even more local coverage, the Corporation for Public Broadcasting developed plans for seven Local Journalism Centers. Coming out of the recession that began in 2007, some local stations were able to add nearby news content, but otherwise the Project for Excellence in Journalism forecast a "bleak long-term picture."[7] Audiences and news producers seem to share an emotional and realist dream about location.

Television is ultimately local and in that sense realist. But by bringing the far away into the privacy of home, TV participates in modernism by making other places part of everyday life, domesticating them, and blurring once-firm distinctions between far away and nearby. The way TV tames location by bringing at-the-scene images into the home produced excitement when the medium first emerged. Its invention would change the world, prognosticators said. Thomas Hutchinson, who helped shape TV programming in its early years and taught the first college course on the subject (at New York University in 1940), believed television would conquer the distance separating nations. It would help bring peace on earth, because all peoples would become like next-door neighbors. His view expresses the optimism of twentieth-century American modernism. To show how TV changed experience, he points to the 1940 Republican Convention: "The television audience saw and heard everything that took place in Philadelphia: the speakers, the demonstrations on the floor, and the final nomination of Wendell Willkie. Actually the television audience knew more about what went on than many people who were there in person."[8]

Television seemed to open a living-room window on the world just outside. Hutchinson describes an incident when a presidential nominee brought in a herd of elephants to parade before the cameras. One of the elephants had a different idea and "affectionately put its trunk around the director's neck." The startled TV director "made a wild rush to leave," just when the cameraman turned toward the scene. The director's wife, "viewing the program in Westchester County in New York, saw him hurrying away from his elephantine *inamorata*." The moral: "When you are away from home, stay away from television cameras unless you want the whole world, and your wife, to know what you are doing."[9]

The all-seeing modern eye on realist local life has guided TV newscasters since then. Early in his more than twenty years as the anchor of *ABC World News Tonight,* Peter Jennings wrote, "It is a simple axiom of journalism that the most effective way to connect with your audience is to make your reporting relevant to an individual's daily life." There is just "no substitute for the powerful impression the local angle makes." According to the Project for Excellence in Journalism, "Newscasts that air more locally relevant stories are significantly more likely to hold onto or attract a larger audience than the preceding program."[10]

How does the "where" look on television? To find out, we took measurements of location on network evening newscasts (figure 11.1).[11] The background surrounding newscasters is one indicator of location. Correspondents appear close to the action by going *on location*, where they stand before the scene itself. Or they

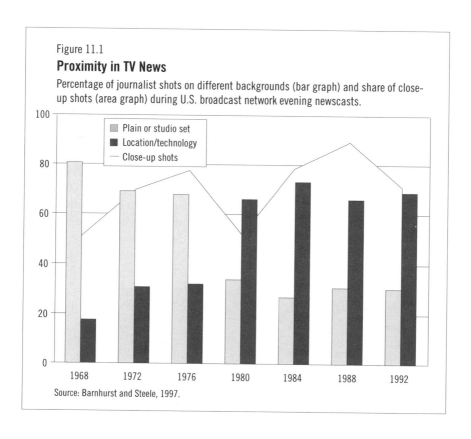

Figure 11.1
Proximity in TV News
Percentage of journalist shots on different backgrounds (bar graph) and share of close-up shots (area graph) during U.S. broadcast network evening newscasts.

Source: Barnhurst and Steele, 1997.

can appear surrounded by the technology needed for direct transmission. Sitting in front of a simple backdrop or a typical TV studio set with a desk and chairs produces the impression of distance from events. Studio shots position the anchor at a vantage point for observing events dispassionately. Besides their relation to the background, we also measured their relation to the camera. Its placement can produce an impression of viewing newscasters up close or from a distance.

We found two main changes in the visual vocabulary of location. Through a quarter century beginning in the 1960s, cameras moved in much closer on the faces of newscasters, conveying visually a sense of their proximity to the audience. Close-ups helped collapse the distance between the viewer and especially anchors. As newscaster images grew more imposing, their on-screen appearances developed a standard length of fifteen seconds and became much more frequent. By the 1990s they appeared three times as often on screen as they had in a typical story of the 1960s. Medium shots (the understated framing that once dominated images of BBC newsreaders, for instance) declined in the U.S. programs, making newscasters appear more dramatic on screen. The small share of long shots increased, but by the end of the period, close-ups—the most intimate shot in film and video—had become predominant.[12]

The other change involved the backgrounds. In the 1960s network news style amounted to a series of moderate shots of talking heads on a bland set. Plain backdrops, the most common in 1968, lent news a cool and neutral distance. During the 1970s, the rise of celebrity newscasters and redesign of sets made news more like other successful genres, following the model of sports on the ABC network. The changes produced a dramatic shift. Images of equipment and technology increased as a background, replacing studio sets and murals. More important, all other backgrounds gradually lost ground to on-the-scene reporting, and by the 1990s the plain backdrop had almost vanished. The growth in shooting on location built proximity between newscasters and events and made reporting more authentic.[13] By the 1990s reporters began to appear on location more often than on any other backdrop.

The changes in television news shots and backgrounds built the dream of nearness. Close-in shots of news personalities blended their presence into the living room, and their stand-up presentations gave viewers a picture of the scene but almost never of the events, which had already occurred or were happening off camera or in the future.[14] With both of the changes, the newscasters' efforts to bring the viewer to the scene brought the news personalities themselves into greater focus. Few studies have measured the local dimension of news content or audiences. In broadcasts originating in Washington, D.C., local coverage had dramatic ups and downs from the 1970s through the next three decades, but its relation to national coverage remained unclear.[15] Critical observers note that in news the "authority has passed to the more central and remote levels of government,"[16] and for news about government, national terms increased and local terms decreased in major news outlets.[17] Styles of news presentation tend to become more alike across markets as newscasters move from job to job, attend industry workshops, and rely on itinerant consultants for packaging content. But local variation still exists, and audiences appear to have their own local news culture that differs from what those in other U.S. regions prefer in the mix of outlets. Those in larger media markets, for instance, experience a richer range of content.[18]

One medium available with some uniformity across the country is National Public Radio (NPR), which has had a history of conveying locations through vivid word-pictures since its founding. Free from the need to provide visual wallpaper, NPR could have focused on small places. But did NPR news go against the trends in other media by depicting realist physical locations, or did it join TV by conveying an audio version of dreamlike modern nearness? To find out, my study of NPR morning and evening news programs recorded all mentions of places for two decades beginning in 1980 and analyzed them based on the smallest to appear in each report. Coding for small places gave the greatest weight to nearby locations and so may overstate their importance (figure 11.2).[19]

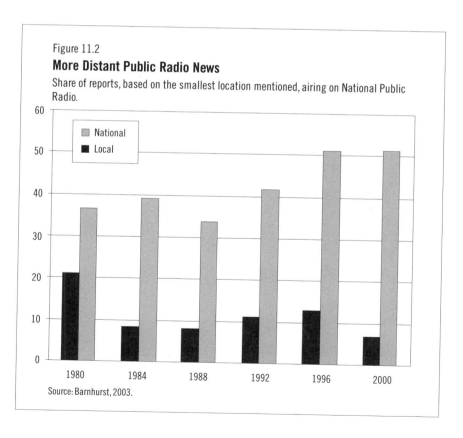

Figure 11.2

More Distant Public Radio News

Share of reports, based on the smallest location mentioned, airing on National Public Radio.

Source: Barnhurst, 2003.

State and regional stories showed no clear trend, but an important shift occurred: NPR moved away from local news, that is, away from mentioning a local town or city either alone or in coverage of other locations. As the share of local stories decreased, international and national news grew. The coverage from other countries increased only somewhat, but national news stories grew to fully half of the reports on the NPR programs after 1992. For all references to locations combined, the trend led away from smaller locations. In other words, the geographic domain of general news became wider, in line with the advance of modern geographic coordination. The changes in reports extended deeply into all topics—accidents, crime, employment, and politics—so that, as historians have noted, NPR reports "abandoned the local."[20] Public radio reporters gained a wider geographic stage and paid less attention to local occurrences.

As NPR reports grew longer and shifted focus to more distant domains in line with news modernism, they added descriptions to retain an element of realism. The period saw an almost fourfold increase in descriptions including characters and settings. The shift emphasized the drama of news. Previous studies found the media adopting stronger forms of news presentation, a general trend toward dramatized reports.[21] Greater dramatization pairs with the growing length of stories. Longer reports tend to make the content of news more abstract and less dynamic, but adding concrete persons and settings counteracts that impression, just as opening anecdotes add realism to newspaper stories. When extending their stories, NPR reporters did not appear to visit more places but found more dramatic ways of presenting the places they did reach. Adding drama and length, the studies say, puts greater emphasis on style over substance. The process enhances the modern authority of newscasters, who talk more often, while adding enough realism and emotional angles to make news memorable.

In serious U.S. radio and television news, the romance with small places nurtures a belief among audiences that news is local. Researchers sometimes find short-term shifts to nearby coverage but rarely study the local in relation to larger domains. TV news researchers, practitioners, and audiences treat the local as the main scene for news, but U.S. newspaper news has been panning away for more than a century, reducing events nearby into the hook or an illustration for news from elsewhere. Television news has been substituting a nearness to the newscaster for proximity to events, and NPR news has been shifting to national coverage, especially on the federal government, and away from local coverage. Broadcast news mystifies the local, domesticating distance by making it a tale told by familiar news personalities. The contradictions in location include enveloping the far away within the viewer's real spaces, creating a modern illusion of global togetherness, and eliding the newscasters while placing them at center stage. How can one make sense of the complex representation of "here" and "there" in the news?

Producers and researchers consider proximity a central attribute of news. Training manuals describe proximity as a core news value, which a textbook used in training several generations of reporters defines this way: "The closer an event is to home, the more newsworthy it becomes."[22] Proximity may include other kinds of nearness, such as making news more emotional for, meaningful in, or relevant to the audience, but it turns up consistently.[23] Educators consider it settled fact that "proximity is a basic news value" for producing content.[24] Most definitions of proximity include the audience and the event, but omit the news practitioners who themselves determine the "where." Ethnographic studies in media organizations show that news usually turns up where reporters look for it, often in official places, such as courts and government offices.[25] Instead of a line between audiences and the sources of news, proximity involves a triangle formed from three points: the reporter, source, and audience. The pattern goes even deeper—each of the points in the triad includes a network of relationships. The reporter has colleagues in the office, in other media, in trade organizations, and so on, to say nothing of other roles in life. Sources and audience members also nest deeply in networks. Each person in each set of networks occupies physical, social, and mental spaces that each perceives, conceives, and lives differently within distinct forms and structures.[26]

In practice, newscasters seem to imagine proximity simply as they assign a location to events and to their audience.[27] Achieving the news value requires connecting events to the audience and making them resonate *as if* they happened next door. For newscasters, proximity occurs along a direct line from audience to event, and the way they present news attempts to shorten that distance. They blend themselves into one of the other two positions in the triad, the anchor in the studio joining the viewer at home in the easy chair (or elsewhere using an electronic device) or the correspondent becoming one with the scene of events. Collapsing their positions produces contradictions. Instead of building proximity between the audience and the events, it contributes to the general placelessness peculiar to watching television and listening to the radio. How could that happen?[28]

Broadcast media have changed the relationship between "here" and "there" by accentuating another order of spaces. Media spaces call attention to the modern malleability of distance rather than reinforcing the fixity of specific realist locations. They suggest a vague citizenship of the world, a public life without roots in a particular locality.[29] Walter Cronkite's early Emmy-winning historical series, *You Are There* (1953–1957), based on the earlier radio series, uses a typical broadcasting phrase that, in effect, makes sense of nonsense. Cronkite was not *there*, nor were the actors playing roles of prominent historical figures, and neither were the writers (who worked at a further remove, some of them pseudonymous because of McCarthy-era blacklists). The viewer was not *there* either. Location in broadcast media involves viewers in modern make-believe.

That fantasy of location depends on a behind-the-scenes economic logic that makes news-casting profitable. Local news producers engage in a complex cartographic exercise that maps affluent places in detail.[30] The places with the largest populations most like educated newscasters receive more coverage per capita than other places. Well-heeled audiences are the upscale market that news organizations need to sell to potential advertisers, and businesses are more likely to see a payoff for their expenditures when their advertising reaches affluent zip codes and neighborhoods nearby. Powerful advertisers connect to the local geography through subsidiaries, franchises, or chain ownership, after decades of buying up or pushing out local businesses. In the modern system, large and reliable sources of income for local stations can be national or international. But the economics of realist place recycles through the system, aligning with the status and reinforcing the connections of newscasters without their paying attention to the underlying logic. The content of news represents itself as an economic activity only by indirection, implying not a market but a particular audience of like-minded hearers and viewers.

In some ways the modern economics of location did become manifest. NPR news oriented itself more toward commercial and entertainment concerns over the period studied. At the beginning of the twenty-first century, a broadcast of *All Things Considered* would be interrupted five times to announce the list of underwriters, along with their slogans and web addresses or toll-free numbers. Nothing similar ever occurred during any of the NPR broadcasts of either major news program in the 1980s. The more-recent *All Things Considered* also ran repeated teasers designed to promote upcoming stories and encourage listeners to stay tuned. The same sort of self-marketing that turns listeners into consumers was also absent in 1980. Promos and donor commercials took up more than three minutes of one broadcast, a small share of the program in the twenty-first century but longer than a typical news report from two decades earlier. Loyal listeners might not have noticed the shift to modern commercial logic, which entered the network in understated ways. Different announcer voices bracketed the promos into the zone with other routine elements such as the station's call numbers, and the practice grew slowly over the decades. Listeners might also have missed the shift toward national and international locations, which aligned the content of news with the geography of its emerging commercial underwriters.

Broadcast news "annihilates" place both ways, by collapsing distant events into real-seeming "here," bringing them into the hearer's home in the voice or visage of the newscaster, and by hiding the modern economic contradiction of distant entities in search of local money to export for the enrichment of other places. Broadcast stations mediate that exchange, and newscasters participate in the geographic contradiction by focusing on "local, local, local" while producing news that has moved continually away from the street address. Listeners to small-town news may not discover their local station uses an automated system, with voice tracks made in a distant city, until a local crisis gets no coverage, exposing the economics of chain-owned radio. News also contributes to the annihilation of some nearby localities by ignoring disadvantaged places, contributing to their symbolic invisibility.[31] Distant locations (whether separated by physical or mental gulfs) present scenes of suffering that cast the audience as spectators, and news supplies them a convenient excuse for looking. They can feel justified in playing voyeur to recorded images and sounds of distant ill fortune by adopting an emotional commitment and "orientation to action" as part of public opinion that stands in symbolic opposition to the distanced distress.[32]

On the larger scene, the modern dream of bringing nations together through television did not make countries better neighbors, although the international reach of TV networks blurred boundaries.[33] The global scope of television and radio made conflict more present and perhaps more likely.[34] Instead of nearness, broadcast media involve more people in a dream, itself a kind of distance. Presentation techniques segue reports from wildly divergent places, so that places become interchangeable parts of the program.[35] Broadcast news tends to turn everywhere into nowhere,[36] but the expert structuring of news packages full of conflict and intrigue excites a desire for more. The correspondent standing just outside the scene of the event keeps the audience in suspension, contemplating what happened when not awaiting the event itself or its next development. But the lesson of broadcast news is local: to stay at home, in front of the receiving set for its emitting signal. Daily news on radio and television fashions a magic place about news, where newscasters tame distance and seem to join the viewing or listening "family." Broadcast news accomplishes "proximity" by bringing practitioners closer to home for the audience while eliding their presence.

Like newspapers, newscasts have increased public distance while seeming to do the opposite. New digital media promise to connect individuals from many places and to make interactions more democratic, at least among those with access. But did the webs of digital media reverse the pattern, moving away from the soaring modern perspective to focus on realist detail and making the distant concrete in other ways?

CHAPTER 12

News Traded Place for Digital Space

The spider's web of computer networks brought a new wave of enthusiasm about the potential for public communication, and pundits said that the internet would change the world—a familiar line repeated whenever a new platform for news emerged during the past century. Creative destruction of old forms is a tenet of modernism, and the first casualty of conflict with new media was expected to be old media. Author Michael Crichton called them "The Mediasaurus," the title of his 1993 *Wired* magazine article that predicts the mass media will "vanish without a trace" within a decade.[1] Writing a year later, technology writer Jon Katz called newspapers "the biggest and saddest losers in the information revolution."[2] Concrete change followed the overstated predictions. By 2010 the Pew Internet and American Life Project found that the "internet has surpassed newspapers and radio in popularity as a news platform."[3] The change illustrates the broader shifts in cultural understanding related to place.

Through the twentieth century, U.S. news organizations had focused on small geographic areas, the sources of ad revenues from local business. Retail stores retain a link to places. Shipping is expensive for big-box items, and shoppers like to see and handle some smaller items before buying. The workforce is also somewhat immobile. Business draws its clerks, laborers, and other entry employees locally and avoids paying moving expenses to fill less-skilled jobs. Television and newspapers built local monopolies on those geographical barriers in the marketplace. "Newspapers' help-wanted ads inch for inch have been their single most profitable product," and news executives watched the internet take away more than 10 percent of classified advertising from newsprint.[4] What did newspapers do? In Colorado, small, local papers at first held back some stories from online editions but recycled staff-produced items instead of using wire copy, so that content online had a higher share of local material.[5] The strategy aimed to shore up local monopolies, but advertising revenues by 2010 had dropped to levels not seen "since the pre-internet year of 1985."[6] Weather, sports, TV listings, obituaries, and school and society events—anything with a local dimension—seemed fair game for online competitors.

News over digital networks seemed to scramble the differences between "here" and "there," the foundation for local newspaper profits. But pressure from competing online news seemed not to affect insiders' assumptions about inadequate foreign news and abundant local coverage. In 2009 George Washington University hosted a roundtable on the topic, "International News Coverage in a New Media World."[7] Speakers included the foreign editor of NPR, representatives from the *American Journalism Review* and the Committee to Protect Journalists, and a spokesperson from the federal Broadcasting Board of Governors. They discussed two interrelated trends: the decline in foreign correspondents and the growth of citizen journalism. Mobile digital media seemed to make everyone a potential reporter, allowing news to reach into the smallest localities.

Online news could have added foreign as well as local citizen reporters, and so what happened to the content of news? To find out I continued the study of mainstream outlets by adding their online sites to the long-term data examining urban, regional, and national newspapers from different U.S. geographical areas.[8] Unlike the Colorado example, the sites of the newspapers included contents almost identical to their print editions (figure 12.1).

Trends occurring in print stories over the previous decades continued when the newspapers moved online. In two key dimensions, the most local and most distant, the trend lines crossed for the newspapers as modernism advanced. References to street addresses had begun a long decline in the 1930s, sinking from a high of three addresses for each two stories to less than one mention per story in the 1990s (see figure 10.1). In the internet editions the trend continued, dropping to about one mention for every three stories. References to countries outside the United States had been inching up since the 1930s, growing from only one mention in ten stories to one in four in the 1990s. By the time the newspapers moved online, foreign places were approaching one reference for every two stories, a tenfold increase in half a century. As the new century began, newspaper reporters for the first time mentioned other countries more frequently than street addresses.

The places of the coverage likely contradicted the readers' experience. A jobs story with a dateline in Phnom Penh, Cambodia, for instance, mentioned labor organizing in Texas and policy debates in Washington (and the World Trade

Figure 12.1
Online Locations
Distance of coverage indexed by events ranging from street address to another nation, overall, by newspaper website, and by topic.

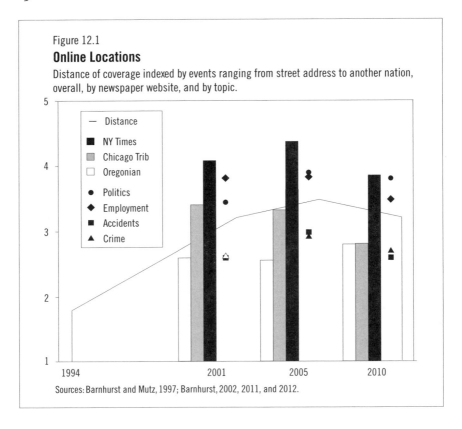

Sources: Barnhurst and Mutz, 1997; Barnhurst, 2002, 2011, and 2012.

Organization) and referred to China, Taiwan, Hong Kong, Singapore, and Mexico, as well as the headquarters of Nike, the Gap, Levi Strauss, and Sears, Roebuck.[9] Readers live out their employment at local addresses, but jobs stories had a modern business perspective, connecting to the reader perhaps through references to products a consumer might buy or chain stores a consumer might visit locally. The content, in short, referred less often to specific places nearby, although it might nod to the local by referring to familiar franchises. The pattern continued through 2010.

The form of the internet sites held a similar contradiction.[10] Where form in newspapers includes the dimensions and numbers of pages, online sites can create any number of pages to fit the width of the screen and can flow a page to any length. The news sites structured stories across more pages, so that they took the reader through more clicks showing more local ads and requiring more screens to navigate. They linked to the news site's own content—its own archive at first, where the user could purchase access though divulging personal details if not paying in dollars—but provided few links to external sites. Aspects of form aimed to hold users within a single online location, so that the sites offered less local content anchored in physical places but sought to keep consumers within local confines anchored in virtual spaces.

News organizations also competed aggressively to control the physical geography of their traditional markets. To protect local ad revenue, news businesses defined a parallel space online. Ethnographic research revealed that internet editions began with a strategy to take possession of that virtual geography. To control the home market, the sites produced most of the content themselves, supplemented by chamber-of-commerce, yellow-page, and other civic information. By encompassing as much as possible related to their market area, the sites become the de facto virtual city. Each site appeared to connect to a larger world but linked mostly to other sites the organization owned or operated. As one executive said, "We are adding to our site with acquisitions and strategic alliances with online companies." Once users entered the organization's hometown site, they could end up staying within the set of interrelated pages without necessarily realizing it.[11]

A strong move involved ownership of domain names, which define the real estate online. In a few cases the principal news organization in a major U.S. market purchased the rights to the locality name. A technology consultant with news experience describes how the *Boston Globe* "rethought old notions of proprietary products. Instead of just taking" the existing newspaper online, the *Globe* editors "opened a gateway—boston.com—to their whole region." Then "all the major television stations and museums in the city" joined "as content partners, creating in the process an impressive new media genre."[12] Owning the name laid claim to geography online and influenced the web presence of cooperating partners. When the main site owns a city name, potential competitors may have difficulty gaining a foothold. The move would then narrow the viable online options for marginalized or alternative voices.

Content changes, design strategies, and market maneuvers are part of a larger transformation around the turn of the twenty-first century. Geographical understanding has changed along with political organization throughout history. When societies first established the means to hold title to land, the understanding of place changed, and private ownership established a system of control. Cultural ideas about location tend to encourage some activities that excite enthusiasm and discourage others that get ignored. The technologies of paper and printing disseminated cultural norms more widely and at a lower cost than older forms of oral communication could achieve. While discouraging older ways, the new means have what historian Harold Innis calls a *spatial bias*. Instead of expanding communication consistently, new technologies result in "monopolies over space" that tend also to "check the movement of ideas."[13]

Technical change can make communication more difficult, but in ways that make avoiding knowledge effortless.[14] After the invention of printing, the then-new technology of printed books was much easier to avoid than the old techniques of storytelling around the hearth. When television diffused into almost every home, the TV set became more difficult to avoid or at least a point of contention about which program to watch. Turning on the news followed a pecking order, but the noise of television news again filled the home as oral stories once had done. A news website online requires different skills and high-cost equipment and imposes access fees but is easier to ignore than a newspaper that lands on the front stoop every day. And a news bulletin that interrupts the flow of entertainment broadcasting is easier to use as a comfort break than a news link that pops up directly on a social-media feed. Online news also restructures control over places.

The cultural transformation that occurred by the early twenty-first century led to a new regime that tends to put less value on concrete *place* than on something more abstract, *space*. Several thinkers identified a change in spatial conceptions.[15] The shifts parallel those a century earlier, and both periods of change linked to an emerging mode of production. The new regime contrasts with the old because place is a product of someone's firsthand *experience*, but space is the product of secondhand *information*. Walter Lippmann called *space* "a good clue" for detecting stereotypes, those oversimplified rubrics so handy for picturing inaccessible places.[16] Space also makes less meaningful the place-based distinctions between authentic and inauthentic experience. Because the mind receives physical seeing and seeing pictures in much the same way, the armchair traveler will recognize the sights when arriving as a tourist or may choose not to travel at all. Recent changes in technology allow a "locational indifference" in the manufacture of things, so that economic activity can happen anywhere.[17]

The new regime had an unexpected impact on political organization. The documentary evidence shows that being able to work or shop at home produced less telecommuting and home shopping than expected at the same time that cities grew and shopping centers proliferated. A "simultaneous spatial dispersion and concentration" occurred.[18] Global and local tendencies came to coexist, shifting political power. Workers can connect to faraway places but do their jobs at home, and they can move to distant suburbs but cluster near industrial parks. The dual tendencies coalesced in the growth of modern news. The shift in content connected news even more to modern systems, but the market strategies online, along with zoned newspaper editions and the illusion of increased televisual proximity, suggest that a kind of realist localizing also occurred. The changes took place online, but print, audio, and video news followed similar distancing and localizing tendencies.

The social theorist Michel Foucault calls the emerging era an "epoch of space," a time of simultaneity, juxtaposition, of near and far, but also side by side, a time of the dispersed and the networked.[19] Space in the new era is holy or sanctified, and Foucault contrasts the sacred quality of private, family, cultural, and leisure space with the secular quality of public spaces. Like others who have considered it, he sees space as a set of relations or interactions, some of them utopias as idealistic as they are unreal, such as the family. Others he calls *heterotopias*, which connect the real and the unreal, as does a mirror that brings the virtual (the viewer's reflection) into view of the real (the viewer). Heterotopias exist to manage deviations, segregating deviants into prisons and hospitals, for instance, and to accommodate liminal phases (like coming of age) and crises like the honeymoon, which places the bride's deflowering outside of the community.

Modern news is one heterotopia. It allows individuals to participate in social control through collective consciousness. Hegel describes news as "the realist's morning prayer,"[20] replacing a deference to God but also tying the act of consuming the news to an awareness that others in many places are following the same ritual—condemning the same deviant, praising the same hero, and so on. News in the twenty-first century began focusing on the distant, where news practice has more control, at least when it comes to substantial shares of U.S. news audiences. It also rejected the street address, where audiences have more knowledge and say. By focusing on the distant while rejecting the most local, modern news sets up a void between lived experience and conceptions of the world out there, a gap that demands filling. News organizations fill the breach by structuring a market around it. They anchor concepts of the local in acts of consumption, and they regularly cover the cycles of holiday or religious activities that invoke hometown feeling. The two together produce a combination of pseudo-religious and commercial fervor.

Ordinary U.S. Americans, with encouragement from news media, also fill the void. When the world has become smaller, at least in modern imagination, audiences can join news producers in fusing foreign places with the living room, so that distance no longer matters, or in turning locations into ideals with sacred qualities, such as home and family. A pronounced aspect in the recent shift in spatial consciousness is "the sentimentalization of home."[21] In a world that seems to have abandoned concrete place in favor of abstract space, the response or reaction has been to enshrine elevator concepts—family, religion, and so-called family values— as placeholders to cover the void. Political organization has followed, establishing monopolies of control in ring cities and on networks online. Modern news helped usher in that wider transformation by covering "calendar events" that mark the cycles of home and community life and by treating readers, viewers, and hearers as potential shoppers seeking amusement in economic activity.

Editors warn each other against "giving people what they *want* instead of what they *need*."[22] The formulation makes modern news an active agent protecting audiences from themselves. But U.S. audiences are not passive, narrow, or parochial followers of local versus foreign coverage. Audiences may be more susceptible to stereotypes in distant news, but they say they want more foreign coverage, not less.[23] As news has changed, what the audience receives has less to do with their public roles as citizens and more to do with their private activities as consumers. At the same time, their social-media sharing of purchases and "clicktivism" on political topics makes their activity public and available for the host sites to "monetize." The shift disperses local interests, encouraging audience members to focus not, for instance, on their collective concerns as workers in a local factory but instead on their interest in, say, discount prices made possible through global connections. Every dimension of the world did get closer, but in ways the founders of television could not anticipate.[24]

When news turns away from the local to give audiences a nourishing dose of the modern big picture, the quality of content may decline. It is the reporter close to an event who quotes more, and more varied, sources; that is, local reports *tell stories*.[25] Reporters without personal knowledge of the community rely on officials and experts farther from the events; that is, they *convey information*. The transformation of locations in the news is a move from event to data, from fact to trend, and from a material "world out there" to the spider's web of networks, or from realist to abstract modernism. Some television industry research indicates that local political news focuses more on concrete problems than does national news, which concentrates more on strategy.[26] Reporters with closer ties to a community have also shown more honesty and less inclination to overstate than do those more distant from events. But as their occupation became itinerant, they had less opportunity to build community ties. News centered on the local can be commercially successful, but occupational aspirations and rewards shift reporting away from that coverage.[27]

All groups use space as a representational strategy, positioning group members in relation to others.[28] News practice is similar. News is a narrative performance, and its reports present "alternative spatial stories."[29] Modern news tends to remove nearby places and substitute unexamined beliefs about other locations. The abstractions about distant places reduce them to fairytale lands,[30] easy to ignore because they lack substance. Daniel Boorstin decades ago identified how pseudo places eliminate physical places by demolishing "sense regimes of place, locale, and history."[31] In the U.S. mythology of modern news, one's city or "America" tends to be superior or mighty, leaving other places primitive and retrograde by comparison.[32]

The realist news of physical proximity grew up more than a century ago along with the rise of the middle classes, and news practices came to focus on the fixed domicile, a factor more important than either commerce or industrialism in implanting the new system of power.[33] News since then has continued to set up a geographical metaphor based on center and periphery. The data show that news has changed beneath the apparent surface to follow a new spatial regime that puts producers at the center and audiences at the periphery, swallowing up the event itself in modern placelessness. News now builds horizontal bonds that bind together news practitioners, although with weak or competitive ties. Two forms of dependency result, so that producers rely on their employers and their occupation, and citizens must rely on the news producer. "More people spend more time," writes James Carey, "dependent on the journalist, the publisher, and the program director," when news supplies information as a commodity instead of telling nearby stories.[34]

Beliefs among news practitioners and researchers, as well as the general public, continue to reflect the realist origins of modern news by expecting stories to focus more on local events. The imagined content of U.S. news has remained true to its roots, while the contents manifest in print, radio, television, and the internet have become modern commodities. Although news prepared the way for the recent changes, transformations in the concepts of space that occurred at the end of the twentieth century seem to have left out news. Smart-phone users employ apps to "check in" at restaurants, shops, and other spaces of consumption and find nearby friends and meet others through interactive location services. But occupational boundaries and standards block the parallel in news and keep "citizen journalism" and "hyperlocal" coverage in continual development, not quite ready for full deployment. Despite the belief that foreign coverage is declining, modern news has put more distance between events and audiences while managing to bring news practitioners themselves into closer focus. The occupation holds a contradictory position, with news industries in turmoil even as some reporters and editors seem more powerful than ever.

"The media have become the power brokers of our time . . . for better or for worse," writes Christiane Amanpour, long-time international correspondent for CNN.[35] When elites disagree about or governments lack a clear policy toward events, news media fill the void with issue coverage. The resulting pressures on political leaders to do something she calls "the CNN factor." Less than a year after her article came out, a CNN freelancer described Sofia, Bulgaria, in January: Crowds demonstrating against the socialist government chanted, "Where is CNN? Where is CNN?" When the network sent in a crew from London, a rally speaker spotted them and shouted, "Christiane Amanpour is here!" and the crowd cheered for her to speak.[36] They saw news as a way to confirm the importance of their location and bring it into existence for others.

Practitioners benefit unequally from the expanded power of news in the era of space. For every Amanpour, many hundreds of others feel powerless, caught in a job squeeze as news businesses reorganize to sustain historical profit margins. But the occupation has also participated perhaps inadvertently in the changed era by striving to incorporate more about distant locations into the news while focusing the form of news on its producers. Modernism provides high-minded reasons—because the world is shrinking and U.S. Americans seem not to know or care—to motivate action within the occupation. Individual workers may not recognize that the rationales of modernism distance them from citizens living at street addresses, while encouraging *hometown* consumption and an artificial localism. The way U.S. news content became modern has redefined the coverage of locations and moved knowledge about the "where" further from the places of everyday life.

THE ART OF SINKING IN POETRY

Ye Gods! Annihilate but space and time,
And make two lovers happy.

> —Alexander Pope, *Martinus Scriblerus*
> *or the Art of Sinking in Poetry* (1727)

PART 5

"When"—The Now of News Pursued Modernism

To every thing there is a season, and a time
to every purpose under the heaven:

A time to be born, and a time to die;

a time to plant, and a time to pluck up that which is planted;

A time to kill, and a time to heal;
a time to break down, and a time to build up;

A time to weep, and a time to laugh;
a time to mourn, and a time to dance;

A time to cast away stones, and a time to gather stones together;

a time to embrace, and a time to refrain from embracing;

A time to get, and a time to lose;
a time to keep, and a time to cast away;

A time to rend, and a time to sew;
a time to keep silence, and a time to speak;

A time to love, and a time to hate; a time of war, and a time of peace.

—Ecclesiastes 2:1–8 (King James Version)

CHAPTER 13

The Press Adopted Linear Time

In popular imagination since the 1980s, America has been "running itself ragged," according to a cover story in *Time* magazine: "These are the days of the time famine."[1] Government officials struggle for "the opportunity to defend" themselves in the accelerating news cycles. Citizens decry the lack of time to make sense of the news.[2] A New Yorker whose kidnapping and release made headlines describes time pressures this way: "You read about it in the *Daily News* while crushed up against people on the subway to work. The story flies past you like a million others; there are far too many . . . to absorb."[3] News insiders have a similar assessment in their own conditions. One cliché is "So many stories, so little time," as *Washington Post* columnist Eugene Robinson puts it.[4] The pace of reporting "inevitably puts more emphasis on efficiency than on depth," says the *Columbia Journalism Review*.[5] Reporters and editors say they focus on the *now* more than ever, and they tend to blame technology for the time pressures they feel. The trade magazine *Editor and Publisher* says, "Heavier work demands are visible" everywhere: "For reporters, it often means taking time . . . to crank out or update the latest web scoop."[6] News reflects the modern experience of time as a scarce resource.

Social scientists and other observers see the broader pattern. Early on, Alvin Toffler identified news among the fast-paced "coded messages [in] industrial society,"[7] and Todd Gitlin decried "the pace of events, the rush of mass-mediated, distanced, and distorted experience" that disorients and deprives groups "of a sense of political context."[8] Anthropologists call the phenomenon a *time famine* peculiar to urban, industrial society. Sociologist Juliet Schor concludes that "nearly all types of Americans" face "a profound structural crisis of time."[9] And the problem has not gone away. Instead, as an analyst puts it, "the rate of change has increased markedly."[10]

News producers, researchers, and observers agree that U.S. American life has become busier, with little time to spare. The time crunch seems to have led newspaper reporters and editors to focus on the real present instead of the modern tasks of gathering background, spotting trends, or ferreting out future problems. Time accelerated especially on television, where competitive pressures to go live have left reporters without time to investigate or even to edit their material. And it results from digital mobile media and the shorter news cycles that emerge along with new technology. By the second decade of the twenty-first century, U.S. newspapers were shutting down or abandoning print, and thousands of reporters had lost their jobs. The time crunch appears among the conditions that made the state of news practice seem dire. Consequences do flow from historical shifts in time regimes,[11] and the press experienced similar disruptions when industrial culture reached its apex around the turn of the nineteenth century. Time again transformed in the nanosecond culture emerging in the late twentieth century.

Did news stories become more centered in the realist present? To test the idea, our long-term study of newspapers looked at how often each article referred to different time points: past, present, and future (figure 13.1).[12] Almost without exception, stories dealt with the present, and those references remained fairly constant over the twentieth century. Although reporters say they refocused on the present, no fundamental change occurred in references to the *now*. Other time mentions did change as news became modern. After a small dip between 1894 and 1914, a slow but steady increase in references to other points in time occurred in news reports. Among the three topics measured—accidents, crime, and employment—coverage of jobs, in general, referred far more often to other points in time, and accident news far fewer. But the trend moved with almost identical timing for each topic as well as for each newspaper.

In shifting focus to other time frames, news stories followed three distinct patterns. The most powerful trend was toward talking about the past. More than twice as many articles included past references in the 1990s than in the 1890s (see the bar graph). Those describing changes over time also increased (see the trend line). In 1894 less than 2 percent of articles talked about change, but a century later more than 7 percent did. Speculation about future events followed a curvilinear pattern, with high points shortly before the turn of each century. The patterns in content reflect changes as news practice shifted toward modern ways.

U.S. news until well into the nineteenth century was haphazard about time. John L. Given, who wrote for the *New York Evening Sun*, remembers the day when a writer could stroll or stand "idle at a street corner waiting for something to happen."

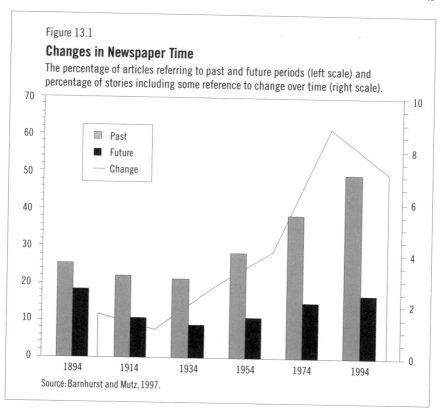

Figure 13.1

Changes in Newspaper Time

The percentage of articles referring to past and future periods (left scale) and percentage of stories including some reference to change over time (right scale).

Legend:
- Past
- Future
- Change

Source: Barnhurst and Mutz, 1997.

There was "no rush or jostle about newspaper establishments," says Colonel A. K. McClure, editor of the *Philadelphia Times*. John Addison Porter of the *Hartford Post* recalls the "leisure in a newspaper office," which valued "literary skill and book knowledge." The prime example (or last hold-out) of deliberate news was Charles A. Dana, editor and publisher of the *New York Sun*, whose adage for success in newspapers was, "Never do anything in a hurry."[13]

News organs of the era still retained some of what scholars call a *classic* sense of time: that events flow through a stable world. In classic time the rhythms of agriculture and the cycles of myth return endlessly, as do impulsive youth and deliberate old age. Philosophers such as Saint Augustine assigned special status to action in the present, but classic time also honors the invariant past. Newspaper operators of the nineteenth century focused on the present but lionized history. Myths of a glorious bygone America emerged in the *New York Times* and some magazines of the era, as editors pursued stories to commemorate national anniversaries from the past.[14]

But ancient and medieval ideas existed alongside a growing *modern* sense of time: linear, measurable, and open to progress or reversals.[15] At the end of the nineteenth century, references to the future were high, as newspapers antici-pated national advances.[16] To illustrate the change, Franc B. "Poliuto" Wilkie, first president of the Press Club of Chicago, begins by describing the timing of mid-nineteenth-century news: "Things that happened in New York were known in their detail three days after they occurred. Events transpiring in London required fifteen days to reach Chicago. Occurrences happening in Central and Southern Europe required not less than three weeks to cross the continent to the metropolis of the West. Northern Africa furnished intelligence that was a full month on its passage. Russia, Siberia, India, Southern Africa only revealed their latest doings to us six months or a year after they happened." But, he continues, all of that had changed by the end of the century: events "of importance" from any "point in civilization" became "known in Chicago the next morning at the very latest."[17] As modern time first took hold, news became more realist and *now* centered, and references to other time periods began declining (trends that would change as modern time matured later in the century). The older generation in newspaper offices felt nostalgia for a work rhythm that retained traces of its ancient and medieval roots.[18]

Newspapers under sensationalist editors like William Randolph Hearst and Joseph Pulitzer became more aggressive in marking linear time: "Evening dailies, multiple editions, and headline rushes . . . narrowed the distance between the news event and its deadline, intensified the pace of office work," and turned news into a perishable product that lost value if "not harvested, processed, and delivered in a matter of hours."[19] As news became distinct from literary work, reporters competed for the stories and stunts that would sell copies on the streets. Under what critics then called the "tyranny of timeliness," John Given recalls, a reporter could get fired for being "a little slow getting to a telephone." Besides the individual advances and reversals registered in the newfangled scoops, exclusives, and deadlines, circula-tion became the measure of success.

By the mid-twentieth century, U.S. news manuals and textbooks treated the new time regime as ordinary, as in the *Introduction to Modern Journalism*: "Reporters' work is almost all extemporaneous. Most of their writing is done under pressure. Generally speaking, news is good only when it is fresh, and reporters find it good routine to write their stories as soon as they return to their desks after gathering the facts for a story."[20]

In a biography of the period, Julius Chambers, who became managing edi-tor of the *New York Herald* and *New York World* in a long career, describes his early adventures in modern news. After a messenger rushed in with a note, the night city editor saw "a great news story was in sight. He glanced at the clock—the hour was eleven." He called on "his star reporter, Daniel Kirwin," saying, "take two men with you. Hire all the cabs you want. Get the story." The account of the murder investigation ran by the clock. Kirwin instructed his subaltern to "hurry to the office and write every line possible." Upon arriving at the scene of the crime, Kirwin uncovered several "mysteries in precisely eleven minutes. He was working against time . . . as a news-hunter." Reaching "the office at 1:30 (having written 1,500 words in the billiard-room of the dead man . . .), he had sufficient facts" to solve the crime, based on precise timings of the victim's movements, such as the word of one witness fixated on time "because his relief was due at nine, hadn't arrived, and he was literally 'watching the clock.'" And in the end, time coordination blended with other stereotypes of the occupation: "The full account of the sensational crime came together into a harmonious whole. At 2.30 a.m., the nine and a quarter column account of the murder of John Hawkins, written and compiled by seven different collaborators, went to press as smoothly as if it had been the work of one hand. . . . Mr. Daniel J. Kirwin, star reporter, ran his critical eyes over the latest proof-sheets, caught a few typographical errors, handed the damp strips of paper to the night editor, . . . lit a cigar, . . . [and] said: 'Let's go down to Charley Perry's and take something.'"[21]

News organizations have generally attributed the need for timeliness to two factors, audience demand and the tools at hand. A booklet for visitors of the *New York Times* printing plant in the 1930s describes how the telegraph and telephone sped newsgathering about a gas explosion that flattened a school building, killing hundreds of children in New London, Texas. The remote town, not on any maps in New York, was reachable by calling officials in Texas, and the *Times* staff then telegraphed "several columns of news, including interviews and eyewitness accounts" and transmitted wire photos by courier and phone lines. *Times* editors called it "one of the most rapid and successful accomplishments in covering news at a distance in recent years."[22] An editor defines news as "current events of interest or importance to the readers" and puts readers first for the *Times*: "Its readers determine what is news" because it "cannot survive one day without readers," who "will switch to another" if the paper fails to publish what they want. And so "speed enters into the gathering, the writing, the editing, and the display of many news stories."[23] The reader-consumer has leverage as long as newspapers face competition to get the most timely news.

The earliest *modern* sense of time emerged along with the communication medium of printing, which scholars in the Renaissance employed to compare the present to the past and test earlier writers' beliefs about nature against their own observations. Modern science and history depended on communication, then as now. Like classic time, the modern sense of time is a flow of events, but modern time puts emphasis on direction, running from past (behind) through present to future (in front).[24] Time also turns into a tool and commodity, leading

Benjamin Franklin to write that time is money.[25] The version of modern time typical of news emerged much later, as newspapers became industrial, shrinking time just as railroads were shrinking space.[26] The factory compresses time, making it seem scarce.[27] "The rhythms of the machine tend to replace human ones. Deadlines reproduce themselves. . . . A generalized hurry makes its entrance," producing social anxiety.[28]

A transformation in modern time sensibilities was occurring by the beginning of the twentieth century, a change that may have accelerated modern time consciousness in news. In the newspapers studied, references refocused on the present, and other periods dropped from prominent view. Talk about change reached a low point by 1914, and references to past and future did the same over the next two decades. The newspapers covered fewer events overall but more foreign events during the same period. It was a phase in history with plenty to cover in the *now*: world war followed by a market crash and economic depression. At the same time, news practitioners were consolidating their claim to expert standing by founding state and national associations and creating codes of ethics. In reporting, they turned to more institutions and groups, along with more officials, to generate stories.[29]

Publishers of the period also rebuilt newspaper form, creating the modernist style that presented the newspaper itself as a social map, re-drawn on a daily basis to emphasize its spatial reach rather than a temporal durability.[30] The older news forms had a temporal bias, meaning a focus on preserving events through time, and the new spatial bias paid more attention to circulation and broad dissemination (through space) in the present. The trends early in the century anticipated the forms of radio and television news that would emerge decades later. As the political economist Harold Innis suggests, the changing biases of communication media have social and cultural consequences and mark shifts in centers of control, and so in newspapers, publishers moved from personalistic to modern corporate patterns of control over communication, and reporters in counterpoint began to push for higher status. Making their occupation professional involved reinterpreting modern time to make news more central in creating a system of knowledge: journalism as the first draft of history.[31]

By the 1930s newspapers began their steep increase in references to other periods, especially the past. One element behind the shifts was that photojournalism established a secure place in news practices. Pictures seemed more direct in describing physical appearance and conveying current emotion, realist tasks that operate in the present tense. News pictures freed reporters to do other things aligned with modernism, such as pointing to earlier events and to the patterns of change from then until now or into the future. Newspaper coverage of the deaths of sitting U.S. presidents over a century illustrates the changes.[32] Pictures of the chief executive grew larger and moved from static, timeless portraits to active and candid shots. As the photographs and their captions took on the realism of presenting the latest news, the surrounding text could turn to other modern tasks, including quoting experts and officials, describing the responses of groups, examining changes through time, and referring to past events.

At midcentury news insiders began to question the slavish emphasis on linear timeliness. One critic, a small-town newsman and journalism professor, argues that "newsdom must confess that it has gone too far" in its zeal "to be up to the moment": some editors have "ruled out a 'yesterday' story" and others proclaim "an event happening at 1 p.m." more newsworthy, "because it is more recent, than one taking place at noon."[33] But the realist emphasis on timeliness was fading. The increase in one-newspaper cities was changing news competition, recent accounts of out-of-date events were receiving wide attention, and reports from military battles in distant places and other foreign news were becoming prominent as editors "geared for years to regard this second [world] war as big news." The editor concludes, "'timely' is being interpreted now much more sensibly than it was a few years ago."

Changes in time sensibilities for news did adjust to economic conditions for the press. In long-term measurements, the realist *now* of news tracked inversely with how many daily newspapers existed in the United States.[34] The number published grew from the 1890s to reach a peak in the early decades of the twentieth century, then began a long, slow decline in 1914, dropping below the initial numbers by the 1960s. Although other factors intervened, news writing tended to focus more on the *now* when daily newspapering as a line of business activity was growing, and then declined as competition waned and reporters could turn their attention to past events and to modern analyses of changing trends to serve a smaller, elite circulation.

Despite redefining time in practice over the course of the century, reporters continued to tell an older, realist story about the "when" of news.[35] It originated in an earlier century when the journalist began to emerge as a separate occupation and assert a respectable pedigree, abandoning previous relaxed and literary routines. As the mainstream occupation became institutional, practitioners did at first focus more on the realist present under the regime of high-speed, intensive labor regulated by deadline pressures. But the newfound status came at a cost. In concert with changes in news form and the rise of photojournalism as an extension, modern news brought the opportunity for reporters to turn more toward long stories that cite previous events and point to extensive patterns. Although the transformation in news time accompanied declines in the newspaper business, the story that reporters and editors tell has still not absorbed the changed environment.

The life cycle of a reporter-editor can illustrate the consequences of modern time sensibilities. Barbara Serrano grew up in Silicon Valley, the daughter of a truck-driver father and a (mostly) stay-at-home mother, on the predominantly Mexican side of Gilroy, California. But she always wanted to leave town, travel, and take part in history. In her early teens, the Watergate hearings on television hooked her. "What are you doing watching that?" her mother asked, and she replied, "It's big. The president's resigning." Her parents seemed to live outside of time. When a local radio station picked up a lunchroom boycott story she wrote for the high school paper, "that was it," she said: "I'm becoming a journalist." She got into Berkeley, landed internships, and got her first jobs for a Gannett paper and the *Orange Country Register*.

In 1990 the *Seattle Times* started Serrano as a general assignment reporter, but about a year later sent her to cover state politics in Olympia, Washington, not a typical assignment for a Latina. After three years she returned to Seattle as a political reporter. Two big stories illustrate her connection to news time. On a proposal to build a central park called the Commons, she wrote seven articles once the Seattle City Council put the project on the ballot. The early stories included a short account with budget projections and then two articles expanding the time frame: a reaction story about the mayor and piece about a Seattle Mariners stadium project competing on the ballot.[36] The stories grew longer as she focused on the future impact of the proposal.

Based on a tip, she began to look at the Commons budget compared with projections that forecast money problems for the city. She talked to the city financial director, residents, and business owners, and the *Times* published her long report detailing the project.[37] The story reviews the four years leading up to the vote, along with earlier projects, such as the Space Needle and related work of 1968, which failed twice before voters approved them. The "dream" the story describes is a blend of business development, affordable housing, and traffic solutions: "How else to explain company CEOs sitting next to labor leaders and environmentalists at the Commons table?" After citing similar ventures in other cities, Serrano raises questions about time: When in U.S. history has a city carved out so many acres for a park? (Answer: never.)

The article balances that possible future with the voices of opponents, who call it "chasing an elusive yuppie rainbow." They consider the Commons an "ideological mantra" and a "utopian concept." An activist "talks history," citing his past going back forty-six years in the district: attending Little League games, working at neighborhood jobs, and driving "city mayors in the annual parade" as far back as the administration of President Lyndon Johnson. Against the solid ground of history, he points to the future uncertainty the proposal creates for park safety, traffic rerouting, tunnels, parking, and the fate of area businesses. Serrano details the past of "one of the biggest urban renewal projects on the planet," concluding that "the Commons might not be the blueprint voters are willing to pay for" in light of an uncertain future, a theme she returned to in two stories leading up to the vote. The following week the front page announced, "Voters Say No to Commons" by a slim margin. Commons supporters "saw me as the enemy," Serrano said in our interview, but newsroom feedback called her coverage the "best reporting in years" for the city. Even so, her predictions did not fare as well; the city's future unfolded as an economic rebound, with surpluses instead of deficits.[38]

In 1997 Serrano followed a similar path in reporting on a Washington legislature handgun proposition, one in a history of gun control bills during the 1990s. She reviewed the fate of four previous bills and investigated what would happen if the new proposal became law, reading the text of the initiative closely and talking to sources in the legislature, law enforcement, hospitals, state government, and both sides of gun-control activism. Shortly before the vote, she published a long, front-page story on the proposal, beginning from the "broader, philosophical questions" that voters faced about gun control, before enumerating doubts about the proposal's future, adding sources: gun owners, their spouses, and children; firearm safety instructors; privacy advocates; and mental healthcare providers working with stalking victims. Her editor David Boardman liked the handgun story, she said in our interview. It was a kind of reporting that began because of time pressures for the *Seattle Times*, then an afternoon paper, to compete with the evening newscasts on local television.[39]

Serrano became political editor in 1999 but remained on the sidelines during the biggest story of the era, the World Trade Organization (WTO) 1999 ministerial meeting in Seattle. *Times* editors assigned it to the business desk, where reporters focused on the Chamber of Commerce and trade, and then the metro desk, staffed with street and police reporters. In 2000 the paper moved to publishing in the morning, and in 2001 Serrano took time off to reflect, spending a year on a Nieman Fellowship. In our interview she was confident about her time orientation: "As an editor now, I really insist" that "for any major initiative," the goal is to show readers "what is really likely to happen." After a year at Harvard, she moved to the *Los Angeles Times*, becoming first a political editor during the 2004 presidential campaign and then an entertainment editor covering television and news media, returning to Washington State in 2006.

Time pressures as well as newsroom procedures can block reporters and editors from covering some events like the WTO story. But with enough autonomy and advance notice, Serrano could pursue hard questions about what led up to a political proposal and what consequences its future passage might reap. In each story, proposal opponents had confidence in the past but expressed uncertainty about the future, painting worst-case scenarios. In modern news, history seems secure and the present clear, despite the persistence of problems, but the future is predictably undependable. Its murkiness makes a compelling story that inherently argues against change.

When news relies on a modern understanding of news time, stories may argue unintentionally against change in society, and the press becomes an institution of stasis, less able to adapt to change itself. The commitment to modern time made news producers resistant to new kinds of information practices and options for conceiving of time. The emergence of other media has been an important element in how the press became entrenched in its version of modern time. The main alternative to newspapers appeared at midcentury: television, a medium that broadcasts in real time and opens the possibility of a return to the realist present. What happened to news time and general ideas of time when live programs entered the media landscape?

CHAPTER 14

Newscasters Seemed More Hurried

Modern time gives a competitive edge to television, and TV newscasters have been pointing to their time advantage since the beginnings of the medium. In a 1938 essay for the magazine *Photoplay*, Gilbert Seldes, who became the first director for CBS News, called television technology "one of the true miracles of modern days" because "mobile units can . . . transmit" events "at the very moment they occur."[1] Newspapers could publish at best a few hours later, and newsreels could update reports appearing in movie houses only twice a week.[2]

The lore of U.S. television cites major benchmarks for in-the-moment coverage in the early 1960s. The first was the televised debates between presidential candidates John F. Kennedy and Richard M. Nixon. Looking back on a long career at ABC News, Pierre Salinger, who worked with the Kennedy campaign, says that live coverage became "*the* factor, anytime anything important happens."[3] Veteran newscaster David Brinkley remembers: "Spending three days and nights with the Kennedy funeral, I think we really saved the country from . . . crisis. I think we calmed [people] down. Kept them informed minute by minute by minute."[4] Dick Salant, a former CBS News president, recalls two other key moments when the network preempted entertainment programs to air events: the Senate Foreign Relations Committee hearings on the Vietnam conflict in 1966 and the Nixon resignation in 1974, both "costly for the network because advertising revenues were lost."[5]

In the late 1970s, Salant moved to NBC and fought for more time—hour-long national evening news, a proposal that failed. But the founding of Cable News

Network (CNN) in 1980 gave newscasters twenty-four hours a day for coverage, along with greater flexibility to use that time.[6] The strategy demonstrated its value when the space shuttle *Challenger* exploded in 1986 and CNN alone had live coverage—the broadcast networks arrived later. They could compete with CNN only with a stroke of luck, such as when the 1989 San Francisco earthquake occurred during live ABC-TV coverage of the baseball World Series or when the O. J. Simpson civil trial verdict came in during broadcast of President Bill Clinton's State of the Union address in 1997. The decision of CNN correspondent Peter Arnett to stay in Baghdad when the Gulf Conflict broke out in 1990 also highlighted the competitive advantage of having more time available on cable.[7]

Although ratings had sunk much lower by the end of the century, MSNBC and Fox debuted twenty-four-hour stations, beginning what became an ongoing cable news race. TV newscasters feel time pressure intensely.[8] Time is a modern commodity that television sells to advertisers, and the value of programming depends on audiences spending time in front of the video feed. Even classic programs like *60 Minutes*, which have a full hour to present investigative work, cannot cover stories "in the depth" they would prefer, says longtime correspondent Morley Safer. Compared with other reporters, broadcasters have greater time constraints, such as the CBS standard that prohibits editing interview segments "out of time sequence," Safer says. "Our rules," he concludes, "are a lot tougher."[9] Time in television news also has consequences for policymakers. Former U.S. Secretary of State Madeleine K. Albright describes "watching CNN" to track others' statements and reacting "much faster," sometimes based on facts that news outlets got wrong.[10] News coverage continues to influence public opinion that then places pressure on policymakers.[11]

Anchors, reporters, and their sources talk about time pressures, but did the time crunch grow worse for television news? Network newscast content suggests that in some ways it did (figure 14.1). The total minutes dedicated to political reporting in network programs (circle size) had become smaller by about a quarter from 1968 to 1988.[12] At the same time, how long newscasters spoke continuously shrank on average, just as the sound bites of politicians had shrunk over the period.[13]

But in other ways no time crunch appeared. If the same economic and competitive pressures newscasters describe, which helped reduce the size of politicians' sound bites, also shortened all dimensions of news reports, everyone should have been talking less. But that was not the case. Beyond political coverage, reports overall did not grow shorter.[14] Of the time available, almost 10 percent shifted away from sources, but correspondents used about the same number of minutes at the start as at the end of the period studied. Newscasters increased their *share* of time compared with the total of their sources' much-reduced sound bites,

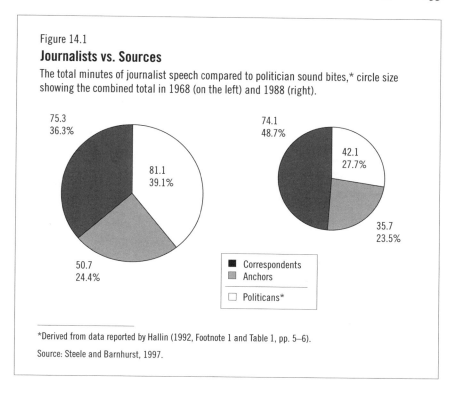

Figure 14.1
Journalists vs. Sources
The total minutes of journalist speech compared to politician sound bites,* circle size showing the combined total in 1968 (on the left) and 1988 (right).

75.3
36.3%

81.1
39.1%

50.7
24.4%

74.1
48.7%

42.1
27.7%

35.7
23.5%

■ Correspondents
■ Anchors
□ Politicans*

*Derived from data reported by Hallin (1992, Footnote 1 and Table 1, pp. 5–6).

Source: Steele and Barnhurst, 1997.

which had declined by half. The pacing of the news reports picked up, leaving the impression that time was at a premium, but on-air time limitations did not grow worse in broadcast for news presenters, even though others lost ground on television. Newscasters experienced more competitive pressures, and in a central area, political coverage, on-air time shrank on the broadcast network evening news, but across all topics and outlets, television newscasters had relatively *more* time on the air. If time gives TV inherent advantages, what can explain the time crunch they describe?

Going live is a kind of pressure unique to broadcasting. On-the-scene reporting supplies realism but adds intensity to meeting a deadline or issuing the latest update. In the late 1990s the industry trade press observed the rise of twenty-four-hour local newscasts and later noted that the "demand for live reports can be so great that there's precious little time for actual reporting" or digging for facts.[15] By providing realism, going live helps television news hold onto viewers who watch for the outcome of a hostage taking, police raid, or fire. The arrival of digital high-definition television a few years later raised greater expectations for live coverage in the industry.

Visual changes in national evening newscasts give credence to the growth of realist on-site coverage. As the backgrounds behind newscasters on screen became more focused on locations, blank walls, once the most common backgrounds, vanished from reports.[16] A plain backdrop behind a talking head is timeless, especially compared with a reporter standing at the location of events, with police investigating or a storm raging. On-location backgrounds doubled, but a more-dramatic visual change was the emergence of on-screen technology for newscast sets. Besides looking current, images of technology convey the power (if not the reality) of news organizations to cover events immediately. The changes gave some substance to—along with the appearance of—focusing on the present, pointing to (if not always carrying out) a core advantage of televised news.

Time on television is multifaceted, and sorting out news time pressures into constituent parts is a valuable exercise that starts from the newscaster's perspective. As early as the 1960s, European researchers identified three time elements typical to coverage of occurrences in news: consonance, unexpectedness, and continuity.[17] U.S. practitioners cover news by employing similar time elements, sometimes under different names.[18] Consonance is the buildup to an expected occurrence, sometimes called a *diary story*, for an item coming up on the newsroom calendar. Unexpectedness is an occurrence that editors cannot predict, also called *spot news*, for items confronting the newsroom unpredictably either in the present or from past occurrences the news staff newly detects. Continuity is an ongoing story, with *running*, developing, or *continuing* coverage of occurrences spanning all three time-elements of news production. The elements align news production with modern time, but spot news or live coverage seems to define the memorable experience for practitioners.

Another way of sorting out news time pressures starts from how sources and audiences experience three dimensions of time in the news: recency, immediacy, and currency.[19] Recency is when the occurrence itself happened, or *event time*, in the lives of sources and actors involved. Immediacy is a lag, the time for production in any medium, called *writer time*. Currency is when the news audience receives the notice and includes listener, viewer, or *reader time*. Reporting conveys a sense of time to audiences at the level of language: the past tense of the context and background details, the present tense of the scoop, and the future (as well as subjunctive or *semiotic*) tense of trends and analysis.[20] The triad of source-reporter-audience is central to witnessing in the news.[21] Live coverage is modernist in its aim to align newsmakers, news producers, and news audiences all at once in time, a precarious performance that depends on the practitioners' understanding of time.

Newscasters' experiences with time reveal their sense of compression in the confrontation with recency or events, their managing of language to collapse time for audiences in the *now*, and their contradictory accounts of the processes of production. Live television can show the scene continuously, let sources speak unedited, and require reporters and anchors to talk impromptu. During periods of intense concentration, individuals may feel time compression,[22] the sensation of time standing still, but at a cost: time becomes an action-chain of scheduled, compartmental tasks with little sense of broader circumstances. The technical challenges and editorial risks of live TV together create stress but also provide what makes television matter, as a medium for covering events right now. The efforts to coordinate with sources and others involved gives the impression of a worsening time crunch, but television news time is contradictory—fast but slow, limited but unlimited.

Because "uncertainty has news value" for audiences, newscasters deploy different expressions of time to make modern news seem more immediate.[23] In the case of Timothy McVeigh, convicted of the bombing that killed 168 at the Alfred P. Murrah Federal Building in Oklahoma City, they used phrases like "due to have happened" and "was to be" done (steps before the execution), inviting the audience to view a future event as having happened recently or as about to happen as the reports aired.[24] When newscasters manipulate time frames verbally to mask the lack of anything new to report, they create the illusion of current news. Those who work at news agencies tend to remodel existing stories, targeting audiences during different time slots rather than doing new reporting. So broadcast news time is malleable. While feeling time compression, newscasters manage to exploit time as a resource in stories.

Newscasters themselves may account for their experiences by taking different and opposing attitudes toward time, *humanistic* or *fatalistic*, but some practitioners exhibit both. A humanistic attitude is a modern sense of control and mastery over activities in time, experienced during planning and carrying out reporting and editing routines. But as deadlines approach or a live broadcast begins, producers feel a fatalistic rush of activity and pressure. The dramatic periods overshadow the rest of the job, reconnect it with realism, and make it meaningful. Newscasters describe their work fatalistically, feeling compelled by time. But that description "diverges from the observed reality" of life in news production. Balancing the two attitudes—staying in control during the mayhem—is the mark of media professionalism. But practitioners' accounts of production give a "spurious coherence" to time in the news.[25] Time compression during reporting veils the clear modern procedures followed to massage time, turning it into an eternal present for audience consumption, while newscasters' accounts are realist, denying their own control over it.

What does television news give the audience through its window on lived events? On twenty-four-hour news channels, "The only live action on view, most of the time, is that provided by the reporters themselves . . . speaking in front of an appropriate location, generally in conversation with an anchor." Rather than reporting as-it-happens news, the cable stations label "breaking news" erratically, to create drama. Even after "an attempted cockpit break-in and a suspected bomb" on a 2004 United Airlines flight to Los Angeles "turned out to be a hoax," some stations continued to label the story *breaking news*. About three-quarters of the time stations dedicate to "breaking news" is recycling previous stories, and the bulk of live coverage involves a few, predictable events, such as press conferences and political debates. Twenty-four-hour news channels "focus on presence and immediacy," favoring not citizenship but spectatorship for "pre-packaged news events (which are easy to cover live)," creating "the *feeling* of discovery."[26]

Audiences differ in their orientations toward time. In rapidly changing conditions, audiences may assign dates to events and then file away or forget the past.[27] Even within a society, time experiences differ by their setting, but U.S. perspectives on news time are surprisingly uniform.[28] Social scientists studying television news tend to mirror newscasters' experiences during production, which training manuals also reflect. Recent textbooks describing news production consider time precious, and they project onto audiences the need for timeliness. U.S. television takes a decidedly modernist view of time as a sequential, scarce resource, like other institutions that "seem to be 'stuck' in" an earlier century.[29]

But for audiences, one of the most powerful aspects of television is the opposite of linear time: its ability to interrupt the "flow of daily life." Media events from the Kennedy funeral to the inauguration of the first black American president, Barack Obama, stopped the profane tasks of advertising and entertaining on national broadcast and cable news to enter sacred time, when television is "actively performing" something "akin to the medieval" staging of holy mysteries. The ritualistic genre of media events creates a time of unity around the goals that newscasters and politicians briefly share during a ceremony requiring the people to act as witness.[30]

A similar logic applies to all types of television content. Daily news can give viewers pleasure partly because it fulfills the expectations of a genre with a beginning ("Good evening") and end ("Good night") that form a time frame for newscasters to fill with something like in-person storytelling. Live events place television spectators outside ordinary time in the continuous cycle of what appears on the monitor, with commentators speaking in the present tense about images from the past. Morning talk shows fuse event time and viewer time into one with producer on-air time by employing an imaginary realism or *liveness*. It overcomes the slowness of real-time experience and the segmentation of television programming made from disparate topical packages, changing scenes, and product ads. The present becomes the present*ation* of the event, built of "a series of juxtaposed 'traces' of absences" that live television glues together with talk during so-called live coverage.[31]

Critics say that time in television is a supply of modules that have modern exchange value. The temporal flow in television implies steady, linear progress that allows newscasters to assign causes and effects. TV news takes a narrative form, and storytelling makes time visible. The story newscasters tell about "working against the clock" in a modern perspective ignores their systematic "over accessing" of the "powerful and privileged,"[32] the few sources reachable now and prepared to respond quickly. Rather than being a scarce resource, time is a malleable aspect of events, giving newscasters much more freedom to select and adjust stories than one would expect given their descriptions of a rush-to-the-present in their work. The urgency and time pressures of television, critics say, are illusory, disconnecting modern TV news from newer perspectives on time.

What does that time experience look like in practice? Scott Talan first experienced news time as an elected official. He became aware of politics in the Reagan era, as an elected student council member at the University of California, Davis. He "was fascinated" by how "all these stories and pictures and headlines . . . came about," he said in our interview. He ran and lost an election for student president and after graduation ran for city council, an unpaid position, but lost. When he ran again in 1989, he finally won. Local media made him a source for routine coverage as the youngest member in Lafayette City Council history, and he got national attention when for safety reasons he blocked Domino's Pizza from building a store at a busy intersection.[33] After three years, the council elected him mayor in 1992, at age twenty-nine the "Youngest Mayor in the Bay Area." Not many months later, when he faced down a proposed 45 percent hike in fees for garbage haulers, the *San Francisco Chronicle* ran a profile of him at age thirty, with a photo and the quotation, "The less I sleep, the more energy I have," in the subtitle.[34] Time was clearly at a premium in his political life.

Despite his popularity, Talan left the council when his mayoral term ended in 1993, but his career in the media had already begun. In college he started with a campus radio talk show and then moved to public-access cable while he was on the city council. The weekly "Bay Area Talks" hosted local worthies such as the general manager of KTVU-2,[35] whom Talan recalled saying, "If you ever want to go into TV, call me." A few months later Talan did just that. It took him two days (rather than the two hours it takes experienced TV reporters) to put together a sample story. With that "introduction into real news in the real world," he left his promising career in government to spend a summer completing a broadcast journalism certificate at Stanford. The training and clips landed him a television news job, but like many broadcast reporters, his career was brief. Starting at an NBC affiliate, KNVN Channel 24 in Chico, California, he would wake up, listen to news on NPR, read the newspaper while watching the local newscast at breakfast, follow radio news during his commute, and work in an office with television news in the background. Coming up with stories usually involved more time off the clock, so that before the morning news meeting, when he had to pitch a story, he had everything ready to pull the story together in a matter of hours. "The quicker your pitch can be," he says, "the better." But then comes the pressure to produce a package.

Working long hours for low pay, he began angling for something better. He won a Radio and Television News Directors Foundation fellowship to Germany and France and then landed work for KRQE-TV, the CBS affiliate in Albuquerque. As a political reporter based in the New Mexico capital, he covered the legislature and governor but also a resident of Chimayo, thirty miles north of Santa Fe, who was "putting up posters" exposing heroin dealers, and Wen Ho Lee, the Los Alamos National Laboratory scientist whose name the *New York Times* published as the target of a spy investigation that fell apart, with recriminations for news credibility. Between the highs in news time were lulls he described in our interview. On July 14, 1998, a summer day with no news, he and a photographer pitched a diary story for Bastille Day. At the French Consulate was a fellow "who could have been an actor in a French movie, sitting poolside" and speaking "with a thick accent." At a French restaurant they found "a guy named Paul Paree," and because "the Tour de France was also happening," they "went to a bike shop." They also visited a French bakery and bought a baguette. "France just won the World Cup," and at a soccer field Talan "was willing for my standup to [use my] head to put a soccer ball in the goal." It "turned out to be a heck of a story" and received raves in the newsroom and from "regular people who saw it." The story illustrates the extreme of malleable news time. But after about two years of serious and sometimes "wacky New Mexico stories," KRQE hired a different news director, who replaced the balding Talan with a TV actress.

By sending in story ideas and studying state politics, Talan then went after and won a job in Florida reporting statewide for NBC affiliates. There he had a formative experience in reporters' timing: while covering the 2000 presidential election recount, he "scooped others in getting the first interview" with the Florida Secretary of State. Reporters "were waiting for Governor Jeb Bush to come down the stairwell." Talan asked his boss, another reporter, "Why don't I scout Katherine Harris?" Talan knew which door she used, but as he waited, "she blew right past us." So he "opened the side door," where the state police said, "You can't come in here." Instead of leaving, Talan asked if the entryway was private. They said, "No," and he had "them on record, the camera rolling":

> And so I just peel open the door, and they let me in. Now they won't let my photographer in, and I pretty much just yanked him in. And the cops—they knew us—they just said, "Go in." We go up to the dais—I told my guy through the mike, "Roll, just roll-roll-roll, have the tape going"—walk up to her. She walks away from us and we kept walking toward her. And all the other reporters are outside waiting for Governor Bush. And I just walked up and first question: "Madame Secretary, how can you tell Florida voters that elected you, that you've done the right thing?" Legitimate, serious question, fair question, tough for her to say, "No comment." She starts talking. I reel off four other questions—even stuff, light stuff like, "What's it like to have Jay Leno talk about you unflatteringly?" So, the bottom line: after that was done, all the networks purchased it from us because it was the first time she'd talked.

The timing for the breaking story involved doing what "a normal person who's not a news reporter" would not likely do, that is, assert public access, move quickly past the guards, keep the camera on, and ask rapid-fire questions. Talan could push because he believed a million Florida viewers had his back. But competition also drove him to the gambit, "because if I walk around and another reporter sees me walk in," others will follow, and "there goes the scoop." The payoff is profit for his news organization and a demonstration of his mastery of time.

Talan won a Nieman Fellowship at Harvard Kennedy School of Government and later worked as a writer-producer for the ABC program *Good Morning America*. He says television leaves viewers with quick impressions, "and if you can do it in less time, that means another story can get in." He prides himself on doing "a story in a minute." "The beautiful part about that," he says, is answering, "What is the story?" The interviews and pictures "are just telling that one sentence thing." The "tight time frame forces you" to ask, "What's this story really about?" His careers in government and media show how TV spot news runs on modern time, with competition for a scarce resource that newscasters use to mediate between the powerful and the people.

TV newscasters experience time in short supply, and the content they produce is modern, shifting time into shapes that fit the needs of news. The present is the basic unit of exchange that allows news media to bring advertisers and other funders together with the viewing audience. The result is television that seems to provide a window on the world, with event time, newscaster time, and audience time in sync. The thrill of live news is its simultaneity—for TV newscasters and their sources a pinnacle moment that joins them with viewers in imagined time. The union is itself transitory, a product of public expectations and production processes defined by modern time. Like money, modern time on television is fungible, one moment readily exchangeable for another. Newscasters project events into a televisual present, and viewers accept multiple times within the *now* of TV. As long as modern time alludes to realism, seeming concrete and solid, television can sustain the transactions it depends on to remain viable. But modern time appears to be losing ground to the greater malleability or further annihilation of time in the digital era.

CHAPTER 15

News Online Reentered Modern Time

In 1969 novelist Kurt Vonnegut Jr. described a character "unstuck in time." Billy Pilgrim, "a senile widower," might wake up on his wedding day or walk from one room in 1951 into another in 1941, then return to find it 1963.[1] Popular commentary about digital mobile media describes a world that also violates modern time expectations. The change fragments time, but a lingering modernist definition—time-as-money—makes filling fragmented time seem more urgent. A growing sense among the general public of being much busier also contradicts documented increases in leisure hours in wealthy countries, where the labor force lives longer and works fewer years.[2] Media critic Jonathan Alter sees the internet as a threat to legacy media, shattering "the old media firmament . . . almost beyond recognition."[3] Social scientists also place digital mobile media "at the heart of the twenty-four-hour news revolution."[4] As part of shifting conditions for news producers and users who enter a web of "time-contracting interconnectedness,"[5] the new time regime seems to weaken news practitioners more as audiences acquire "powers of their own."[6] News insiders say that the advent of digital media accompanied profound social changes. After becoming president of the Associated Press, Tom Curley wrote that "a journalist's job is actually harder" to manage in time.[7]

Practitioners treat the new time regime as added labor, in line with modernist time expectations. "Goodbye Gutenberg," a special issue of *Nieman Reports*, the Harvard quarterly, describes how the interconnections online still embed news stories in a matrix with the past but fill the present with continuous updating. Because "deadlines are gone" (and were "artificial constructs" in the first place), the *New York Times* began handling the extra workload by creating a *continuous news desk* and began asking reporters to contribute to blogs and other new content by "sneaking in bits of online work whenever there's time" or by engaging in "smart time management."[8] The technology increases "the urgency of getting things out," says a managing editor of Wall Street Journal Online.[9]

A main component in the story that online practitioners tell about time involves the accelerating *news cycles*. Each new technology has accompanied a speed up in work routines. Larger, faster presses made more editions possible for newspapers, and successive waves of communications technology led newscasters to give the audience more free headlines over the air, eroding the market for newspapers and forcing print producers to rethink their content.[10] The emergence of twenty-four-hour news on cable erased the older broadcast cycles that used to reset after the daily deadline for evening network news. Since then competition increased and cycles stepped up along with the introduction of digital and mobile devices, and news producers anticipate consequences for themselves and for citizens.

Social science has tended to accept that view of time-obsessed, present-focused practices and a chronic scarcity of time in news. Research replays the accounts of accelerating news cycles as a frame for study or as a background for declines in news quality. The studies then find that leaders in news and politics seem less able to reflect and so make more mistakes, that practitioners find "less time for serious reporting" and fact checking, and that legacy news outlets serving local communities are especially vulnerable.[11] The logs of the wire services document the view common among producers that continuous cycles increase competitive pressures. And comparing campaign advertisements to news content shows that reporters are relying more on candidate press releases as original reporting declines. Digital mobile media seem to increase the disparities among news outlets as smaller news outlets lag behind larger ones in interactive capabilities.[12]

Critics and social scientists agree that time has shifted in news production. They tend to cite technology as the cause, especially felt under competitive market conditions, so that reporters must race in faster cycles that debase content. How solid are the assertions? In their prior history as print-only outlets, the national *New York Times*, regional *Chicago Tribune*, and Portland *Oregonian* serving its city and state had slowly increased references to the past, to changes over time, and, as the turn of each century approached, to the future (figure 15.1).[13]

After moving online, the papers' electronic editions went through a period of adjustment, initially increasing time references, but then returning to levels that continued the earlier trend of gradual increases. In the initial, volatile transition to the digital era, the time aspects of news form and content began changing in almost every way.[14] References to past and future per story jumped by 2001, and references to change over time also increased. But the differences were not uniform. Politics and jobs coverage developed a much more intricate presentation

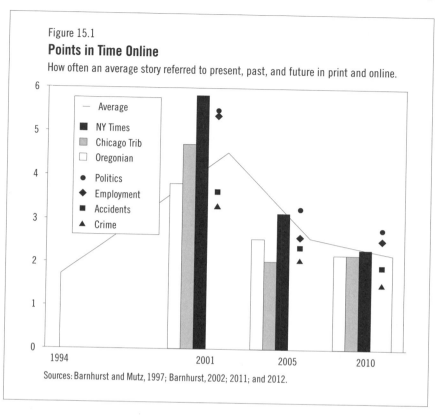

Figure 15.1
Points in Time Online
How often an average story referred to present, past, and future in print and online.

Sources: Barnhurst and Mutz, 1997; Barnhurst, 2002; 2011; and 2012.

of time than did stories about accidents and crime. And NYTimes.com had more complicated ways of handling time especially compared with the *Oregonian* site, a disparity that might seem obvious but had emerged slowly beginning in the 1950s.

Over the decade, the older trends of modernism reasserted themselves. After the initial jump in time references, the topics became more uniform in 2005, so that employment stories briefly became more like crime and accident stories in mentioning fewer time frames. In political stories, reporters made more than twice as many references to distinct periods as they had for the general run of reporting a century before. But by 2010 the topics had returned to the older pattern, with crime and accidents presenting time more simply. The differences among the newspapers had all but vanished, and the online editions diverged only somewhat from the print editions. Although a majority of online and print stories were identical or had only minor changes to the headline or dateline in 2001, full stories online were appearing as digest items or briefs in print by 2005, especially for wire-service copy. By 2010 more wire stories online never saw print, but in-house stories still appeared much the same in both venues.

The initial experimentation with news time online did not last, but talk about accelerating news cycles continued. The term *news cycle* emerged in the 1920s,[15] when newspapers were issuing multiple editions daily but time references were in decline. The ramp-up in "when" references in newspapers coincided with television becoming a news outlet, which began with an evening broadcast and added morning news in 1952. TV loomed larger for newspapers, but radio stations had covered important news events since the 1920s and were distributing regular news content by the 1940s. Their cycles were hourly by the 1960s. And all news media had ways of covering unexpected stories by breaking the normal cycles. After the founding of cable news in the 1980s, along with the emergence of satellite transmissions when the phrase "twenty-four-hour news cycle" appeared, newspapers slowed their rate of increasing time references. Wire services preceded the internet in moving toward a continual cycle and finally abandoned the AM and PM cycle designations by the beginning of the twenty-first century.

Events in news cycle history as well as the news content published are inconsistent with the story that editors tell about newspapers responding to the increasing competition from other media with shorter cycles. Despite the prominence of news cycles in the imagination of news practitioners and academics, research on the phenomenon has been rare. Content differences among news outlets appear to result less from their positions in the news cycle than from other organizational conditions: staff size, total amount of content, and audience size.[16] But news does appear to be an important conduit for popular ideas about time management. As modern time concepts dominated in the twentieth century, references to different periods shifted slowly. Once the internet emerged, reporters responded by expanding time references more quickly for a period, but then they returned to levels that continued the trend followed for almost a century.[17]

The availability of electronic news archives and search engines made referring to other times more convenient, perhaps sparking an upturn in time references within stories, but convenience cannot explain the later decrease. After the internet and social media became commonplace, news practice seems to have entered a period of adjustment, returning to the older process that retained vestiges of realism as modernism advanced. Reporters and editors, who point to competition and digital mobile media, no doubt felt busier and overworked: they were persisting in and also *accelerating* for a brief period their progress toward longer, more temporally complex news. The causes news producers and researchers point to and the consequences they see for the quality of news and policymaking may follow from economic crisis but also flow from news returning to reinforce the modern sense of time.

As modernism waned in U.S. culture, an age of simulation appears to have emerged, replacing facts with scenarios at the end of the twentieth century.[18] The transformation grew in part from perspectives on time. One proposes that time in the twenty-first century has become postmodern. In *The Condition of Postmodernity*, cultural geographer David Harvey says that modes of production embody time. He cites the view of German existentialist philosopher Friedrich Nietzsche that, in the modern world, the newspaper replaced prayer to mark the passing of the day.[19] Newspapers came to narrate present events as if they were a raw or realist succession of causes and effects. Modern time grew out of the medieval invention of clockworks coupled with an early-modern awareness of multiple times across continents, which arose during the era when Europe "discovered" and conquered distant colonies. The existence of different clock time especially in the newly colonized Americas made coordination seem necessary. Modern time then came to synchronize multiple, disparate events across space, making them present all at once. Before modern time, the idea of multiple co-existing times may have seemed mere madness, but newspapers managed to make them seem ordinary by presenting them daily cheek-by-jowl on the page. In the twentieth century, modern aesthetics considered that traditional design too messy and set out to tame the jumble of co-present times. Modern newspapers began arraying events on the page in orderly, balanced ways that seemed to map conditions across societies. One of Harvey's main arguments is that a sea change occurred when those new ways of experiencing time came to dominate. But the postmodern sensibility collapses events and time into images, so that "aesthetics predominate over ethics," presaging the unhinged period of *rusé* realism.[20]

In *The Network Society*, sociologist Manuel Castells calls the new temporal concept *timeless* time, a "space of flows" where global capital works. Simultaneous "real time" around the globe manufactures value by capturing upcoming time using tools like futures markets. Buying and selling potential value in a sense absorbs time itself into trading and also damages the "correspondence between production and reward" as expectations about a commodity replace its value when traded in the present.[21] Network time breaks down the connection between biology and society, producing a kind of arrhythmia by ignoring vital elements in the cycle of life and society such as death and war—events that seem only to happen to others and repeat numbingly in the news. Narratives such as history become mere collections of images from the available stock, reassembled for each genre, including news, to guide consumer decisions.

Although aiming to encompass news along with entertainment and advertising, the postmodern or network concept of time does not describe the texts that mainstream news practitioners have been producing. News content is growing longer and more elaborate in references to time, not eliminating sequencing as theorists expect. News texts may persist in modern temporal narrative because of producer aspirations and entrenched newsroom practices, where modernist ideas linger. But like others, Castells acknowledges that the "new concept of temporality" leaves behind some functions and persons.

The twenty-first-century shift in understanding time also fits within a longer history. Modern time first emerged as an external flow in the physics of Sir Isaac Newton and then became a chain of causality in the eighteenth-century philosophy of Immanuel Kant.[22] Linear, clock time worked in modern thinking as an *a priori* intuition about the world.[23] In the nineteenth century, sociologists such as Émile Durkheim proposed the idea of *social* time, which goes in cycles in response to natural time, and later Anthony Giddens argued that social time takes the form of change and movement of resources. But modern time contains a dichotomy, being linear (moving from past, through present, to the future) but simultaneously cyclical, and by the early twentieth century other dimensions of time emerged. The phenomenologist Edmund Husserl added *inner* time, the subjective flow of time within each person, and the sociologist of phenomenology Alfred Schütz added *world* time, the wider sense of historical flow.[24]

A full sense of time early in that century included clock time, calendar time, private time, and public time, but later in the century scholars proposed further dimensions. The idea of the social construction of time acknowledges differing temporal senses for each cultural group.[25] Women might have distinct experiences, and feminists have argued that women must defend private moments as markets invade. But how groups experience time may differ from what they believe about it. News producers appear to practice their craft within a temporal paradox, firmly planted in modern clock deadlines, calendar events, and even history (from the "morgue" or digital archive of news), but without similar routines for feminist or ethnic rhythms and also out of sync with recent change in time regimes.[26]

By the twentieth century's end, questions arose about the dualities in concepts of time: social vs. natural, cyclical vs. linear, plural vs. universal. Contrasting social to natural time, for instance, obscures how humans are as natural as other social creatures. Equating clock time to objective and quantifiable nature makes no sense because all concepts of time are integral to the natural world and its cycles, *except* for clock time. Unlike the cyclical time of subjective social life, "universal" clocks impose an abstraction through a technology at odds with the everyday experiences of humans in many cultures. Michael Crichton had a similar insight in the novel *Timeline*: "Time doesn't flow. The fact that we think time passes is just an accident of our nervous systems—of the way things look to us. In reality, time doesn't pass; we pass."[27]

Crichton arrives at something like the understanding of time found in Chicago Sociology from a century ago.[28] For George Herbert Mead acts are events that emerge and *make* the present, simultaneously making the past and future instead of moving along a line from yesterday to tomorrow. From the present as a perspective, the past and future are horizons. But events themselves constitute time. Through what Mead calls *emergence*, any surprise that interrupts the continuity of life is what marks time. The present is reality, the past is made of hypotheses about what preceded, and the future is made of conjectures about what may lead out from the event. But they all emerge in every act. Humans are "activity-matter, . . . communication networks, biological clocks that beat in 'off-beat' to the rhythms of our earth," and so time itself evolved from sociality.[29]

News plays a central role in defining acts—such as the risks growing out of, say, nuclear disaster and the potential for political responses[30]—and an *act* is distinct from *action*. Action is the ongoing present, but humans separate out parts of the ongoing action and define them as acts. An act is known *retrospectively*, as humans look back and explain, and *prospectively* as humans project forward and attribute potential meanings. The producers of news select acts from an unlimited array of actions (or *occurrences*), and only those acts can then become news events. But occupational expectations shape their choices[31]—which acts they recognize as events through all aspects of their efforts, words, and dreams. Their world in the newsroom, television studio, or computer workspace makes its version of time "interactively and subjectively,"[32] but following institutional expectations established under earlier, modern concepts of time. Whether an event is tragic or comic, practitioners impose order and sequencing and present the event in relation to the three time dimensions: other events in the present, the past of previous news stories, and the future of policy options and decisions.

In its history, news has hewed to the mainstream, usually lagging behind other cultural institutions. Newspapers are stuck in late-nineteenth-century modern time, raising complaints and objections to the new time regime much as the Editor and Journalist did to the Time Traveller in *The Time Machine,* H. G. Wells's 1898 futuristic novel. Television news is mired in mid-twentieth-century modern time, and the web editions of legacy media, after a moment of turbulence, returned to reflect the modernist time of an institutional memory they share. New interactive and mobile technologies create for news media a space of temporal discomfort. The modern sense of time empowered practitioners, giving them clear tools for selection and sequence, the discipline of deadlines, and the competition of the scoop and the exclusive, with the underlying assumption that time is money. The new sense of time removes their illusion of some control in a political life formerly attuned to their own news cycles.[33]

If communication is a ritual, then news is a prime means of arresting time, akin to monumental architecture, the plastic arts, and myth. Media scholar James Carey wrote: "Journalism is the keeping of a serial biography of a community in a more or less fixed and regular way."[34] But the producers of news content, like many others, now realize they must create (not spend) time through "cultural rhythms, sequences, and duration."[35] Suddenly it seems news practice must become more improvisatory, a performing art like jazz, popular dance, and oral narrative. News faces the imperative to turn into another art, needed sometimes with urgency but sadly underpaid for all but the lucky few. Modern news does compress and process time, especially on television, but perhaps its competitors, the news aggregators, bloggers, and portals, are more adept in the time regime of the twenty-first century. And that may be why news insiders see the old ways failing. They embody an institution already fixed in time more than a century ago. Their predicament highlights how times have changed for knowledge about time.

THE TIME MACHINE

"It seems a pity to let the dinner spoil," said the Editor of a well-known daily paper. . . . [But then] the door from the corridor opened slowly. . . . and the Time Traveller stood before us.

His coat was dusty and dirty. . . . ; his chin had a brown cut on it—a cut half healed. . . .

The Editor began a question. "Tell you presently," said the Time Traveller. . . .

Then, "Remarkable Behaviour of an Eminent Scientist," I heard the Editor say, thinking (after his wont) in headlines. . . .

The dinner was resumed. . . . and then the Editor got fervent in his curiosity. "Does our friend eke out his modest income with a crossing? or has he his Nebuchadnezzar phases?" he inquired. "I feel assured it's this business of the Time Machine," I said. . . . The Editor raised objections. "What was this time travelling? . . ." And then, as the idea came home to him, he resorted to caricature. Hadn't they any clothes-brushes in the Future? The Journalist too, would not believe at any price, and joined the Editor in the easy work of heaping ridicule on the whole thing. They were both the new kind of journalist—very joyous, irreverent young men. "Our Special Correspondent in the Day after To-morrow reports," the Journalist was saying—or rather shouting. . . .

"I say," said the Editor hilariously, "these chaps here say you have been travelling into the middle of next week! . . ."

The Time Traveller . . . smiled quietly, in his old way. . . .

"Story!" cried the Editor.

"Story be damned!" said the Time Traveller. "I want something to eat. . . ."

"One word," said I. "Have been time travelling?"

"Yes," said the Time Traveller. . . .

"I'd give a shilling a line for a verbatim note," said the Editor. . . . The rest of the dinner was uncomfortable. . . . The Journalist tried to relieve the tension by telling anecdotes. . . . At last the Time Traveller pushed his plate away, and looked round us. * * *

"I will . . . tell you the story of what has happened to me, if you like, but you must refrain from interruptions. . . . Is it agreed?"

"Agreed," said the Editor, and the rest of us echoed "Agreed." And with that the Time Traveller began his story. . . . Most of us hearers were in shadow, . . . and only the face of the Journalist [was] illuminated. . . .

—H. G. Wells, *The Time Machine*, 1895

"Crossing" means "swindle," and "Nebuchadnezzar phases" are "strange dreams." A "shilling a line" is about 2.5 current U.S. pennies per line of newspaper column text.

PART 6

"Why"—Against All Odds, Interpretation Advanced

All that dabble in the Ink, . . . can think,
Conceive, express, and steer the Souls of Men,
As with a Rudder, round thus, with their Pen.
[Which] must be one that can instruct your Youth,
And keep your Acme in the state of Truth . . .
—Ben Jonson, *The Staple of News* (1692)

Acme, as "mature age."

CHAPTER 16

The Press Grew More Interpretive

On a Wednesday afternoon in 2009, the U.S. Senate subcommittee on communications convened on the Future of Journalism. Sen. John Kerry began with a welcome to the brave new world where "newspapers look like an endangered species."[1] After comments by senators and testimony from press executives and others, online *Huffington Post* founding editor Arianna Huffington criticized the old system of news that failed to explain "the run-up to the war in Iraq and the financial meltdown" but instead let "publishing Pooh-Bahs" dictate "what is important." Those days "are over," she said, "and thank goodness."[2] Legislators asked whether online editions can produce reporting that explains events, and newspaper publishers said no. When asked whether not-for-profits could fill the gap, a foundation witness said no. Sen. Kerry closed by noting that all sides agree on the need to preserve a kind of in-depth reporting that goes into *quality* news. His was an argument for explaining processes and causes in news.

Scholars complain that U.S. news falls short when it comes to making sense of events, especially compared with the press in Europe. An article in *The Nation* on "the collapse of journalism" argues that other countries spend more on informing their public through media, an investment that yields "dramatically more detailed and incisive" news.[3] Another commentary points to the French press[4] as an example of analysis and depth for American news to follow, and a study of the Finnish press[5] found an increase since the 1990s in commentary about events within front-page stories. But the U.S. press, sociologists report, fails "to produce reasonably unambiguous explanations," and "answering the 'why' questions," they conclude, "might have attracted" a larger audience.[6]

Critics have called regularly for more interpretive news. The Left worries about commercial and public relations influences, and the Right about reporters' biases, but both sides call for news that gives more context.[7] They say the press should also do a better job of explaining where information comes from. News content producers want to supply more and better interpretations and have called for more context that "makes the complex coherent and meaningful,"[8] decried a growing tendency of science news reports to manipulate facts,[9] and warned against surrendering "their functions of analysis and explanation."[10] Pulitzer Prize winner Jack Fuller argued as publisher of the *Chicago Tribune* that audiences find "perfectly neutral accounts" uninteresting and expect news to do "much of the analytic work for them,"[11] but amid the newspaper crisis he wondered where the reading public would "find adequate explanation."[12]

The usual remedy practitioners, scholars, and critics prescribe is modern: for reporters to include more context and background in their stories, but not more judgments, which they say belong on the editorial pages. The financial crisis of newspapers in the early twenty-first century made a remedy seem urgent. But was the news failing to supply citizens with the fifth W, the "why" making sense of events? Did the content of news stories lack explanations of how events occurred? A closer look shows a broad interpretive turn toward modern news, with explanations along with judgments and opinions increasing in the news content of daily papers, network television, public radio, and mainstream sites online. Newspapers we studied expanded their emphasis on interpretations overall and their references to how and why events occur (figure 16.1). Compared with a one-paragraph story on a factory adding jobs in 1894, a 2005 story on layoffs at IBM ran twenty paragraphs (about average for *New York Times* staff pieces that year) analyzing global markets where jobs migrate to places like India and presenting IBM as "a corporate laboratory that highlights the trend." Reporting on an event triggered something else, the larger making-sense activity called *interpretation*.[13]

Since it first emerged, the journalist occupation has harbored an explanatory urge. The November 21, 1885, issue of *The Journalist* announced "Explanatory Journalism" on its cover page. In the early twentieth century, the majority of stories containing no interpretations began to shrink as newspapers confronted competition from radio and the newly invented news magazine. Briton Hadden and Henry Luce founded *Time* in 1923, and the Mellon family and other investors in the 1930s backed a former *Time* foreign editor to found what became *Newsweek*. A third competitor, *U.S. News and World Report*, started as a newspaper in the 1930s, and all three provided something newspapers lacked: summaries that made sense

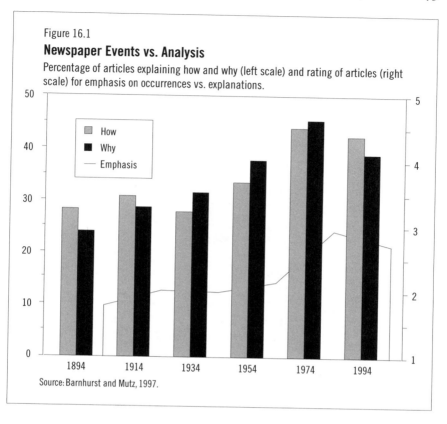

Figure 16.1
Newspaper Events vs. Analysis
Percentage of articles explaining how and why (left scale) and rating of articles (right scale) for emphasis on occurrences vs. explanations.

Source: Barnhurst and Mutz, 1997.

of the week's events. Radio news commentaries on current events had also begun drawing large audiences, creating pressure for the newspaper industry.[14]

The American Society of Newspaper Editors in 1933 resolved, "Editors should devote a larger amount of attention and space to explanatory and interpretive news, and to presenting a background of information which will enable the average reader more adequately to understand the movement and significance of events."[15] Practitioner trade outlet *The Quill* then took up the cause. "The newspaper of tomorrow," writes Charles Poe, managing editor of the *Chattanooga News*, "will interpret in its news coverage."[16] And Mark Ethridge, publisher of the Richmond, Virginia, *Times-Dispatch*, says that readers demand "to know not only what is happening, but why it is happening."[17]

Pressure to provide explanations also came from Progressives. Lincoln Steffens, dean of muckraking journalists, had long "wanted to know about motives"—not just what individuals did in society "but why they did what they did."[18] His modern stance contrasted with the older, realist focus on facts from detailed accounts. After U.S. publishers told Raoul de Roussy de Sales: "We *believe* in facts, . . . facts and nothing else but facts," the former reporter from leftist *Paris-Soir* wrote, "When it comes to informing the public," facts "are of less value than the analysis." U.S. editors had already begun experimenting, he says, pointing to the weekly summaries of the Sunday *New York Times* as evidence of a new tendency toward interpretation.[19]

Modern news presents an intelligible account by laying out and making events plain (*ex* means *out* and *planare* means *level* in Latin, the roots of the word *explain*), providing the careful, detailed, and illustrated facts (*expounded* with care, *explicated* with details, and *elucidated* with examples—three other synonyms for *explain*), and drawing them all together in an act of imagination and sympathy that goes below the surface to *interpret* the events. Although Webster's dictionary defines explanation as the central term, interpretation gathers together all related senses into an overarching idea. The interpretive move in modern news tells the meaning of events, construed in light of general beliefs and judgments and particular interests. To interpret is to "represent by means of art," Webster says.

In the 1930s "interpretative" news seemed admirable for attracting audiences, making sense of events, and doing public good. All three qualities were modern: functionalism in the market, reliance on big-picture abstractions, and the hope and push for progress. By 1939 a former Illinois editor noted, "The trend is unmistakably in the direction of combining the function of interpreter with that of reporter" and called "the ability to interpret . . . a prerequisite" for "keeping the public informed."[20] The Hutchins Commission report in 1947 reasoned that new technologies like radio and movies and more concentrated ownership had sparked a "communications revolution." To represent faithfully the disconnected groups of modern U.S. America to each other and to societies abroad, a responsible press must reject the "isolated fact" in favor of reporting "the truth about the fact." Press responsibility means acting in the public interest by interpreting events and placing them in context, but the existing interpreters—columnists and commentators—focused on entertainment, deviance, and violence in an effort to reach larger audiences. Modern interpretation had a complex relationship with commerce. The report says big business was biasing press content and advertisers were dictating radio programming. Instead of representing society to itself, communications industries provided a "miscellaneous succession of stories and images, which have no relation to the typical lives of real people anywhere."[21]

The modern ideal of social responsibility soon entered university training in news. A 1949 textbook, *Exploring Journalism*, included a full chapter on Press Interpretation, where the two authors, an editor and a professor, argue, "It is not enough for the public to have the facts, for it also must know the meaning of the facts," and so a majority in newsrooms were acting responsibly when they "stress interpretative reporting."[22] The ideal became entrenched in education once the Cold War–era *Four Theories of the Press* placed social responsibility opposite totalitarian news practice. But the authors said reporters and editors were "deficient in performing" their task of "enlightening the public" and should do more so that the people can self-govern in democracy.[23]

Working reporters and news executives had qualms. In a 1954 collection, *Newsmen Speak*, insiders write unanimously about accuracy and about separating opinion from facts, but not about interpretations. Some say coverage "should go a step further by explaining the news," but a New York AP bureau chief calls for a facts-only news story "so written that the reader will understand it easily and completely." William Randolph Hearst Jr. takes a lukewarm stance, calling for news to interpret "if necessary." But another publisher says reporters had moved "from scoop to scope" and were writing "with deepened perspective and understanding." And a news agency president says his services provide "the best possible coverage" by reporting "news events themselves" along with "what the facts of a news story mean" to make them understandable "for the average citizen."[24]

Despite objections in the trade press, "interpretative" news did grow from the 1930s to the 1950s in our data. The magazine *American Journalism* voiced concern in 1941 that interpreting events slides quickly into expressing opinion; an early issue of *Nieman Reports* criticized editors in 1949 for letting too much opinion enter into interpretive stories; and the monthly *Bulletin* of the American Society of Newspaper Editors continued the controversy later.[25] But the turn toward interpretation continued amid concerns that new communication technologies of the period threatened to produce a press deficient in explanations.

By the 1960s mainstream newspapers began shifting toward "explanatory" news. The owners of the *Wall Street Journal* in 1962 founded *The National Observer*, a weekly newspaper of interpretation that pioneered articles on trends and current event analysis, genres that the daily press imitated.[26] The *New York Herald Tribune*, despite its demise in 1966, provided another model of explanatory news under former *Newsweek* editor John Denson.[27] Movements from beyond the American occupation and from its fringes pressed for more explanatory content. News practitioners and academics of the 1960s shared a faith in the potential for poor countries to advance through the miracles of agricultural innovation. News practice seemed capable of helping transform economic conditions, leading in turn to individual freedom and democracy. In the Philippines, agriculture extension communicators ran a successful media campaign to inform small farmers about new rice varieties.[28] A press institute and later an academic program in the Philippines founded *development journalism*, meant to boost national advancement through explaining the Green Revolution and economic change.[29] Similar efforts emerged in India, and seminars of the Press Foundation of Asia trained reporters to interpret development projects, rather than merely passing on government claims. U.S. press workers saw no ready application at home and objected that governments abroad co-opted development journalism to restrict press freedom, which the annual Associated Press survey found "seemed to lose more ground than it gained" around the globe in 1966.[30]

Another movement to explain and interpret news in the 1960s, the alternative press, drew inspiration from an earlier model, the *Village Voice*.[31] Its news combined reviews of art, movies, and theater with rambling personal stories about local events. The weekly did no editing and paid writers little or nothing at all. Alternative newspapers used modern news methods to attack the mainstream press and foster activist writing about the counterculture. But within a decade mainstream news co-opted radical weeklies by expanding alternative coverage and explaining new trends such as youth culture. Some alternative papers still survived in major cities by following standard business models, like the *Voice*, while continuing to challenge objective writing and push for explanatory articles.

The *Voice* was a model for New Journalism, which burst on the scene by the mid-1960s.[32] Reportage by Norman Mailer and others for *Esquire* magazine inspired writers to experiment, and Truman Capote's *In Cold Blood* became a classic of the genre because its modern interpretation followed realist facts. Reporters in the daily press began doing interpretive writing: Tom Wolfe at the *New York Herald Tribune*, Gay Talese for the *New York Times*, and others. But news industry leaders had doubts. A former *New York Times* editor issued a screed (his word) saying New Journalism was not new, not journalism, and "cannot and should not take the place of the misnamed 'Old Journalism'" that critics scorned as the "who-what-when-where-how-and-why school." Even if New Journalism strained credibility, old journalism was "increasing . . . interpretation"—the effort to make the news clear and relevant for the reader.[33]

As modern interpretation advanced, the American right wing took up press bashing.[34] During the 1964 National Convention, when Dwight D. Eisenhower urged Republicans not to let outsiders from the press divide them, the delegates directed "a deafening roar of boos . . . at the press stands flanking the speakers' platform and many on the convention floor jumped up and shook their fists." Tom Wicker, a *New York Times* staffer, remembers "those shouting, livid delegates, rising almost as one man, pointing, cursing, in some cases shaking their fists, not just at the men in the glass [television] booths but at *me*." He sat with other "reporters gazing in astonishment at this sudden surge of hatred." His paper could not report what happened, he says, because the account would have introduced subjective explanation. But the era had begun when conservatives saw the press as a powerful agent of "menacing, hateful, corrupt" interpretation.[35]

Mainstream reporting on youth culture and protest made major daily newspapers an easy target as the radical press declined. The advocacy *I. F. Stone's Weekly*, which predicted and then protested the Vietnam conflict, had seventy thousand subscribers when it closed in 1971,[36] but analysts suggested that all news would move toward interpretation. *Chicago Sun-Times* and Associated Press reporting are just two examples of the spreading influence of immersion experiences and literary writing to interpret them. In the sixth edition of his textbook, MacDougall lists "activist, advocacy, participatory, . . . investigative," and "reformist" among the new kinds of writing that expanded interpretation in the press.[37] New Journalism continued the historical link between news and literature, extending how news "explores how and why."[38] By the mid-1970s, when interpretation had become widespread in American news,[39] mentions of how and why events occurred and emphasis on explanations reached a zenith in our study newspapers, just as movements to make reporting more explanatory pressed on mainstream news from all sides.

Practitioners and academics pushed other interpretive reforms to modernize the occupation. Peace journalism had origins in the pacifist societies of the early nineteenth century but formed part of peace initiatives in the 1970s.[40] Peace instruction entered U.S. colleges of the Vietnam War era, sometimes at the urging of students who had studied journalism.[41] But in the buildup to subsequent wars,[42] news routines still failed to provide the context for people to judge events. In surveys, practitioners agreed that explaining was their greatest challenge, and so other reforms emerged. One from within the occupation was the application of data analysis to news, called *precision journalism*.[43] To cover race riots in Detroit, the *Free Press* sent reporters to cover events, but to explain them the editors teamed up with the University of Michigan to survey households in search of patterns. They found that rising expectations, not lack of education or recent migration from the South, drove those who participated in the riots. Data analysis techniques soon grew for criminal cases, election claims, drug trafficking, and civic engagement, especially among reporters and editors dissatisfied with traditional tools of interpretation.[44]

Investigative journalism—a third impulse of the period—fired imaginations in the occupation and the reading public with how modern news could change public affairs. Its early roots were in muckraking and crusading news, but the 1970s movement was mainstream. The *Plain Dealer, Miami Herald*, and *Newsday* set up investigative efforts, and the *Boston Globe* and other papers followed suit. Investigative news gained national attention in 1969, when atrocities in My Lai, Vietnam, came to light. Other investigations exposed crooked fundraising at the Nebraska Boys Town orphanage and documented the harsher sentences that black and poor defendants faced in Philadelphia. Richard Nixon resigned the presidency in 1974 once other institutions intervened, but the *Washington Post* Watergate investigation and media coverage kept the scandal alive. Skepticism grew toward government, and a romantic notion of the news occupation arose. Trade schools soon produced a glut of graduates, and a mainline Protestant church then helped organize Investigative Reporters and Editors, its acronym IRE expressing a moral stance. Critics objected that investigative reporting tended not to focus on corporations or advertisers, ignored marginal groups, and made the work of news political, aiming to expand beyond social into *moral* responsibility that usurped "the functions of institutions." The new interpretive impulse was open to abuse, but in its heyday even government officials criticized the press for not doing enough investigating.[45]

Investigative, precision, and peace journalism were exceptional, a few reporters usually working on their own time and without much support from skeptical management. Even in boom years, conditions always worked against them: chain ownership, market competition, government deregulation, commodity-style information, and underfunded news operations. But modern interpretation had become basic to news writing by the 1980s, and in 1985 the Pulitzer board began awarding a prize for explanatory work. In its first quarter century, the winners were primarily complex stories that explained the human consequences of medicine and science, economics, and government policies.[46]

At the height of modern news, a top-down interpretive pattern had come to permeate the occupation from beginner training to Pulitzer Prizes and helped give rise to civic or public journalism. After news media interpreted the 1986 and 1988 elections as a game of insider jockeying and failed to counter manipulative political ads, public journalism began to emerge mostly at small heartland newspapers. Reporters and editors again felt restless with just-the-facts news and wanted to re-engage citizens facing too much information. Within a decade more than two hundred projects sprang up, got attention, and began influencing mainstream practices. But heavy hitters from the elite press, especially the *New York Times*, soon condemned the idea. Critics said public journalism was doing only what news should be doing anyway—describing and explaining events—but in ways that distorted newsroom budgets and compromised press independence.[47]

U.S. news in our study became more interpretive as waves of modern reform demanded: "interpretative" news of the 1930s; New Journalism of the 1960s; the surge of peace, precision, and investigative work in the 1970s; and public journalism arising in the late 1980s.[48] The prominent rejection of each movement denied the changes underway, so that practitioners misrecognized they were explaining more. Interpretations did decline somewhat in news of the late 1980s and early 1990s, but the interpretive turn rebounded over the next two decades.[49] Despite persistent complaints that the news explained too little, the content was doing the opposite. News had become a modern system of knowledge interpreting public life. How did it look in practice?

Deborah Lohse's career spanned a period of high levels of modern interpretation along with growing partisanship. She worked as a financial reporter for the *Wall Street Journal* and other publications, fulfilling a childhood dream. For a fourth-grade project she interviewed pupils about their sleep habits and found that eighth graders slept less than sixth graders. She wondered why, but "really wasn't comfortable interpreting," she said in our interview. The realist "idea of being a conduit" is what got her started in news, first in college as an assistant at *Barron's*, and then at her first job at *Money* magazine, where she would "write, write, write," and editors would add the big-picture interpretation for her to okay. She began with brief items in 1989 and was writing longer bylined articles by 1991.[50] She led a "simple tax life" herself, but offered tax advice and began analyzing tax policy by 1993. That year conservatives in Congress reacted to Clinton's tax proposal by renewing a claim that it would impose the biggest increase in history.

Money editors wanted the story and assigned Lohse—by then a Washington correspondent—but the only way "the math would verify it" was by adding in Medicare and increases "even further down the road." She checked sources she knew, the editors did their interpretive magic, and the story landed on the cover. The article ran with anti-proposal graphics, cast doubts on Democratic claims, and did predict "the biggest tax hike in history," but Lohse concentrated on details: tax rates and tips for taxpayers, especially in high-income brackets.[51] When *Money* hit the newsstands, opponents in Congress began citing it. The "huge cover story" was a coup, but Lohse felt uncomfortable, thinking, "I've just become really partisan here." Her editors "liked that *Money* magazine was being held up on TV" during congressional debate, and she saw how facts turn "into a *story*," that is, how realist reporting fed into modern interpretation.

She remembers her editors would always ask, "Well, what does this mean?" "Why should I care?" or "So what?" Calling Clinton's tax the "biggest in history" gave an attention-grabbing and arguably partisan answer to the so-what question. Republicans had been using the phrase at least since the early 1980s to attack Democrats.[52] The 1993 article in *Money* helped move the slogan into the limelight. Republicans renewed the charge in the next election cycle, when the phrase reached a high point in news coverage and spread to popular culture such as an episode of *The Simpsons*.[53] In 2001 Republicans labeled their temporary tax *cuts* the biggest ever, and the theme continued in politics for another decade, with Republicans returning to the original charge when their temporary cuts were to expire.[54]

Lohse's work in 1993 caught the attention of personal-finance editors who hired her at the *Wall Street Journal*. There her regular spot noted the "emerging market meltdown" in 1995 and tracked the technology bubble bursting through 1999. Major news organizations like the *Journal*, Lohse said, want reporters to aim for page 1. Her stories covering the last days of an insurance company that failed after investing in risky bonds made the front page in 1999 by their realism, describing employees working "late into the night" and "canceling vacations," drivers shuttling "visitors to their hotels," "secretaries and mail clerks" buying food and "delivering documents," as well as the CEO's fateful Jefferson City meeting that put the company under Missouri insurance supervision. The details gave her explanation of what happened solidity. Editors "want that" kind of reporting "for every story," she said.[55]

But she saw limitations for modern explanation. What a story means depends on which sources reporters have talked to, and in business news, major companies can "shut off my access to information." Outsiders doing serious work to question corporate actions tend to be shrill to get attention, but their lone-wolf status makes reporters nervous, keeping "fringe sources on the fringe." She saw her job as giving "a full view of things," rather than saying what they mean. But "some of the best" reporters she knew "are completely comfortable being the voice of authority." The interpretive pattern held especially at major news media: "Everybody at the *Wall Street Journal* has to have that voice." When powerful institutions "say something is news, everybody else will follow it," but for a good reason. Her experiences in Washington and New York showed her how much effort goes into finding occurrences for realist reporting and also into creating modern interpretations for big stories.

By the end of the twentieth century, reporters like Lohse lived in the contradiction between the common idea of news as just realist facts and the practice of news as modern interpretation. For decades disparate movements had pushed and critics had prodded the press toward an interpretive turn, which occurred despite industry leaders' protesting too much. Practitioners learned to go along with modern ways, knowing their stories had to interpret or perish, ending up buried on an inside page and forgotten. The patterns help explain how news as a system of general knowledge could change unnoticed. A main impetus for the change at newspapers was television, which stole breaking news and seemed to push print reporters into writing more-interpretive follow-up stories. But what happened in the contents of television news?

CHAPTER 17

Broadcast News Became Less Episodic

After "the nightly 'front page' on television"[1] began scooping the latest events, newspaper reporters were left to write follow-up stories, a more explanatory mode in line with modernism. TV images seem to show breaking events with realism and without the delays of print production and distribution, but critics soon complained that broadcasting lacked interpretation. In a 1980 *New Yorker* essay, staff writer George W. S. Trow laments that television unravels events from their contexts. Twenty years later he found newscasters still failing to connect the dots between events: "Television news people," he says, "value and love the episodic" — events left to stand without interpretation. The critiques called for modern sense making. In the ensuing decades analysts agreed that television fails to supply "the context and analysis necessary to turn facts into real understanding."[2] In 2010 another *New Yorker* analyst saw even more declines in "seeking context."[3]

U.S. Americans have tended to be realist, viewing problems as "concrete rather than abstract" and relying more on television for news, which simplifies "complex issues to the level of anecdotal evidence."[4] Episodic newscasts may lead audiences to ignore the modern big picture of social conditions and public policy behind problems. For a century the U.S. population has scored poorly on standard memory tests of political knowledge,[5] leading political scientists to wonder how democracy is possible, especially if television, as a primary source for news, adds little depth to what citizens know. An uninformed audience may need more explanations, but did the interpretive turn fail to spread to television as critics suggest?

Just the opposite occurred, so that television news adopted the wider modern perspectives that critics demanded. Since the 1960s, newscasters have expanded interpretation on national evening news (figure 17.1).[6] After beating newspapers to the newest stories, network newscasts themselves began shifting into modern interpretive styles instead of sticking with realist, episodic coverage.

An overview of the decades since the 1960s can illustrate how modern interpretation advanced and evening newscasts moved from election by election. In 1968 political reports on national television gave a direct description of events, some with film segments of candidates talking.[7] With each passing election, newscasters delivered more frequent opinion. In a 1972 news package, NBC Anchor John Chancellor lists facts (*who* was speaking *where* in the campaign) to introduce a story on George McGovern's stump speech in Chicago. Reporter Richard Valeriani then ticks off more facts about the candidate endorsing "federal aid to parochial

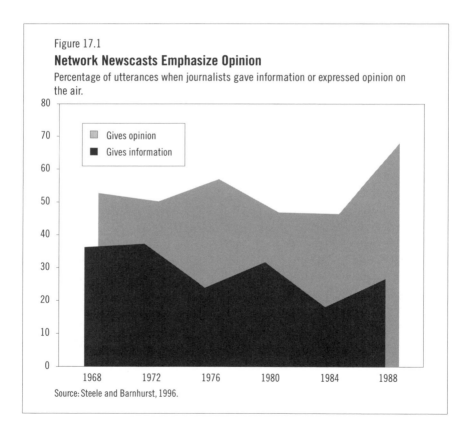

Figure 17.1
Network Newscasts Emphasize Opinion
Percentage of utterances when journalists gave information or expressed opinion on the air.

Source: Steele and Barnhurst, 1996.

and other non-public schools." McGovern gives his reasons, and Valeriani adds a list of upcoming campaign events, describes McGovern's strategy "to concentrate heavily on the big electoral vote states," and explains that McGovern may give a national speech on television because "his image is still blurred among many regular Democrats." Chancellor's opening is neutral and informational, as is Valeriani's first voice-over. After McGovern's sound bite, Valeriani adds a small contextual interpretation drawn from a campaign spokesperson.[8]

Television news of the 1970s began limiting politicians' sound bites, deferring less to what the campaigns were showing, and interpreting candidates' appearances.[9] In 1980 Ronald Reagan countered by issuing pithy made-for-television phrases on eye-catching backdrops that his opponents tried to emulate. The evening news responded by shortening sound bites further, being more selective about images, and trying to explain "the issues," in line with modernism, although the segments NBC initiated that year fared poorly in the ratings. In 1984 Walter Mondale presented documents on an un-filmable subject, the budget deficit, to which newscasters gave little play in a year when his most quoted phrase was the fast-food slogan, "Where's the beef?" Reagan took the opposite approach, refining the visual equivalent of "no comment": "For television . . . couldn't show something that wasn't happening. And Reagan was not giving them anything to take a picture of . . . so television covered what Reagan was doing, rather than covering what he wasn't."[10]

Campaign coverage data by 1988 show a clear increase in modern interpretation, mostly in the form of expressing opinions. A report from ABC News explains why George H. W. Bush was making appearances in shirtsleeves: to portray himself "as a man in tune with rural America." With a description of the candidate's luxury tour bus, correspondent Brit Hume interprets the Bush image as misleading or cynical and complains that the Bush campaign controls the flow of information by making the press travel separately and refusing to answer questions. In NBC coverage that year, correspondent Lisa Myers also hammers the point that politicians were not talking to her. The election campaigns used images to sway interpretations.[11] Michael Dukakis postured for cameras in media events designed to convey his message, and both candidates' political handlers set up scenes for the media and distributed video press releases. The networks, hampered by declining audiences, staff, and budget, cut back on their own visuals but treated campaign images with disdain,[12] making light of Dukakis riding a tank wearing a helmet, for instance. But modern interpretation put newscasters front and center.

Broadcasters say that new technologies of the 1980s—video cameras and satellite feeds—made "spicing up stories with visual imagery" irresistible for television.[13]

Local news became especially vulnerable to the new video press releases or "wall-paper" that politicians, political parties, and lobbyists provided and stations used without citing sources. NBC Anchor Tom Brokaw worried that "context will be overrun,"[14] and critic Walter Goodman called the new visual style of the network news divisions, "MTV journalism, images with little context."[15] The term *context*, which gained broad currency for describing any kind of background, has roots in linguistics and literature, where a word or passage appears surrounded by language that helps explain its meaning.[16] Context is a mark of modern news. Newscasts used visual images less to document unfolding events than to show a backdrop for reporters, providing only a particular kind of context to grab viewers and keep them watching. But TV news uses context to focus on the newscasters providing modern interpretation.

Network newscasts did show more images at a much faster pace; video clips, graphics, and captions peaked; and the length of newscaster shots reached a plateau as their frequency of appearing on-screen climaxed in the 1980s. By the 1990s the pattern for covering U.S. politics was set: candidates responded to the visual rhythms of television news, and newscasters competed to capture voters' imaginations through modern, interpretive visual styles. In the 1992 elections, the pacing of news had resumed its climb and reached all-time highs, and backgrounds became more varied. Candidates tried to circumvent the national networks: Bush used local news and satellite feeds to reach small groups and individual stations, independent Ross Perot used "infomercials" and went on *Larry King Live*, and Bill Clinton found alternatives like *Saturday Night Live* and set a daily agenda to dominate the "media spin." At stake was the authority of modern news casting.[17]

Television required an ever-better show, and networks displayed newscasters' images more often and closer up in political reports, centering coverage more on news processes.[18] Political parties were no longer the main focus in campaigns overshadowed by personalities, and the new visual style of news reports person-alized candidates but treated the viewing public as passive observers,[19] supplying images that tended to work against learning. Although rich in information, the routine scenes could show little "about complex social and political problems" and instead reinforced stereotypes. The newscasters' voice-overs interpreted, and the "visual themes proved to be more memorable than verbal ones."[20] As context, visuals added variety to the public airwaves, but may have impeded careful thought or reflection among viewers.

By the 2000s newscasts had abandoned their early realist style, but modern interpretive reporting "did not translate into higher-quality analysis."[21] At presidential news conferences, newscasters had become more aggressive interviewers by moving from simple questions to opinionated statements.[22] After facing widespread criticism for calling the 2000 election winner too early, TV news divisions promised changes, but in 2004 they continued their "journalism of assertion,"[23] despite some changes in handling exit-poll data. Candidates influenced newscasters, and through them the broader public, by staying on message and managing imagery. But assertive news influenced voters and policymakers by analyzing events and judging politicians and their proposals as the supply of modern interpretation grew in TV news coverage.[24]

The weather, a most-watched but lower-status segment of local news, shows how deeply the modern interpretive turn affected newscasts.[25] TV forecasters have long been the butt of jokes if not joking themselves, but when Boston hosted a political convention, the morning weather forecasts were serious about the national political ritual. The chitchat among announcers and other on-air personalities and the visuals during report segments on three network affiliates illustrate how weathercasters acted as explainers for the viewing public, combining complex visual and narrative elements to heighten the drama. They featured themselves at times—and surprisingly—as controllers of the capricious weather that might threaten the political event. The viewing public rarely figured at all in weather segments and received mention or comment only in passing during news-team banter. The interpretive turn had reached the margins of modern news.

On television, newscasters expressed opinions more than their print counterparts did, but both media added opinions, as critics feared. News insiders said they were responding to pressures from markets and new technologies, a pattern deserving a closer look. But modern interpretive news shifted attention to the occupation itself, especially on TV. Perhaps television, with its reliance on imagery, was more vulnerable. Did the move toward opinion occur elsewhere?

Radio seemed a likely place to find an answer because it uses only mental imagery and might have bucked the content trends in newspapers and television. Radio moved into commentary early in the twentieth century and honored a long tradition of explanatory news: Edward R. Murrow's CBS radio reports from London during the German bombing blitz of World War II. "He was trying to explain" the British events to U.S. Americans and "explain America to Britons."[26] By the 1980s, U.S. commercial radio had moved to narrower music formats with less news, but National Public Radio (NPR) became a home for pieces interpreting events. NPR founded *Morning Edition* and *All Things Considered* as its main news programs, which became outlets for extended audio reporting. Did they follow the modern interpretive turn? And did they rely on opinions as television did?

Given the history of radio, it should come as no surprise that reports on NPR in 1980—the first election year both programs were on the air—began with more interpretation than newspaper articles had.[27] But contrary to expectation, NPR reports became even more interpretive (figure 17.2). That emphasis peaked in 1996 and by 2000 was a third higher than where it began. The changes also occurred over a relatively short period.[28]

Political stories on NPR illustrate what the numbers show. In 1980 reporter Linda Wertheimer opened her report on Jimmy Carter and some hecklers by focusing on facts, and any terms expressing an opinion, such as *mincing* and *defect*, she attributed to the candidate. In 1996, a year when modern interpretation crested in the newscasts, Joanne Silberner opened a report on the presidential debate and healthcare with the big-picture interjection, "What a difference four years makes!" Then, after an archival sound bite of Clinton, came the reporter's judgment that his healthcare proposals were "vaguer, less-ambitious" than in the past.

As modern interpretation advanced on NPR, reporters began interviewing each other "to present their different points of view."[29] In a segment on September 11, 2001, host Noah Adams asks, "What do you think is going to happen [to the

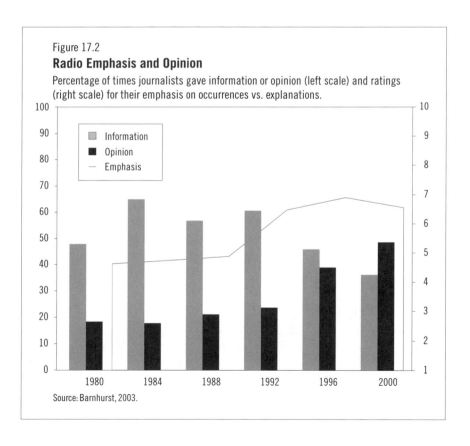

Figure 17.2
Radio Emphasis and Opinion
Percentage of times journalists gave information or opinion (left scale) and ratings (right scale) for their emphasis on occurrences vs. explanations.

Source: Barnhurst, 2003.

Reform Party]?" And reporter Andy Bowers answers, "Well, Noah, unless something changes" in the divided party, there "could be even more chaos." Adams counters, "Is it fair to say, though," to introduce a doubt, and Bowers begins, "In a way," to yield the point. Adams then asks him to venture a guess about contact with the party. He responds by invoking collective opinion: "I think most people would agree that . . ." Then Adams asks, "What do you think will happen [with funding]?" Bowers begins, "Well, it depends . . . ," explains what one official says, and ends with, "But this could very well end up in court." After another round of similar Q&A, the two thank each other before Adams moves on. Similar examples became more common, with NPR news personalities in the role of sense-makers. Asking questions, an archetypal task for reporters, declined sharply as they paraphrased their sources instead of airing questions and answers. The main task of giving information also seesawed down, so that by 2000 it no longer represented the largest share of speech, and newscasters expressed opinions more than twice as often as they had in 1980. In the hotly contested election that year, NPR newscasters focused less on action, so that more than half the times they spoke, they were interpreting. As in network TV news, how NPR correspondents and anchors explained the meaning of events shifted, but not to providing more of the context; the share of times newscasters gave background declined by more than half.[30]

NPR moved into the modern mainstream, becoming more like the daily press and network television. As it grew prominent and attracted larger audiences, its programs expanded their political reporting, a premier beat for reporters and marker of authority. Reports became less neutral in tone and more polarized, making the news more dramatic for listeners but also a target for critics and for attacks on its public funding.[31] Like television news, NPR relied on more opinions to interpret events, a tendency common to the modern turn in news but more pronounced in broadcasting. And NPR also faced charges that its reports failed to give *enough* context for events, especially in the 1990s after Congress cut the network budget amid objections that NPR lacked balance.[32] As elite insiders had feared earlier, news came under fire the more its interpretive style shifted the focus of news onto modern sense making and sense-makers.

The experiences of an investigative reporter can show what interpretive news looks like in practice. Roberta Baskin started her career at a local network affiliate in Chicago before going to Washington, where she moved between competing local and network news outlets during a long career. Instead of going for jobs to get into larger markets with better pay, Baskin started in a big market, and she sometimes had to move after trying to make sense of major products and the companies that advertise or make them. "I'm trying to present information that you otherwise wouldn't have access to. I want you to see one of my reports and say, 'Wow, I didn't know that,'" she said in our 2001 interview at Harvard, while she was on leave from

ABC News. The statement points to her commitment to realist facts, common among practitioners.

Baskin developed one of her first big stories after reading, in the trade journal *Brewer's Digest*, that German scientists had found nitrosamines in beer. The U.S. Department of Agriculture had begun regulating the cancer-causing agent in smoked foods and had shut down some plants for producing bacon with nitrosamines above permissible levels. It was the late 1970s, and she was in her first job at WMAQ-TV in Chicago, an NBC-owned station. She wanted to get measurements for U.S. beer, a product in a lot of local advertising. WMAQ managers objected to the story, refused her requests to pursue it, and then exercised their option not to renew her contract.

After a weekend in despondence, she wrote a one-page "treatment" to pitch the story to the competition, ABC-owned WLS-TV in Chicago. To get the story, the station agreed to lab-test beers and send Baskin to interview scientists in Germany. Of the eighteen beers tested, all but Coors contained nitrosamines. Drinking a bottle of Heineken delivered as much as eating more than 175 slices of bacon produced at the maximum legal limit. The U.S. Food and Drug Administration knew of the problem, and so Baskin interviewed FDA officials. Her report says scientists found that nitrosamines resulted from a direct firing process during malting, but to avoid the problem, brewers could shift to indirect firing while making beer. Once the story broke in 1980, Walter Cronkite cited it during the *CBS Evening News*, editorial cartoonists showed drinkers puzzling over the bacon content of their beer, and Johnny Carson made jokes in his monologues on the *Tonight Show*. Coors began advertising itself as "The Beer with No Nitrosamines." Phil Donahue invited Baskin onto a segment of the *Today Show*, where he was a contributor, and so she returned to tell the story on NBC, in the studios of the employer that had blocked the story and let her go. Within months the FDA set standards for nitrosamine content in beer, and media attention helped change beer processing worldwide. The story had on-the-ground realism plus the wider perspective and promise of progress from modernism.[33]

Baskin also reported on corruption in Illinois and among federal workers, setting her pattern of winning national recognition and building a network of contacts in Washington, D.C. In 1984 she moved to the ABC affiliate there, WJLA-TV, where her reporting reached regulators and elected officials, "getting them at home," she said, "on the six and eleven o'clock news." Her reports made radon a national issue, and her coverage of drug testing led to national standards and accrediting for drug-testing labs and to the firing of the NFL drug-testing chief by National Football League Commissioner Paul Tagliabue, who called her the "Molotov cocktail of journalists."[34] After CBS News lured her away by offering the chance to work at "the Tiffany network," with its tradition of high quality, the daily *CBS Evening*

News with Dan Rather ran her stories on oil leaks, lead poisoning, consumer product dangers, corporate bid rigging, airport irregularities, and other topics. She won industry acclaim and moved quickly to an evening magazine program, where she did in-depth reporting with more time to explain her findings on the air.

Her biggest story, on sneaker manufacturers' contracts for cheap labor in Asia, appeared on *Eye to Eye* with Connie Chung, but the 1996 follow-up while she worked as chief investigative reporter for another magazine program, *48 Hours*, received much more attention. "I've always wondered how things are made," she said, and the price tags on athletic shoes got her asking what went into them. In the first story she visited a factory in Indonesia, where companies under contract with Nike were paying below the local minimum wage to workers living in poverty. Her report three years later shows Niketown in Chicago selling shoes for $140 and then takes viewers to Vietnam, where Nike had moved to new contractors paying women below the legal minimum of $40 a month for working ten-hour days and six-day weeks. Baskin's reporting is realist, showing pay slips that document the low wages and interviews on tape about the workers' declining health and cases of physical abuse for talking on the factory line or for sewing that their employers considered unacceptable.[35]

After the story appeared, activists began quoting from it in leaflets distributed outside of Niketown, a short distance from the CBS offices. Georgetown University students began protesting in Washington, and boycotts of Nike products spread. The *Wall Street Journal* published an op-ed piece saying that Baskin had "trashed Nike."[36] Following the usual procedure, she wrote a response, but CBS News President Andrew Heyward blocked its release. An internal audit Nike commissioned from Ernst & Young—leaked to the media—corroborated the report.[37] CBS normally repeated stories that got attention and developed further after the first airing, and Baskin was working on an update when its slot disappeared from the schedule for July 24, 1997. CBS News stalled further coverage, and a few months later she could surmise why.

CBS had the exclusive contract to cover the Winter Olympics in Japan in early 1998, and Baskin noticed colleagues from *48 Hours* doing pre-game coverage wearing jackets with Nike swooshes. Nike had provided CBS Sports and CBS News employees with wardrobes bearing prominent monograms of the logo, requiring correspondents to wear them or be sent home, and Baskin objected to the violation of network ethics standards. The internal memo she sent to CBS News managers, along with Heyward's angry "Dear Roberta" response, reached other media. CBS nominated her Nike coverage for the highest honor in television news, the Alfred I. du Pont–Columbia University Award, but the network moved her off *48 Hours* in 1999, demoting her to the morning news with assignments on soft-news shows. Later that year she resigned from CBS. Her next move, to senior producer for investigations at the news magazine *20/20*, allowed her to pursue serious work but took her off the air, which in television means a loss of pay and prestige.[38]

Television newscasters who cover the activities of corporations and advertisers test the boundary between the public-service aims of the occupation and the profit motive for broadcasting enterprises. Colleagues gave Baskin high honors for television news—National Press Club Awards, an Investigative Reporters and Editors Award, and an Edward R. Murrow Award from the Radio and Television News Directors Association. And the television industry gave her Peabody awards and a raft of Emmy awards. But advertisers and companies doing business with her employers and in "a cozy relationship with regulators" have called her "a vulture" and worse.[39]

As the news budgets for investigations declined and investigative news teams disappeared, the realist, factual details typical of Baskin's reporting shrank. But modern interpretive news continued to grow. In the tradeoff between concrete reporting and interpretive judgments, broadcast news supplied more opinions in response to critics' demands for "context." But soon the spider's web of connected information would supplant television as the go-to outlet for news. As a condition of general knowledge in the new century, the rise of digital mobile media could promise access to more realist facts and to more modernist opinions. What happened to news as it moved online?

CHAPTER 18

Online News Reverted to Sense-Making

At an important city newspaper, with statewide circulation and regular national attention, an editor recalls a scene. A fellow from a small town nearby bumps into him socially and describes a scandal at an apartment development for seniors. The commercial management company receiving federal subsidies has thrown out an eighty-year-old former engineer for doing things like gardening, painting the peeling benches on the grounds, and organizing a regular Saturday breakfast, all at his own expense. The housing manager dislikes these activities and labels them dangerous, so that her eviction warnings turn them into something else. For instance, she calls planting flowers digging too close to underground utility connections. She issues a series of memos with new rules against gardening and putting out bird feeders and also limiting use of the community kitchen, which the residents find padlocked. The editor says honestly, "Thanks for the tip," but knows no one will follow up. The newspaper has laid off so many reporters that the newsroom lacks resources to cover anything but big and essential stories. In our interview he calls the scene typical in the 2010s. When concerned citizens call in news tips, the few remaining editors listen carefully and even take notes, then say thanks and hang up. End of story.

The digital era seems to offer a public information utopia: plentiful headlines from aggregators delivered free based on reporting from news outlets and linked to government and other online sources, with open commentary from bloggers and others. News practitioners in mainstream organizations experienced the opposite, hamstrung in a digital spider web. The move online has cost reporting jobs and disconnected readers' stories. Editors say that with the rise of internet news circulation, the damage to "news-gathering is too high." Their expressions of concern echo responses to earlier shifts in news distribution, when radio, news magazines, and later television challenged the press, but no previous era approached the speed and magnitude of digital change. After a few years of trial and error, practitioners reasserted the continued need for the real reporting and modern analysis developed in the previous century. Awash in data without much contextual analysis, voters cannot "separate reported fact from fabricated fiction," news insiders say. Critics agree that the mass of information online makes it hard for attentive readers to "sift fact from rumor or evaluate sources or gauge context."[1]

The spread of internet access and invention of websites created a conundrum for news. Manufacturers could post product information and expand sales via links to online shopping or finding a nearby retailer, and service providers could offer some add-on web services to enhance their reach and effectiveness in person. The changes added value and cut some costs but left the core activity intact. News sites instead posted online all or part of their core product—news—usually for free. The move made sense for their public-service mission but undermined profits. News sites at first resembled the web presences of public utilities, clunky and basic, because news is like a utility providing a necessity. The sites were adequate for the essentials of keeping watch on government and other institutions and so required few digital whistles and bells. Despite having some qualities of a manufactured product and of a personal service, news is easy to deliver electronically, unlike most output of the industrial and service economy. The web trapped and held the core of modern news because stories require no physical container for or personal encounter with its consumers.

Twentieth-century news lacked competitors in supplying citizens with information. Newspapers in their heyday deployed a share bordering on monopoly for reporting general knowledge about politics, the economy, culture, and other dimensions of complex society. The barriers to entry—from investments in costly equipment to compliance with government regulations—insulated news businesses from open competition. Modern news practitioners soon came to see themselves as essential to the public good, especially as regulation or protection for public utilities waned late in the century. But as informal production and free product substitution grew online,[2] digital media reduced the value of and need for legacy formats, spelling the end of some news outlets and many news jobs. The shift to online information helped undercut the resources for serious reporting, except for the showy, prize-winning kind.

One way out of the conundrum, which practitioners say they use online, is to spend "more time looking for something to add to the existing news, usually interpretation."[3] Modern news aims to serve its audience by explaining the flood of information and providing the context, something aggregators can hardly reduce to headlines. To "monetize" context in the new era required rethinking the core unit of news—the story—and shifting to something with a longer "shelf life." Here digital thinkers jumped in. At South by Southwest Interactive, an annual new-tech event associated with the music festival labeled SXSW, they reached consensus that news online should use "*topics* instead of stories as the atom of news,"[4] a major shift away from the realism of concrete storytelling to the categories of modernism. The *Huffington Post, New York Times*, and other sites began offering topical links, making news resemble then-emerging social media. Besides linking related content, top-ics interpret, panning away from events to show how and why patterns emerge or tracking a story long term instead of offering an isolated daily update.[5] Interpreta-tion became "one of the key concepts" in "the style and character" of news by the first decade of the 2000s.[6] But as news became more interpretive, those producing news seemed more like direct participants, "no longer constrained by a need to place newsmakers' words and actions at the center of the story."[7]

The malleability of online media might serve realism or modernism. It could add to the flow of realist information, and it could add to the flowering of modern interpretation. In the case of newspapers at least, the complex process involved both (figure 18.1).[8] After going online in the 1990s, the news websites exploded with

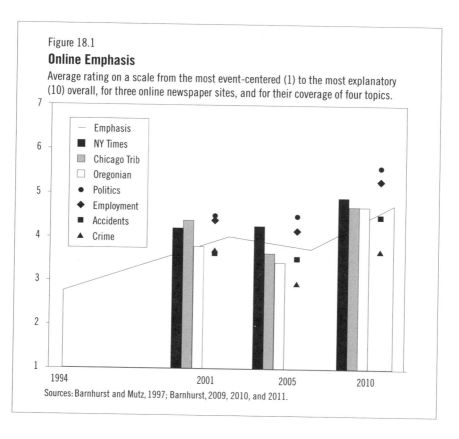

Figure 18.1
Online Emphasis
Average rating on a scale from the most event-centered (1) to the most explanatory (10) overall, for three online newspaper sites, and for their coverage of four topics.

Legend:
— Emphasis
■ NY Times
▨ Chicago Trib
□ Oregonian
● Politics
◆ Employment
■ Accidents
▲ Crime

Sources: Barnhurst and Mutz, 1997; Barnhurst, 2009, 2010, and 2011.

interpretations by 2001. For a brief period the sites became more denotative (see the chart for 2005), especially for some topics. Then the phase of experimenting ended, and the century-long march to interpretive news returned more than ever by 2010, in line with the historical trend. The reporting shown on the scale from the most event-centered to the most interpretive coverage was approaching the tendencies in media known for news analysis, such as NPR.[9]

Explanatory tendencies grew consistently at NYTimes.com, even while dipping briefly at the news sites run by the *Chicago Tribune* and especially the *Oregonian*. The articles that changed came from news columns, not the opinion or editorial pages, and lacked the label News Analysis because they were simply news. The coverage of politics, employment, crime, and accidents aligned predictably, with stories about politics and jobs including much more interpretation than those about crime and accidents. Topics spread further apart, so that especially accident stories, a staple of online news, ended lower in interpretations by 2010. But any news story tended to be more interpretive the longer its text ran.

Two examples can illustrate the range from short and factual to long and interpretive news. A *Tribune* crime story in 2010 says police are investigating the drive-by shooting of a twenty-four-year-old man who died in the Humboldt Park neighborhood. The five short sentences contain little interpretation. At the other extreme, a *Times* article in 2001—at one of the high points for interpretation—takes several screens of text to describe a report from the U.S. Conference of Mayors. The story runs long by reviewing the urban rebirth of the 1980s, the way cities created jobs in the 1990s, and urban decay and suburban sprawl. Citing economic forecasts and authoritative sources and providing links to census maps and interactive features all take space. Political reports became longer and more interpretive than other topics by 2005 and grew even more so by 2010.

Those in online news practice noticed the move to modern interpretation. Lisa Stone, the first from online news media awarded a Harvard Nieman Fellowship, spotted the trend by 2001 and expected it to grow, she said in our interview. After working for print as a reporter at the *Oakland Tribune* and in broadcast news for CNN, she concluded that the "entrenched" older media were taking "fear-based baby steps" online. Layoffs had already begun in the 1990s, stripping newsrooms of young, diverse, and female reporters and leaving older staff routines intact, including their old "way of building a Rolodex of sources" instead of using interactivity to expand participation in news. She observed that newspapers like the *San Jose Mercury News* and *Boston Globe* and other print publishers, such as Time-Warner as it first developed Pathfinder sites, separated their web and print operations, improving the creativity and profitability of online operations in the short term but at the cost of trapping the print side in older ways. Print remained "a source of interpretation of events," she said, but what would "make that institution answerable"? And how could website interactivity generate audience feedback for older news media?

To pursue her questions online, Stone joined first WebTV and then the startup Women.com, a group of integrated sites affiliated with Hearst magazines, where she became executive producer and then a programming VP and editor-in-chief developing content for women in partnerships with HBO, E!Online, MSNBC, CNN, and PBS. For a project called Majority 2000, Women.com did a baseline and follow-up surveys with Harris Interactive and Gallup on what American women were thinking that election year. *Good Housekeeping* promoted the survey, and *Good Morning America* reported the results on ABC. The survey found, for instance, that "women care about gun control," a surprising result that "it's a girl thing," she said, when common wisdom identified guns as a men's issue. When the *New York Times* covered the report, she said, "I knew we'd made a difference."

But ABC News had "a complete discomfort with the idea of an internet panel" that drew on audience participation along with traditional telephone surveying. The unease of traditional news outlets hindered their getting a "payoff for context" that digital mobile media could deliver, she said. Organizations like CNN missed the chance to move audiences "back and forth between the website and the broadcast." Older news operations where she worked did have data about audiences, but only in marketing departments, and editors failed "to march across the hall, take the numbers," and consider ways of "reaching peoples' lives." Online news could allow more "interpreting from the perspective of the audience." But during the experimentation phase of the new century's early years, legacy media instead focused their websites on accidents and other eye-catching news.

The trend toward modernism returned in force after industry leaders said interpretation could counter online competitors like bloggers. Mainstream practitioners held fast to the realist idea that they were delivering denotative reports of events, and they thought their stories lacked *enough* context and explanation even after news websites expanded interpretive reporting. The gap persisted between insiders' assumptions about their work and the news content they produced. Their beliefs about news had continually made stories more interpretive across venues as the industry adapted to each new competitor, and the web was no different.

How did practitioners sustain their beliefs in spite of the gap? One pattern was by describing changes as financial but not part of news. In the early decades of the twenty-first century, the news audience increased for news content, but executives reported having fewer paying customers because competitors were distributing news for free or below cost. The financial argument recycled from earlier crises. Cheap industrial newspapers of the nineteenth century, radio commentators and television newscasts of the early and mid-twentieth century, and online news aggregators and blogs of the twenty-first century used newer technologies to undercut older news outlets. The alternatives might be cheap or convenient for the reading public, but the new ways tended to debase news content, insiders argued. Newer outlets would reuse facts from old media and add opinions, producing a more appealing package, so that editors saw and repeatedly warned of a crisis for public life. In each era they described cheaper outlets leaching from mainstream media and threatening access to the deeper information citizens need.

News occupations also responded to different pressures in a surprising way, by doing more of the same, each time aligning further with modern interpretation. When news magazines and radio commentaries began supplying more interpretations, practitioners at newspapers said they had to *do the same* to compete. After midcentury, television news began supplying more breaking news of events, and print editors and reporters saw themselves pushed to do the opposite of news flashes, that is, *more of the same* interpretive news they had already been adding, again to compete. In the new century digital mobile media began supplying more interpretive opinions, and those at legacy news media saw the need to *do more of the same* by sorting out and making better sense of events, expanding interpretation. In each period different innovations that seemed to threaten mainstream news in different ways met with the same general response, a demand for more interpretive news and an expanded role for practitioners to act as explainers.

But prominent leaders in news organizations had a negative reaction in each period. They disparaged "interpretative" news of the 1930s, New Journalism of the 1960s, and public journalism of the 1990s. Policing the boundary between an ideal of realist facts and the slippery slope of comment and opinion diverted attention from the trends, but modern interpretation continued to advance. Leaders who objected were themselves proposing other kinds of interpretation. Each movement in modern news since the era of Mister Pulitzer aimed to tell the truth in ways that would protect the people and make for a better world. The leaders' objections echoed that aim without resisting an interpretive urge basic to modern news. Facing critics of a deficient press, big-time editors and publishers called for a return to the basics of explaining events, while they cautioned against opinions and judgments that erode news credibility. But finding, selecting, and laying out the facts—in careful, detailed, and lucid description—are all interpretive. Explanation is inherent in and basic to modernism. The project to make the world intelligible to people is interpretive to its core, contradicting the just-the-facts beliefs at the heart of realism.

As debates over interpretive news spread beyond practitioners, the political right and left swapped positions. Progressive reformers of 1900 saw fact-centered news as an antidote to the excesses of partisan reporting, but the ground had shifted after midcentury, when conservative convention delegates jeered at the press boxes.[10] The political right began demanding what the Left once proposed. A conservative magazine editor charges the *New York Times* with a "yawningly predict-able" perspective that treats "the facts . . . as so much tedious filler" in "so-called hard news." After reciting the claim of liberal newsroom bias, he calls for a return of "integrity and impartiality" toward facts based in reasoned argument about concrete reality.[11]

Equally serious commentary from the Left tends to worry less about bias than about superficiality in news. A *New Yorker* critic writes that the loss of "professional expertise" as newspapers cut reporting jobs leaves a hole in what citizens need to know, one that cheap "aggregation and opinion" cannot fill.[12] Online news lacks the staff and resources to replace legacy outlets, and peddling the party line is shallow whether at the *Huffington Post* or Fox News.[13] Liberals argue in *The Nation* maga-zine for government to shore up credible news analysis and insight by providing subsidies that would reverse the "lowering quality and . . . trivializing" of news.[14] Corporate ownership has either watered down news content or replaced it with fluff, they say, and relying on images makes TV news especially vulnerable.[15] The solution to the problem of superficiality, say liberal critics, is better explanations. Where the Left has become modern, the Right has become realist (in a shrewd *rusé* fashion), a surprising about-face.

Questions of power underlie the debate. A line between news and opinion is difficult to draw where the news moves beyond "superficial" facts into interpre-tive "bias." Over the past century, each new technology accompanied a crisis that threatened the authority of mainstream news practice. The response from the press consistently pushed toward greater interpretation, an activity of the powerful and of news modernism. The industry leaders who objected also saw the political risks of looking like interpreters instead of realist messengers, and their protests attempted to redraw the line, a moving border that shifted the ground between political positions on interpretive news.

The realism within news grew from roots in the nineteenth century, follow-ing European movements centered on the reality of objects, words, and images. In the sciences realism asserts that a world exists independent of any observer, and humans can either take the measure of objects or come up with theories that describe unobservable but solid dimensions. Early in the twentieth century, when Albert Einstein won the Nobel Prize, his theory of relativity produced "a profound sensation," and a few years later quantum theory reached wide public attention through physicist Nils Bohr's series of lectures at Yale. The new science called into question commonplace ideas about a fixed reality at the macro, interplanetary scale, and also at the micro scale, where atomic objects can at once behave as particles *and* as waves.[16] Religious fundamentalist leaders reacted to the emerg-ing science by reasserting naïve realism, following a long tradition of common sense ideas in American history. In the sphere of objects, realist or objective views continued to pervade American culture, news, and even some fields of science for most of the twentieth century.[17]

In the sphere of language, American literary realism expressed progressive urges for reform. Growing industrial production, migration into urban areas, and distribution of goods for mass consumption produced a chaotic new world, and so writers felt compelled to help manage the complexity and control the confusion of rapid social change. The new journalists of that era tended to explain and interpret conditions by presenting facts and narrating a closely observed reality, and novelists did something similar, some of them using the literary conceit of calling their accounts factual. In a precursor to literary realism, *The Scarlet Letter* (1851), Nathaniel Hawthorne claims to base the story on a recovered old Salem Custom House document. Realist writers such as Mark Twain and Stephen Crane—both with experience at newspapers—aimed to redress social injustice by pursuing verifiable truths through science-like methods. Those writing news and those writing novels held out hope for a new coherent, open, and democratic world.[18]

In the visual sphere, still and motion photographers of the Progressive Era hoped that documenting the reality of modern mass-scale industrial life would make the downtrodden visible and spur improvements in the lives of immigrants, workers, and ghetto dwellers. Reformer Lewis Hine tracked three decades of immigration, exposed child labor, and revealed workers on the Empire State Building to show that a modern visual imagination could bring life "to facts, to science, and to common lives."[19] The new picture press and halftone photographs in daily newspapers seemed to give readers witness to current events.[20] Philosopher John Dewey said the art of "presentation is fundamentally important." Because "artists have always been the real purveyors of news," democracy would flourish through "the art of full and moving communication."[21] Only art had enough power to map the emerging twentieth-century world.

Visual realism, the idea that optical lenses and camera technology can take a true measure of reality, persisted through most of the twentieth century. In the 1960s, newspapers were already losing influence and closing down editions—consequences of their focus on entertainment instead of "real news" based on facts. Daniel Boorstin exposed the pseudo image, "the making of our illusions—'the news behind the news'" that aimed to "clear away the fog so we can face the world."[22] But his critique reasserted realism. Visual historian and theorist E. H. Gombrich later called for a modern alternative that would accept the camera image as "an objective record" that "has to be interpreted." To overturn the commonsense realism that he called "copy theories" of representation, he still proposed "a universal science" that excluded values, and so his modernism became "just another realism."[23]

Only by century's end did realism lose some force. For objects, the theories of relativity and quantum mechanics became ordinary. Newtonian science seemed less apt when new ways of living alongside electronic devices defied time and place. For language, a less-sanguine view of realism emerged. One literary editor objected that successors to realism simplified complex problems and reduced the social to the individual.[24] But lecturing in the early 1960s, essayist Mary McCarthy worried that a focus on facts, fairness, and fidelity in the "journalistic frame" would doom the modern novel, which, "with its common sense, is of all forms the least adapted to encompass [a] world, whose leading characteristic is irreality" (the term Gombrich used).[25] *Irreality* expresses not the unreal but the sense of estrangement from realism which had emerged. Realism became a minor or naïve, beginner's view of the concrete world and the literary world.[26]

Critical scholarship implicated realism in the rise of consumer culture. Reporting on everyday life displayed events for consumption and brought consumers under surveillance but also alleviated their fears of powerlessness under the new industrial order. Instead of "a progressive force exposing social conditions," realism tended to make consumer relations the norm. Mass circulation newspapers—the new medium of the era—competed to do the same, promising "a coherent and a cohesive world" but delivering only more problems. The "attempt to imagine and contain social change," which made "the problems visible," also made "their resolution impossible."[27] Realism was an early strain of modernism, not its opposite, and both strains played a role in the adaptation to industrial conditions. To open a hope for progress and vision of an intelligible world, realism proposed close and accessible observation, and American modernism proposed an encompassing view that required expertise. In the course of the twentieth century, as political positions on objective reality changed sides, the language of realism lingered in news and other literary genres.

For visuals, essayist Susan Sontag proposed in the 1970s that expert photography made people into passive onlookers, not activists. Science and government used photos to monitor and control the populace, and politicians, celebrities, and pornographers used them to make themselves into mythic icons. The media used photos to support dominant ideas about nature and society, and advertisers and marketers immersed the viewing public in a "commodity dream"[28] about products and tourism that promised an escape from the mundane industrial world. The ensuing critique of positivism—a philosophical position that makes sensory experience of the concrete world the source of authoritative knowledge—accompanied the rise of digital picture manipulation. As the twentieth century ended, objectivity seemed less neutral and solid once audiences became aware of photo faking and grew more skeptical of visual images.[29]

The twenty-first century presents a terrain of contradictions,[30] where the solidity of things sits alongside quarks and chaos from "postmodern science," the realism of language alongside post-realist literature, and the specificity of images alongside new forms of manipulated irreality in the camera arts. But philosophers thinking about modern news had already posed the idea of irrealism a century earlier. Italian writer and political theorist Antonio Gramsci attacked the press for injecting the people with "ways of feeling and judging the facts" to benefit the press itself and serve the dominant classes.[31] American newsman and commentator Walter Lippmann, after echoing Gramsci, wrote that for occurrences "outside the direct experience" of reporters and others, news "abstracts" by using catchwords imbued "with feelings" to produce "realities."[32] And Argentine writer Jorge Luis Borges imagined interpretation as a "labyrinth of symbols"[33] where humankind would become lost—like today's digital news, massively multiplayer online games, or hypertext novels hosting worlds lacking the solidity of Newtonian physics.

But U.S. news has retained an element of and commitment to realism. At mid-century neither the working press nor its readers saw "explanation to be news."[34] Editors ridiculed "the long report [or] 'think piece,'" calling the articles "thumb sucking," and continued "to revolve around the immediate, the flash, the shock, the punch." Event-centered, episodic news did come under intellectual attack. The semiologist Roland Barthes wrote in a 1964 essay that fact-based items—what the French call *Fait-Divers*—were not news that occurs within history but mere filler, trivialities made interesting by a suspicious or astonishing cause or by a peculiar coincidence without requiring knowledge beyond the item itself. Later in the century, *Fait-Divers* still seemed the realist, U.S. model, an ideal of the body oriented "in a geo-astronomical space," said semiologist Umberto Eco, because humans would "follow certain 'directions' [e]ven if the world were a labyrinth."[35] Realism was one direction, but U.S. news was changing. Historian Robert Darnton, in a memoir of his time at the *New York Times*, recalled one reporter telling him, "The game is to sneak some color or interpretation past" the copyeditors.[36] Over time the reporters succeeded.

One might describe the intellectual landscape using the two-sides trope of modern news. Anthropologist Clifford Geertz observes that genres once separated out fact, blurring "what goes on in the world."[37] From the Left that favors modernism, news pursues broad, complex purposes, but follows rituals, performs like a medieval bard, and builds cultural memories and myths[38]—a far cry from the realist ideal. From the Right that favors the return of realism, social scientists wonder about "The Future of Fact" and push to make news scientific.[39] News practitioners have engaged in a rearguard action in the face of critiques from the left by abandoning the term *objectivity*, only to discover that its alternatives, *fairness* and *balance*, opened another interpretive quagmire on the right. There politicians invented *rusé* realism to invoke concrete reality, as in cynical Bush-era phrases like "Blue Skies Initiative" or the "Healthy Forest Act," to pursue policy aims wildly contrary to the terms' concrete meanings.[40] But between the two sides of modern news, concrete daily life goes on. The view of news as a modern battle between social forces leads to choices with economic and personal as well as political costs.[41] If news is a product in search of high-end markets, it makes sense to move content behind pay-walls. If news provides a bird's-eye perspective, its content will serve high-level corporate and institutional interests.

An example can illustrate. In late June 2008, Loyola University Chicago security took a graduate student into custody and turned him over to Lake Shore Hospital.[42] The psychiatric facility kept him without food or a bed for twenty hours, five hours in isolation, before transferring him. His mistake was sending fantasy poetry referring to the death of an Archangel to his psychologist on the Loyola staff, who complained, and Illinois law had just made a complaint sufficient for anyone's involuntary detention. For the next nine days the state maximum-security mental facility held him with patients known to be violent. Finding no evidence, the state dropped the case against him, but by then he had lost his job, his apartment, his degree status, and his sense of safety in the world. Hoping to warn others, he talked to a higher education reporter at the *Chicago Sun-Times*, who spent three days interviewing the family, getting releases to read private documents, and collaring Loyola students and staff.

The September 8 story, "Getting Students to ID Troubled Students," was a model of modernism. Pointing to the context of campus shootings at Virginia Tech and Northern Illinois University, it uses a military frame—"an army" of students as "the front lines"—to laud Loyola's institutional response to "behavioral concerns." It quotes one opposing voice, the "graduate student who believes the school over-reacted to some 'strange' emails he sent over the summer." Online reader comments go on to interpret, calling him "a punk" who deserved what he got. That is the whole coverage of the student's story, which says nothing about his detention and mistreatment. The reporter, a specialist in higher education, does the usual realist reporting but ends up seeing a higher-ed problem to solve, leaving untold the story of personal tragedy. The report typifies the tilt of U.S. news away from realism and toward high modernism, away from memorable stories to share and toward forgettable abstractions.

For a century, the occupation of journalist has attempted to become professional, with access to scarce, authoritative information and with analytical skills to explain events. But if a journalist provides knowledgeable interpretations, the audience must start each interaction under-informed, so that news remains necessary for making sense of events. Intelligent, expert news envisions audiences who need its ministrations. Modern news then relies on top-down authority and a one-to-many model of public information. The resulting perception—that news lacks interpretation—blocks an understanding that sense-making news accelerated in U.S. America. The contradiction between the imagined episodic news and the growing thematic coverage invokes a sociological fact: that what societies define as real *is* real in its consequences. Perceiving an urgent need for news to make sense of a world too complex for citizens to understand led modern explanation to expand as it did.[43]

But in interactive media, news practice faces contradictory expectations. Instead of delivering hard-to-get news, reporters seem like just another supplier of opinion among many competing on legacy media—cable outlets, talk radio, and comedy newscasts—and online. Instead of off-stage observers in search of reality, editors seem to play on-stage roles making social knowledge. And the persistent clinging to the idea and markers of realism disguised the growing modernism of U.S. news, which was losing the advantage that realism once provided. The modern vision of news never quite reflected public intelligence or engagement with news media from the Progressive Era to the crowd-sourcing era. Somehow the social definition of the situation—not some external nature—then made a world that seems less welcoming to modern news even as blogs and reader comments join in interpreting it. Or might there be some other way to understand the long-term changes in all five W's of the general knowledge that news once cultivated?[44]

THE DEVIL'S OWN WAY: A FABLE

What I saw startled me. I saw a man reach up into the sunshine and grasp a piece of truth. It was a little bit of a piece, but it was truth. No wonder the devil was interested.

I looked at him, expecting to see alarm on his countenance. There was none. He was so utterly untroubled that I couldn't be sure he had either seen or understood what had happened. I sounded him.

"Did you see that man get that piece of truth?" I asked.

He nodded, but he made no reply.

"You don't seem to be disturbed by it."

"No," he answered absently.

"But you see how it would hurt business; don't you?" I urged.

"Yes." He smiled. "It would ruin mine."

"Well, then," I persisted impatiently, "why do you take it so easily?"

"Because," he answered patiently, "I know what to do about it."

"What will you do?"

"Why," he said, "I shall tempt them to organize it."

—Journalist Lincoln Steffens, "The Devil's Own Way, A Fable,"
The Century, June 1922

PART 7

News Transformed:
So What and Now What?

It is a misfortune that necessity has induced men to accord greater license to this formidable engine, in order to obtain liberty, than can be borne with less important objects in view; for the press, like fire, is an excellent servant, but a terrible master.

It may be taken as a rule, that without the liberty of the press, there can be no popular liberty in a nation, and with its licentiousness, neither publick honesty, justice, nor a proper regard for character. Of the two, perhaps, that people is the happiest which is deprived altogether of a free press, since private honesty, and a healthful tone of the publick mind are not incompatible with narrow institutions though neither can well exist under the constant corrupting action of a licentious press.

The governing principle connected with this interest, would seem to depend on a general law, which, under abuses, converts the most beneficial moral agents to be the greatest enemies of the race. The press is equally capable of being made the instrument of elevating man to the highest point of which his faculties admit, or of depressing him to the lowest.

—James Fenimore Cooper, *The American Democrat* (1838)

CHAPTER 19

Social Values Enabled Change

News elites converged on Cambridge, Massachusetts, in 2001—a handful of fellows at the Shorenstein Center in the Kennedy School of Government, several times that number at the Nieman Foundation, and others scattered across campus—to spend a semester or two away from the din of daily news to think, study, and reflect at Harvard. The few researchers arriving among the fellows anticipated a rare chance to talk not as professor-sources but on equal footing with reporters. Our class pictures in September show smiles and high hopes. Two weeks later, we made our way across a Harvard Yard glorious in early fall for what should have been an ordinary day at the office. Instead of chat over coffee, the news pros in the break room encountered a plane crashing into a World Trade Center tower on television news, and researchers powering up computers at our desks caught the same news over web browsers and email.

Those in the break room hardly left. They watched and compared reports on the main broadcast networks—ABC, CBS, NBC, and Fox—along with cable news channels. The morning newspapers sat on the large break table. The main question after "What happened?" was "What to do with ourselves?" At the computer I tried to concentrate on writing my first study of how news was moving online, steadying myself with the idea that in a crisis the best course is to do one's job, whatever it is. But I found myself constantly stopping to check the unfolding events online and wander back into the break room to watch my colleagues from industry watching news. They sat on the sofa and chairs or stood around, reduced to onlookers. They critiqued the coverage—Fox News was the best by consensus (its critics seem not to notice what they saw)—and lamented being sidelined during one of the most important stories during their careers.

Over the next few days, they found a way to renew their mission to serve the public, either as commentators and advisors to those in the field or by returning to work temporarily alongside their colleagues in New York and elsewhere. On Boston newsstands, the press proclaimed the meaning of the attacks within a day: that the world had changed forever.[1] U.S. news itself changed during and right after what the media dubbed 9/11. After initial missteps into objectivity, news media producers lined up in patriotic unity. They pushed aside commercial concerns, stopping broadcast advertising during the initial days, and absorbed the high costs of coverage. Individual reporters put themselves in danger to serve the better good and revitalized their occupation's service mission. Scandals that absorbed news time and space before the attacks evaporated. Audiences returned to news in droves, boosting ratings and circulation and confirming in surveys their opinions on the importance of news as an occupation.[2]

But one of the Shorenstein fellows, former *Times of India* Resident Editor Ramindar Singh, a few weeks later remarked at a campus event that the world had not changed; instead, it had come to visit America for a change.[3] The thought was prescient at least for news because its practitioners and audiences resumed familiar routines in the years to follow. The politicized reporting of Fox News spread to other outlets, and minor scandals reentered daily coverage as mainstream news businesses focused again on profit margins and news competition. Trends among consumers returned to older patterns, so that the aging readers and viewers of major outlets remained loyal and the young continued to abandon those venues in favor of digital, mobile platforms and satirical "fake-news" formats. But in government and politics a growing surveillance environment solidified. The U.S. administration used the "world has changed" idea to pass the 2001 USA PATRIOT Act that made human rights at home secondary and to pass the Homeland Security Act of 2002, restructuring government to make national security supreme. Changes also led into wars and nation building abroad. U.S. news organizations eager to make sense of events went along with administration explanations in their news coverage and returned to the previous century's patterns of interpretive news.

What had happened over the century to U.S. news? The headline of the story is clear: reports grew longer in mainstream news, but few seemed to notice. The rest of the story shows what filled up the longer reports. Was it people, events, places? No, not the "who," "what," or "where." The most denotative and realist of the Five Ws all declined in different ways. But the other two Ws, "when" and "why," did expand the connotative, modern dimension. While references to the present remained fairly constant in stories, the past grew more important along with the future and change over time. The pattern of explaining how and why events happened also expanded but shifted in particular ways that opened space within news for opin-ions and judgments, especially in broadcast and online. The evidence is clear.

One way to understand the changes is by looking at what practitioners do. If news is supposed to be short and denotative but measuring news content shows otherwise, then they must have changed their practices. Holding writers to account for what they publish is part of the American tradition of individualism. Personal accountability for press content has a long history in the United States, going back to the tarring and feathering of editors for views they expressed in print.[4] Before the twentieth century, the editor might be the only one writing for a local newspaper, and by riding (usually) him out of town on the rail, a mob effectively closed the paper, although some destroyed the presses or even burned down the print shop. But audiences seem unaware of how news practices may have changed as U.S. news content transformed over the past century.

When asked about what happened to their practices, news insiders point pri-marily to market competition and technology affecting what they do. Those with long careers at newspapers remember the shift from metal type to photo processes and remember when television news was new. Broadcasters remember moving from cumbersome film to videotape and then digital recording. Content changes did accompany the entry of new competitors in the market and new contenders in the news arena. But the changes also preceded technical transformations in print-ing, innovations in formats for radio and newsweeklies, and rivalries with televi-sion and online news. The account insiders give falls short of explaining how news content evolved when they infer the shifts in competition and technology made their reports even shorter. Besides leading to the wrong conclusion, focusing on individual actions alone may place unfair blame. The practitioners I interviewed made choices that harmed their own interests on the job and resulted in setbacks in their personal lives. They are hardly deserving of censure.

Daily actions and decisions of individuals cannot alone explain the transforma-tion of news content, but a faith in the power of individual action to effect social change has been a central tenet for imagining U.S. news. Once they come to absorb the evidence that their decisions have transformed the "who," "what," and "where," the big question is what kind of stories news producers want. Individual report-ers and editors can ask whether writing longer or shorter serves readers better or invites more readers into the news arena. Does a longer report crowd out other news? Editors and publishers can reconsider decisions about resources, the profit margin versus the reporting staff they field. It takes more time to talk to people about their lives. Adding a local angle to national and international stories also adds length but not much local content. How can news pay more attention to the zones citizens inhabit? Existing beliefs about short news stories focusing on local people and events clearly have not carried news in that direction.

In light of changes in the "when" and "why" of news, producers can continue asking what news is for.[5] For it to serve the public good, how much context and history should stories include? News producers explain to make it easier for citizens to understand events, but history and context also tend to make news more authoritative. The interaction around news becomes asymmetrical, rather than a conversation among peers. Previous debates have taken place on a backdrop that assumes reporters interpret too little, but now studies show the opposite. A better question might be what interpretive moves are adequate and succinct, whether opinion-free news is possible, and how to make a routine of revealing underlying opinions.[6] Asking about basic news values could then shift the focus from individual workers onto their collective aims.

Looking at the news occupation is another way to understand what happened since the nineteenth century. News practice did change, organizing along professional lines, pushing universities to provide training programs, and absorbing new technologies. It improved in standing from a job based on piecework to an occupation based on knowledge. An outcome of its growing confidence was a pattern of "journalists interviewing each other."[7] On NPR, for instance, one might expect reporters in Washington, D.C., to interview an Israeli about events in Israel, but producers began to bring American or other colleagues working in Israel on the air instead of local sources. The shift in group practices accompanied a growing reliance on the collective intelligence and judgment within the occupation.[8] The contradiction between expectations and news content was most notable on national TV and radio network newscasts but also present in other media.[9] Upon seeing the results showing that news has grown longer but less focused on local people and places, mainstream practitioners dismissed the data and reasserted the conventional wisdom that news has grown shorter but more local and personal.

Contradictions between common belief and practice can reveal ideologies, the shared ideas that cloak how powerful groups dominate others.[10] In a limited, critical sense, each journalist shares an ideology, as in any other occupation. But its operations and values are "one of the most opaque structures of meaning in modern society," according to Stuart Hall. He writes that news seems to happen to its producers, as if "events select themselves," revealing "a 'deep structure'" that functions in ways "un-transparent even to those who professionally most know how to operate it."[11] But mainstream practice does leave traces of that structure in news texts, a kind of documentary evidence showing the mutable social status of the occupation. Its position is ideological in the Marxian sense, working within a pattern of dominance—called *hegemony*—that secures a place for social groups among the elite.[12] Those among or hoping to join the elites tend to promote dominant views, make them seem natural and universal, and denigrate other perspectives and anyone who holds them, while obscuring all of the foregoing operations.

In the world of the twentieth century, the main tools for exerting dominion in stable societies had shifted from the sword to language and the media.

Occupational ideology might shed more light on modernist changes especially in the "when" and "why" of news. Increasing attention to the past and the future can *over-determine* the meaning of events in ways that support existing or emerging power relations.[13] The growth in stories that point to why and how events happened tend to position reporters as a source of explanations, and a reliance on more opinions and judgments shifts the occupation nearer to the center of public life. The higher standing that the occupation acquired in comparison with other groups and the general public might help account for the tendency of audiences, especially the young, to abandon mainstream news media. Expert news also becomes a clear target for cultural resistance among particular social groups, political blocs, and economic strata and in the culture more broadly. Novelist Tim O'Brien—whose story "The Things They Carried" became an anthology standard by piling up realist, denotative lists to convey the weight of battle—disparaged efforts to make meaning from the Vietnam War. The same might be said of the accidents and crimes that attract reporters beyond wartime.[14]

The occupational view wants to forgive individuals and show that larger forces account for lapses into *false consciousness*, the patterns that lead groups to act against their own interests.[15] But the ideological argument also places blame, treating the occupation as unintelligent and unwittingly in league with hegemons. News practice does confront the power of government at all levels, of institutions such as hospitals, and of corporations and businesses—even news media headquarters—while pursuing ways to bring events to light and serve the public good.[16] The stance has come to mirror the focus of cultural criticism on the origins and consequences (past and future) and on the processes and reasons (how and why) for what happens. But critique has its limits, which are mainly to do with getting "closer to" concrete or material "matters of concern," as sociologist of science Bruno Latour suggests.[17] In making content that reaches others, producers make news a *thing* that has collectively understood meanings, and the gathering of meanings around it produces more than the news story as a mere object. Occupational ideology has difficulty dealing with the stubborn fact of American realism in denotative news but does give some insight into the rise of modernism in interpretive news.

What can the occupation do about its contradictions? The key to ideological change is awareness, and the main way to build it is consciousness-raising. The term arose in the late 1960s among women working for equal rights. Within news, professional associations in workplaces and annual meetings could spread awareness about how news transformed in the past century. Knowing what happened to the denotative stuff of news might galvanize workers around ways to respond to specific changes in events, people, and local places within news reports. Outside of news production, attention in the media might shift awareness in unexpected ways, perhaps realigning objections to interpretive news among the political left or right. Consciousness-raising had earlier been a tool for countering workers' passive attitudes toward industrial conditions and can succeed by disarming hidden ideological processes. Beyond the occupation, a wide understanding of what news has become may help slow or reverse the periodic crises undermining mainstream news by helping rebuild rapport between producers and the publics they aim to serve. Reconsidering that mission might build new connections for news practice in the surrounding society.

The broadest way to understand what happened is by looking at news as an expression of social values.[18] The journalist entered popular imagination once the occupation had formed an identity in the late nineteenth century. Within a few decades, a stock character had emerged in literature and the arts, best known from the hard-bitten smoker-drinker reporter of *The Front Page*. Commonplace procedures of news also appear: a breaking news event, the scurry to compete for the scoop, a once-in-a-lifetime exclusive, and the news interview. And so do the dingy pressrooms and courthouses, telephones and typewriters, and corruption of police and politicians. The sets, props, characters, and ideas define an industrial occupation at the margins of institutional power but with a high purpose, to serve ordinary, blameless folk by exposing chicanery among the supposedly upright. After the play became a Broadway hit in 1928, a dozen productions on stage and in film helped define the terrain of social values surrounding news in the twentieth century.[19]

Like Clark Kent of Superman comics, daily newsgathering hides its heroism behind an oafish façade. That value for news held up through the 1970s, with the film *All the President's Men*, when U.S. American news reached the height of its modern moment.[20] In a broad, descriptive sense, the position of an occupation is ideological because in sociology ideologies are the shared beliefs that groups use in shaping their world.[21] Like other occupations, news practice operates under a descriptive ideology that envisions a kind of Utopia[22]: the journalist as Everyman who does a thankless job that plays a surprising role in making the world a better place. But societies also define ideals by negation, the villain in contrast to the hero, and so U.S. popular culture "captures the sleazy side of the journalist."[23] In *The Front Page*, that face shows up in the character of the editor, whose deep knowledge of practice has turned cynical and serves dark money-spinning interests. The journalist as villain was prominent in the U.S. media during the last decades of the twentieth century.[24]

Considering news part of broader social ideals helps explain some of the ways individuals carry out their work and some of the moves and blind spots within the occupation. How workers see themselves and their collective purposes to serve the general public is not peculiar to the news industry. English teachers and the bright "good writers" they choose for high school news media express the same individual satisfactions and collective aims,[25] which experienced practitioners talk about in interviews and the occupation has built into its codes of ethics. The contradictions—between what individuals say they *believe* and how their stories end up reporting on people, places, and events—may spring from the values surrounding news. And cultural expectations of news may account for the contradictions between how news content tackles the "how" and "why" of events and what the occupation accepts as common wisdom: the need for news to become more contextual and explanatory. The social ideals surrounding news also bring to light the cultural predicament of U.S. news practice.

The quandary of any occupation intertwines with the fate of individual workers, and their experiences can illuminate the larger backdrop of society. Those I interviewed arrived at Harvard with substantial experience as news insiders (anyone from public relations, for instance, is ineligible to apply).[26] The Nieman Foundation selected them for their accomplishments, for their individual "aspirations for the years ahead," and for their diversity—how as a group they could "represent the changing face of journalism." Their applications had to show a "capacity for growth and leadership," and their study proposals had to suggest how they could influence "the broader world of journalism." A requirement to return to their former employment aimed to assure their places as future leaders in the field.

But over the next decade and a half, only some remained in mainstream news and few in full-time daily reporting. Changes leading into the 2000s "created turbulence in journalists' work environment,"[27] but in surveys more workers expected to stick with their careers. By late in the first decade of the century, blogs and magazines began following "life after journalism," suggesting that the high rate of layoffs had increased some patterns already well established for the occupation. After spending their early years in mainstream news production, reporters move on, usually out of news-gathering into management, commentary, or another end of the business, or they might find work outside mainstream news organizations as consultants and freelancers. But many "defect" from news into public relations, consulting, education, or government—fields that can use their skills.[28]

The Harvard fellows well advanced in their careers moved around but rejoined the ranks of managers or commentators. Rick Kaplan returned to ABC in 2003 to become senior vice president of news and then served as MSNBC president from 2004 to 2006. In 2007 he became executive producer of the CBS Evening News and in 2011 moved back to ABC, producing *This Week* and running political coverage until 2012, when he became a network contractor. Ramindar Singh led a TV channel and then directed corporate communication at its parent, Hinduja Group, before spending time as a visiting lecturer first at the Times School of Journalism and then at the Indira Gandhi National Open University. He eventually became consulting editor and chief trainer for Press Trust of India, New Delhi. Andy Glass joined *The Hill* newspaper as a senior editor in 2002, becoming managing editor in 2003, writing his weekly column until 2006, and teaching media ethics for a time at the University of Maryland. Then he joined the staff of *Politico*, a multi-platform outlet on Washington, D.C., politics, where he moved into history by writing a column about past news, beginning with the phrase "On this day in" a given year.

Some younger fellows stayed in mainstream news. Matt Bai, after a brief stint at *Rolling Stone*, joined the *New York Times Magazine* as a political reporter and staff writer in 2002, covering the 2004 and 2008 presidential campaigns and becoming chief political correspondent at the magazine. In 2007 he published *The Argument*, a book about how progressive activists and leaders of the Democratic Party moved into the digital era, and in 2013, after a fellowship at the Wilson Center to write a book about how a past political scandal influenced political coverage, he moved to Yahoo News as a national political columnist. But others moved into writing even longer works or away from big, legacy news outlets. Tim Sullivan worked at Court TV and American Lawyer Media, then spent time as a freelance writer in New York and part-time instructor at Marist College before returning to the Associated Press as an Asia writer and then senior correspondent based in New Delhi, India. He was exceptional; those in freelance work, commentary, and literary pursuits are not at a far remove from reporting on news events.

Consulting based on their expertise was a short-term stop for a majority of the Harvard interviewees on the road out of daily news. Barbara Serrano, after leaving the *Seattle Times* in 2003 to become an editor for the *Los Angeles Times*, then took over as managing editor of the *Yakima Herald-Republic*, a property of the Seattle Times Company. In 2010 she turned her editorial skills to other areas, including a task force on higher education, a medical center, and, later, a nonprofit in post-conflict Cambodia. But she went back to school and completed a law degree in 2013, interning with the Seattle city attorney and with the Washington State Supreme Court, before entering practice as a criminal prosecutor. In 2014 she joined the Seattle city attorney's office. Consulting turned into more for Michel Marriott, who stayed at the *New York Times* until 2007, when he joined Baruch College as an assistant professor in the journalism program. He wrote a thriller published in 2008 and left Baruch to become a literary consultant.

Education became a next career for others after they left Harvard. Michele McLellan held fellowships or directed projects at the independent Poynter Institute journalism training center, Northwestern University Medill School of Journalism, University of Missouri School of Journalism, and USC/Annenberg Knight Digital Media Center. Along the way she ran a Community News Summit meeting for three years in support of online local news and founded Michele's List, a database of local news startups online. After leaving ABC News, Scott Talan worked briefly for UNICEF, then taught part-time at George Washington and Johns Hopkins Universities before settling in 2005 as communications director for the National Association of Schools of Public Affairs and Administration. In 2010 he became a member of the faculty of American University.

Along with education, external and media relations became a destination. Deborah Lohse, tired of the "ten hour days" and pressure to produce interpretive stories at the *Wall Street Journal*, moved to the *San Jose Mercury News* to find more balance in life. In 2008 she joined the media relations staff at Santa Clara University in the San Francisco Bay Area. Roberta Baskin left ABC News *20/20* to spend a year as an investigative reporter for *Now with Bill Moyers*. In 2005 she joined the Center for Public Integrity in Washington, D.C., as executive director, before returning in 2007 to the local ABC affiliate to direct an investigative-news team, a position she later lost during layoffs. For five years she directed media communications in the Office of Inspector General, U.S. Department of Health and Human Services, and in 2014 she created a global online storytelling project, AIM2Flourish.com, at Case Western Reserve University in Cleveland, Ohio.

Among the Harvard visitors, one who returned to the same medium and stayed was Lisa Stone, the first Nieman fellow from online news. She continued blogging, wrote for outlets like the *New York Times* and *Los Angeles Times*, and helped Law.com create a sponsored blog network. Then in 2005 she co-founded and became CEO of BlogHer.com Inc., a meta-network to promote women in social media, funnel brand marketing into their blogs, and circulate news and information among women in social media. In 2014 the company merged into SheKnows Media, and as its chief community officer she still considered her activities, such as moderating a town hall meeting with President Barack Obama, part of news practice, committed to "excellent hard-news journalism and storytelling about women."[29]

What happened to her and the other future news leaders after their time in the Ivy League is revealing. Their fate exposes inconsistencies in the social values surrounding news not unlike the contradictions within individual practitioner responsibility and news occupational ideology. News practice may seem to stand opposite politics and public relations, but Serrano's move to a city agency in Seattle and Baskin's move to a project seeking uplifting stories involved transitions into another phase in their commitment to serve society. In some ways, Stone's career in online media resembles where her colleagues went later, especially the entrepreneurial roles as consultants, freelancers, and independent authors and contractors. Digital media may shed light on old roles in news and on new kinds of involvement with news for the public of informed citizens, consumers, and audience members. What kind of "news space" do those publics occupy? Answering that question can help explain what has happened to news and its place in building general knowledge in U.S. America.

CHAPTER 20

Modernism Exposed the Flaws of News

In spring 2009, students at the Northwestern University journalism school developed Stats Monkey, software to turn box scores and similar sports data into a news story, like this one: "BRADENTON, Fla.—Northwestern held off a late comeback bid by Georgetown to defeat the Hoyas 5–3 Friday. Trevor Stevens led the Wildcats with two hits and one run scored. . . ."[1] In the Northwestern magazine published that autumn, the machine-written lines introduced an article that an alum then blogged for the *Hartford Courant* online. NPR picked up the news in January, followed by technology bloggers. The students' professor-developers raised $6 million in venture capital to found Narrative Science, and in 2011 the *New York Times* reported that a joint venture of the college Big Ten conference and Fox was among twenty clients signed up for the story-generating service. By 2015 the firm had become a "Partner" with a regular byline in *Forbes*, the AP was employing a competitor's software called Wordsmith, and the *Los Angeles Times* was using another called Quakebot. Digital technology began absorbing the real labor of news.[2]

News stories about automation focused on whether software would help or replace reporters and editors, a theme the trade press picked up after *Wired* magazine predicted a "robonews tsunami" based on Narrative Science claims that computers would win a Pulitzer within five years and write "more than 90 percent" of news within fifteen years.[3] The main role the stories implied for audiences was to guess whether a machine wrote the story (conclusion: unlikely). People would be getting coverage of events that the established media ignore, such as Little League games, or no longer cover enough, from business earnings to school-board meetings. The developers claim the software can produce financial and political insights people need and can also entertain, ranging from breathless breaking news to snarky restaurant reviews. The understandable job fears highlight a gap between the ambitions of modern news and its reception among audiences.

Modern news practice aims to perfect the accuracy, reliability, and insight of reporting.[4] *Accuracy* requires mature judgment about the facts. *Reliability* requires making those facts clear in the context of the past, present, and future. And *insight* requires conveying the story in ways that reveal what the facts mean. But news practice operates under conditions placing all three dimensions beyond its grasp.

Can citizens expect the *accurate* performance that modern news pursues and that the machine apparently delivers? Probably not.[5] Daily news gathering of the early twentieth century was an activity of the youthful,[6] and today the labor of reporting what happens each day to local people is still a "young man's game."[7] Lawyers or doctors join their profession early and then pursue its public-service mission late in life, but the news arena operates amid centripetal forces that spin off practitioners into adjacent roles or into defection. The careers of those I interviewed show the pattern. Daily news reporters who stay put seem stuck in a dead-end jobs, watching others who merely pass through. Because reporting the day's events tends to happen only early in the typical career, citizens tend to get an inexperienced account of events, which invites them to respond by adding their hard-won know-how. But the modern hope for an accurate story, despite inspiring admiration, would end the conversation, exposing a contradiction of news. The public at large may benefit more from a callow rendition of events that invites completion than from perfected coverage that modern news seems to promise. A core assertion of professionals is consistent performance, that any reporter following news routines will produce much the same account. Achieving that aim in the machine version may replace news laborers or free them for knowledge work, but in either case, the engaged public could suffer.[8]

Can citizens expect the *reliable* news that modern practice aims to achieve and that its automation might deliver? Probably not. Telling a news story involves weaving a plot built around available information through known procedures. Its actors perform roles in a story that reaches climax and resolution through the mediation of news practice.[9] Although modern reports decenter the practitioner, news is by definition a secondhand account. It first emerged from the convergence of keeping physical records, new printing technology, and a human desire to hear and believe something new has happened. Stories going through a mediator are hearsay in courts of law, unreliable as any retold tale. But words disseminated as news seem authoritative *because of* mediation. The technologies of reproduction and physical distribution lend them and their purveyors a kind of clout. That power operates *in spite of* a close involvement of news organs with political power, which through modern history has regulated but also relied on news media to advance policy. Those involved have tended in recent decades to think of news and politics as healthful activities; they express surprise when the audience treats both with a measure of condescension. But if news is unreliable, its recipients end up considering the sources and triangulating among them, and so a contradiction of news is that unreliable stories about current events can serve the public good. News software could produce public forgetfulness about the unreliability of second-hand accounts, leaving citizens without the task of considering the forces that supply events in the ways peculiar to news.[10]

Can citizens expect the *insight* that news practitioners want to supply and the machine might generate? Probably not. My studies found that news reports included more explanations and references to the past and future, adopting critics' expectations. But its practitioners have little time or payoff for looking back in depth. In broadcasting especially, they express opinions, but even newspapers may serve up a quick perspective drawn from individual and collective memory in the newsroom, from the digital or old-time "morgue" of internal clipping files, or from external searches. Historians do a better job of assessing what happened, but because they wait a decade or more before taking on the task, they leave an opening that news fills. Working in relative haste, reporters then give a middling, predictable account of what went just before. Audiences, not least of all politicians and citizens, want to know what happened in the last election or other event, but no one can venture with much surety into that opening. Modern practitioners undertake a fool's mission and get it wrong often enough to expose a contradiction of news as a kind of knowledge.

In the early years of the twenty-first century, U.S. news media missed or ignored the most important stories, got them wrong, or reached them late. Examples of the bad "first rough draft of history" abound.[11] Business news fueled the rise of Enron, once the world's largest energy corporation, and its fall into bankruptcy in 2001, the first huge business failure of the century.[12] Mainstream news and especially the *New York Times* fell short during the false weaponry (called WMD) claims justifying the 2003 invasion of Iraq.[13] The war led to the Halliburton contracting scandal, exposure of CIA operative Valerie Plame, torture of Abu Ghraib prisoners, and controversies surrounding the U.S. military prison in Guantánamo Bay, Cuba. But the recent record is probably no worse than the erroneous coverage of World War I.[14]

Modern news works under an assumption about what society must do to succeed, expressed in the aphorism of George Santayana: "Those who cannot remember the past are condemned to repeat it."[15] News practice tries to make the *now* into a draft historical record, in the optimistic hope for bettering society. But any insights that machines could produce might make matters worse, not better. So-called big data or "precision" gives solidity to news conclusions. Within its short time frame, news rushes into the gap that legitimate history leaves open and inevitably fails. Insights published on demand about past events reaffirm the contradiction that news may perform a public service by supplying unsound accounts that prove wrong just often enough to keep the citizenry alert.

News practitioners probably do better with the past than with trends leading into the future. Audiences, especially the political elite, want to know how the story will end, but the future is the stuff of soothsayers. By finding patterns and making assumptions about stability and change, physical science can sometimes predict what comes next. Weather reporting shows how forecasts fail as they reach further out, and viewers likely benefit from daily lessons on the unreliability of weather prediction. Other news occupies similar shaky ground, less like physical than social science, which cannot predict any but gross aggregate behavior as long as individuals do the sublime, unexpected, and ridiculous. When social scientists try to provide knowledge to direct future action, whether individual or social, they enter an ethical quagmire. The future is a matter of speculation that scientists rule out, but when editors risk a guess about, say, impending government action, their fallible attempt opens a chance for voters to do something about it. Unerring modern insight would settle the matter, exposing the contradiction that the guesswork inherent in news may also serve the public good by keeping hopes for news content modest and expectations for citizenship ambitious.

Modern news aims for accuracy, reliability, and insight, and the effort does some good while also making its contradictions inescapable. They follow from the position news occupies in the lives of reporters, audiences, and society. If callow, unsound, and fallible news does more good than modernists expect, understanding the contradictions may lead to a better sense of what news can supply, how the labor of news can prosper, and which contents politicians and people need. Understanding the contradictions of news may also help close the gap between modern news producers and audiences, which opened as news transformed through the twentieth century.[16] Mister Pulitzer's journalist quickly came to occupy a distinct space that set the main conditions and problems news confronts, such as cynicism, sensationalism, and the bias of partisanism. Like the high aims of the occupation, the -isms that journalism resists may not bedevil audiences, especially in the era of the spider's connective web.

Partisanism became a target for the journalist as soon as the emerging occupation rejected the model of the partisan press. Attacking opposition newspapers was routine in the nineteenth century, and *partisanism*, meaning partisanship or the partisan spirit, was a prominent feature in U.S. public discussion by midcentury. The poet Rob Morris was among the first to introduce the term, remarking that "newspaper reading . . . was a pleasant compound" that included "bitter partisanism."[17]

Newspaper publishers like Robert R. "Colonel" McCormick of the *Chicago Tribune* were partisans in one way, and in another, Progressives turned partisanism into a movement. When founding the *St. Louis Post-Dispatch*, Pulitzer set out to put people before party, criticize government administrations, and advocate "principles and ideas rather than prejudices and partisanship."[18] Its neutrality opened the door to other modern tasks.

Modern news worked to segregate opinion and remove it entirely from most pages. U.S. newspapers quarantined it, so that the partisan press survived only on the editorial pages of the next century.[19] The feat required editors to work more in abstraction, applying practical epistemology to root out opinion.[20] News facts align with previous events that reporters have covered, in a process parallel to the way judges consider precedent when deciding a case. Impartiality excludes feelings and ideas that incline one to judge occurrences without forethought, and news facts came to stand opposite partisanship, turning the party spirit into a kind of prejudice resulting in biased news. Reporters undertook other basic tasks of epistemology such as verification. One standard is to corroborate facts by drawing evidence from at least two sources. In U.S. partisan affairs, facts emerge from treating both parties with fairness by giving voice to each. The two-party model in politics extended into other news, so that reporters began looking for binaries, assuming each source has an opponent. Opinion then resides outside of news, and editors become arbiters in the balance of opinion. Under that standard, mainstream news practitioners by the late twentieth century shunned the expression of partisan opinion, refusing in some instances to declare a party affiliation.[21]

Modern news adapts facts to market conditions. One of the intangible values that publishers and media owners accumulate is credibility, combining believable contents, which varies, and a level of affinity that remains stable between the news organ and its audience.[22] Credible news usually manages to present accounts that readers or viewers find plausible. After a lapse in credibility, published corrections attempt to repair the record of an event but also reassert the believability of the outlet as a connection to consumers. Factual news supposedly makes money when highly credible content leads to higher circulation and better ratings. The added number of readers and viewers generates little revenue itself but increases what media owners can charge for advertising, which may produce more profits. But U.S. news stories shifted back into giving opinions over the twentieth century, especially on television, perhaps because markets rewarded outspoken opinion and because audience allegiance to modern news waned.

News practitioners seem to find the citizenry imponderable, reliable only at the macro level, in the aggregate. At the micro level, individual citizens, unlike reporters, are expected to have opinions, even baseless and bigoted ones, because partisan choices lead into the voting booth. Polling emerged in the twentieth century as a tamer of public opinion by finding the center of the bell curve, the polite consensus that pushes the rabble aside as statistical outliers. The idea of one person, one vote seems to apply to opinion surveys, which ask a narrow range of questions on topics the respondents may know little or care less about. By damping the cacophony of individual voices, polling makes democracy manageable for elites. News content then cites the surveys, tempering them with creditable sources to control news quality. But reader opinion, corralled into comments and letters to the editor, is content that engages the audience, even though editors view the writers as something close to lunatics whose words require domestication. Quality-control measures to keep modern news credible have failed to manage audiences. When the number of paying customers for legacy media eroded in the twenty-first century, some news outlets took up a partisan model, still claiming fairness and balance in the case of Fox News, and others put content behind pay walls.[23]

Media businesses seem to treat customers at the micro level, as individuals voting for news products with their eyeballs and subscriptions, expressing opinions of news by investing time and money. News outlets also compete for audience attention, but competitive processes tend to make the content of different outlets interchangeable, so that the news is similar but arrives in different packages. Consumers then make micro "purchases" based on delivery style and presenter personality. Citizens' awareness of an outlet's partisan leanings may work at the macro level, applying to the whole enterprise and emerging from partisan cues in the content and the reactions of a citizen's personal connections. News practice makes fine distinctions among genres belonging in different sections of its output, labeling some elements Analysis or sections Opinion. But the effort is lost on audiences who occupy a news space that views an outlet through a broader, macro lens on its political leanings.

News producers and audiences may simplify the complex interplay of macro and micro judgments by being dismissive of each other and by agreeing a citizen should embrace partisanship where reporters and editors should not. But the opposite seems to occur, so that news takes control of the space of citizenship. Generating the meanings for what happens defines modern news, asserting its neutrality and definitiveness even though the work of making meaning is political, a task once reserved to citizenship. Pushing partisan content into separate places appears to tame the bias of politics but also hides other ways that news conveys the partisan spirit. Nineteenth-century partisan news asserted its party affiliation, but modern news asserts a kind of partisan spirit of the occupation toward itself. A focus on credibility and quality concentrates on content and elides its producer, veiling the contradictions within news at the risk of deactivating the citizen. By avoiding overt partisanship while defining always-political meaning, modern news also opens the occupation to partisan attack, spurring politically active audiences to find other ways of staying informed. And so fighting the bias of partisanism may be fruitless.

Sensationalism is another problem that the occupation has targeted since the rise of modernism. The term *sensationalism* appeared in nineteenth-century philosophy to describe human sensation as the source of knowledge, harking back to earlier theories such as idealism.[24] Chosen to avoid association "with what is *morally* vicious,"[25] *sensationalism* soon came to brand novelists, dramatists, and journalists as amoral.[26] Sensational practice peaked with yellow journalism in the 1890s.[27] Progressive Era muckrakers and crusading writers argued that exciting human sensation could generate moral indignation and action against injustice, sustaining the press crusades boosting legislation against tainted food and other social ills. To show children, immigrants, young women, and others beyond the view of polite society, news practice developed a kind of fieldwork in factories, brothels, and other sites of realism also found in art and literature.[28]

In the twentieth century, the project to make news modern diverged from nineteenth-century practice by rejecting the subjective appeals underlying sensationalism and adopting routines to make coverage objective.[29] The objective account may dissociate news from its realist roots by accepting occurrences as inherent in the world and regarding them without flinching either morally or emotionally. News stories could still show the underdog, but dispassionately, through expert observation committed to social change. Objective reports were also versions of events that trainees could learn to produce respectably. In the tacit bargain between publishers seeking profit and employees seeking better working conditions, objective news could build occupational expertise while commanding high-end markets, outweighing the mass readership that sensationalism attracted. The cheap sensational press made money from selling copies, but as advertising revenues grew around affluent consumers, news became what marketers later came to call a "loss leader." Gathering sensational stories attracted more readers but tended to lose money for publishers. Modern news instead allied producers with advertisers, demoting citizens by making them into economic actors under the emerging idea of consumerism.[30]

Standing against sensationalism also placed mainstream practice opposite the shrill voice of the then-new tabloid newspapers.[31] Sensational news reeks of danger or appeals to base instincts that educated audiences can conquer to resist demagoguery, or so the argument goes, but only the *other* person is ever likely to succumb. Seeing oneself as immune to sensational accounts lets the tabloid news consumer adopt moral outrage, reinforcing assumptions about the world. But the sensational lurks everywhere in efforts to make "news" from what occurs. Serious news also speaks in the peculiar voice that makes each story sound important and urgent but without the breathless or screaming text of tabloids. Patrons of serious news then adopt a merely different moral stand, leading to the continual criticism that news needs to improve.

The distinction between tabloid and serious news denies what practitioners do when they tell the story. The coin of the trade is a kind of exaggeration, not because human nature makes news what it is but because its producers make their output that way.[32] In news through the twentieth century, milder kinds of intrigue, excitement, and suspense over what will happen next made serious news texts a literary performance the audience could easily recognize. The ordering of story content puts the most surprising and important stuff early in a plot that news producers master. News is an act that calls for a listening ear and plants a question for practitioners to answer, and so its content points inward to news itself by signaling what its producers make: news events. Giving away too much too soon is the essence of sensational overstatement. The revelation incites a passion for more, for news itself.

Unlike the uniformity and abstraction of modern news, readers and viewers can occupy a subjective and contradictory realist landscape, where sensationalism is a guilty pleasure or minor annoyance.[33] Audiences can also recognize the voice that pumps up occurrences to make them into news, especially on local newscasts.[34] Survey respondents' demands for better quality may help restrain the overstatement inherent in news.[35] Audiences then take the macro view, seeing news as knowledge presented in the imperative, where practitioners take the micro view, hoping to make news into knowledge presented in the declarative.[36] As income from circulation and market share eroded late in the twentieth century, news organs returned to scandal, negativity, and so-called infotainment. Older generations accustomed to objective news felt nostalgia, and critics decried the return of sensationalism. But new media users adapted to the weird and shocking in social media feeds tumbling alongside data graphs and kitten videos. Just as skilled social beings sift through self-interest, gossip, and speculation, users manage to sort out the personal, commercial, and political interests behind the new media. The measures of digital traffic reveal now what readers once did in newspapers, scanning headlines and skipping to the funny papers. Online news sites promote connections to social media, where the labor of reporting sinks into the background and the tone of news makes it easy to discount. Sensationalism in new and old media exposes the contradictions inherent in news and the peculiar kind of knowledge it produces. Savvy audiences can then take news as a contradictory thing easily dismissed.[37]

Modern news keeps at bay another of its problems, public cynicism toward media and politics, by building trust—a high but likely unattainable aim. The journalist's occupation emerged not long after the discipline of history, but academic historians in most instances rejected news as a primary source that grows from the direct experience of participants in events.[38] Historians' efforts to approximate truth invoked realism by cutting out "secondary" sources that talk *about* events or interpret them. By that definition, news media are secondary historical sources. Journalists found their own ways to approach realist truth, by inventing the interview for witnesses and the press conference to question authoritative elites and by extending the press pass from its origins in the military to enter other official spaces and get records.[39] The emerging occupation also added tools such as the camera, and it earned expertise through following standards, all of which seemed to make possible a positive account of real occurrences. By the mid-twentieth century modern news outlets could make a reasonable claim to public trust. And connections with elites allowed news practitioners to share the stage with powerful actors in politics and society.

At the height of modern news, mainstream outlets held monopolies in the main distribution formats.[40] Whether the power of newspapers like flagships in the Hearst chain at its peak, of radio commentators like Paul Harvey, of magazines like *Newsweek*, or of newscasters like Walter Cronkite was real matters less than the *belief* among politicians, news practitioners, and active citizens that it was. The objections of those left out of news also reinforced the dominant social pattern from the end of World War II until the 1980s. But trust in news media began dropping, and surveys found "The Trust Gap" between citizens and social institutions.[41] Social scientists say confidence in institutions matters to society, but then contrast trust with alarmist terms: a growing *cynicism*, or contempt for institutions, and *mistrust*, the doubt that paralyzes society.[42] Trust in news may seem an asset and its loss an evil, as the choice of terms like *cynicism* suggests, but trust is more complex.[43] It grows from personal experience but changes when extended to society, which involves groups with collective powers unavailable in personal life. What serves persons can harm society. For instance, smart individuals or small businesses reduce their non-investment debt and build reserves to secure their private stability, but more saving in the aggregate tends to produce a higher savings *rate*, a drag on the macro economy.

Practitioners who pursue trust in their individual performance also stand at a distance from what serves audiences in general. A lack of trust in the aggregate may indicate not cynicism but heightened interest in current affairs.[44] In a macro sense, trust in news may decline as citizens think for themselves, employing *skepticism*, a moderate description. When readers place little faith in the press, as Jefferson recommended, distrust could be an indicator of healthy polity.[45] Emerson likewise saw news as mere "circumstance" and called for people to exercise independent judgment.[46]

The pursuit of trust exposes how the contradictions underlying news may have unintended consequences. The more people trust modern news, the less homework they have to do to make sense of the world. Some citizens continue consuming news while disengaging from public tasks, a source of concern, but others instead disengage from news.[47] Audiences who reject mainstream newspapers, news-weeklies, and newscasts may still pay attention to news through digital channels that seem less connected with claims to trust. And citizens may join with others in the hope for trustworthy news, without believing it attainable. The hope may benefit society by animating practitioners' micro desires without materializing at the macro level.

By ministering to its public, modern news opened a kind of misrecognition that distanced it from its profane roots in the realism of daily life.[48] Its self-promotion may have contributed a share to the polarization, extremism, and doubt that worry observers, but are the bugaboos of modern news necessarily harmful? Worries such as partisanship, sensationalism, and cynicism may instead spur the citizenry. Daily encounters with partisanship might teach voters to compare sources and discuss events, looking for consensus. Daily encounters with sensationalism might teach consumers to wink at the media, practicing moderation. Daily encounters with untrustworthy news might teach audiences to depend less on media, practicing self-reliance. The media version of twentieth-century American modernism exposes the contradictions inherent in news, which underlie the current crisis as much as market forces, technical innovations, or the scurrying after scoops. But all is not lost for the purveyors of general knowledge if the labor of news from an earlier era can point to a way forward.

CHAPTER 21

Realism Could Rekindle Hope

In 2013 Rolf Dobelli's pop psychology book, *The Art of Thinking Clearly*, already in translation into several languages, appeared in the United States with a marketing splash.[1] In op-ed and online commentaries, aided by press headlines like "News Is Bad for You," Dobelli described an experiment he tried on himself: he stopped paying attention to the news. His how-to list of ninety-nine things that clutter the mind does include daily news, but the marketing effort went further. Users could download a longer essay on the experiment and the problems with attending to news. Reviewers—mostly news insiders—dug out assertions from different chapters to lament the attack on the public usefulness of news, panning the book.[2] But within half a year its worldwide sales exceeded a million copies.

A pitch that gets traction by recommending audiences abandon news casts a shadow over the industry and its employees. And that pessimism seemed justified as software threatened to automate news writing, promising reporters left mainstream news, and news businesses struggled beyond the Great Recession of 2008. In digital times, news no longer worked as it had when editors managed the flow to an audience of opinion leaders and avid followers.[3] In mobile, digital media, reporting and editing of news slipped into the background, and legacy media seemed like dinosaurs about to join other industries in the tar pits of history. The gloomy side of the digital era may trap individuals, groups, and sectors of life in a cultural paradox, a sticky web that the Arachne of fracking capitalism[4] is building strand by strand to extract value from daily living.

In some ways mainstream news may be a relic, but is there hope for its future? One source of optimism is that news practitioners have managed to hold on through a century of tough transitions, a tenacity that also makes news an apt case study of current transformations. Another is that news organizations have been creative.[5] Despite the usual view that legacy media fail to innovate, concrete evidence shows their contributions to the digital boom. News organizations at first built free-access sites online, contributing to the euphoria about the democratic potential of the web. As the internet became more commercial, mainstream news sites joined the competition for traffic, claiming local turf, buying up competitors, and redesigning content to capture more page views for advertisers, but they also allied with information sources like movie houses and sports organizations to reproduce the omnium-gatherum of the old-time newspaper. Ubiquitous links to social media invited readers to clip and send news stories using digital tools, another adaptation from the heyday of print news.

But the main cause for hope may spring from the contradictions of news, which seem to have stymied the lofty strain of twentieth-century modernism without rejecting the down-to-earth strain from nineteenth-century realism. The modernist focus on big-picture explanations from big-name practitioners at big-time media undermines the enduring cultural idea that news provides many small encounters with the human condition. But realist reporting of what happens to the little guy at places nearby remained an attraction for audiences online and on mobile social media and a factor pushing government and political action.[6] News content illustrates the uneven course of modernism and its tensions and contradictions with realism in U.S. culture, which contributed to the misrecognition of the changing content best illustrated in the certainty that news is brief. Brevity marked the early forms of the new journalism with a quality that settled into cultural expectations, but over the century, stories grew longer first in newspapers and then on television after newscasts began scooping the press. They continued that growth across media, even without commercial and visual pressures, such as on NPR.

The change received little attention, although practitioners were clearly adding more words. In the "who," ordinary persons could no longer stand alone in stories, distancing news especially from the laborer or wage worker.[7] Stories lost their common touch despite the sense of realism that reporters gained on the ground during their early careers. But as socioeconomic status and education levels in the occupation rose, stories shifted to modern modes that emphasized abstract groups, supervising officials, and distant experts. The belief in expert knowledge endured at the expense of realist accounts about people. The shift away from persons also accompanied declines in the usual measures of citizen activity and related attention to news, such as newspaper readership. During the span when modernism became ascendant, U.S. news moved away from the substance of realism about persons.

A similar change occurred in the "where." Street addresses disappeared, following cultural shifts in the understanding of public and individual safety but also contrary to the practitioner mantra of making reports "local, local, local."[8] Moving locations farther from the places people live might reflect an effort to address the geographic ignorance of audiences, but it accompanied their waning direct engagement with mainstream news outlets. In television, place-relations among actors in and audiences for events became more complex but overall made anchors and correspondents more central. The transformation followed the modernist penchant for elites to provide broader-based views for citizens and downplayed the realist trust in publics that form around their own issues. Under ascendant modernism, news provided less realism about places.

The "what" might be the most realist of the Ws because news depends on what happens, but events became less abundant in stories. Reports retained some realist effects, but modern analysis crowded out other occurrences. The changes in the "what" were complex and interacted with the "why." News of World War I relied on dispatches that turned out to be a kind of wishful thinking, interpretations based what correspondents hoped events would mean. In the aftermath of that revelation and the discovery of large-scale internal U.S. propaganda, the press refocused on event coverage. But denotative news then came into question in the McCarthy era, when reporting the baseless accusations of a U.S. senator ruined lives and disrupted government while objective standards kept reporters from saying what they knew was happening. Stories then became less centered on events after midcentury. Both the reactions, which seem to contrast, responded to crisis—World War I and the McCarthy era—by seeking much the same end, the high-modern goal to explain events better. Both also asserted news practitioners' role as sense-makers, serving an ideological process that advanced the occupation. Overall a commitment to the abstract strain of modernism pulled news away from realism about events.

The denotative three of the Five Ws tended to move away from realist accounts of events affecting people in nearby places, but in the other two, modernism reigned. The "why" along with the "when" of news transformed as demanded by critics, who for much of the century complained that news lacked enough context and background to make the origins and effects of events understandable and to explain their meanings and significance.[9] Although unrecognized, the time dimension of news grew more varied, enlarging the background in news content over the century. More references to the past and to future expectations, along with references to change over time, fit the modernist understanding of time that stresses the long view. And in the "why," the explanatory element also expanded, adding more about how events work, what causes them to happen, and which purposes they serve. News practitioners no longer wrote as if their main task were to report what happened for the public to process. Instead they presented themselves as modern experts making sense of events and spotting issues and trends. Especially on television, the growth in expressing opinions may have prompted critics to urge news toward further and better explanations. Turning stories toward explanation required expertise, but in interviews, practitioners espoused the realist humility of down-to-earth, episodic news.

Realism lost ground during the ascendancy of twentieth-century modernism in the news. The descriptive facets, "who," "where," and "what," at the center of realism, declined over the century, and the contextual facets, "when" and "why," expanded at the center of the newer modernism. All five Ws had moved largely in a direction opposite from what observers expected, so that news was no longer what all but the best-informed insiders, students, or policymakers tended to assume. At its height, modern news seemed to reveal a great deal about the world without any reflection on the messenger.[10] Practitioners came to stand on a detached, authoritative ground. The use of the opening anecdote[11] emerged as a way to say that the story matters in realist terms, in the places where life goes on. But for the body of the story, news aligned with social sciences, precision data analysis, and other ways for arriving at an abstract account. Other arts and literature had shifted into naturalism and on through other movements, embracing the underside of U.S. life, but news practice resisted efforts to realign news with human expression. Rejecting them helped practitioners retain the hope for progress and helped the occupation retain its claim to serve the public.

But by century's end, U.S. society and concepts of time and space had again entered flux, with publics forming around fleeting issues within mobile, networked space shown in tag clouds and new-media visualizations. Digital society seemed to break with previous realist concepts of stable persons, contiguous places, and concrete events, as well as with modernist concepts of linear progress and expert explanation. Take location services.[12] In the digital era a place comes into existence not because an Internet Service Provider finds a user or brings one onto the network, the way news once brought places into existence for distant others by telling a story set there. No new-media executive can put anyone on the digital map. Instead a place emerges and appears online and on GPS systems when enough users pinpoint and identify its location. A home at the end of the telephone lines in rural America is "no place" on any digital device for about a month after its broadband service goes live. It becomes a location only after multiple users leave tracks using online maps, mobile apps, and GPS to find it. And it disappears if it falls out of use. A worrisome visibility system replaced the old authority system. No one can impose top-down information, but neither has the physical dropped out of play for locations.

For news a similar pattern exists for the "where" and extends to the other Ws of online lives and occurrences. People and events "go viral" because of user traffic, and from it aggregators have found a way to turn a profit. The main search engines operate much as newspapers had after display advertising became a major source of revenue.[13] Selling ad space to department stores could make up for giving away or selling more copies at a loss. Digital businesses hand out free content but make smaller amounts of money from advertisers who want to reach the much larger volume of self-selecting digital views. As conditions changed, news organizations seemed capable of going in any direction, putting all five Ws of content into play online. Their websites left a record of the period, showing they later chose to stay the course of modernism. The patterns for each of the five Ws were strong across the news sites and ran deep in the four topics studied: accidents, crime, jobs, and politics. By 2000 the websites in the study, which differed in size and spanned the U.S. geography, had built online editions that closely matched what they were already doing in print. By 2005 social interactivity was emerging in a new iteration of the web, and the sites had expanded their experimentation online. But by 2010 the content had reverted, returning to the tendencies of the previous century, as leaders of major media called for reporters and editors to recommit to earlier values for news. That advice meant going back to authoritative and explanatory news, aspects of modernism that became more elite when NYTimes.com and ChicagoTribune.com put their content behind pay walls. There a reader of the *Times* online found virtual pages in high-modern design, enhanced with digital navigation, zooming, and interactivity.

For the referential Five Ws, the pattern played out with some variations. The "who" changed to match the length of news. Stories were growing longer in 2000 and ebbing in 2005, but returned to the longer flow by 2010. In the "who" of mobile, digital media, people play a more active role, and the initial increase in persons on the sites seemed to realign news with the zeitgeist, possibly returning news to its realist roots. But over the ensuing decade, fewer people populated stories on home pages and throughout the sites. For the "what," events bucked the long-term trend at first but then returned to the declining levels of the previous half century. The new era seemed to provide access to more events, and the sites did that at first, suggesting a comeback for the multiple occurrences from realism. But here again, the content turned away from that course. And for the "where" of news, places, after a slight reversal, moved more distant from the street address. Place and space interact in contradictory ways under digital conditions, with possibilities that news practice rejected after an initial flirtation. The pauses and accelerations in how news presented persons, places, and events registered a moment when the sites tried new things, some of them concrete aspects of realism, with brief accounts of events focused on persons at local places.

The inferential side of the Five Ws stayed with the modern course online. The context of "when" and explanations of "why" continued moving away from the realist assumption that audiences would make sense of the news for themselves. Collapsing and coordinating time characterizes the digital era, but the "when" of news online *expanded* while coordinating time, so that the trend toward more references to more time frames and periods peaked and then resumed. Producers of news content added points along a time continuum, falling into an incongruity with digital possibilities as well as with the *now*-focus of realist time. Multiple, contradictory, and individual interpretations may have become more available in the digital era, but the "why" of news content pushed forward on the project of providing easy or binary explanations of trends and problems. Following American modernism contradicted how audiences were adapting, making sense for themselves and resisting expectations in the new-media era. Practitioners misrecognized that news had become a powerful interpreter and that people could use new media to resist.

News producers were not alone in that misrecognition. In his 2010 commencement address at the University of Michigan in Ann Arbor, President Barack Obama described citizens actively seeking and sorting out information.[14] He went on to explain—

> That's why we need a vibrant and thriving news business that is separate from opinion makers and talking heads. [*Applause.*] That's why we need an educated citizenry that values hard evidence and not just assertion. [*Applause.*] As Senator Daniel Patrick Moynihan famously once said, "Everybody is entitled to his own opinion, but not his own facts." [*Laughter.*]
>
> Still, if you're somebody who only reads the editorial page of the *New York Times*, try glancing at the page of the *Wall Street Journal* once in a while. If you're a fan of Glenn Beck or Rush Limbaugh, try reading a few columns on the *Huffington Post* website. It may make your blood boil; your mind may not be changed. But the practice of listening to opposing views is essential for effective citizenship. [*Applause.*] It is essential for our democracy. [*Applause.*]

Obama's remarks assert the realism of "hard evidence" but also accept the modernist ideal of the media sorting content into abstract categories. He invokes the usual justification that separating fact from opinion is essential for democratic life. His advice refers mostly to opinion columns, as if elite outlets succeed in dividing the news into two clear categories. His view shows how the nineteenth-century realist and twentieth-century modernist strains of modernism may fuse, but careful thinking about their differences can reduce confusion and point a course out of the current crisis.

In her masterwork, *The Human Condition*, political thinker Hannah Arendt distinguishes between labor and work.[15] In one sense she defines labor as ephemeral and work as more permanent. A cook labors by making everyday foods, where the wider occupation of chefs works within a larger tradition or cuisine that endures. She also defines work as the way humans transform the world into something designed, contrived, or simulated. A builder labors by constructing common-place but authentic shelters, and architects work by applying the artifice needed for memorable or unique structures that give a city or landscape its character. Journalists labor when they go out into the streets, workplaces, eateries, and dwellings to gather stories, then write and edit them to convey what people experience. The labor of news may occur once and evanesce or recur in the round of seasons and anniversaries. Practitioners seem to misrecognize their labor by discounting gumshoe reporting as beginners' drudgery, handing it over to interns, or farming it out to stringers. One way to reimagine news would be to restore the dignity and value of news labor, along with other kinds of labor in society.[16]

Practitioners also misrecognize the work of journalism, treating it as the product of individual effort, achievement, and recognition. The work of journalism builds something larger than any individual. It is certainly more than a collection of stories reprinted in an anthology, although that book may endure for a while, and probably more than inventing a genre such as "explanatory writing" or founding a news institution, although both involve originality and artifice in Arendt's sense. From another perspective, the work of news is centripetal, and its labor is centrifugal.[17] Centrifugal forces flee from, and centripetal forces draw to, the center. Think of centrifugal forces as Ray Bradbury described them in *Fahrenheit 451*, flinging off wasteful thoughts, and think of centripetal forces as gravity in the cosmos, drawing moons to planets and planets to the sun by counterbalancing the outward momentum of their orbital spin.[18] The commercial side of news media tends to be centrifugal, spinning off audience members as individual consumers, but the political side can be centripetal, pulling citizens together toward the center of majoritarian democracy.[19]

Practitioners may misrecognize the distinction by assuming that the work of journalism will flow directly from its labor. But the relation between its work and labor is more complicated because, among other things, the two are opposing forces and involve long-lasting culture on one hand and a short-term interaction on the other. The view of practitioners might spring in part from misconceptions about how audiences watch and read news, especially in the digital era.[20] Citizens may not engage with news in the way Obama recommends, but they are as knowledgeable as they need to be and continue to form into publics around emerging issues. In Dewey's sense, the public is not a dummy. As news grew distant from the working classes and others, audiences found alternatives. Replacing the hope for an attentive and engaged citizenry with cynicism about a browsing audience that skims and dismisses stories makes it even more difficult for news practitioners and outlets to build bridges to the emerging era. Revaluing the labor of journalism might shift responsibility for citizenship back to audiences, aiding them as the main participants in democracy.[21]

The work of journalism first defines what news is or can be, how it should be made, and which uses and purposes it serves. The "journalist" was its first invention, defining the occupation and sustaining that definition for more than a century.[22] By positioning itself in relation to others and society, journalism creates a view of the world, a system of ideas surviving in collective life. That perspective inheres in stories, genres, and institutions, but arises more from shared beliefs within the occupation and society than from individual actions. By the end of the twentieth century, news had become one of the central ways of asserting what *is* and what one can know about the world. Even science was turning to news, having abandoned its ivory tower of a century before to focus on "impact," "outreach," and "communication," to cite the recent language of research funding agencies.[23]

Studying the work of news texts requires going beyond them to the surrounding history and society and below their surface to the philosophy underpinning them, the ontology and epistemology of news. Like any general kind of knowledge, news turns out to have a complicated and contradictory history. One way to understand it is through the intellectual strains from its origins, the intertwining of nineteenth-century realism and twentieth-century modernism. Realism provided a baseline in persons, places, and events, and modernism supplied an overlay of temporal context and explanatory power. But the strains of modernism had unequal influence. The record of content from the invention of the journalist around the 1880s to the aftermath of the digital crisis in the 2010s shows a long if uneven pattern of realism declining into the background as modernism ascended. No matter what new technology, new kind of medium, or new form of market or content competition emerged, news overall grew longer and more abstract, interpretive, and temporally complex. That those involved assumed news was much the same as it had been a century before is testament that journalism is more than an occupation and that its product, news, sheds light on the cultural transformation now in progress.

The reasons for what happened to U.S. news content are complex. At times the changes emerged from occupational conditions and ambitions for those creating news, at times from the economic context for news organs and their goods, at times from the political moves of parties and editors in relation to partisanship, at times from the responses of audiences and publics, and at times from technical changes that seemed to intervene on their own. The causes worked in concert as well as alone—but also in conflict—across the levels of social analysis, and the power relations among levels had critical consequences. Viewing the competing forces using the lens of modernism assumes that they worked through the symbols and representations available in the culture. In that sense, news played a central role in creating the modern world of the twentieth century.

The grandiosity and elitism of modernism are difficult to mourn, but realism presents a different picture. In the latter half of the nineteenth century, when the journalist emerged amid the ideas abroad in U.S. literature and society, its practical realism built on assumptions similar to what emerged in other realist writing of the era: that readers and producers shared an earthy skepticism about reports, enjoyed encountering graphic details and felt motivated by them, and embraced the rough-and-tumble of party politics. News practitioners in the twentieth century produced stories that slowly abandoned those assumptions, distancing the news from audiences who appeared always on the verge of contempt, vulnerable to sensational content, and blinded by partisan politics. The gritty labor of news production, imagined with its original typographic and photographic tools even after they left common use, tended to veil how news transformed. And the process opened a kind of misrecognition, so that practitioners saw themselves doing the labor of reporting while their output did other work, which may have advanced careers or the occupation but also served the modern ideal.

U.S. intellectual life of the late twentieth century engaged in several decades of cultural critique and responded to die-hard realists in a period of "culture wars," which spawned the hybrid *rusé* realism among extremists on the right. Its rhetoric hides a tacit, contemptuous application of constructivism behind lip service to the ideals of observing and reporting on the concrete world. The result is a systematic misrepresentation of knowledge to manipulate public opinion.[24] But by a few years into the new century the severest critics of realism had turned a corner.[25] When French sociologist Bruno Latour, an early constructionist student of scientific practice, paused to ask for a return to realism in 2004, he pointed to a twentieth-century philosopher with expanding influence, Alfred North Whitehead, a mathematician whose later work turned to metaphysics. American thinkers like John Dewey, William James, George H. Mead, and others associated with Chicago sociology developed pragmatism as a philosophy with concrete application, but the Englishman Whitehead took the idea of symbolic interaction to its root. His masterwork, *Process and Reality*, asserts that Western philosophy went astray by considering matter fundamental. He decries the "ingrained tendency . . . to look below what we are aware of for the substance in the sense of the 'concrete thing,'" which "is the origin of the modern scientific concept of matter."[26]

His view would seem to destroy the basis of news in concrete persons or things, but there is more. He also dismisses the possibility of concrete places and times. "What we find in space are the red of the rose and the smell of the jasmine and the noise of the cannon," he says. "We have all told our dentists where our toothache is." It is not the things in a place but the experience of ongoing processes that makes what is. To dismiss time, he argues that the Greek philosopher Zeno "had an obscure grasp" of process in his paradox that an arrow in flight is motionless at any point in time: "The introduction of motion brings in irrelevant details. The true difficulty is to understand how the arrow survives the lapse of time." Not the arrow, its line of motion, or lapse of time makes the arrow's flight but the interaction with human subjectivity. Whitehead's "process philosophy" argues that any baseline "reality" observable in the sciences, for instance, is an illusion because all supposed "objects" are instead processes that humans experience.

Whitehead shares with the American pragmatists and others in rejecting the grand view from the heights of philosophy in favor of a homemade kind of thinking that emerges in experience.[27] People make the world through interactions together, and what they produce, from home life to international cooperation, works because of interaction and not because of "hard" matter or preconceived notions like science or democracy. For news and the belief system called *journalism* that produces it, experience is at the core because people and places are always in process, captured by the idea of events. Whitehead calls events "actual objects" or "actual occasions" and places them at the center, as what humanity grasps in the moment of emotional engagement. They "are drops of experience, complex and interdependent," and "the final real things. . . . There is no going behind actual entities to find anything more real."[28] The shock or amazement in the voice of "news" is much the same, and so process philosophy does two things. It fits with the realist aspects of news but also anticipates postmodern conditions, opening the way to adapt to the digital era. It is not hard to imagine what news-as-process would look like because it is already there in the best of news.

A recent example is *Serial*, the first podcast to win a Peabody award, taking a seat alongside legacy media like CNN, NBC, and NPR.[29] The series is not short, each segment running about fifty minutes and appearing weekly in twelve installments during in 2014. Nor is the event, a 1999 murder in Baltimore, new. Besides the unsolved crime, what makes the content riveting is the sound of everyday people from places surrounding Hae Min Lee, a Baltimore high school student, and her ex-boyfriend Adnan Syed, convicted and imprisoned for her strangling and death. Series creator Sarah Koenig said in an interview, "These are real people with families and lives, who have trusted me with their information or with their anonymity, and so it makes it nervous."[30] The reporters were also frank about *not* having answers and explanations. Halfway through the series, Koenig told *Nieman Storyboard*, "We've always known we don't know exactly how it's going to end." By digging out details without prejudging them, the series producers brought audiences into the making of content, drawing in more than 80 million listeners, who commented on the blog and generated external discussion boards. And the story was not even local for listeners like Ewan McGregor, the Scottish actor. "To say it was addictive is an understatement," he wrote in *Time* magazine. "People were talking about it everywhere you went."[31] It's not about length, or the nuts and bolts of the Five Ws, but about news as a source of knowledge about the world, which comes inflected with assumptions that worked well a century ago but no longer reign supreme. The key would be to imagine the journalist refocusing so that those assumptions continue working today.

Since it first emerged from rumor and gossip in the handwritten and printed news sheets of the fifteenth century, news has always met strong reactions, and that is a strength. The past century of modernist improvement has not made much difference, as the lapses in *New York Times* coverage of WWI and WMD which bookend the period illustrate.[32] War is the ultimate government policy decision, one that the press seeks to mediate in the public interest. But the press and politics are an alliance of two unsavory activities, an irony often lost on practitioners and academics, if not on audiences. News may be great stuff for the people, its excitement over accidents a cautionary tale, its exposure of crime a comfort to the compliant, its analysis of unemployment a daily sermon on work and capital, and its pontificating on politics a foil for the active citizenry. And during times of great danger, the press can steady the nation, as it did in the Great Depression and the most recent of the Great Recessions, which the news helped name.[33] At other times journalists tend to fall into mischief but also into fun, as interviews with reporters and editors demonstrate here. Their line of work should not go away, but if it does, another version of news practice will turn up, producing another kind of news content for audiences to heed and resist.[34]

News content since the Mister Pulitzer era moved away from its roots in storytelling to embrace sense making as the contours of generally available knowledge also shifted from realism to modernism. But the digital spider's era has undermined the position of mainstream news. While promising greater democracy, its web has fed the advance of a new kind of realism, the *rusé* version that exploits the "construction" of facts to serve reactionary elites. News practice may continue aspiring to deliver solid explanations, sound history, and safe predictions, pursuing ends that lend the occupation authority by colonizing the terrain of citizenship. But journalism as a system that once counteracted other -isms could plausibly foster general knowledge another way, by recording real events in the locations of everyday life, telling the stories of, by, and for the people.

THE CRITIC AS ARTIST

There is much to be said in favor of modern journalism. By giving us the opinions of the uneducated, it keeps us in touch with the ignorance of the community. By carefully chronicling the current events of contemporary life, it shows us of what very little importance such events really are. By invariably discussing the unnecessary, it makes us understand what things are requisite for culture, and what are not.

—Oscar Wilde, "The Critic as Artist," *Intentions* (1891)

Notes

Preface

1. Weber 1946, 196–98.
2. See Noel Mwakugu, "Money Transfer Service Wows Kenya," BBC News, April 3, 2007.
3. See Thomas Macaulay, "Hallam's Constitutional History," *Edinburgh Review* 48 (September 1828): 165.
4. The man-dog aphorism is of uncertain nineteenth-century origin.
5. Quoted in Kutrovátz and Zemplén 2011, 282.
6. December 2014. Part 2 chapter edited by Marcel J. Broersma (Leuven, Belgium: Peeters, 2007, 219–34). Part 3 article (vol. 2, no. 2: 84–95) named International Communication Association (ICA) Journalism Studies Outstanding Article of 2014. Part 5 article (vol. 11, nos. 1–2: 98–123) was the first to receive the same award (2011). Part 6 chapter edited by Clemens Zimmermann and Martin Schreiber (Chicago: University of Chicago Press, 2014, 111–14).
7. Quotation from Barnhurst and Mutz 1997. See *Chicago Tribune*, April 10, 1894.
8. See chapter 3. Quotation from Benjamin 1986, 83. See especially his essay on the storyteller.
9. Thanks to John Nerone for identifying the bias and its implications.
10. Barnhurst 1991.
11. Barnhurst and Mutz 1997, 27.
12. See for example, Høyer and Nossen 2014; Esser and Umbricht 2014.
13. See Mott 1942. A Sunday-school example is Trumbull 1888. On Progressive origins, see Errico 1997. On connections to Aristotle and Burke, see Abbot 2004, 50.
14. Kipling, *Just So Stories* (New York: Doubleday, 1902), 63–83.

Chapter 1. Industrial News Became Modern

1. Bradbury 1953, 84–85. On the transformations see Kern 2003. On metaphors see Barnhurst and Nerone 2001; Lizcano 2006.

2. On machine understanding see Juergens 1966. On progressivism and sensationalism see Soderlund 2013. On older "viral" news see Aleszu Bajak, "How Newspaper Stories Went Viral in the 19th Century," *Storybench*, December 10, 2014, www.storybench.org.

3. Barnhurst and Nerone 2001.

4. See Carey 1989, on the telegraph. Quotation from Emma Lazarus, "The New Colossus," 1893. On department stores see Leach 1993.

5. Adams 1918. On electric industry see Hughes 1983; Nye 1990. On rotogravure and news production, see the report The WGN (Chicago Tribune, 1922), http://tinyurl.com/wgn-handbook-1922.

6. On the popular icon see Ehrlich and Saltzman 2015. On the front page see Barnhurst and Nerone 2001.

7. Barnhurst and Mutz 1997. On horoscopes in newspapers see Campion 2009, and compare Adorno 1994.

8. Bradbury 1953, 84–85. On privatization see Williams 1974. On art trends see Minissale 2013. A changeable art example is Jane Ingram Allen, *Every Drop Counts*, Tenri Cultural Institute, New York, May 2008, www.tenri.org. On place and space see part 4 and Castells 2000. On irrealism see chapter 18; McCarthy 1960; Swinford 2001. On physics and mathematics see Shrader-Frechette 1979.

9. On paradigm shift see Castells 2000; Schudson 2011; Jenkins 2008; Jay Blumler, "The Fourth Age of Political Communication," *Politische Kommunikation in der Online-Welt*, September 17, 2013, www.fgpk.de. On reading changes see Maria Konnikova, "Being a Better Online Reader," *New Yorker*, 2007, www.newyorker.com. Quotations from "Paper Industry Facts," 2007, www.cpbis.gatech.edu.

10. Fidler 1997 described mediamorphosis. On trains see Meyer 2009; compare Lule 2001. On the crisis see Barnhurst and Nerone 2013. Michael Crichton, "The Mediasaurus," *Wired*, December 1993. "Legacy media" appeared in Jakob Nielsen, "The End of Legacy Media," *NN/g*, August 23, 1998, www.nngroup.com, and reached general circulation in Joseph Kahn, "Between Wall Street and Silicon Valley, a New Lexicon," *New York Times*, January 1, 2000.

11. On boards and tickers see Barnhurst and Nerone 2001. On the conditions see Tewksbury and Rittenberg 2012; Boczkowski 2005. Quotation from Dean Starkman, "Tracking Digital-era News Quality Declines," *Columbia Journalism Review*, January 14, 2014, www.cjr.org.

12. Sara Dickenson Quinn, "Looking Back at EyeTrack." Poynter.org, March 14, 2007; Garcia and Stark 1991.

13. The project began in 1984 and grew to a dozen studies, which began with newspapers, sampling at twenty-year intervals through a century. Several compared three outlets, either the *New York Times*, *Chicago Tribune*, and Portland *Oregonian* (see Barnhurst and Mutz 1997) or the *San Francisco Chronicle*, (Illinois) *State Journal-Register*, and *Peterborough Transcript*, of New Hampshire (see Barnhurst and Nerone 1991). Commentary reached the mainstream with Michael Kinsley, "Cut This Story!" *The Atlantic*, January–February 2010, 35.

14. For the long period, topics were general enough to appear regularly but specific enough to be identifiable. We began with three to track natural, social, and economic dimensions (Barnhurst and Mutz 1997). Accidents present surprises, often involving nature, and happen with regularity. Crimes offer human interest, and job or employment stories further involve

social actors with economic institutions. The topics proved consistent and reliable. Study after midcentury added politics for comparability. Visual studies followed research on news form that displays content across topics (Barnhurst and Nerone 2001). Coding the Five Ws followed a simple, extensive strategy. The "who" counted individuals, their identification (name and/or description) and role (main actors or victims, direct responders, officials, or outside experts). The "what" counted events mentioned, and the "where" all locations mentioned. The "when" counted mentions of present or past, the future, and change over time. The "how" counted processes, and the "why" any causal explanations. Coders rated length of stories and their position on the range from event centered to meaning centered. Ratings proved consistent across print, audio, video, and web platforms, following protocols for consistency.

15. See part 1. Interviews included a dozen identified plus two anonymous news practitioners, selected through fellowship programs in 2001. They ranged across local, regional, and national media and from old-timers at newspapers, through network newscasters, to new-media reporters. Initial meetings ran sixty to ninety minutes and were transcribed. News stories from archives included any mentioned in interviews and related coverage. Participants reviewed the interview write-up, made corrections, and were invited to review passages of the book manuscript for feedback. Tracking careers involved a decade of periodic correspondence, some telephone conversations, and online searches along with reviews of social media feeds.

16. On ideology see chapter 19.

17. Also called "fallacy of misplaced concreteness" (Whitehead 1929).

18. On the Marxian definition see Althusser 1996. One study is Clark and Monserrate 2011; for other studies see Barnhurst, Besel, and Bodmann 2011.

19. See Thompson 1995; Barnhurst 2002b.

20. Eisenstein 2012; Chartier 1988. On ceremony and print see Jouhaud 1987.

21. See Harvey 2003.

22. From an 1888 letter (Chipp 1968, 60). On the goblet see Beatrice Ward, "Printing Should Be Invisible," speech to British Typographers' Guild, London, October 7, 1930. On style obsolescence see Illich 1973; Nerone and Barnhurst 1995.

23. Chipp 1968, 502. On the real see Orvell 1989. On photography see Barnhurst and Nerone 2001.

24. Holmes, "The Stereoscope and the Stereograph." *Atlantic*, June 1, 1859, 738–48.

25. On mechanical reproduction see Benjamin 1986. For Linotype history see www .linotype.com.

26. A detail of the Englebright photograph appears on the book cover. The full image contains the spectacular stainless-steel sculpture, *News* (1938–1940), soaring above the entrance to what was the Associated Press Building. The artist, Isamu Noguchi, depicts with vibrancy and power five newsmen using machine-era technology: the telegraph, teletype, and telephone along with camera and paper. See www.rockefellercenter.com.

27. See chapter 20. On the value of realism see chapter 21.

Chapter 2. Stories Only Seemed Shorter

1. Gleick 1999, 140. The next quotation is from David Carr, "Magazines," *New York Times*, April 1, 2002.

2. Quotations from Jon Franklin, "When to Go Long," *American Journalism Review*, December 1996, 36–39.

3. The spread of killer bees was a recurring story. The conference arrived from and later returned to Boston University with its founder Mark Kramer. Quotation from Larry Burrough, "The Long and Short of It," *American Editor*, August 2001, 5.

4. Glass, interview with the author, Cambridge, Mass., December 3, 2001.

5. Kinsley, "Cut This Story!" *Atlantic*, January–February 2010, 35. The newspaper study, Barnhurst and Mutz 1997, includes the quotations and citations.

6. Barnhurst and Nerone 1991.

7. See Chapman 2005, a media history textbook that implies journalism remained much the same throughout the century.

8. Daniel Riffe, "A Deeper Look at the 'Superficiality' of Television News," paper presented to AEJMC, Anaheim, California, August 1996; Riffe and Budianto 2001; Daniel Riffe and Lori Spiczka Holm, "A Quarter Century of Television Network News," paper presented to AEJMC, New Orleans, August 1999. The two studies are Whitney et al. 1989; Jones 2008.

9. Hallin 1994.

10. See Steele and Barnhurst 1996, for the following quotations.

11. Results and quotations from Barnhurst and Steele 1997.

12. Barnhurst 2003a; Steve Oney, "The Philosopher King and the Creation of NPR," Paper D-87, July 2014, http://shorensteincenter.org.

13. The study included only regular stories, not roundups and teasers.

Chapter 3. Longer News Turned Elite

1. Koch 1991, xxiii. See the issue titled "Technology Is Changing Journalism Just as It Always Has," *Nieman Reports*, Winter 2000, http://niemanreports.org.

2. Cyra Master, "Media Insiders Say Internet Hurts Journalism," *Atlantic*, April 10, 2009.

3. Barnhurst 2010b; Barnhurst 2012a; and Barnhurst 2013a. The baseline research is Barnhurst and Mutz 1997, and the television study is Steele and Barnhurst, 1996.

4. Barnhurst 2009.

5. Donovan and Scherer 1992, 281.

6. Donovan and Scherer 1992, 302–3.

7. Donovan and Scherer 1992, 273.

8. Donovan and Scherer 1992, 258.

9. Donovan and Scherer 1992, 272, 306.

10. Barnhurst 2010b; Barnhurst 2012a; and Barnhurst 2013a.

11. Quotations from the TV show *Headlines and Sound Bites: Is That the Way It Is?* (New York: Media Studies Center, 1995).

12. Barnhurst and Nerone 2001. The graph represents changes schematically, using numbers of pages as a scale, the other dimensions indicate general directions, not equivalent measurements.

13. McGerr 1986, 134.

14. Kaplan 2002, 107.

15. Kaplan 2002.

16. Kaplan 2002, 131n20.

17. Barnhurst and Nerone 2001. On distant affairs at home see part 4.

18. See Hardt 1998.

19. See part 5.

20. Pasley 2001.

21. On Greeley see McGerr 1986.

22. Matheson 2000, 569.

23. McGerr 1986.

24. Weber 1946, 196–98.

25. See part 2.

26. On Cronkite see Donovan and Scherer 1992. For examples see part 7.

27. See part 6.

28. Pascal 1941, 571.

29. "The Housekeeper," *North of Boston*, 1915.

30. See part 3.

Chapter 4. Groups Supplanted Persons

1. On the *Times* column see James F. Clarity, "Reconciling the Past," *New York Times*, October 27, 1971. On television see "Changing Definitions of News," Journalism.org, March 6, 1998.

2. Quotations from Danielson and Lasorsa 1997, 109. On the brief reversal of 2005, see Weldon 2007; Barnhurst 2012a.

3. Quotations from Barnhurst and Mutz 1997. Groups ranged from small clubs to large institutions, and descriptions included such factors as age, gender, or race, but a person's specific location counted as a place (see part 4). Follow-up studies include Barnhurst 2010b; Barnhurst 2012a; and Barnhurst 2013a.

4. Marx 1965, 8.

5. Quotations from Barnhurst and Nerone 2001, 32–33, 41–42.

6. Ekecrantz 1997.

7. Barnhurst and Nerone 2001.

8. Barnhurst and Nerone 2001.

9. Barnhurst and Mutz 1997, 27.

10. Quotations from Bradlee 1995, 37.

11. On the name and address norm see Ettema and Peer 1996. Quotation from Mills 1956, 71–72.

12. Janes 1958.

13. Feldman 2008; Barnhurst and Nerone 2010.

14. Byron, "English Bards and Scotch Reviewers: A Satire." In *The Complete Poetical Works of Lord Byron* (Boston: Houghton Mifflin, 1905), line 51.

15. Nerone 1994.

Chapter 5. Authorities Replaced Others

1. Hall et al. 1978; Fishman 1980; Ericson, Baranek, and Chan 1989. On the news net see Tuchman 1978. Sigal 1973, showed officials predominated. The later study is Brown et al. 1987. The word-count study is Danielson and Lasorsa 1997; a related study is Barker-Plummer 1988.

2. Gans 1979.

3. Whitney et al. 1989, updated in Jones 2008.

4. Barnhurst and Mutz 1997.

5. On political stories and changes since the 1990s, see Barnhurst 2010b; Barnhurst 2012a; and Barnhurst 2013a.

6. See Barnhurst 2010b.

7. Whitney et al. 1989. On exemplars see Zillmann and Brosius 2000.
8. Berger 2001.
9. Byatt 2000, 26.
10. Ericson, Baranek, and Chan 1989.
11. Lelyveld 1985, 113.
12. Gans 1979.
13. Stempel and Cuthbertson 1984.
14. Atwater and Green 1988.
15. Jones 2008.
16. Brint 1994.
17. See Danielson and Lasorsa 1997.
18. Barnhurst and Mutz 1997.
19. Soley 1992.
20. Steele 1995.
21. Hallin, Manhoff, and Weddle 1993.
22. David Barstow, "Message Machine," *New York Times*, April 20, 2008.
23. Page, Shapiro, and Dempsey 1987.
24. See part 3.
25. Hugh M. Culbertson, "Veiled News Sources," *News Research Bulletin*, American Newspaper Publishers Association, Washington, D.C., May 14, 1975; Sundar 1998.
26. Gibson and Hester 2001.
27. Hallin 1994.
28. Transcription and quotations from Barnhurst 2003a.
29. Steele and Barnhurst 1996, the source for the quotation.
30. Hallin 1994, 146.
31. Hallin, Manoff, and Weddle 1994. See Hall et al. 1978.

Chapter 6. News Gained Status but Lost Touch

1. Quotations from Grant 1974, 263.
2. Bradlee 1995.
3. Moynihan 1971, 43.
4. The degree research is Rosten 1937; the midcentury report is William Rivers, "Washington I," *Columbia Journalism Review*, Spring 1962, 4–10; the later one is Hess 1981.
5. Weaver 1999; Weaver et al. 2006; Beam, Weaver, and Brownlee 2009. The census puts racial minorities at a quarter of the U.S. population.
6. Mills 1956, 75. Quotations from Dreier 1982, 298. On local powers see Soloski 1989.
7. Hardt 1998.
8. Brint 1994.
9. Mellinger 2013.
10. Byerly and Ross 2006.
11. On diversity efforts see the ASNE.org and annual reports at http://stateofthemedia.org.
12. Gans 1979, 126.
13. Hess 1981.
14. Sumpter 2000.
15. Hess 1981, 126.
16. Weber 1958.

17. Hallin and Papathanassopoulos 2002.

18. Gans 1979, 126.

19. Goldenberg 1975.

20. Sumpter 2000.

21. Gans 1979.

22. Herbst 1993.

23. See "Public Knowledge of Current Affairs Little Changed by News and Information Revolutions," April 15, 2007, http://people-press.org.

24. Gans 1979.

25. Barnhurst 2009.

26. Sumpter 2000.

27. Jacobs 1996.

28. Ericson, Baranek, and Chan 1987, 362.

29. Martin 1988, 986–89, 1043.

30. Hansen 1991.

31. Seymour-Ure 1974.

32. Dautrich and Hartley 1999.

33. Confidence differs from trust, described in chapter 20.

34. "Press Accuracy Rating Hits Two Decade Low," September 13, 2009, www.people-press.org.

35. Mutz 2006; Gentzkow and Shapiro 2010.

36. Eliasoph 1988.

37. Garcelon 2006. "FBI Shutdown of Indymedia Threatens Free Speech," Fairness and Accuracy in Reporting, action alert, October 15, 2004, www.fair.org. See https://docs.indymedia.org.

38. Owens 2008.

39. Mitchelstein and Boczkowski 2009.

40. On newspaper online market actions see Barnhurst 2002a. On digital news see Tewksbury and Rittenberg 2012.

41. Emerson 1841, 41. A sensitive study from the perspective of voters is Coleman 2013.

42. Barnhurst 2003b.

43. Barnhurst 2003b.

44. Leibler, Schwartz, and Harper 2009.

45. Grant 1974, 263.

46. Feldman 2008.

47. Zelizer 1992.

48. Sumpter 2000.

49. Levy 1981.

50. Robbins 1993.

51. Eco's remarks are from Authors and Artists After Hours, Public Square, Chicago, October 19, 2002.

52. Bourdieu 1990.

Chapter 7. Events Dwindled in Print Stories

1. Irwin 1969, 34. See also Reese and Ballinger 2001.

2. White 1950.

3. Iyengar (1991) investigated episodic news.

4. Winburn 2003, 114.

5. Rosenblum 1981, 3.

6. See Floyd Abrams, "The Press, Privacy and the Constitution," *New York Times Magazine*, August 21, 1977, 12.

7. Rosenblum 1993, 9.

8. Rosenblum 1981, 14.

9. Alex Williams, "Overfeeding on Information," *New York Times*, October 10, 2008.

10. See "Online Papers Modestly Boost Newspaper Readership," July 30, 2006, and compare other years at www.people-press.org, and "The Mobile Difference," March 25, 2009, www.pewinternet.org. On crises see Fuller 2010.

11. On workers see Mike Walsh and Michele Vivons, "New Survey Reveals Extent, Impact of Information Overload on Workers," October 20, 2010, www.multivu.com. On the young see Bree Nordenson, "Overload!" *Columbia Journalism Review*, November–December 2008, www.cjr.org.

12. Jack Rosenthal, "What to Do When News Grows Old Before Its Time," *New York Times*, August 8, 2004.

13. Barnhurst and Nerone 2001.

14. Barnhurst and Mutz 1997.

15. Fishman 1980; Schudson 2001.

16. Irwin 1969, 8, 30, 36.

17. Feldman 2008.

18. Sinclair 1936, 412; Goldstein 1989, 157.

19. "A Test of News," *New Republic*, August 4, 1920, 2–3.

20. Frederick Lewis Allen, "Newspapers and the Truth," *Atlantic*, January 1922, 44.

21. Mock and Larson 1968; Sproule 1987.

22. Mott 1952.

23. Casey 1963, xi; the source for Davis information.

24. Kuhn 1996, 113.

25. Vaihinger 1968.

26. Lippmann 1922, suggested the stereotype, for instance.

27. Vaihinger 1968. The classic study is Molotch and Lester 1974.

28. Molotch and Lester 1974, 101, citing Dewey 1927.

29. Molotch and Lester 1974.

Chapter 8. The "What" Waned in Broadcast News

1. James F. Widner, "Radio News," *Old Time Radio*, www.otr.com.

2. Quotations from Casey 1963, 57, 61–64.

3. Marcus and Marcus 1998, 149–50.

4. Quotations from Casey 1963, 79–80, 84, 91.

5. Mott 1952, 31.

6. Griffith 1970, 318.

7. Riffe and Budianto 2001, 23, 25.

8. Project for Excellence in Journalism, "Network TV," www.stateofthemedia.org/2006.

9. See Steele and Barnhurst 1996.

10. Barnhurst 2003a.

11. See Donovan and Scherer 1992.

12. Chafets 1990, 30, 63.

13. Laura Pierce, "Crime Stories, You and Kent," *Kent Reporter*, January 22, 2010.

14. Rosenblum 1993, 1.

15. Phyllis Lyons, "Making World News Matter in Hometown Daily USA," *Freedom Forum Online*, December 8, 1998, www.freedomforum.org.

16. Chris Roush, "Unheeded Warnings," *American Journalism Review*, December–January 2009, www.ajr.org.

17. Casey 1963, 51, 82.

18. Irwin 1969, 30.

19. Alterman 2003.

20. See Gitlin 1980; Gitlin 1987; Iyengar 1991.

21. Jane Feinberg, "How Framing Influences Citizen Understanding of Public Issues," March 2009, www.frameworksinstitute.org.

22. Paul Bedard, "Media Graveyard: Hard News 'In Danger,'" *Washington Examiner*, November 11, 2011, www.washingtonexaminer.com.

23. Ranney 1983, 18.

24. Goldberg 2001, 15–18.

25. Hellmann 1981.

26. Boyle and Hoeschen 2001.

27. See Darcia Narvaez, "Myths about Circumcision You Likely Believe," *Psychology Today*, September 11, 2011, www.psychologytoday.com.

28. White 1970.

29. *New York Times*, August 31, 2001.

30. Winburn 2003, 105.

31. Jeff Madrick, "The Business Media and the New Economy," R-24, Shorenstein Center, Harvard, December 2001, http://shorensteincenter.org.

32. "Early Scrutiny," *New York Times*, January 28, 2002.

33. "The Times and Iraq," *New York Times*, May 26, 2004; "A Mea Culpa, and a Debate," May 27, 2004; Howard Kurtz, "The Post on WMDs: An Inside Story," *Washington Post*, August 12, 2004.

34. Lakatos 1974, 137. See also Katz 1989.

Chapter 9. Modern Events Resumed Online

1. Quoted in Terry Gross, "Alex Jones on *Losing the News*, and Why It Matters," *Fresh Air*, NPR, August 18, 2009, www.npr.org; Jack Shafer, "Ink Hole," Slate.com, August 27, 2009.

2. "Sustaining Quality Journalism," *Dædalus*, Spring 2010, 39, 43.

3. See chapter 20.

4. Mears 2009, 424.

5. Barnhurst 2010b.

6. Barnhurst 2013a.

7. Pew Project for Excellence in Journalism, "State of the News Media 2006," March 13, 2006, http://stateofthemedia.org. See also James Rainey, "More News Outlets, Fewer Stories," *Los Angeles Times*, March 13, 2006.

8. See issue titled "Technology Is Changing Journalism," *Nieman Reports*, Winter 2000, http://niemanreports.org.

9. Barnhurst 2002a.

10. Ross 1998; compare Marriott interview, part 2.

11. Barnhurst 2012a.

12. "Understanding the Participatory News Consumer," March 1, 2010, www.journalism .org and www.pewinternet.org.

13. Mulkay 1979, 35.

14. "Changes at the *New York Times*," *Daily Briefing*, 2003, www.journalism.org.

15. Mulkay 1979, 46.

16. See Daniel Zwerdling, "Shattered Myths," *Gourmet*, August 2004, 72–73, 126.

17. "The Times and Iraq," *New York Times*, May 26, 2004.

18. Juntunen and Väliverronen 2010.

19. Mulkay 1979.

20. Romano 2012.

21. Knorr-Cetina 1981.

22. Hacking 1990.

23. Barnhurst 2007b.

24. Barnhurst and Nerone 2002.

25. Further discussion and quotations from Hacking 2000, 4, 23.

26. Darnton 1975, 192.

27. Hall et al. 1978, 57.

28. Hartley 1996; Esch 1999.

29. "Love and Race Caught in the Public Eye," *Chronicle of Higher Education*, June 8, 2001, B9.

30. Lewis and Ardizzone 2001.

31. Nora Ephron, "Telling a Story," Narrative Journalism Conference, Cambridge, Mass., November 30, 2001.

Chapter 10. Local Lost Ground to Distant News

1. Desmond 1937, vii, 96.

2. Schulten 2001.

3. Hamilton 1988, 152, 154.

4. Markel and March 1976, 16.

5. *Foreign Affairs* editor James F. Hoge Jr., "Foreign News: Who Gives a Damn?" *Columbia Journalism Review*, November/December 1997, 49.

6. Bree Nordenson, "Overload!" *Columbia Journalism Review*, November–December 2008, www.cjr.org.

7. Lippmann 1922, 332. Foreign news bounced up and down from 1910 to 1940 (Mott 1942, 64).

8. Desmond 1937, xxiv, quotes Harold Laski.

9. Kaplan 1979.

10. Lent 1977.

11. Hamilton 1988, 5.

12. "ABC, CBS, NBC, Downsizing Overseas Bureaus, Discuss Shared Effort with CNN," AP, October 27, 1998.

13. For industry see John Maxwell Hamilton, "The Great Experiment," *American Editor*, Spring 2009, 8; "backing away" quotation from Sherry Ricchiardi, "Covering the World," *American Journalism Review*, December/January 2008, 32; lament from Marisa Guthrie, "News Purges Cutting Into Muscle," *Broadcasting and Cable*, March 1, 2010, 4.

14. Hamilton 1988, 5–6. "Local" is within the news outlet's audience as employed here.

15. See www.latimes.com.

16. Rem Reider, "Retreating from the World," *American Journalism Review*, June/July 2007, 6.

17. Kliesch 1991; Hamilton and Jenner 2004.

18. Carey 1989, 152.

19. Polelle 1999.

20. Kern 2003, 132.

21. Buchanan 2009.

22. Rantanen 1997.

23. Brooker-Gross 1985.

24. Barnhurst and Nerone 1999.

25. Carey 1989.

26. Soja 1989.

27. For U.S. flows see Husselbee and Stempel 1997; for foreign flows see Walmsley 1980. Historical studies include Woodward 1930; IPI 1953; Kayser 1953; Hester 1971; Wu 1998. On the metaphor see Hjarvard 1995. On gatekeepers see White 1950; Galtung and Ruge 1981, 52–63; Hester 1978. On the news hole see Bogart 1992; Riffe et al. 1994; Wu 1998. On news-flow predictors see Östgaard 1965; Hester 1971; Roessler 2004.

28. Compare Gerbner and Marvanyi 1977; Emery 1989; Riffe et al. 1994. For Europe see Wouters 2009. Television news flow research suffers similar problems see Hester 1971; Nordenstrang and Varis 1974; Larson and Hardy 1977; Norris 1995. For an industry view see "Year in Review 2008," Tyndall Report, http://tyndallreport.com. Parallel research looks at foreign correspondents: see Wilhelm 1963; Onu 1979; Kliesch 1991. But the foreign corps waxes and wanes slowly, and U.S. organizations rely on others—U.S. and foreign nationals—for reporting. On how news flows influence the public see Tichenor, Donohue, and Olien 1970; Althaus, Cizmar, and Gimpel 2009. A thorough study is Gonzenbach, Arant, and Stevenson 1992; and see Weaver Porter, and Evans 1984. The editor quotation is from Markel and March 1976, 53.

29. Hjarvard 2000.

30. On the ideology behind news see Relph 1976; Hartley 1982; Tunstall 1999; Golding and Elliott 1999; and compare Corner 2001. On the free information flow see Schiller 1974; on free trade and Canada see Carey 1989.

31. Gerbner and Marvanyi 1977; Stevenson 1996; Robert L. Stevenson, "Other Research and the World of the News," appendix 5, *Foreign News in the Media: International Reporting in 29 Countries*, 71–80, IAMCR Report (Paris: UNESCO, 1985).

32. Gonzenbach, Arant, and Stevenson 1992, 71.

33. Barnhurst and Mutz 1997, includes quotations in subsequent paragraphs.

34. "Sierra Leone Cleans Up after War," AP, August 30, 1999.

35. "In Freetown, a Faded Remnant of Colonial Gentility Quietly Crumbles," AP, September 14, 1999.

36. "Hoping for Peace, Sierra Leone Grudgingly Accepts Its Torturers," AP, September 4, 1999.

37. "Background of Sierra Leone Rebels," AP, January 7, 1999. Quotation from Auletta 2003, xvii.

38. "Joy of Youth, Pain of War: Sierra Leonean Girl Endures with a Smile," AP, October 17, 1999; "Children of Sierra Leone's War Find One Small Haven," AP, October 21, 1999.

Chapter 11. Newscasters Appeared Closer

1. Hero 1959, 6. On department stores see Leach 1993; on radio in stores see Victor Rawlings, "Radio in Department Stores," *Radio News*, December 1921, 485.

2. Peterson 1956, 392. On how form and content registered space transformations see Buchanan 2009. On pictures in the news see Barnhurst and Nerone 2001. On photography and space see Schwartz and Ryan 2003.

3. "Middletown Revisited, with Ben Wattenberg," WIPB/PBS-TV, Muncie, Indiana, April 28, 1982.

4. Hamilton 1988, 1.

5. Phyllis Lyons, "Making World News Matter in Hometown Daily USA," *Freedom Forum Online*, December 8, 1998, www.freedomforum.org.

6. "Going Local, Not AWOL," *Editor and Publisher*, December 1, 2006, 19.

7. "Local TV: Good News after the Fall," Pew Research Center, http://stateofthemedia .org. The CPB announcement is in "Citing Newspaper Reporting Void," *Editor and Publisher*, March 31, 2010, www.editorandpublisher.com.

8. Hutchinson 1946, 227.

9. Hutchinson 1946, 227.

10. Jennings quoted in Hamilton 1988, xii–xiii. Quotation from Tom Rosenstiel, "Special Report: Local TV News," *Columbia Journalism Review*, November/December 2002, 92.

11. Barnhurst and Steele 1997.

12. Steele and Barnhurst 1996.

13. Zelizer 1990; Raymond 2000.

14. Huxford 2007.

15. Dominick 1977; Whitney et al. 1989; Jones 2008.

16. Relph 1976, 111.

17. Danielson and Lasorsa 1997.

18. Althaus, Cizmar, and Gimpel 2009.

19. Barnhurst 2003a.

20. McCourt 1999, 183.

21. See for instance Bennett 2008.

22. Bender et al. 2010, 110.

23. Campbell 2004 summarizes nearness concepts.

24. Traquina 2004, 97.

25. Tuchman 1978.

26. On networks see, for reporters, Larson 1984; for others, Lefebvre 1991.

27. Hallin 1986.

28. On placelessness see Meyrowitz 1985. On pliable distance see Williams 1989.

29. On malleability see Williams 1989, on rootlessness see Relph 1976, and for its emergence see Soderlund 2013.

30. Howe 2009. See part 2 on changing demographics of news workers.

31. Gerbner, Morgan, and Signorielli 1976; Tuchman 1978; Shapiro 1999.

32. Boltanski 1999.

33. Friedland 1992.

34. Kern 2003, 132.

35. Relph 1976.

36. Epstein 1973.

Chapter 12. News Traded Place for Digital Space

1. Crichton, "Mediasaurus," *Wired*, December 1993, www.wired.com.

2. "On Line or Not, Newspapers Suck," *Wired*, September 1994.

3. "Understanding the Participatory News Consumer," Project for Excellence in Journalism, March 1, 2010, www.pewinternet.org.

4. Saul Hansell, "The Monster That's Feasting on Newspapers," *New York Times*, March 24, 2002.

5. Singer 2001.

6. Mark Fitzgerald, "Newspaper Ad Slump," *Editor and Publisher*, September 7, 2010, www.editorandpublisher.com.

7. UChannel, December 8, 2008, www.youtube.com.

8. Barnhurst 2010b; Barnhurst 2012a; and Barnhurst 2013a.

9. *New York Times*, "The A.F.L.-C.I.O. Organizes in Cambodia," July 12, 2001.

10. Barnhurst 2002a.

11. Riley et al. 1998, jcmc.indiana.edu, is the ethnographic study.

12. Katherine Fulton, "A Tour of Our Uncertain Future," *Columbia Journalism Review*, March/April 1996, 19.

13. Innis 1964, 129.

14. Carey 1989.

15. Lefebvre 1991; Harvey 1989. On experience and information see Burgess and Gold 1985.

16. Lippmann 1922, 133.

17. On authenticity see Morris 1988. On location indifference see Kellerman 1984, 231.

18. Castells 2000, 428.

19. Foucault 1999, 237.

20. Hegel 2002, 247; see also Anderson 1991, and compare Nietzsche's view in Harvey 1989.

21. Relph 1976, 82.

22. George Garneau, "Foreign News Grows, but It Is Reported Here Less," *Editor and Publisher*, February 10, 1990, 18, 51; see also "Age Before Beauty," *Editor and Publisher*, October 1, 2008, www.editorandpublisher.com.

23. Gilliam, Valentino, and Beckmann 2002.

24. On foreign news demand see Cohen et al. 1996. On shifts to consumer perspectives see Gimpel and Schuknecht 2003.

25. Martin 1988. On community ties see Neveu 2002.

26. See for example Martin Kaplan and Matthew Hale, "Local TV Coverage of the 2000 General Election," Norman Lear Center, USC Annenberg, February 2001.

27. On overstatement see Neveu 2002. On local news success see Hjarvard 1995; "Local TV: Good News after the Fall," Project for Excellence in Journalism, 2011, http://stateofthemedia.org.

28. Crang and Thrift 2000.

29. Shapiro 1999, 159.

30. Burgess and Gold 1985.

31. Morris 1988, 3.

32. Lule 2001.

33. Virilio 1986; Seamon and Sowers 2008.

34. Carey 1989, 168.
35. *Quill*, May/June 1996, 16.
36. Flournoy and Stewart 1997, 203.

Chapter 13. The Press Adopted Linear Time

1. April 24, 1989, 58–67.
2. Kurtz 1998, 322.
3. Alpert 2007, 301.
4. March 6, 2007, washingtonpost.com.
5. May–June 2004, 65–66.
6. May 2007, 36.
7. Toffler 1970, 147.
8. Gitlin 1980, 235–36.
9. Schor 1991, 5.
10. Stille 2002, xv. See also Parkes and Thrift 1980.
11. Rifkin 1987.
12. Barnhurst and Mutz 1997.
13. All quotations from Wilson 1985, 26–28.
14. See O'Malley 1990 on "classic"; Thompson 1967 on agriculture; May and Thrift 2001 on age; Adam 1990 on Augustine; Winfield and Hume 2007 on magazines.
15. Adam 1999.
16. Winfield and Hume 2007; Väliverronen 2003.
17. Wilkie 1891, 323.
18. Rifkin 1987.
19. Wilson 1985, 26, 38, and 31.
20. Robertson 1930, 25. See also Campbell and Wolseley 1949.
21. Chambers 1921, 81–90.
22. "News: The Story of How It Is Gathered and Printed," New York Times Company 1937, 10.
23. MacNeil 1945, 126–27, 129.
24. Giddens 1987; Lawrence 1971 (1993). On earlier time reckoning see Nilsson 1920.
25. "Advice to a Young Tradesman" in *Poor Richard's Almanack* (1748). On time as commodity see Bauman 2000.
26. Schivelbusch 1986.
27. May and Thrift 2001.
28. Ferrarotti 1990, 92.
29. Kern 2003; Rifkin 1987. Data from Barnhurst and Mutz 1997. See part 3 for events, part 4 for foreign coverage, part 2 for officials.
30. Nerone and Barnhurst 1995.
31. On communication biases see Innis 1951. On professionalization see Barnhurst 2013b.
32. Barnhurst and Nerone 1999.
33. Neal 1947, 55–56.
34. Census Bureau (1976, 810, series 246) reports 1,610 dailies for the 1890s, a 61 percent increase to 2,600 newspapers in the 1910s, and a 68 percent decrease to 1,766 dailies by the 1960s.
35. But see Rantanen 2009.
36. *Seattle Times*, July 8, 1995; August 20, 1995.

37. "61 Acres and Counting," *Seattle Times*, August 27, 1995.

38. *Seattle Times*, September 5, 1995; September 11, 1995; and for results September 20, 1995.

39. *Seattle Times*, March 29, 1997; September 26, 1997; October 17, 1997. Front-page story, "Gun Measure Isn't as Simple as Seems," October 26, 1997. For context on her editor's feedback see lead-up, October 27, 1997; October 29, 1997; and follow-up: "Handgun Proposal Is Trounced," and "Voters Mostly Say No," November 5, 1997.

Chapter 14. Newscasters Seemed More Hurried

1. Quoted in Slide 1987, 107.
2. Barkin 2003.
3. Cunningham 1995, 61.
4. Marlane 1999, 113.
5. Buzenberg and Buzenberg 1999, 54.
6. See part 4; Barkin 2003.
7. On Simpson see Hilliard and Keith 2005. On the news race see "The Cable News Battle," *Television Quarterly*, Fall 1997, 49–53.
8. Plasser 2005.
9. "*60 Minutes*: A Candid Conversation," *Playboy*, March 1985, 160, 168.
10. Albright 2001, 105.
11. Seib 2009.
12. Steele and Barnhurst 1996.
13. Hallin 1994.
14. See part 1.
15. Quoted from "Satellite Extravaganza," *American Journalism Review*, September 2001, 51; see also "The Rise and Rise of 24-hour Local News," *Columbia Journalism Review*, November–December 1998, 54–57; "Great Expectations," *Broadcasting and Cable*, July 19, 2004, 26; and Seib 2001.
16. Barnhurst and Steele 1997.
17. Galtung and Ruge 1965. See also Fowler 1991; Schulz 1982.
18. For U.S. research see Tuchman 1978; Gans 1979; Fishman 1980.
19. Roshco 1975.
20. Manoff and Schudson 1986.
21. Peters 2012.
22. Hall 1983.
23. Jaworski, Fitzgerald, and Morris 2003, 47.
24. Niblock and Machin 2007.
25. Schlesinger 1977, 348, 339.
26. Lewis, Cushion, and Thomas 2005, 465, 467–68.
27. Hall 1980; Gell 1992.
28. Across researchers, media, and audiences see Line 1979; Donnelly and Blaney 2003; and compare Knox 2007.
29. Wilson 1999, 171.
30. Quotations from Dayan and Katz 1992, 89, 91. See also Pantti and Sumiala 2009.
31. van Loon 1997, 96. See Stam 1983 on genre; Marriott 1996 on tense; Feuer 1983 on liveness.
32. Hall et al. 1978, 58. See also van der Poel 1997; Pan et al. 2001; and Ricoeur 1984.

33. *San Francisco Chronicle*, September 6, 1991; September 17, 1991; October 3, 1991.

34. November 25, 1992; see also December 14, 1992; April 19, 1993.

35. The station later affiliated with Fox: see *Chronicle*, November 9, 2001.

Chapter 15. News Online Reentered Modern Time

1. Vonnegut 1969, 20.

2. Castells 2000.

3. Alter 2000, 89–90.

4. Kansas and Gitlin 1999, 73.

5. *New York Times Magazine*, Sunday, June 3, 2001, 17.

6. Rheingold 2003, 197.

7. *Quill*, September 2004, 40; and see *Quill*, "Time-Saving Tips," May 2006, 26.

8. *Nieman Reports*, Winter 2006, 67, 66.

9. *Media Business*, October 1, 2007, 29.

10. See part 1.

11. Plasser 2005, 59.

12. See Briggs 1982 on social science; Wicks and Kern 1995 on cycles; and, for quality, Williams and Delli Carpini 2000 on news; Gilboa 2003 on government. See also, on the internet, Thomas Patterson, "Creative Destruction," Shorenstein Center, August 2007, http://shorensteincenter.org; on radio Riffe and Shaw 1990; on agencies, Palmer 2003; on agendas, Ridout and Mellen 2007; on the divide, Greer and Mensing 2004.

13. Barnhurst and Mutz 1997.

14. Barnhurst 2002; Barnhurst 2010b; Barnhurst 2010a; Barnhurst 2012a; Barnhurst 2012b; and Barnhurst 2013a.

15. Jenson White 2008.

16. Lacy and Bernstein 1988.

17. See Ballard and Webster 2008 on time management; Kern 2003 on modern time. Memetracker.org includes research on internet time.

18. Rifkin 1987.

19. Compare Anderson 1991 on Hegel's view of news and prayer.

20. Harvey 1989, 322. On news form see Barnhurst and Nerone 2001.

21. Castells 2000, 467, 465.

22. See Nowotny 1992.

23. Peters 2011.

24. See Bergmann 1992 on time sociology

25. See Berger and Luckmann 1966.

26. See Nowotny 1994 on women; Fraser 2003 on groups.

27. Crichton 1999, 108. See Adam 1988 on clock time.

28. See Nowotny 1992. See also Bergmann 1992.

29. Adam 1988, 218.

30. Adam 1999; Adam 2004.

31. Bell 1995. On occurrences see part 3.

32. Adam 2004, 66.

33. Barnhurst and Owens 2008; Barnhurst and Nerone 2001; Nerone 2014.

34. Carey 2007, 8.

35. Adam 2004, 97.

Chapter 16. The Press Grew More Interpretive

1. "Future of Journalism," Hearings, U.S. Senate Committee on Commerce, Science, and Transportation, Washington, May 6, 2009, commerce.senate.gov.

2. "Future of Journalism," Hearings, commerce.senate.gov/HuffingtonTestimony FutureofJournalism.pdf.

3. John Nichols and Robert McChesney, "The Death and Life of American Newspapers," *Nation*, April 6, 2009, 18.

4. Rodney Benson, "Journalism, French and American Style," *PressThink*, December 5, 2003, archive.pressthink.org

5. Väliverronen and Kunelius 2012.

6. Adkins-Covert et al. 2000, 241–42. See also Fink and Schudson 2014.

7. See Stauber and Rampton 2002; Weaver 1994; "Net Is New Political Ground," *Times-Picayune*, October 11, 1998.

8. "The News and What It Means," *Times-Picayune*, December 28, 1997.

9. Crossen 1994.

10. David Shaw, "On Your Day's To-do List, Is Reading the Paper a Must?" *Los Angeles Times*, October 27, 2002, latimes.com.

11. Fuller 1996, 30.

12. Fuller, "What Is Happening to News?" *Dædalus*, Spring 2010, 111. See also Fuller 2010.

13. Barnhurst and Mutz 1997, 33 (figure), and for examples and quotations.

14. For staff details and opinion in *Time* see Wilner 2006; Brinkley 2010.

15. American Society of Newspaper Editors convention, Washington, D.C., April 28–29, 1933, 74.

16. "Changing News Values in a Fumbling World," *Quill*, August 1934, 10.

17. "Newspapers in Flux," *Quill*, March 1936, 4.

18. Winter and Shapiro 1962, xiii.

19. Raoul de Roussy de Sales, "Notes on American Newspapers." *Atlantic*, January 1937, 30–31.

20. MacDougall (1938) 1972, v.

21. Commission on Freedom of the Press 1947, 4, 16, 22, 58.

22. Wolseley and Campbell 1949, 359, 360. "Interpre*ta*tive" comes from the noun *interpretation*, *interpretive* from the verb, a little-observed distinction that shifts notice away from what practitioners do and onto news as an object.

23. Siebert, Peterson, and Schramm 1956, 74.

24. Coblentz 1954, 47, 139, 74, 191, 148.

25. See Landers 2005 for citations.

26. John Morton, "Great While It lasted," *American Journalism Review*, December 2002, 64.

27. Landers 2005.

28. Shafer 1991.

29. Ogan 1982.

30. "Fight against News Censorship Set Back," *New York Times*, January 2, 1966.

31. A contemporary account is McAuliffe 1978. See Louis Menand, "It Took a Village," *New Yorker*, January 5, 2009, 36–45.

32. See F. W. Dupee, "Truman Capote's Score," *New York Review of Books*, February 3, 1966, 3–5; Dwight Macdonald, "Parajournalism II," *New York Review of Books*, February 3, 1966, 18–24; David McHam, "The Authentic New Journalism," *Quill*, September 1971, 9–13.

33. Lester Markel, "So What's New?" *ASNE Bulletin*, January 1972, 6, 8, 9.

34. How the trends relate deserves study.

35. Quotations from Wicker 1978, 1–4, 16.

36. Christopher Lydon, "I. F. Stone to Suspend 19-Year-Old Leftist Biweekly," *New York Times*, December 7, 1971; Murphy 1974.

37. MacDougall 1972, v.

38. Connery 1992, 5. See also Fishkin 1985; Aucoin 2008.

39. Johnstone, Slawski, and Bowman 1976 identified libertarians favoring neutral roles and social responsibility advocates following participant roles.

40. See Roberts 2008 on history; Lee and Maslog 2005 on later peace journalism.

41. Joseph F. Sullivan, "Wayne College Plans a Peace-Science Course," *New York Times*, March 26, 1972.

42. Machin and Niblock 2006.

43. Everette Denis coined the term: see Philip Meyer, "Precision Journalism and Narrative Journalism," *Nieman Reports*, Fall 2011, www.nieman.harvard.edu, which describes the Detroit example.

44. For other accounts see Meyer 1973; Mosier and Ahlgren 1981; Robert Reinhold, "Computer Joins the Typewriter among News Reporter's Tools," *New York Times*, September 1, 1974; and David Halvorsen, "Entering the Strange New World of Precision Journalism," *Chicago Tribune*, April 25, 1976.

45. See Armao 2000 on "mainstream." On beats see Donald Barlett and James Steele, "Reporting Is Only Part of the Investigative Story," *Nieman Reports*, Spring 2008, www.nieman.harvard.edu. On Watergate see "The *Post* Investigates" and "Nixon Resigns," *Washington Post*, 2009, www.washingtonpost.com; Lang and Lang 1983; Kutler 1990; Schudson 1992; Greenberg 2003. On students see Jan Schaffer, "Blame Woodward and Bernstein," *Chicago Tribune*, March 24, 1974. On IRE see Houston 2010. On abuse see Roger Morris, "The Press as Cloak and Suitor," *New York Times*, May 11, 1974; de Burgh 2000; and J. Carey, "What Does 'Good Work' in Journalism Look Like?" *Nieman Reports*, Spring 2002, nieman.harvard.edu.

46. On skepticism see Barlett and Steele 2008, www.nieman.harvard.edu. On later conditions see Deborah Chambers, "The Changing Context for Investigative Journalism," in de Burgh 2000, 89–107; and survey results in "Investigative Journalism Despite the Odds," *Columbia Journalism Review*, November–December 2002, 102–5.

47. On training see Kennedy, Moen, and Ranly 1984; English, Hach, and Rolnicki 1990. For journalists, interpretive, investigative, and adversarial roles outweighed neutral, information disseminator roles (see Weaver and Wilhoit 1991). On prizes see Harris 2007; www.pulitzer.org; Forde 2007. On civic journalism see Merritt 1998; Rosen 1999; Gade et al. 1998; Lambeth 1992; Charity 1995. Critics include Paul S. Voakes, "A Brief History of Public Journalism," *National Civic Review*, September 22, 2004, 25–35; Max Frankel, "Fix-it Journalism," *New York Times Magazine*, May 21, 1995, 28, 30. On the outcome see Edwin Diamond, "An Experiment That Didn't Work," *Columbia Journalism Review*, July/August 1997, 11–12; Gartner 1997; Corrigan 1999.

48. Philip Meyer, "Public Journalism and the Problem of Objectivity," IRE conference, Cleveland, Ohio, September 1995, tied investigative and precision journalism to public journalism, www.unc.edu.

49. Esser and Umbricht 2014.

50. Lohse examples in *Money* include "Smart Ways to Cut your Taxes," May 15, 1991; tax advice in "Where Retirees Save," July 1, 1992, and "The Greenest Tax Breaks of All Go to

the Self-Employed," August 1, 1992; and tax policy in "Bill Clinton's First 100 Days Could Surprise You," January 1, 1993.

51. Lohse, "How to Beat the Biggest Tax Hike Ever," *Money*, August 1993, 58–63 (protest photo, 58; later quotations, 59–61, 63). G. H. W. Bush used the phrase in 1992 campaigning, footage on *NBC Nightly News*, August 27. Conservative claims include "Media Accuracy Patrol Only Shoots GOP," *MediaWatch*, September 1992, archive.mrc.org.

52. Helen Dewar, "Senate Endorses Balanced Budget," *Washington Post*, March 26, 1980. On the history phrase see Clinton-Dole debate transcripts, *Washington Post*, October 7, 1996. The exact phrase appeared thirty-nine times in major newspapers that year (Lexis-Nexis). U.S. Treasury Department analysis found the 1993 tax fell below top increases since 1942 and tied for third among hikes since 1968, see "Revenue Impacts of Major Tax Legislation 1940–2006," Office of Tax Analysis, 2006, www.treasury.gov.

53. The "bear tax" episode (3F20).

54. Molly Ivins, "Bush Tax Cuts Mean State's Cupboard Is Bare," May 28, 2001, www.creators.com; Robert Dodge, "Congress Passes Tax Cut," *Dallas Morning News*, May 27, 2001; Daniel J. Parks, "Tax Debate Assured a Long Life," *Congressional Quarterly Weekly*, June 1, 2001. Rep. Charles B. Rangel (D-NY) used the argument against Republicans, "Final Tax Bill Contains 'Biggest Tax Increase in History,'" press release, May 26, 2001 (author's collection). See also Jake Berry, "Charlie Bass Says Expiration of Bush Tax Cuts Would Be Highest Tax Increase in History," *Tampa Bay Times*, May 11, 2012.

55. Jonathan Clements and Deborah Lohse, "How to Play the Emerging-Market Meltdown," *Wall Street Journal*, January 13, 1995. Deborah Lohse, "Some IPOs Hold a Fire Sale for Investors," *Wall Street Journal*, June 24, 1996. On the company see Lohse, "Too Little Coverage," *Wall Street Journal*, September 3, 1999.

Chapter 17. Broadcast News Became Less Episodic

1. Wicker 1978, 16.

2. "Within the Context of No Context," *New Yorker*, November 17, 1980, 63–171; Trow 1999, 44.

3. Critics include Robert Jensen, "Embedded Media Give up Independence," *Boston Globe*, April 7, 2003, and Ken Auletta, *New Yorker*, "Non-Stop News," January 25, 2010, 42.

4. Iyengar 1991, 136.

5. See Barnhurst 2013c for a summary.

6. Steele and Barnhurst 1996.

7. See part 2.

8. Quotations from Steele and Barnhurst 1996, which uses conversation analysis to distinguish information from opinion utterances.

9. Henry 1985.

10. Schram 1987, 303–4.

11. Adatto 2008.

12. Levy 1981.

13. Carol Matlack, "Live from Capitol Hill," *National Journal*, February 18, 1989, 390.

14. "A Network Anchorman on the Fate of TV News," *Washington Post*, April 19, 1987.

15. "Networks Look Back at What They Saw," *New York Times*, December 28, 1989.

16. Oxford English Dictionary and Historical Thesaurus.

17. Trends from Barnhurst and Steele 1997. See also Cushion 2015. On the 1992 election see Goldman et al. 1994.

18. Hallin 1994.

19. Patterson 1993; Cook 1998.

20. Graber 1990, 139, 145.

21. Thomas Patterson, "Diminishing Returns," Shorenstein Center RWP03-050, 7, December 2003, http://shorensteincenter.org.

22. Clayman et al. 2010; Heritage and Clayman 2013.

23. Marriott 2007, 699; compare Kovach and Rosenstiel 2007.

24. Barnhurst 2013c; Graber 2006.

25. Doherty and Barnhurst 2009.

26. Sevareid 1995, 178; Seib 2007, 125.

27. Barnhurst and Mutz 1997.

28. Barnhurst 2003a.

29. Barnhurst 1991, 17.

30. Steele and Barnhurst 1996.

31. Bennett 2008; and compare McCourt 1999.

32. Mark Sommer, "Public Radio's Future Depends on Government and Listeners," *Christian Science Monitor*, December 5, 1994.

33. Baskin, "Investigative Reporting," News Media and Politics: Independent Journalism conference, Budapest, October 7, 2000, www.europatarsasag.hu, cites Coors and FDA; other outcomes from our interview.

34. Baskin, "Radon: The Invisible Menace," *Focus 7 Extra*, WJLA-TV, March 22, 1986, follows local reports of February 11–13. See file 3600, www.ire.org. The Peabody went to WLS-TV *Eyewitness News*, see www.peabody.uga.edu. Baskin, "Testing the Drug Testers," February 15–19, 1987; and "Illegal Procedure," January 24–25, 1990, WJLA-TV. See files 5463 and 7366, www.ire.org. See also Sheila Gibbons, "News Layoffs Aren't All Bad for Female Veterans," *Women's eNews*, March 30, 2009, womensenews.org. For industry attention see "CBS Buckles Down over Seat Belts," *Washington Journalism Review*, January–February 1993, http://ajr.org.

35. Baskin, "Just Do It," *Street Stories*, July 2, 1993; Baskin, "Controversy Surrounds Nike" and "Investigation into Nike's Overseas Operations," *48 Hours*, CBS News, October 17, 1996.

36. Greg Rushford, "Nike Lets Critics Kick It Around," *Wall Street Journal*, May 12, 1997.

37. On the audit see *New York Times*, November 8, 1997.

38. On the dispute see Howard Kurtz, "CBS Reporter Creates Internal Furor over Nike," *Washington Post*, February 11, 1998; Bernard Kalb, Greta Van Susteren, and Howard Kurtz, "The Dangerous Backlash against the Media," *CNN Reliable Sources*, February 14, 1998; Larry Stewart, "CBS Woes Go beyond the Ratings to a Swoosh," *Los Angeles Times*, February 15, 1998. Press commentators continued the controversy: Todd Gitlin, "Maybe that Swoosh Was CBS," *New York Observer*, May 11, 1998.

39. Baskin, "Investigative Reporting," October 7, 2000, www.europatarsasag.hu.

Chapter 18. Online News Reverted to Sense-Making

1. Cyra Master, "Media Insiders Say Internet Hurts Journalism," *Atlantic*, April 10, 2009; Mears 2009, 424; Tom Bettag, "Evolving Definitions of News," *Nieman Reports*, Winter 2006, 37; Allegra Goodman, "Lost in the Internet Age," *Boston Globe*, August 18, 2008.

2. Lobato, Thomas, and Hunter 2011.

3. Kovach and Rosenstiel 2001, 77.

4. See comments on Future of Context, SXSW Interactive, Austin, March 2010, www .futureofcontext.com.

5. Early topical media include Digg (founded 2004) and Reddit (2005).

6. Salgado and Strömbäck 2012, 144.

7. Thomas Patterson, "Doing Well and Doing Good," Shorenstein Center, Harvard, 2000, 14, http://shorensteincenter.org.

8. Barnhurst and Mutz 1997.

9. Studies are Barnhurst 2002; Barnhurst 2010b; Barnhurst 2010a; Barnhurst 2012b; Barnhurst 2012a; and Barnhurst 2013a.

10. Wicker 1978.

11. Joseph Epstein, "Are Newspapers Doomed?" *Commentary*, January 2006, 47, 48, 51.

12. Eric Alterman, "Out of Print," *New Yorker*, March 31, 2008, 48–59.

13. The most partisan TV news programs provide the least information; see the Fairleigh Dickinson University PublicMind survey results reported May 22, 2012, at www .businessinsider.com.

14. John Nichols and Robert McChesney, "How to Save Journalism," *Nation*, January 7, 2010, 4, 6. See also Bagdikian 2004.

15. Adatto 2008.

16. See Albert Einstein, "Theory of Relativity Does Not Overthrow Newtonian Creation," *Washington Post*, January 18, 1920; "The Ten Great Discoveries of the New Physics," *Current Opinion*, no. 1 (January 1921); and "Dr. Bohr Expounds Theory of Atoms," Special to the *New York Times*, November 7, 1923.

17. On realism see "Epistemological Problems of Perception" (2007) and "The Problem of Induction" (2010), *Stanford Encyclopedia of Philosophy*, plato.stanford.edu. On the fundamentalist movement see Marsden 2006; on American "common sense" following the Baconian tradition see Rosenfeld 2011. A newer realism emerged by the 1950s (Rudner 1953).

18. On literary realism see Auerbach 1953. See Kaplan 1992 on views of social chaos and improvement; Davis 1983, on the trope of factuality. On social justice, objectivity, and science, Pizer 1998 gives examples such as novelist Henry James's 1884 defense of realism (p. 11) and critic Alfred Kazin's 1930s observation that "realism in America . . . engaged in . . . elementary truth-telling" (p. 217).

19. Trachtenberg 1997, 132; see also Barnhurst 1996.

20. Barnhurst and Nerone 2001.

21. Dewey 1927, 183–84.

22. Boorstin 1961, 33, 5–6.

23. Gombrich 1980, 238; and critic: Mitchell 1991, 25, 33.

24. Cowley 1947.

25. McCarthy 1960, 433, 455–56.

26. See also Kazin 1942.

27. Kaplan (1988) 1992, 7, 13, 160.

28. Berger 1980, 58.

29. See Sontag 1977. A critique of positivism and objectivity is Said 1983; see Orvell 1989. See Perlmutter 2005, on photo manipulation; Haskell (1998) 2000, on objectivity. Examples of public skepticism range from popular (Errol Morris, "Photography as a Weapon," *New York Times*, August 11, 2008) to high culture (Mia Fineman, curator, "Faking It," Metropolitan Museum of Art, 2012).

30. Merchant 2004; see also Toulmin 1983; Gorak 1987; Swinford 2001.

31. Antonio Gramsci, "I giornali e gli operai," *Avanti!* December 22, 1916.
32. Lippmann 1922, 348–49.
33. "The Garden of Forking Paths," *Ellery Queen's Mystery Magazine*, August 1948, 107.
34. Breed 1955, 264, 317–18. Barthes 1972; see also Boudana 2012.
35. Eco 1990, 2.
36. Darnton 1990, 69.
37. Geertz 2001, 179.
38. Hartley 1982; Carey 1988; Carey 1989; Meyrowitz 1991; Corner 1995; Schudson 2011.
39. Strange and Katz 1998; compare critic Fallows 1996.
40. See Bush-era terms in discussion boards such as www.democraticunderground.com.
41. On inequality see A. O. Scott, "The Squeeze on the Middlebrow," *New York Times*, August 1, 2014; Prior 2007.
42. Barnhurst 2009.
43. James Carey, "What Does 'Good Work' in Journalism Look Like?" *Nieman Reports*, Spring 2002. See Carey 1986; Thomas and Znaniecki 1927.
44. See Goffman 1959 for off stage; Thomas and Znaniecki 1927 on social definition.

Chapter 19. Social Values Enabled Change

1. See "U.S. Must Respond with Courage, Resolve," *Kansas City Star*, September 11, 2001, one of eighty-eight uses of the "changed forever" phrase in general news a month after the attacks (Lexis-Nexis). The previous year saw only five uses, all in political-cultural contexts. An early demurrer is William Raspberry, "Suspect Thinking," *Washington Post*, October 15, 2001.
2. On changes to news see Zelizer and Allan 2002. On public responses see Andrew Kohut, "The Press Shines at a Dark Moment," *Columbia Journalism Review*, January 2002, 54; compare Kellerman 1992.
3. From the author's notes. In later remarks Singh, who had a long career in print journalism culminating in six years as resident editor at the *Times of India*, Delhi, called for more analysis and forecasts responding to crisis (White Lecture 2001) and wrote a paper, "September 11 and Its Consequences," WP2002-4, http://shorensteincenter.org. On the new climate of fear see Kellner 2004.
4. Nerone 1994.
5. Kovach and Rosenstiel 2007.
6. On interpretive news see Barnhurst 1991; Salgado and Strömbäck 2012.
7. Barnhurst 2005, 239.
8. Barnhurst 2003a; Barnhurst 2003b.
9. Steele and Barnhurst 1996; Barnhurst and Steele 1997; Barnhurst 2003a.
10. Barnhurst 2005; compare Corner 2001.
11. Hall 1981, 234.
12. Eagleton 1991; and see Gitlin 1980.
13. Althusser 1969 borrowed *over-determine* from Freud.
14. See Barnhurst, Besel, and Bodmann 2011 on youth; Hallin 2006 on resistance; Gibson 2007 on culture; O'Brien 2009 on moral lessons.
15. A term attributed to Engels (see Eagleton 1991, 89) and introduced by Lukács 1971.
16. On the status of news practice see Weber 1958.
17. Latour 2004, 231; see 231–32 on Heidegger and the etymology of *thing*—a gathering like parliament vs. mere object—and on "stubborn realism."

18. See Barnhurst 2013b; Hardt and Brennen 1995.

19. On the journalist in literature see Good 1986; in film see McNair 2010.

20. Hallin 1994.

21. Barnhurst 2005.

22. Mannheim 1985.

23. Loren Ghiglione, "The American Journalist," American Antiquarian Society, Worcester, Mass., October 17, 1990, www.americanantiquarian.org.

24. On the ideal see Courson 1976; a popular view is Casey Pittman, "In the Movies, Journalists Are No Longer Heroes," Observations, 2001, www.ijpc.org.

25. Schofield Clark and Monserrate 2011.

26. Fellowship details and quotations from http://nieman.harvard.edu.

27. Weaver et al. 2006, 55.

28. Few have expected to remain in mainstream news since the 1970s (Weaver and Wilhoit 1996), but even fewer women and minorities, and more managers, say they will (Weaver et al. 2006, 115–16). The surveys do not track those who leave.

29. Lisa Stone, "It's Time We Recognized How Influential Women's Lives Are to News and Media," SheKnows.com, July 16, 2015.

Chapter 20. Modernism Exposed the Flaws of News

1. Angela Dee Kwan, "When Journalists and Technologists Monkey Around," *Medill Magazine*, Fall 2009, 13–15.

2. Rick Green, "Robot Reporters," *CT Confidential*, October 12, 2009, blogs.courant.com. Guy Raz, "Program Creates Computer-Generated Sports Stories," NPR *Weekend All Things Considered*, January 10, 2010, www.npr.org. Steve Lohr, "In Case You Wondered, a Real Human Wrote This Column," *New York Times*, September 11, 2011. Shelley Podolny, "If an Algorithm Wrote This, How Would You Even Know?" *New York Times*, March 7, 2015.

3. Steven Levy, "Can an Algorithm Write a Better News Story Than a Human Reporter?" *Wired*, May 2012, www.wired.com. Andrew Beaujon, "Journalists Debate Value of Robots," *Poynter*, April 26, 2012, www.poynter.org. By 2015 the estimate was ten years (Podolny, "If an Algorithm Wrote This"). Another developer of newswriting software is Stat Sheet in North Carolina.

4. Kovach and Rosenstiel 2007.

5. The logic follows Eco 1989, arguing for open instead of closed texts.

6. See Hardt and Brennen 1995.

7. Epstein 1991, 392.

8. On the profession see Barnhurst 2013b. Schudson 2011, 219, draws parallels between news and the arts "people enter because they love" them.

9. White 1973; Ricoeur 1984.

10. On news origins see Barnhurst and Owens 2008. On form see Barnhurst and Nerone 2001. Some journalists see the problem, "Breaking News Consumer's Handbook," NPR *On the Media*, September 20, 2013, www.onthemedia.org.

11. Jack Shafer, "Journalism Is the 'First Rough Draft of History,'" Slate.com, August 30, 2010.

12. Sridharan, Dickes, and Caines 2002; Howard Kurtz, "The Enron Story that Waited to Be Told," *Washington Post*, January 18, 2002; Kelly Heyboer, "The One That Got Away," *American Journalism Review*, March 2002, www.ajr.org; compare Paul E. Steiger, "Not Every Journalist 'Missed' the Enron Story," *Nieman Reports*, Summer 2002, www.nieman.harvard.edu.

13. Daniel Okrent, "Weapons of Mass Destruction?" *New York Times*, May 30, 2004; Franklin Foer, "The Source of the Trouble," *New York Magazine*, June 7, 2004, http://nymag.com.

14. See chapter 16.

15. Santayana 1905, 284, whom pragmatist William James mentored at Harvard.

16. A gap noted in Boczkowski and Mitchelstein 2013.

17. Morris 1860, 302; the compound included "more bitter sectarianism, and most bitter antimasonry," 302–3.

18. On Pulitzer's views see "Joseph Pulitzer Dies Suddenly," *New York Times*, October 30, 1911.

19. Barnhurst and Nerone 2001.

20. Park 1940.

21. On facts see part 3, chapter 8.

22. See Meyer 2009.

23. See part 2 on imponderable citizens and audience roles. On one-purchase–one-vote see Barnhurst and Nerone 2001. On public opinion see Herbst 1993. On audience opinions see Wahl-Jorgensen 2007. On journalist disdain for sources' events, see Levy 1981.

24. Stephens 1988 suggests ancient antecedents; compare Jouhaud 1987 on *occasionnels* in early modern France. Phenomenology succeeded "sensationism" in philosophy. On sensationalism history see Stevens 1985; Francke 1985; Shaw and Slater 1985.

25. Morell 1846, vol. 1, xi.

26. The first to publish the term was the *Saturday Review*, calling the *London Journal* "that well of sensationalism pure and undefiled" ("Uncle Silas," February 4, 1865, 145, col. 2).

27. See Campbell 2013; Juergens 1966.

28. On Progressive sensationalism see Soderlund 2013. See also Park 1923. On realism in literature see Auerbach 1953.

29. Schudson 2001.

30. On economics see McChesney 1987.

31. For definitions see Sachsman and Bulla 2013; Stevens 1991. On drawing boundaries see Stevens 1985.

32. Sensational news combines racy topics, hyped language, and exaggeration, then adds a moral (Sachsman and Bulla 2013).

33. See Sparks and Tulloch 2000; Lull and Hinerman 1997, especially chapters by Bird.

34. Drake Bennett, "The Sensationalism Sweeping Local News Is Bad for Ratings," *Boston Globe*, October 14, 2007, and Peter Dominowski, "The Local News Project II," *Market Trends Research*, October 2003, www.markettrendsresearch.com/pubradio.

35. Stevens 1985; compare John Zaller, "Market Competition and News Quality," paper presented to APSA, Atlanta, 1999.

36. Schelling 1978.

37. On scandal see Lull and Hinerman 1997; Thompson 2000; on negativity see McGrail 2008. On critics' views see part 6. On sensationalism online see chapter 18. On news and gossip see Pettegree 2014; Barnhurst and Owens 2008. On scanning see Garcia and Stark 1991. Sparks and Tulloch 2000 shows sensation replacing analysis.

38. Townsend 2013.

39. On historians' primary and secondary texts see Mortimer 2008. On interviews and factual news aspects see part 3.

40. Hallin 1994.

41. On declining audiences and engagement see Barnhurst 1997. See "The Trust Gap," *Forbes*, July 2010, www.forbes.com, for commentary from business, philosophy, law, and media on faith in institutions.

42. Alarmist terms occur in political communication research (see Cappella and Jamieson 1997) and in the trade (see Kovach and Rosenstiel 2007).

43. See Luhmann 1979; Misztal 1996; an overview is Barnhurst 2011; Barnhurst 2013c; Wijfjes 2004. On professionalism see Barnhurst 2013b.

44. On trust relating inversely to engagement see Wijfjes 2004; Barnhurst 2011; and Barnhurst 2013c.

45. Jefferson to Edward Carrington, January 16, 1787, http://press-pubs.uchicago.edu/founders.

46. Emerson said a person "of ideas, accounting the circumstance nothing, judges of the commonwealth," 1849, 271.

47. On news practice colonizing citizenship see Carey 1978; compare Pooley 2011.

48. Nerone 2013.

Chapter 21. Realism Could Rekindle Hope

1. Dobelli, "News Is Bad for You—and Giving up Reading It Will Make You Happier," *Guardian*, April 12, 2013.

2. See, for example, Philip Delves Broughton, "Decision Theories," *Wall Street Journal*, May 22, 2013.

3. White 1950.

4. Ian Martin, "Fracketeering," Guardian.com, June 30, 2015.

5. John O'Sullivan et al., "Innovators and Innovated: Newspapers and the Post-Digital Future Beyond the 'Death of Print,'" unpublished manuscript; Barnhurst 2002. See Boczkowski 2005; Anderson 2013; Usher 2014.

6. Young readers find breaking stories attractive: see "Social and Demographic Differences in News Habits and Attitudes," *Personal News Cycle* report, March 17, 2014, www.americanpressinstitute.org. Critical theory wrestles with realist policy in Duggan and Hunter 2006.

7. Nerone 2009. On audiences see Barnhurst 1997; Barnhurst 2000.

8. "Going Local, Not AWOL," *Editor and Publisher*, December 1, 2006, 19. Audiences first left newspapers, then television: see "Trends in News Consumption, 1991–2012," September 27, 2012, www.people-press.org.

9. Patterson 2013.

10. Barnhurst and Nerone 2001.

11. See Part 2.

12. The example comes from the author's discussions with GPS, ISP, and map providers affecting service in rural New Hampshire.

13. Barnhurst and Nerone 2012. On finances underpinning the crisis see Crain 2009; Almiron 2010.

14. "Transcript of Obama's Remarks at U. Mich. Commencement," *Wall Street Journal*, May 1, 2010.

15. Arendt 1958.

16. On authenticity see Orvell 1989. On time see Innis 1964.

17. Carey 1965; Innis 1964.

18. Bradbury 1953, 85.

19. For the press see Nerone 2015, 111.

20. Tewksbury and Rittenberg 2012; on reading see Maria Konnikova, "Being a Better Online Reader," *New Yorker*, July 16, 2007, www.newyorker.com.

21. On audience knowledge see Graber 1990. Dewey 1927 contrasts with unproved claims that calls persons smart but "people" stupid. On alternatives and responses see Ladd 2011; Barnhurst 2000; Barnhurst 2011.

22. See part 2.

23. Funding language appears in National Science Foundation (NSF) and other agency and foundation announcements. The site www.nsf.gov returns 132,000 hits for impact, 106,000 for outreach, and 84,700 for communication, but only 36,400 for evidence and 4,270 for facts (Google, June 2015).

24. Examples include the global warming controversy (see chapter 3) and the abuse of realist language during the George W. Bush era (see chapter 18). Rusé realism includes but is broader than the demand for constant war, which C. Wright Mills called "crackpot realism"; see Pinkindustry (blog), 2007, https://pinkindustry.wordpress.com/c-wright-mills-2.

25. Latour 2004.

26. Whitehead 1929, 18, 21, 68–69.

27. On experience and knowledge see Bachelard 1988, and compare Auerbach 1953 and Steward 2012.

28. Whitehead 1929, 18

29. The series appeared on http://serialpodcast.org; award listed at www.peabody awards.com.

30. The interview is with Louise Kiernan, *Nieman Storyboard*, October 30, 2014, http://niemanstoryboard.org.

31. McGregor, "The Investigator in your Ear," *Time*, April 16, 2015, http://time.com.

32. Barnhurst and Owens 2008.

33. Catherine Rampell, "'Great Recession': A Brief Etymology," NYTimes.com, March 11, 2009, http://economix.blogs.nytimes.com.

34. On the fate of journalism see Paul Starr, "Goodbye to the Age of Newspapers," *New Republic*, March 4, 2009, 28–35, and Victor Pickard, "Wither(ing) Journalism?" *Public Books*, July 1, 2014, www.publicbooks.org.

Bibliography

Abbott, Andrew. 2004. *Methods of Discovery*. New York: Norton.

Adam, Barbara. 1988. "Social versus Natural Time, a Traditional Distinction Re-Examined." In *The Rhythms of Society*, edited by Michael Young and Tom Schuller, 198–226. New York: Routledge, 1988.

———. *Time and Social Theory*. 1990. Philadelphia: Temple University Press.

———. "Radiated Identities." 1999. In Featherstone and Lash, 1999, 138–58.

———. *Time*. 2004. Cambridge, Mass.: Polity.

Adams, Henry. 1918. *The Education of Henry Adams*. Boston: Massachusetts Historical Society.

Adatto, Kiku. (1993) 2008. *Picture Perfect*. Princeton, N.J.: Princeton University Press.

Adkins-Covert, Tawnya, Denise P. Ferguson, Selene Phillips, and Philo C. Wasburn. 2000. "News in My Backyard." *Sociological Quarterly* 41, no. 2 (Spring): 227–44.

Adorno, Theodor W. 1994. *The Stars Down to Earth, and Other Essays on the Irrational in Culture*. Edited by Stephen Crook. London: Routledge.

Albright, Madeleine K. 2001. "Around-the-Clock News Cycle a Double-Edged Sword." *Press/Politics* 6, no. 1 (Winter): 105–8.

Almiron, Nuria. 2010. *Journalism in Crisis*. Cresskill, N.J.: Hampton.

Alpert, Stanley N. 2007. *The Birthday Party: A Memoir of Survival*. New York: Putnam's.

Alter, Jonathan. 2000. "Print Journalism." *Press/Politics* 5, no. 1 (January): 89–91.

Alterman, Eric. 2003. *What Liberal Media?* New York: Basic.

Althaus, Scott L., Anne M. Cizmar, and James G. Gimpel. 2009. "Media Supply, Audience Demand, and the Geography of News Consumption in the United States." *Political Communication* 26, no. 3 (July): 249–77.

Althusser, Louis. 1996. *For Marx*. London: Verso.

Anderson, Benedict. 1991. *Imagined Communities*. Rev. ed. London: Verso.

Anderson, C. W. 2013. *Rebuilding the News*. Philadelphia: Temple University Press.

Arendt, Hannah. 1958. *The Human Condition*. 2nd edition. Chicago: University of Chicago Press.

Armao, Rosemary. 2000. "The History of Investigative Reporting." In *The Big Chill*, edited by Marilyn Greenwald and Joseph Bernt, 35–50. Ames: Iowa State University Press.

Aronson, James. 1970. *The Press and the Cold War*. Indianapolis: Bobbs-Merrill.

Atwater, Tony, and Norma Green. 1988. "New Sources in Network Coverage of International Terrorism." *Journalism Quarterly* 65, no. 4 (Winter): 967–71.

Aucoin, James L. 2008. "Investigative Reporting." In Donsbach, vol. 6, 2529–32.

Auerbach, Erich. 1953. *Mimesis: The Representation of Reality in Western Literature*. Translated by Willard R. Trask. Princeton, N.J.: Princeton University Press.

Auletta, Ken. 2003. *Backstory: Inside the Business of News*. New York: Penguin.

Bachelard, Gaston. 1988. *Air and Dreams*. Dallas, Tex.: Dallas Institute.

Bagdikian, Ben. (1983) 2004. *The Media Monopoly*. 6th ed. Boston: Beacon.

Ballard, Dawna I., and Sunshine Webster. 2008. "Time and Time Again: The Search for Meaningfulness through Popular Discourse on the Time and Timing of Work." *KronoScope* 8, no. 2 (June): 131–45.

Barker-Plummer, Bernadette. 1988. "Look Who's Talking: Trends in Attribution and Sources in Two Elite Newspapers." *Southwestern Mass Communication Journal* 4, no. 2 (Fall): 55–62.

Barkin, Steve M. 2003. *American Television News*. New York: Sharpe.

Barnhurst, Kevin G. 1991. "The Great American Newspaper." *The American Scholar* 60, no. 1 (Winter): 106–12.

———. 1994. *Seeing the Newspaper*. New York: St. Martin's.

———. 1996. "The Alternative Vision." In *Photo-Textualities*, edited by Marsha Bryant, 85–107. London: Associated University Presses.

———. 1997. "Media Democracy: How Young Citizens Experience News in the United States and Spain." PhD diss., University of Amsterdam.

———. 2000. *Political Engagement and the Audience for News*. Vol. 2, no. 1 (Spring) of *Journalism and Communication Monographs*. Chapel Hill, N.C.: AEJMC.

———. 2002a. "News Geography and Monopoly: The Form of Reports on U.S. Newspaper Internet Sites." *Journalism Studies* 3, no. 4 (November): 477–89.

———. 2002b. "Postscript: Beyond the Frame." In John T. Waisanen, *Thinking Geometrically*, edited by Jennifer Daryl Slack, 149–92. New York: Peter Lang.

———. 2003a. "The Makers of Meaning: National Public Radio and the New Long Journalism, 1980–2000." *Political Communication* 20, no. 1 (January–March): 1–22.

———. 2003b. "Queer Political News: Election-Year Coverage of the LGBT Communities on National Public Radio, 1992–2000." *Journalism* 4, no. 1 (Winter): 5–28.

———. 2005. "News Ideology in the Twentieth Century." In *Diffusion of the News Paradigm, 1850–2000*, edited by Svennik Høyer and Horst Pöttker, 239–62. Gothenburg, Sweden: Nordicom.

———. 2007a. "Ideology and the Changing Representations of Persons in U.S. Journalism." In *Form and Style in Journalism*, edited by Marcel J. Broersma, 219–34. Leuven, Belgium: Peeters.

———. 2007b. "Visibility as Paradox: Representation and Simultaneous Contrast." In *Media/Queered*, 1–20. New York: Peter Lang.

———. 2009. "The Fate of Two Stories: How U.S. Journalism Is Forgetting the People." *Journalism* 10, no. 3 (Spring): 282–85.

———. 2010a. "The Form of Reports on U.S. Newspaper Internet Sites: An Update." *Journalism Studies* 11, no. 4 (July): 555–66.

———. 2010b. "Technology and the Changing Idea of News." *International Journal of Communication* 4 (October): 1082–99.

———. 2011. "The New 'Media Affect' and the Crisis of Representation for Political Communication." *Press/Politics* 16, no. 4 (October): 573–93.

———. 2012a. "The Content of Online News in the Mainstream U.S. Press, 2001–2010." In Jones, 2012, 231–53.

———. 2012b. "The Form of Online News in the Mainstream U.S. Press, 2001–2010." *Journalism Studies* 13, nos. 5–6 (Spring): 791–800.

———. 2013a "Newspapers Experiment Online." *Journalism* 14, no. 1 (January): 1–19.

———. 2013b. "The Rise of the Professional Communicator." *Media History and the Foundations of Media Studies*, edited by John Nerone, 463–76. London: Blackwell.

———. 2013c. "'Trust Me, I'm an Innovative Journalist,' and Other Fictions." In *Rethinking Journalism*, edited by Chris Peters and Marcel Broersma, 210–20. New York: Routledge, 2013.

Barnhurst, Kevin G., Richard Besel, and Christopher Bodmann. 2011. "Subjective Posture and Subjective Affluence." *Communication Theory* 21, no. 4 (November): 436–55.

Barnhurst, Kevin G., and Diana C. Mutz. 1997. "American Journalism and the Decline of Event-Centered Reporting." *Journal of Communication* 47, no. 4 (Autumn): 27–53.

Barnhurst, Kevin G., and John Nerone. 1991. "Design Changes in U.S. Front Pages, 1885–1985." *Journalism Quarterly* 68, no. 4 (Winter): 796–804.

———. 1999. "The President Is Dead: American News Photography and the New Long Journalism." In Brennen and Hardt, 1999, 60–92.

———. 2001. *The Form of News, A History*. New York: Guilford.

———. 2010. "Concentrated Power v. Anglo-American Free Expression." *Political Communication* 27, no. 3 (July): 326–29.

———. 2012. "The Media in North America." *The USA and Canada 2012*, www.europaworld.com. Edited by Neil Higgins. Europa Regional Surveys of the World. Oxford: Routledge.

Barnhurst, Kevin G., and James Owens. 2008. "Journalism." In Donsbach, 2008, Vol. 6, 2557–69.

Barnhurst, Kevin G., and Catherine A. Steele. 1997. "Image Bite News." *Press/Politics* 2, no. 1 (February): 40–58.

Barthes, Roland. "Structure of the *Fait-Divers*." (1964) 1972. In *Critical Essays*, 185–95. Evanston, Ill.: Northwestern University Press.

Bauman, Zygmunt. 2000. "Time and Space Reunited." *Time and Society* 9, nos. 2/3 (September): 171–85.

Beam, Randal A., David H. Weaver, and Bonnie J. Brownlee. 2009. "Changes in Professionalism of U.S. Journalists in the Turbulent Twenty-First Century." *Journalism and Mass Communication Quarterly* 86, no. 2 (Summer): 277–98.

Bell, Allan. 1995. "News Time." *Time and Society* 4, no. 3 (October): 305–28.

Bender, John R., Lucinda Davenport, Michael Drager, and Fred Fedler. 2011. *Reporting for the Media*. 10th ed. New York: Oxford.

Benjamin, Walter. 1986. *Illuminations*. New York: Schocken.

Bennett, W. Lance. 2008. *News: The Politics of Illusion*. 8th ed. White Plains, N.J.: Longman.

Berger, Charles R. 2001. "Making It Worse Than It Is: Quantitative Depictions of Threatening Trends in the News." *Journal of Communication* 51, no. 4 (December): 655–77.

Berger, John. 1980. "Another Way of Telling." *Journal of Social Reconstruction* 1, no. 1 (January–March): 57–75.

Berger, Peter L., and Thomas Luckmann. 1966. *The Social Construction of Reality*. Garden City, N.Y.: Anchor.

Bergmann, Werner. 1992. "The Problem of Time in Sociology." *Time and Society* 1, no. 1 (January): 81–134.

Blumer, Herbert. 1969. *Symbolic Interactionism: Perspective and Method*. Berkeley: University of California Press.

Boczkowski, Pablo J. 2005. *Digitalizing the News*. Cambridge, Mass.: MIT Press.

Boczkowski, Pablo J., and Eugenia Mitchelstein. 2013. *The News Gap: When the Information Preferences of the Media and the Public Diverge*. Cambridge, Mass.: MIT Press.

Bogart, Leo. 1992. "The State of the Industry." In *The Future of News*, edited by Phillip S. Cook, Douglas Gomery, and Lawrence W. Lichty, 86–103. Baltimore, Md.: Johns Hopkins University Press.

Boltanski, Luc. 1999. *Distant Suffering*. Cambridge: Cambridge University Press.

Boorstin, Daniel. 1961. *The Image: A Guide to Pseudo-Events in America*. New York: Harper.

Boudana, Sandrine. 2012. "The Unbearable Lightness of the Fait Divers." *Critical Studies in Media Communication* 29, no. 3 (September): 202–19.

Bourdieu, Pierre. 1990. "The Uses of the 'People.'" In *Other Words: Essays towards a Reflexive Sociology*, 150–55. Stanford, Calif.: Stanford University Press.

Boyle, Elizabeth Heger, and Andrea Hoeschen. 2001. "Theorizing the Form of Media Coverage over Time." *Sociological Quarterly* 42, no. 4 (Fall): 511–27.

Bradbury, Ray. 1953. *Fahrenheit 451*. New York: Ballantine.

Bradlee, Ben. 1995. *A Good Life*. New York: Simon and Schuster.

Breed, Warren. 1955. *The Newspaperman, News, and Society*. PhD diss., Columbia University.

Briggs, Asa. 1982. *The Future of Broadcasting*, edited by Richard Hoggart and Janet Morgan, 20–41. London: Macmillan.

Brinkley, Alan. 2010. *The Publisher: Henry Luce and His American Century*. New York: Knopf.

Brint, Steven. 1994. *In an Age of Experts*. Princeton, N.J.: Princeton University Press.

Brooker-Gross, Susan R. 1985. "The Changing Concept of Place in the News." In Burgess and Gold, 1985, 63–85.

Brown, Jane Delano, Carl R. Bybee, Stanley T. Wearden, and Dulcie Murdoch Straughan. 1987. "Invisible Power: Newspaper News Sources and the Limits of Diversity." *Journalism Quarterly* 64, no. 1 (Spring): 45–54.

Buchanan, Carrie. 2009. "Sense of Place in the Daily Newspaper." *Aether* 4 (Spring): 62–84.

Bureau of the Census. 1976. "Historical Statistics of the United States: Colonial Times to 1970." Communications, 775–810. Washington, D.C.: U.S. Department of Commerce.

Burgess, Jacquelin A., and John R. Gold, eds. 1985. *Geography, the Media, and Popular Culture*. London: Croom Helm.

Buzenberg, Susan, and Bill Buzenberg, eds. 1999. *Salant, CBS, and the Battle for the Soul of Broadcast Journalism*. Boulder, Colo.: Westview.

Byatt, A. S. 2000. *The Biographer's Tale*. London: Chatto and Windus.

Byerly, Carolyn M., and Karen Ross. 2006. *Women and Media*. Malden, Mass.: Blackwell.

Campbell, Laurence R., and Roland E. Wolseley. 1949. *Newsmen at Work*. Boston: Houghton Mifflin.

Campbell, Vincent. 2004. *Information Age Journalism*. London: Arnold.

Campbell, W. Joseph. 2013. "Yellow Journalism" In Sachsman and Bulla, 2013, 3–18.

Campion, Nicholas. 2009. *The Medieval and Modern Worlds*. Vol. 2 of *A History of Western Astrology*. New York: Continuum.

Cappella, Joseph N., and Kathleen Hall Jamieson. 1997. *Spiral of Cynicism*. New York: Oxford University Press.

Carey, James W. 1965. "The Communications Revolution and the Professional Communicator." *Sociological Review* 13, no. S1 (May): 23–38.

———. 1978. "A Plea for the University Tradition." *Journalism Quarterly* 55:846–55.

———. 1986. "How and Why: The Dark Continent of American Journalism." In Manoff and Schudson, 1986, 149–96.

———, ed. 1988. *Media, Myths, and Narratives*. Newbury Park, Calif.: Sage.

———. 1989. *Communication as Culture*. New York: Routledge.

———. 1997. "A Short History of Journalism for Journalists." *Press/Politics* 12, no. 1 (Winter): 3–16.

Casey, Ralph D., ed. 1963. *The Press in Perspective*. Baton Rouge: Louisiana State University Press.

Castells, Manuel. 2000. *The Rise of the Network Society*. 2nd ed. London: Blackwell.

Chafets, Ze'ev. 1990. *Devil's Night*. New York: Random House.

Chambers, Julius. 1921. *News Hunting on Three Continents*. New York: Mitchell Kennerley.

Chapman, Jane. 2005. *Comparative Media History*. Cambridge: Polity.

Charity, Arthur. 1995. *Doing Public Journalism*. New York: Guilford.

Chartier, Roger. 1988. *The Cultural Uses of Print in Early Modern France*. Princeton, N.J.: Princeton University Press.

Chipp, Herschel B. 1968. *Theories of Modern Art*. Berkeley: University of California Press.

Clayman, Steven E., Marc N. Elliott, John Heritage, and Megan K. Beckett. 2010. "A Watershed in White House Journalism: Explaining the Post-1968 Rise of Aggressive Presidential News." *Political Communication* 72, no. 3 (August): 229–47.

Coblentz, Edmond D. 1954. *Newsmen Speak*. Berkeley: University of California Press.

Cohen, Akiba A., Mark Levy, Michael Gurevitch, and Itzhak Roeh. 1996. *Global Newsrooms, Local Audiences*. London: Libbey.

Cohen, Stanley, and Jock Young, eds. 1981. *The Manufacture of News*, rev. ed. London: Constable.

Coleman, Stephen. 2013. *How Voters Feel*. Cambridge: Cambridge University Press.

Commission on Freedom of the Press. 1947. *A Free and Responsible Press*. Report. Chicago: University of Chicago Press.

Connery, Thomas B. 1992. *A Sourcebook of American Literary Journalism*. New York: Greenwood.

Cook, Timothy E. 1998. *Governing with the News*. Chicago: University of Chicago Press.

Corner, John. 1995. *Television Form and Public Address*. London: Arnold.

———. 2001. "'Ideology': A Note on Conceptual Salvage." *Media, Culture, and Society* 23, no. 4 (July): 525–33.

Corrigan, Dan. 1999. *The Public Journalism Movement in America*. New York: Praeger.

Courson, Maxwell Taylor. 1976. "The Newspaper Movies." PhD diss., University of Hawaii.

Cowley, Malcolm. 1947. "A Natural History of American Naturalism." *Kenyon Review* 9 (Summer): 414–35.

Crain, Matthew. 2009. "The Rise of Private Equity Media Ownership in the United States." *International Journal of Communication* 3:208–39.

Crang, Mike, and Nigel Thrift, eds. 2000. *Thinking Space*. London: Routledge.

Crichton, Michael. 1999. *Timeline*. New York: Knopf.

Crossen, Cynthia. 1994. *Tainted Truth*. New York: Simon and Schuster.

Cunningham, Liz. 1995. *Talking Politics*. London: Praeger.

Curran, James, and Toril Aalberg, eds. 2012. *How Media Inform Democracy*. New York: Routledge.

Cushion, Stephen. 2015. *News and Politics*. New York: Routledge.

Danielson, Wayne A., and Dominic L. Lasorsa. 1997. "Perceptions of Social Change." In *Text Analysis for the Social Sciences*, edited by Carl W. Roberts, 103–15. Mahwah, N.J.: Erlbaum.

Darnton, Robert. 1975. "Writing News and Telling Stories." *Daedalus* 104, no. 2 (Spring): 175–94.

———. 1990. "Journalism." In *The Kiss of Lamourette*, 60–93. New York: Norton.

Dautrich, Kenneth, and Thomas H. Hartley. 1999. *How the News Media Fail American Voters*. New York: Columbia University Press.

Davis, Lennard J. 1983. *Factual Fictions*. New York: Columbia University Press.

Dayan, Daniel, and Elihu Katz. 1992. *Media Events*. Cambridge, Mass.: Harvard University Press.

de Burgh, Hugo, ed. 2000. *Investigative Journalism*. London: Routledge.

Desmond, Robert W. 1937. *The Press and World Affairs*. New York: D. Appleton-Century.

Dewey, John. 1927. *The Public and Its Problems*. New York: Holt, Rinehart.

Dobelli, Rolf. 2013. *The Art of Thinking Clearly*. New York: Harper.

Doherty, Richard, and Kevin G. Barnhurst. 2009. "Controlling Nature." *Journal of Broadcasting and Electronic Media* 53, no. 2 (June): 1–16.

Dominick, Joseph. 1977. "Geographic Bias in National TV News." *Journal of Communication* 27, no. 1 (March): 94–99.

Donnelly, Gerard, and Joseph R. Blaney, eds. 2003. *Technological Issues in Broadcast Education*. Westport, Conn.: Praeger.

Donovan, Robert J., and Ray Scherer. 1992. *Unsilent Revolution*. New York: Cambridge University Press.

Donsbach, Wolfgang. 2008. *International Encyclopedia of Communication*, 12 vols. Oxford: Blackwell.

Dreier, Peter. 1982. "The Position of the Press in the U.S. Power Structure." *Social Problems* 29, no. 3 (February): 298–310.

Duggan, Lisa, and Nan Hunter. 2006. *Sex Wars*. New York: Routledge.

Eagleton, Terry. 1991. *Ideology*. London: Verso.

Eco, Umberto. 1989. *The Role of the Reader*. Bloomington: Indiana University Press.

———. 1990. *The Limits of Interpretation*. Bloomington: Indiana University Press.

Ehrlich, Matthew C., and Joe Saltzman. 2015. *Heroes and Scoundrels*. Urbana: University of Illinois Press.

Eisenstein, Elizabeth L. 2012. *The Printing Revolution in Early Modern Europe*. 2nd ed. Cambridge: Cambridge University Press.

Ekecrantz, Jan. 1997. "Journalism's 'Discursive Events' and Sociopolitical Change in Sweden, 1925–87." *Media, Culture, and Society* 19, no. 3 (July): 393–412.

Eliasoph, Nina. 1988. "Routines and the Making of Oppositional News." *Critical Studies in Mass Communication* 5, no. 4 (December): 313–34.

Emerson, Ralph Waldo. 1841. "Self-reliance." In *Essays*, 1841, 37–73.

———. 1849. "Introductory Lecture on the Times." In *Nature*, 1849, 249–82.

Emery, Michael. 1989. "An Endangered Species." *Gannett Center Journal* 3, no. 4 (Fall): 151–64.

English, Earl, Clarence Hach, and Tom E. Rolnicki. 1990. *Scholastic Journalism*. 8th ed. Ames: Iowa State University Press.

Epstein, Edward Jay. 1973. *News from Nowhere*. New York: Vintage.

Epstein, Joseph. 1991. *Partial Payments*. New York: Norton.

Ericson, Richard V., Patricia M. Baranek, and Janet B. L. Chan. 1987. *Visualizing Deviance*. Toronto: University of Toronto Press.

———. 1989. *Negotiating Control*. Toronto: University of Toronto Press.

Errico, Marcus. 1997. "The Evolution of the Summary News Lead." *Media History Monographs* 1, no. 1.

Esch, Deborah. 1999. *In the Event*. Stanford, Calif.: Stanford University Press.

Esser, Frank, and Andrea Umbricht. 2014. "The Evolution of Objective and Interpretative Journalism in the Western Press." *Journalism and Mass Communication Quarterly* 91, no. 2 (June): 229–49.

Ettema, James S., and Limor Peer. 1996. "Good News from a Bad Neighborhood." *Journalism and Mass Communication Quarterly* 73, no. 4 (Winter): 835–56.

Fallows, James M. 1996. *Breaking the News*. New York: Pantheon.

Featherstone, Mike, and Scott Lash, eds. 1999. *Spaces of Culture*. London: Sage.

Feldman, Stephen M. 2008. *Free Expression and Democracy in America*. Chicago: University of Chicago Press.

Ferrarotti, Franco. 1990. *Time, Memory, and Society*. New York: Greenwood.

Feuer, Jane. 1983. "The Concept of Live Television." In *Regarding Television*, edited by E. Ann Kaplan, 12–21. Los Angeles: University Publications of America.

Fidler, Roger F. 1997. *Mediamorphosis*. Newbury Park, Calif.: Pine Forge.

Fink, Katherine, and Michael Schudson. 2014. "The Rise of Contextual Journalism, 1950s–2000s." *Journalism* 15, no. 1 (January): 3–20.

Fishkin, Shelley Fisher. 1985. *From Fact to Fiction*. New York: Oxford University Press.

Fishman, Mark. 1980. *Manufacturing the News*. Austin: University of Texas Press.

Flournoy, Don M., and Robert K. Stewart. 1997. *CNN: Making News in the Global Market*. Luton, U.K.: University of Luton Press.

Forde, Kathy Roberts. 2007. "Discovering the Explanatory Report in American Newspapers." *Journalism Practice* 1, no. 2 (June): 227–44.

Foucault, Michel. 1999. "Of Other Spaces." In *Visual Culture Reader*, edited by Nicholas Mirzoeff, 237–44. London: Routledge.

Fowler, Roger. 1991. *Language in the News*. New York: Routledge.

Francke, Warren. 1985. "Sensationalism and the Development of 19th-Century Reporting." *Journalism History* 12, nos. 3–4 (Winter–Autumn): 80–85.

Franklin, Benjamin. 1950. "Advice to a Young Tradesman." *Poor Richard's Almanack*, 132–34. New York: Modern Library.

Fraser, Julius T. 2003. "Time Felt, Time Understood." *KronoScope* 3, no. 1 (January): 15–26.

Friedland, Lewis A. 1992. *Covering the World*. New York: Twentieth Century Fund.

Fuller, Jack. 1996. *News Values*. Chicago: University of Chicago Press.

———. 2010. *What Is Happening to News*. Chicago: University of Chicago Press.

Gade, Peter, Scott Abel, Michael Antecol, Hsueh Hsiao-Yin, Janice Hume, Jack Morris, Ashley Packard, Susan Willey, Nancy Fraser, and Keith Sanders. 1998. "Journalists' Attitudes toward Civic Journalism Media Roles." *Newspaper Research Journal* 19, no. 4 (Fall): 10–26.

Galtung, Johan, and Mari Holmboe Ruge. 1965. "The Structure of Foreign News." *Journal of Peace Research* 2, no. 1 (January): 64–90.

———. 1981. "Structuring and Selecting News." In Cohen and Young, 52–63.

Gans, Herbert J. 1979. *Deciding What's News*. New York: Pantheon.

Garcelon, Marc. 2006. "The 'Indymedia' Experiment." *Convergence* 12, no. 1 (February): 55–82.

Garcia, Mario R., and Pegie Stark. 1991. *Eyes on the News*. St. Petersburg, Fla.: Poynter Institute.

Gartner, Michael. 1997. "Public Journalism." *Media Studies Journal* 11, no. 1 (Winter): 69–73.

Geertz, Clifford. 1980. "Blurred Genres." *American Scholar* 29, no. 2 (March): 165–79.

Gell, Alfred. 1992. *The Anthropology of Time*. Oxford: Berg.

Gentzkow, Matthew, and Jesse M. Shapiro. 2010. "Ideological Segregation Online and Offline." National Bureau of Economic Research Working Paper 15916, Cambridge, Mass.

Gerbner, George, Larry Gross, and Nancy Signorielli. 1976. "Living with Television." *Journal of Communication* 26, no. 2 (Spring): 172–94.

Gerbner, George, and George Marvanyi. 1977. "The Many Worlds of the World's Press." *Journal of Communication* 52, no. 1 (Winter): 52–66.

Gibson, Mark. 2007. *Culture and Power*. Oxford: Berg.

Gibson, Rhonda, and Joe Bob Hester. 2001. "Reporters as Sources." *Web Journal of Mass Communication Research* 5, no. 1 (December), www.scripps.ohiou.edu/wjmcr.

Giddens, Anthony. 1987. *Social Theory and Modern Sociology*. Cambridge: Polity.

Gilboa, Eytan. 2003. "Television News and U.S. Foreign Policy." *Press/Politics* 8, no. 4 (Fall): 97–113.

Gilliam, Franklin D., Jr., Nicholas A. Valentino, and Matthew N. Beckmann. 2002. "Where You Live and What You Watch." *Political Research Quarterly* 55, no. 4 (December): 755–80.

Gimpel, James, and Jason E. Schuknecht. 2003. *Patchwork Nation*. Ann Arbor: University of Michigan Press.

Gitlin, Todd. 1980. *The Whole World Is Watching*. Berkeley: University of California Press.

———, ed. 1987. *Watching Television*. New York: Pantheon.

Gleick, James. 1999. *Faster*. New York: Pantheon.

Goffman, Ervin. 1959. *The Presentation of Self in Everyday Life*. New York: Anchor.

Goldberg, Bernard. 2001. *Bias*. Washington, D.C.: Regnery.

Goldenberg, Edie N. 1975. *Making the Papers*. Lexington, Mass.: Heath.

Golding, Peter, and Philip Elliott. (1979) 1999. "Making the News." In *News: A Reader*, edited by Howard Tumber, 112–20. Oxford: Oxford University Press.

Goldman, Peter, Thomas M. DeFrank, Mark Miller, Andrew Murr, and Tom Mathews. 1994. *Quest for the Presidency*. College Station: Texas A&M University Press.

Goldstein, Tom, ed. 1989. *Killing the Messenger*. New York: Columbia University Press.

Gombrich, Ernst H. 1980. "Standards of Truth: The Arrested Image and the Moving Eye." *Critical Inquiry* 7, no. 2 (Winter): 237–73.

Gonzenbach, William J., M. David Arant, and Robert L. Stevenson. 1992. "The World of U.S. Network Television News." *Gazette* 50, no. 1 (August): 53–72.

Good, Howard. 1986. *Acquainted with the Night*. Metuchen, N.J.: Scarecrow.

Gorak, Jan. 1987. *God the Artist*. Urbana: University of Illinois Press.

Graber, Doris A. 1990. "Seeing Is Remembering." *Journal of Communication* 40, no. 3 (September): 134–55.

———. 2006. *Mass Media and American Politics*. 7th ed. Washington, D.C.: Congressional Quarterly Press.

Grant, Gerald. 1974. "The 'New Journalism' We Need." In *The Reporter as Artist*, edited by Ronald Weber, 263–70. New York: Hastings House.

Greenberg, David. 2003. *Nixon's Shadow*. New York: Norton.

Greer, Jennifer, and Donica Mensing. 2004. "U.S. News Web Sites Better, But Small Papers Still Lag." *Newspaper Research Journal* 25, no. 2 (Spring): 98–112.

Griffith, Robert. 1970. *The Politics of Fear*. Lexington: University Press of Kentucky.

Hacking, Ian. 1990. *The Taming of Chance*. Cambridge: Cambridge University Press.

———. 2000. *The Social Construction of What?* Cambridge, Mass.: Harvard University Press.

Hall, Edward T. 1980. *The Silent Language*. Westport, Conn.: Greenwood.

———. 1983. *The Dance of Life*. Garden City, N.Y.: Anchor.

Hall, Stuart. 1981. "The Determination of News Photographs." In Cohen and Young, 1981, 226–43.

Hall, Stuart, Chas Crichter, Tony Jefferson, John Clarke, and Brian Roberts. 1978. *Policing the Crisis*. New York: Holmes and Meier.

Hallin, Daniel C. 1986. "Where?" In Manoff and Schudson, 1986, 109–45.

———. 1994. *We Keep America on Top of the World: Television Journalism and the Public Sphere*. New York: Routledge.

———. 2006. "The Passing of the 'High Modernism' of American Journalism Revisited." *Political Communication Report* 16, no. 1 (Winter), www.political communication.org.

Hallin, Daniel C., Robert Karl Manhoff, and Judy K. Weddle. 1993. "Sourcing Patterns of National Security Reporters." *Journalism Quarterly* 70, no. 4 (Winter): 753–66.

Hallin, Daniel C., and Stylianos Papathanassopoulos. 2002. "Political Clientelism and the Media: Southern Europe and Latin America in Comparative Perspective." *Media, Culture, and Society* 24, no. 2 (March): 175–95.

Hamilton, John Maxwell. 1988. *Main Street America and the Third World*. Cabin John, Md.: Seven Locks.

Hamilton, Maxwell, and Eric Jenner. 2004. "Redefining Foreign Correspondence." *Journalism* 5, no. 3 (August): 301–21.

Hansen, Kathleen A. 1991. "Source Diversity and Newspaper Enterprise Journalism." *Journalism Quarterly* 68, no. 3 (Fall): 474–82.

Hardt, Hanno. 1998. *Interactions: Critical Studies in Communication, Media, and Journalism*. Lanham, Md.: Rowman and Littlefield.

Hardt, Hanno, and Bonnie Brennen, eds. 1995. *Newsworkers: Toward a History of the Rank and File*. Minneapolis: University of Minnesota Press.

Harris, Roy J. 2007. *Pulitzer's Gold: Behind the Prize for Public Service Journalism*. Columbia: University of Missouri Press.

Hartley, John. 1982. *Understanding News*. Edited by John Fiske. London: Routledge.

———. 1996. *Popular Reality: Journalism, Modernity, Popular Culture*. London: Arnold.

Harvey, David. 1989. *The Condition of Postmodernity: An Enquiry into the Origins of Cultural Change*. London: Basil Blackwell.

———. 2003. *Paris, Capital of Modernity*. New York: Routledge.

Haskell, Thomas. (1998) 2000. *Objectivity Is Not Neutrality: Explanatory Schemes in History*. Baltimore, Md.: Johns Hopkins University Press.

Hegel, Georg Wilhelm Friedrich. 2002. *Miscellaneous Writings of G. W. F. Hegel*. Translated by Jon Bartley Stewart. Evanston, Ill.: Northwestern University Press.

Hellmann, John. 1981. *Fables of Fact: The New Journalism as New Fiction*. Urbana: University of Illinois Press.

Henry, William A., III. 1985. *Visions of America: How We Saw the 1984 Election*. Boston: Atlantic.

Herbst, Susan. 1993. *Numbered Voices: How Opinion Polling Has Shaped American Politics*. Chicago: University of Chicago Press.

Heritage, John, and Steven E. Clayman. 2013. "The Changing Tenor of Questioning over Time: Tracking a Question Form across U.S. Presidential News Conferences, 1953–2000." *Journalism Practice* 7, no. 4 (August): 481–501.

Hero, Alfred O. 1959. *Mass Media and World Affairs*. Boston: World Peace Foundation.

Hess, Stephen. 1981. *The Washington Reporters*. Washington, D.C.: Brookings.

Hester, Al. 1971. "An Analysis of News Flow from Developed and Developing Nations." *Gazette* 17, no. 1 (February): 29–43.

———. 1978. "Five Years of Foreign News on U.S. Television Evening Newscasts." *Gazette* 24, no. 1 (February): 86–95.

Hilliard, Robert L., and Michael C. Keith. 2005. *The Broadcast Century and Beyond: A Biography of American Broadcasting*. 4th ed. Boston: Elsevier/Focal.

Hjarvard, Stig. 1995. "TV News Flow Studies Revisited." *European Journal of Communication* 5, no. 2–3 (Summer–Autumn): www.cios.org/getfile/Hjarvard_V5N2395.

———. 2000. "Proximity: The Name of the Ratings Game." *Nordicom Review* 21, no. 2 (June): 63–81.

Houston, Brant. 2010. "The Future of Investigative Journalism." The Future of News issue. *Daedalus* 139, no. 2 (Spring): 45–56.

Howe, Peter D. 2009. "Newsworthy Spaces: The Semantic Geographies of Local News." *Aether: The Journal of Media Geography* 4 (Spring): 43–61.

Høyer, Svennik, and Hedda A. Nossen. 2015. "Revisions of the News Paradigm: Changes in Stylistic Features between 1950 and 2008 in the Journalism of Norway's Largest Newspaper." *Journalism* 16, no. 4 (May): 536–52.

Hughes, Thomas P. 1983. *Networks of Power: Electrification in Western Society*. Baltimore, Md.: Johns Hopkins University Press.

Husselbee, Paul L., and Guido H. Stempel. 1997. "Contrast in U.S. Media Coverage of Two Major Canadian Elections." *Journalism and Mass Communication Quarterly* 74, no. 3 (Autumn): 591–601.

Hutchinson, Thomas H. 1948. *Here Is Television: Your Window to the World*. Rev. ed. New York: Hastings House.

Huxford, John E. 2007. "The Proximity Paradox: Live Reporting, Virtual Proximity, and the Concept of Place in the News." *Journalism* 8, no. 6 (December): 657–74.

Illich, Ivan. 1973. *Tools for Conviviality*. New York: Harper and Row.

Innis, Harold. 1964. *The Bias of Communication*. 2nd ed. Toronto: University of Toronto Press.

International Press Institute. 1953. *The Flow of the News*. Zurich: IPI.

Irwin, Will. 1969. *The American Newspaper*. Ames: Iowa State University Press.

Iyengar, Shanto. 1991. *Is Anyone Responsible? How Television Frames Political Issues*. Chicago: University of Chicago Press.

Jacobs, Ronald N. 1996. "Producing the News, Producing the Crisis: Narrativity, Television, and News Work." *Media, Culture, and Society* 18, no. 3 (July): 373–97.

Janes, Robert W. 1958. "A Technique for Describing Community Structure through Newspaper Analysis." *Social Forces* 37, no. 2 (December): 104–5.

Jaworski, Adam, Richard Fitzgerald, and Deborah Morris. 2003. "Certainty and Speculation in News Reporting of the Future: The Execution of Timothy McVeigh." *Discourse Studies* 5, no. 1 (February): 33–49.

Jenkins, Henry. 2008. *Convergence Culture*. New York: NYU Press.

Jenson White, Kathryn. 2008. "News Cycles." In Donsbach, 2008, vol. 7, 3241–43.

Johnstone, John W. C., Edward J. Slawski, and William W. Bowman. 1976. *The News People: A Sociological Portrait of American Journalists and Their Work*. Urbana: University of Illinois Press.

Jones, Steve. 2008. "Television News: Geographic and Source Biases, 1992–2004." *International Journal of Communication* 2 (February): 223–52.

———. 2012. *Communication @ the Center*. New York: Hampton.

Jouhaud, Christian. 1987. "Printing the Event: From La Rochelle to Paris." In *The Culture of Print: Power and the Uses of Print in Early Modern Europe*, edited by Roger Chartier, 290–335. Translated by Lydia G. Cochrane. Princeton, N.J.: Princeton University Press.

Juergens, George. 1966. *Joseph Pulitzer and the* New York World. Princeton, N.J.: Princeton University Press.

Juntunen, Laura, and Esa Väliverronen. 2010. "Politics of Sexting: Re-negotiating the Boundaries of Private and Public in Political Journalism." *Journalism Studies* 11, no. 6 (November): 817–31.

Kansas, Dave, and Todd Gitlin. 1999. "What's the Rush?" *Media Studies Journal* 13, no. 2 (Spring/Summer): 72–77.

Kaplan, Amy. (1988) 1992. *The Social Construction of American Realism*. Chicago: University of Chicago Press.

Kaplan, Frank L. 1979. "The Plight of Foreign News in the U.S. Mass Media." *Gazette* 25, no. 4 (November): 233–43.

Kaplan, Richard L. 2002. *Politics and the American Press*. Cambridge: Cambridge University Press.

Katz, Elihu. 1989. "Journalists as Scientists." *American Behavioral Scientist* 33, no. 2: 238–46.

Kayser, Jacques. 1953. *One Week's News*. Paris: UNESCO.

Kazin, Alfred. 1942. *On Native Grounds*. New York: Harcourt Brace.

Kellerman, Aharon. 1984. "Telecommunications and the Geography of Metropolitan Areas." *Progress in Human Geography* 8, no. 2 (June): 222–46.

Kellerman, Donald. 1992. "America's Love-Hate Relationship with the Press." *Media Studies Journal* 6, no. 4 (Fall): 80–92.

Kellner, Douglas. 2004. "9/11, Spectacles of Terror, and Media Manipulation." *Critical Discourse Studies* 1, no. 1 (April): 41–64.

Kennedy, George, Daryl R. Moen, and Don Ranly. 1984. *The Writing Book*. Englewood Cliffs, N.J.: Prentice-Hall, 1984.

Kern, Stephen. 2003. *The Culture of Time and Space*. Cambridge, Mass.: Harvard University Press.

Kliesch, Ralph E. 1991. "The U.S. Press Corps Abroad Rebounds." *Newspaper Research Journal* 12, no. 1 (Winter): 24–31.

Knorr-Cetina, Karen. 1981. *The Manufacture of Knowledge*. Oxford: Pergamon.

Knox, John. 2007. "Visual-Verbal Communication on Online Newspaper Home Pages." *Visual Communication* 6, no. 1 (February): 19–53.

Koch, Tom. 1991. *Journalism for the 21st Century*. New York: Greenwood.

Kovach, Bill, and Tom Rosenstiel. 2007. *The Elements of Journalism*. Revised edition. New York: Three Rivers.

Kuhn, Thomas S. (1962) 1996. *The Structure of Scientific Revolutions*. Chicago: University of Chicago Press.

Kurtz, Howard. 1998. *Spin Cycle: Inside the Clinton Propaganda Machine*. New York: Simon and Schuster.

Kutler, Stanley I. 1990. *The Wars of Watergate*. New York: Knopf.

Kutrovátz, Gábor, and Gábor Á. Zemplén. 2011. "Experts in Dialogue." *Argumentation* 25, no. 3 (August): 275–83.

Lacy, Stephen, and James M. Bernstein. 1988. "Daily Newspaper Content's Relationship to Publication Cycle and Circulation Size." *Newspaper Research Journal* 9, no. 2 (Winter): 49–57.

Ladd, Jonathan M. 2011. *Why Americans Hate the Media and How It Matters*. Princeton, N.J.: Princeton University Press.

Lakatos, Imre. 1974. "Falsification and the Methodology of Scientific Research Programmes." In *Criticism and the Growth of Knowledge*, edited by Imre Lakatos and Alan Musgrave, 91–196. New York: Cambridge University Press.

Lambeth, Edmund B. 1992. *Committed Journalism*. Bloomington: Indiana University Press.

Landers, James. 2005. "*The National Observer*, 1962–77." *Journalism History* 31, no. 1 (Spring): 19–22.

Lang, Gladys Engel, and Kurt Lang. 1983. *The Battle for Public Opinion*. New York: Columbia University Press.

Larson, James F. 1984. *Television's Window on the World*. Norwood, N.J.: Ablex.

Larson, James F., and Andy Hardy. 1977. "International Affairs Coverage on Network Television News: A Study of News Flow." *Gazette* 23, no. 4 (November): 241–56.

Latour, Bruno. 2004. "Why Has Critique Run Out of Steam? *Critical Inquiry* 30, no. 2 (Winter): 225–48.

Lawrence, Nathaniel. (1971) 1993. "Time Represented as Space." In *Basic Issues in the Philosophy of Time*, edited by Eugene Freeman and Wilfrid Sellars, 123–32. LaSalle, Ill.: Open Court.

Leach, William. 1993. *Land of Desire*. New York: Pantheon.

Lee, Seow Ting, and Crispin C. Maslog. 2005. "War or Peace Journalism?" *Journal of Communication* 55, no. 2 (June): 311–29.

Lefebvre, Henri. 1991. *The Production of Space*. London: Basil Blackwell.

Leibler, Carol M., Joseph Schwartz, and Todd Harper. 2009. "Queer Tales of Morality." *Journal of Communication* 59, no. 4 (December): 653–75.

Lelyveld, Joseph. 1985. *Move Your Shadow*. New York: Times Books.

Lent, John A. 1977. "Foreign News in American Media." *Journal of Communication* 27, no. 3 (March): 46–51.

Levy, Mark R. 1981. "Disdaining the News." *Journal of Communication* 31, no. 3 (Summer): 24–31.

Lewis, Earl, and Heidi Ardizzone. 2001. *Love on Trial*. New York: Norton.

Lewis, Justin, Stephen Cushion, and James Thomas. 2005. "Immediacy, Convenience, or Engagement?" *Journalism Studies* 6, no. 4 (November): 461–77.

Line, W. C. 1979. *News Writing for Non-Professionals*. Chicago: Nelson-Hall.

Lippmann, Walter. 1922. *Public Opinion*. New York: Harcourt, Brace.

Lizcano Fernández, Emmánuel. 2006. *Metáforas que nos piensan*. Madrid: Ediciones Bajo Cero.

Lobato, Ramon, Julian Thomas, and Dan Hunter. 2011. "Histories of User-Generated Content." *International Journal of Communication* 5:899–914.

Luhmann, Niklas. 1979. *Trust and Power*. New York: Wiley.

Lukács, György. 1971. *History and Class Consciousness*. Cambridge, Mass.: MIT Press.

Lule, Jack. 2001. *Daily News, Eternal Stories*. New York: Guilford, 2001.

Lull, James, and Stephen Hinerman, eds. 1997. *Media Scandals*. London: Polity.

MacDougall, Curtis D. (1938) 1972. *Interpretive Reporting*. 6th ed. New York: Macmillan.

Machin, David, and Sarah Niblock. 2006. *News Production*. London: Routledge.

MacNeil, Neil. 1945. "The Presentation of News." In *The Newspaper: Its Making and Its Meaning*, 125–45. New York: Scribner's.

Manoff, Robert Karl, and Michael Schudson, eds. 1986. *Reading the News*. New York: Pantheon.

Mannheim, Karl. 1985. *Ideology and Utopia*. New York: Harcourt.

Marcus, Robert D., and Anthony Marcus, eds. 1998. "Red Scare." In *On Trial*, vol. 2, 136–51. St. James, N.Y.: Brandywine.

Markel, Lester, and Audrey March. 1976. *Global Challenge to the United States*. Cranbury, N.J.: Associated University Presses.

Marlane, Judith. 1999. *Women in Television News Revisited*. Austin: University of Texas Press.

Marriott, Stephanie. 1996. "Time and Time Again." *Media, Culture, and Society* 18, no. 1 (January): 69–86.

———. 2007. "American Election Night and the Journalism of Assertion." *Journalism* 8, no. 6 (December): 698–717.

Marsden, George M. 2006. *Fundamentalism in American Culture*. 2nd ed. New York: Oxford University Press.

Martin, Shannon Rossi. 1988. "Proximity of Event as a Factor in Selection of News Sources." *Journalism and Mass Communication Quarterly* 65, no. 4 (December): 986–89, 1043.

Marx, Groucho. 1965. *The Groucho Letters*. New York: Simon and Schuster.

Matheson, Donald. 2000. "The Birth of News Discourse." *Media, Culture, and Society* 22, no. 5 (September): 557–73.

May, Jon, and Nigel Thrift. 2001. *Timespace*. London: Routledge.

McAuliffe, Kevin Michael. 1978. *The Great American Newspaper*. New York: Scribner's.

McCarthy, Mary. 1960. "The Fact in Fiction." *Partisan Review* 27, no. 3 (Summer): 438–58.

McChesney, Fred S. 1987. "Sensationalism, Newspaper Profits and the Marginal Value of Watergate." *Economic Inquiry* 25, no. 1 (January): 135–44.

McCourt, Tom. 1999. *Conflicting Communication Interests in America*. Westport, Conn.: Praeger.

McGerr, Michael E. 1986. *The Decline of Popular Politics*. New York: Oxford.

McGrail, J. Patrick. 2008. "Sensationalism, Narrativity and Objectivity." PhD diss., Syracuse University.

McNair, Brian. 2010. *Journalists in Film*. Edinburgh: Edinburgh University Press.

Mears, Walter R. 2009. "Finding News Despite the Noise." *Journalism Studies* 10, no. 3 (May): 423–26.

Mellinger, Gwyneth. 2013. *Chasing Newsroom Diversity*. Urbana: University of Illinois Press.

Merchant, Carolyn. 2004. *Reinventing Eden*. New York: Routledge.

Merritt, Davis "Buzz." 1998. *Public Journalism and Public Life*. 2nd ed. Mahwah, N.J.: Erlbaum.

Meyer, Philip. 1973. *Precision Journalism*. Bloomington: Indiana University Press.

———. 2009. *The Vanishing Newspaper*. 2nd ed. Columbia: University of Missouri Press.

Meyrowitz, Joshua. 1985. *No Sense of Place*. New York: Oxford University Press.

———. 1991. "The Questionable Reality of Media." In *Ways of Knowing*, edited by John Brockman, 141–60. New York: Prentice Hall.

Mills, C. Wright. 1956. *The Power Elite*. New York: Oxford University Press.

Minissale, Gregory. 2013. *The Psychology of Contemporary Art*. Cambridge: Cambridge University Press.

Misztal, Barbara A. 1996. *Trust in Modern Societies*. Cambridge: Polity.

Mitchell, W. J. T., ed. 1983. *The Politics of Interpretation*. Chicago: University of Chicago Press.

Mitchelstein, Eugenia, and Pablo J. Boczkowski. 2009. "Between Tradition and Change." *Journalism* 10, no. 5 (October): 562–86.

Mock, James R., and Cedric Larson. 1968. *Words that Won the War*. New York: Russell and Russell.

Molotch, Harvey, and Marilyn Lester. 1974. "News as Purposive Behavior." *American Sociological Review* 38, no. 1 (February): 101–12.

Morell, J. D. 1846. *An Historical and Critical View of the Speculative Philosophy of Europe in the Nineteenth Century.* Vol. 1.

Morris, Meaghan. 1988. "At Henry Parkes Motel." *Cultural Studies* 2, no. 1: 1–47.

Morris, Robert. 1860. *Tales of Masonic Life.* Louisville, Ky.: Morris and Monsarrat.

Mortimer, Ian. 2008. "What Isn't History?" *History* 93, no. 312 (October): 454–74.

Mosier, Nancy R., and Andrew Ahlgren. 1981. "Credibility of Precision Journalism." *Journalism Quarterly* 58, no. 3 (Autumn): 375–81, 518.

Mott, Frank Luther. 1942. "Trends in Newspaper Content." *Annals of the American Academy of Political and Social Science* 219, no. 1 (January): 60–65.

———. 1952. *The News in America.* Cambridge, Mass.: Harvard University Press.

Moynihan, Daniel P. 1971. "The Presidency and the Press." *Commentary* 51, no. 3 (March): 41–52.

Mulkay, Michael. 1979. *Science and the Sociology of Knowledge.* London: Allen and Unwin.

Murphy, James E. 1974. *The New Journalist.* Journalism Monographs 34. Lexington, Ky.: AEJ.

Mutz, Diana C. 2006. *Hearing the Other Side.* Cambridge: Cambridge University Press.

Neal, Robert M. 1947. *News Gathering and News Writing.* New York: Prentice-Hall.

Nerone, John. 1994. *Violence Against the Press.* New York: Oxford University Press.

———. 2009. "The Death (and Rebirth?) of Working-Class Journalism." *Journalism* 10, no. 3 (June): 353–55.

———. 2013. "The Historical Roots of the Normative Model of Journalism." *Journalism* 14, no. 4 (May): 446–58.

———. 2014. "Temporalities of News." *Journalism and Technological Change,* edited by Martin Schreiber and Clemens Zimmermann, 53–79. Frankfurt: Campus Verlag.

———. 2015. *The Media and Public Life: A History.* London: Polity.

Nerone, John, and Kevin G. Barnhurst. 1995. "Visual Mapping and Cultural Authority." *Journal of Communication* 45, no. 2 (Spring): 9–43.

Neveu, Erik. 2002. "The Local Press and Farmer's Protests in Brittany." *Journalism Studies* 3, no. 1: 53–67.

Niblock, Sarah, and David Machin. 2007. "News Values for Consumer Groups." *Journalism* 8, no. 2 (Spring): 184–204.

Nilsson, Martin P. 1920. *Primitive Time-Reckoning.* London: Lund.

Nordenstrang, Kaarle, and Tapio Varis. 1974. *Television Traffic: A One-Way Street?* Paris: UNESCO.

Norris, Pippa. 1995. "The Restless Searchlight." *Political Communication* 12, no. 4 (October): 357–71.

Nowotny, Helga. 1992. "Time and Social Theory." *Time and Society* 1, no. 3 (September): 421–54.

———. 1994. *Time.* Cambridge: Polity.

Nye, David E. 1990. *Electrifying America.* Cambridge, Mass.: MIT Press.

O'Brien, Tim. 2009. *The Things They Carried.* New York: Mariner.

Ogan, Christine L. 1982. "Development Journalism/Communication." *Gazette* 29, nos. 1/2 (February): 3–13.

O'Malley, Michael. 1990. *Keeping Watch.* Washington, D.C.: Smithsonian Institution Press.

Onu, P. Eze. 1979. "The Dilemma of Presenting an African Image Abroad." *African Studies Review* 22, no. 2 (September): 95–110.

Orvell, Miles. 1989. *The Real Thing*. Chapel Hill: University of North Carolina Press.

Östgaard, Einar. 1965. "Factors Influencing the Flow of News." *Journal of Peace Research* 2, no. 1 (March): 39–63.

Owens, James E. 2008. "Who Produces the Means of Democracy." Master's thesis, University of Illinois at Chicago.

Page, Benjamin I., Robert Y. Shapiro, and Glenn R. Dempsey. 1987. "What Moves Public Opinion?" *American Political Science Review* 81, no. 1 (March): 23–43.

Palmer, Michael. 2003. "News: Ephemera, Data, Artifacts." *Journalism* 4, no. 4 (Fall): 459–76.

Pan, Zhongdang, Chin-Chuan Lee, Joseph Man Chan, and Clement Y. K. So. 2001. "Orchestrating the Family-Nation Chorus." *Mass Communication and Society* 4, no. 3 (Summer): 331–47.

Pantti, Mervi, and Johanna Sumiala. 2009. "Till Death Do Us Join." *Media, Culture, and Society* 31, no. 1 (January): 119–35.

Park, Robert E. 1923. "The Natural History of the Newspaper." *American Journal of Sociology* 29, no. 3 (November): 273–89.

———. 1940. "News as a Form of Knowledge." *American Journal of Sociology* 45, no. 5 (March): 669–86.

Parkes, Don, and Nigel Thrift. 1980. *Time, Spaces, and Places*. New York: Wiley.

Pascal, Blaise. 1941. *Pensées: The Provincial Letters*. New York: Modern Library.

Pasley, Jeffrey L. 2001. *"The Tyranny of Printers."* Charlottesville: University Press of Virginia.

Patterson, Thomas E. 1993. *Out of Order*. New York: Knopf.

———. 2013. *Informing the News*. New York: Vintage.

Perlmutter, David D. 2005. "Photojournalism and Foreign Affairs." *Orbis* 49, no. 1 (Winter): 109–22.

Peters, John Durham. 2001. "Witnessing." *Media, Culture, and Society* 23, no. 6 (November): 707–23.

———. 2012. "Calendar, Clock, Tower." In *Deus in Machina*, edited by Jeremy Stolow, 25–42. New York: Fordham University Press.

Peterson, Theodore. 1956. *Magazines in the Twentieth Century*. Urbana: University of Illinois Press.

Pettegree, Andrew. 2014. *The Invention of News*. New Haven, Conn.: Yale University Press.

Pizer, Donald. 1998. "The Late Nineteenth and Early Twentieth Centuries, 1874–1914." In *Documents of American Realism and Naturalism*, edited by Donald Pizer, 3–17. Carbondale: Southern Illinois University Press.

Plasser, Fritz. 2005. "From Hard to Soft News Standards?" *Press/Politics* 10, no. 2 (Spring): 47–68.

Polelle, Mark. 1999. *Raising Cartographic Consciousness*. Lanham, Md.: Lexington.

Pooley, Jefferson. 2011. "Another Plea for the University Tradition." *International Journal of Communication* 5, no. 2 (September): http://ijoc.org.

Prior, Marcus. 2007. *Post-Broadcast Democracy*. Cambridge: Cambridge University Press.

Ranney, Austin. 1983. *Channels of Power*. New York: Basic.

Rantanen, Terhi. 1997. "The Globalization of Electronic News in the 19th Century." *Media, Culture, and Society* 19, no. 4 (October): 605–20.

———. 2009. *When News Was New*. Oxford: Wiley-Blackwell.

Raymond, Geoffrey. 2000. "The Voice of Authority." *Discourse Studies* 2, no. 3 (August): 354–79.

Reese, Stephen D., and Jane Ballinger. 2001. "The Roots of a Sociology of News." *Journalism and Mass Communication Quarterly* 78, no. 4 (Winter): 641–58.

Relph, Edward. 1976. *Place and Placelessness*. London: Pion.

Rheingold, Howard. 2003. *Smart Mobs*. New York: Perseus.

Ricoeur, Paul. 1984. *Time and Narrative*. Chicago: University of Chicago Press.

Ridout, Travis N., and Rob Mellen Jr. 2007. "Does the Media Agenda Reflect the Candidates' Agenda?" *Press/Politics* 12, no. 2 (Spring): 44–62.

Riffe, Daniel, Charles F. Aust, Ted C. Jones, Barbara Shoemake, and Shyam Sundar. 1994. "The Shrinking Foreign Newshole of the *New York Times*." *Newspaper Research Journal* 15, no. 3 (Summer): 74–88.

Riffe, Daniel, and Arianne Budianto. 2001. "The Shrinking World of Network News." *International Communication Bulletin* 36, nos. 1–2 (Spring): 18–35.

Riffe, Daniel, and Eugene F. Shaw. 1990. "Ownership, Operating, Staffing and Content Characteristics of 'News Radio' Stations." *Journalism Quarterly* 67, no. 4 (Winter): 684–91.

Rifkin, Jeremy. 1987. *Time Wars*. New York: Holt.

Riley, Patricia, Colleen M Keough, Thora Christiansen, Ofer Meilich, and Jillian Pierson. 1998. "Community or Colony." *Journal of Computer-Mediated Communication* 4, no. 1 (September): doi/10.1111/j.1083–6101.1998.tb00086.x.

Robbins, Bruce. 1993. *Secular Vocations*. London: Verso.

Roberts, Nancy L. 2008. "Peace Journalism." In Donsbach, 2008, vol. 8, 3531–33.

Robertson, Stewart. 1930. *Introduction to Modern Journalism*. New York: Prentice-Hall.

Roessler, Patrick. 2004. "Political Communication Messages." In *Comparing Political Communication*, edited by Frank Esser and Barbara Pfetsch, 271–92. Cambridge: Cambridge University Press.

Romano, Carlin. 2012. *America the Philosophical*. New York: Vintage.

Rosen, Jay. 1999. *What Are Journalists For?* New Haven, Conn.: Yale University Press.

Rosenblum, Mort. 1981. *Coups and Earthquakes*. New York: Harper and Row.

———. 1993. *Who Stole the News?* New York: Wiley.

Rosenfeld, Sophia. 2011. *Common Sense*. Cambridge, Mass.: Harvard University Press.

Roshco, Bernard. 1975. *Newsmaking*. Chicago: University of Chicago Press.

Ross, Steven S. 1998. "Journalists' Use of Online Technology and Sources." In *The Electronic Grapevine*, edited by Diane L. Borden and Kerric Harvey, 143–60. Mahwah, N.J.: Erlbaum.

Rosten, Leo. 1937. *The Washington Correspondents*. New York: Harcourt, Brace.

Rudner, Richard. 1953. "The Scientist Qua Scientist Makes Value Judgments." *Philosophy of Science* 20, no. 1 (January): 1–6.

Ryfe, David. 2012. *Can Journalism Survive?* Cambridge: Polity.

Sachsman, David B., and David W. Bulla, eds. 2013. *Sensationalism*. New Brunswick, N.J.: Transaction.

Said, Edward W. 1983. "Opponents, Audiences, Constituencies, and Community." In Mitchell, 1983, 7–32.

Salgado, Susana, and Jesper Strömbäck. 2012. "Interpretive Journalism." *Journalism* 13, no. 2 (January): 144–61.

Santayana, George. 1905. *The Life of Reason*. New York: Scribner's.

Schelling, Thomas C. 1978. *Micromotives and Macrobehavior*. New York: Norton.

Schiller, Herbert I. 1974. "Freedom from the 'Free Flow.'" *Journal of Communication* 24, no. 1 (Winter): 110–17.

Schivelbusch, Wolfgang. 1986. *The Railway Journey*. Berkeley: University of California Press.

Schlesinger, Philip. 1977. "Newsmen and Their Time-Machine." *British Journal of Sociology* 28, no. 3 (September): 336–50.

———. 1978. *Putting "Reality" Together*. London: Sage.

Schofield Clark, Lynn, and Rachel Monserrate. 2011. "High School Journalism and the Making of Young Citizens." *Journalism* 12, no. 4 (May): 417–32.

Schor, Juliet B. 1991. *The Overworked American*. New York: Basic.

Schram, Martin. 1987. *The Great American Video Game*. New York: Morrow.

Schudson, Michael. 1992. *Watergate in American Memory*. New York: Basic.

———. 2001. "The Objectivity Norm in American Journalism." *Journalism* 2, no. 2 (August): 149–70.

———. 2011. *The Sociology of News*. 2nd ed. New York: Norton.

Schulten, Susan. 2001. *The Geographical Imagination in America, 1880–1950*. Chicago: University of Chicago Press.

Schulz, Winfried F. 1982. "News Structure and People's Awareness of Political Events." *Gazette* 30, no. 3 (December): 139–53.

Schwartz, Joan M., and James R. Ryan, eds. 2003. *Picturing Place*. London: Tauris.

Seamon, David, and Jacob Sowers. 2008. "Place and Placelessness." In *Key Texts in Human Geography*, edited by Phil Hubbard, Rob Kitchin, and Gill Valentine, 43–51. London: Sage.

Seib, Philip M. 2001. *Going Live*. Lanham, Md.: Rowman and Littlefield.

———. 2007. *Broadcasts from the Blitz*. Washington, D.C.: Potomac.

———, ed. 2009. *Toward a New Public Diplomacy*. New York: Macmillan.

Sevareid, Eric. 1995. *Not So Wild a Dream*. Columbia: University of Missouri Press.

Seymour-Ure, Colin. 1974. *The Political Impact of Mass Media*. Beverly Hills, Calif.: Sage.

Shafer, Richard. 1991. *Journalists for Change*. Manila: Philippine Press Institute.

Shapiro, Michael J. 1999. "Triumphalist Geographies." In Featherstone and Lash, 1999, 159–74.

Shaw, Donald L., and John W. Slater. 1985. "In the Eye of the Beholder?" *Journalism History* 12, nos. 3–4 (Winter–Autumn): 86–91.

Shrader-Frechette, Kristin S. 1979. "High-Energy Models and the Ontological Status of the Quark." *Synthese* 42, no. 1 (September): 173–89.

Siebert, Frederick S., Theodore Peterson, and Wilbur L. Schramm. 1956. *Four Theories of the Press*. Urbana: University of Illinois Press.

Sigal, Leon V. 1973. *Reporters and Officials*. Lexington, Mass.: Heath.

Sinclair, Upton. 1936. *The Brass Check*. 11th rev. ed. Pasadena, Calif.: printed by author.

Singer, Jane B. 2001. "The Metro Wide Web." *Journalism and Mass Communication Quarterly* 78, no. 1 (Spring): 65–78.

Slide, Anthony, ed. 1987. *Selected Radio and Television Criticism*. London: Scarecrow.

Soderlund, Gretchen. 2013. *Sex Trafficking, Scandal, and the Transformation of Journalism*. Chicago: University of Chicago Press.

Soja, Edward W. 1989. *Postmodern Geographies*. London: Verso.

Soley, Lawrence. 1992. *The News Shapers*. New York: Praeger.

Soloski, John. 1989. "Sources and Channels of Local News." *Journalism Quarterly* 66, no. 4 (Winter): 864–70.

Sontag, Susan. 1977. *On Photography*. New York: Farrar, Straus, and Giroux.

Sparks, Colin, and John Tulloch, eds. 2000. *Tabloid Tales*. Lanham, Md.: Rowman and Littlefield.

Sproule, J. Michael. 1987. "Propaganda Studies in American Social Science." *Quarterly Journal of Speech* 73, no. 1 (February): 60–78.

Sridharan, Uma V., Lori Dickes, and W. Royce Caines. 2002. "Enron: The Social Impact of Business Failure." *American Journal of Business* 17, no. 2 (Fall): www.emeraldinsight .com/journal/ajb.

Stam, Robert. 1983. "Television News and Its Spectator." In *Regarding Television*, edited by E. Ann Kaplan, 23–43. Los Angeles: University Publications of America, 1983.

Stauber, John, and Sheldon Rampton. 2002. *Trust Us, We're Experts! How Industry Manipulates Science and Gambles with your Future*. New York: Tarcher Putnam.

Steele, Catherine A., and Kevin G. Barnhurst. 1996. "The Journalism of Opinion: Network Coverage in U.S. Presidential Campaigns, 1968–1988." *Critical Studies in Mass Communication* 13, no. 3 (September): 187–209.

Steele, Janet E. 1995. "Experts and the Operational Bias of Television News: The Case of the Persian Gulf War." *Journalism and Mass Communication Quarterly* 72, no. 4 (Winter): 799–812.

Stempel, Guido H., III, and Hugh M. Cuthbertson. 1984. "The Prominence and Dominance of News Sources in Newspaper Medical Coverage." *Journalism Quarterly* 61, no. 3 (Autumn): 671–76.

Stephens, Mitchell. 1988. *A History of News: From the Drum to the Satellite*. New York: Viking.

Stevens, John D. 1985. "Sensationalism in Perspective." *Journalism History* 12, nos. 3–4 (Autumn–Winter): 78–79.

———. 1991. *Sensationalism and the New York Press*. New York: Columbia University Press.

Stevenson, Robert L. 1996. "Remapping the News of the World." *Medien Journal* (Austria) 20, no. 4: 41–48.

Steward, Helen. 2012. *A Metaphysics for Freedom*. Oxford: Oxford University Press.

Stille, Alexander. 2002. *The Future of the Past*. New York: Farrar, Straus, and Giroux.

Strange, Jeffrey J., and Elihu Katz, eds. 1998. "The Future of Fact." Special issue. *Annals of the American Academy of Political and Social Science* 560, no. 1 (November).

Sumpter, Randall S. 2000. "Daily Newspaper Editors' Audience Construction Routines: A Case Study." *Critical Studies in Media Communication* 17, no. 3 (September): 334–46.

Sundar, S. Shyam. 1998. "Effect of Source Attribution on Perception of Online News Stories." *Journalism and Mass Communication Quarterly* 75, no. 1 (March): 55–68.

Swinford, Dean. 2001. "Defining Irrealism: Scientific Development and Allegorical Possibility." *Journal of the Fantastic in the Arts* 12, no. 1 (November): 77–89.

Tewksbury, David, and Jason Rittenberg. 2012. *News on the Internet: Information and Citizenship in the 21st Century*. Oxford Studies in Digital Politics. Oxford: Oxford University Press.

Thomas, William I., and Florian Znaniecki. 1927. *The Polish Peasant in Europe and America*, 2 vols. New York: Knopf.

Thompson, E. P. 1967. "Time, Work-Discipline, and Industrial Capitalism." *Past and Present* 38 (December): 56–97.

Thompson, John B. 1995. *The Media and Modernity: A Social Theory of the Media*. Stanford, Calif.: Stanford University Press.

———. 2000. *Political Scandal: Power and Visibility in the Media Age*. Cambridge: Polity.

Tichenor, Phillip J., George A. Donohue, and Clarice N. Olien. 1970. "Mass Media Flow and Differential Growth in Knowledge." *Public Opinion Quarterly* 34, no. 2 (Summer): 159–70.

Toffler, Alvin. 1970. *Future Shock*. New York: Bantam.

Toulmin, Stephen. 1983. "The Construal of Reality." In Mitchell, 1983, 99–117.

Townsend, Robert. 2013. *History's Babel*. Chicago: University of Chicago Press.

Trachtenberg, Alan. 1977. "Ever—the Human Document." In *America and Lewis Hine*, 118–38. New York: Aperture.

Traquina, Nelson. 2004. "Theory Consolidation in the Study of Journalism." *Journalism* 5, no. 1 (February): 97–116.

Trow, George W. S. 1997. *Within the Context of No Context*. New York: Atlantic Monthly Press.

———. 1999. *My Pilgrim's Progress: Media Studies, 1950–1998*. New York: Pantheon.

Trumbull, H. Clay. 1888. *Teaching and Teachers; or, The Sunday-School Teacher's Teaching Work and the Other Work of the Sunday-School Teacher.*

Tuchman, Gaye. 1978. *Making News*. New York: Free Press.

———. 1978. "The Symbolic Annihilation of Women by the Mass Media." In *Hearth and Home*, edited by Gaye Tuchman, Arlene Kaplan Daniels, and James Benet, 3–38. New York: Oxford University Press.

Tunstall, Jeremy. 1999. *The Anglo-American Media Connection*. Oxford: Oxford University Press.

Usher, Nikki. 2014. *Making News at the* New York Times. Ann Arbor: University of Michigan Press.

Vaihinger, Hans. 1968. *The Philosophy of "As if."* New York: Barnes and Noble.

Väliverronen, Esa. 2003. "Mediating Time." In *Media Culture Research Programme*, edited by Päivi Hovi-Wasastjerna, 83–99. Helsinki: Academy of Finland, 2003.

Väliverronen, Jari, and Risto Kunelius. 2012. "From Reporting to Storytelling." In Jones, 2012, 215–29.

van der Poel, Hugo. 1997. "Leisure and the Modularization of Daily Life." *Time and Society* 6, nos. 2/3 (July): 171–94.

van Loon, Joost. 1997. "Chronotopes of/in the Televisualization of the 1992 Los Angeles Riots." *Theory, Culture, and Society* 14, no. 2 (May): 89–104.

Varis, Tapio. 1974. "Global Traffic in Television." *Journal of Communication* 24, no. 1 (March): 102–9.

Virilio, Paul. 1986. *Speed and Politics*. New York: Semiotext(e).

Vonnegut, Kurt, Jr. 1969. *Slaughterhouse-Five*. New York: Delacorte.

Wahl-Jorgensen, Karin. 2007. *Journalists and the Public*. Cresskill, N.J.: Hampton.

Walmsley, D. J. 1980. "Spatial Bias in Australian News Reporting." *Australian Geographer* 14, no. 6: 342–49.

Weaver, David H. 1999. "Who Will Be Journalists in the Next Century?" *Media Studies Journal* 13, no. 2 (Spring/Summer): 24–31.

Weaver, David H., Randal A. Beam, Bonnie J. Brownlee, Paul S. Voakes, and G. Cleveland Wilhoit. 2006. *The American Journalist in the 21st Century*. New York: Routledge.

Weaver, David H., and G. Cleveland Wilhoit. 1991. *The American Journalist*. Bloomington: Indiana University Press.

———. 1996. *The American Journalist in the 1990s*. New York: Routledge.

Weaver, James B., Christopher J. Porter, and Margaret E. Evans. 1984. "Patterns in Foreign News Coverage on U.S. Network TV." *Journalism Quarterly* 61, no. 2 (Summer): 356–63.

Weaver, Paul H. 1994. *News and the Culture of Lying*. New York: Free Press.

Weber, Max. (1958) 1991. "Politics as a Vocation." In *Max Weber: Essays in Sociology*, edited by H. H. Gerth and C. Wright Mills, 77–128. London: Routledge, 1991.

Weldon, Michele. 2007. *Everyman News*. Columbia: University of Missouri Press.

White, Alan. 1970. *Truth*. Garden City, N.Y.: Anchor.

White, David Manning. 1950. "The 'Gate Keeper.'" *Journalism Quarterly* 27, no. 4 (Fall): 383–96.

White, Hayden. *Metahistory*. 1973. Baltimore, Md.: Johns Hopkins University Press.

Whitehead, Alfred North. 1929. *Process and Reality*. New York: Macmillan.

Whitney, D. Charles, Marilyn Fritzler, Steven Jones, Sharon Mazzarella, and Lana Rakow. 1989. "Geographic and Source Biases in Network Television News 1982–1984." *Journal of Broadcasting and Electronic Media* 33, no. 2 (Spring): 159–74.

Wicker, Tom. 1978. *On Press*. New York: Viking.

Wicks, Robert H., and Montague Kern. 1995. "Factors Influencing Decisions by Local Television News Directors to Develop New Reporting Strategies during the 1992 Political Campaign." *Communication Research* 22, no. 2 (Spring): 237–55.

Wijfjes, Huub. 2004. "Getting Truth or Getting Pizzas." In *Trust*, edited by Frank R. Ankersmit and Henk Te Velde, 125–43. Leuven, Belgium: Peeters.

Wilhelm, John. 1963. "The Re-Appearing Foreign Correspondent." *Journalism Quarterly* 40, no. 2 (June): 147–68.

Wilkie, Franc B. 1891. *Personal Reminiscences of Thirty-Five Years of Journalism*.

Williams, Bruce A., and Michael X. Delli Carpini. 2000. "Unchained Reaction." *Journalism* 1, no. 1 (April): 61–85.

Williams, Raymond. 1974. *Television*. London: Fontana.

———. 1989. "Distance." In *Raymond Williams on Television*, edited by Alan O'Connor, 13–21. New York: Routledge.

Wilner, Isaiah. 2006. *The Man Time Forgot*. New York: Harper-Collins.

Wilson, Christopher P. 1985. *The Labor of Words*. Athens: University of Georgia Press.

Wilson, H. T. 1999. "Time, Space and Value." *Time and Society* 8, no. 1 (March): 161–81.

Winburn, Jan. 2003. *Shop Talk and War Stories*. New York: Bedford/St. Martin's.

Winfield, Betty Houchin, and Janice Hume. 2007. "The Continuous Past." *Journalism and Communication Monographs* 9, no. 3 (Autumn): 119–74.

Winter, Ella, and Herbert Shapiro, eds. 1962. *The World of Lincoln Steffens*. New York: Hill and Wang.

Wolseley, Roland E., and Laurence R. Campbell. 1949. *Exploring Journalism*. New York: Prentice-Hall.

Woodward, Julian Laurence. 1930. *Foreign News in American Morning Newspapers*. New York: Columbia University Press.

Wouters, Ruud. 2009. "The Nature of Foreign News." In *News in Europe, Europe on News*, edited by Agnieszka Stepinska, 43–62. Berlin: Logos-Verlag.

Wu, Denis Haoming. 1998. "Investigating the Determinants of International News Flow." *Gazette* 60, no. 6 (December): 493–512.

Zelizer, Barbie. 1990. "Where Is the Author in American TV News?" *Semiotica* 80, nos. 1–2 (June): 37–48.

———. 1992. *Covering the Body*. Chicago: University of Chicago Press.

Zelizer, Barbie, and Stuart Allan, eds. 2002. *Journalism After September 11*. New York: Routledge.

Zillmann, Dolf, and Hans-Bernd Brosius. 2000. *Exemplification in Communication*. Mahwah, N.J.: Erlbaum.

Index

THE HISTORY OF COMMUNICATION

KEVIN G. BARNHURST is a writer and retired university professor. He has been a shoe salesman in Utah and a farm hand in Idaho, was in the U.S. Army Infantry, and has worked as an economist and as an editor and graphic designer. His first book, *Seeing the Newspaper*, was named a Best Book of 1994 by *In These Times* magazine and received a Lowell Mellett Awards Special Citation. *The Form of News*, with John Nerone, received the Outstanding Book Award from the International Communication Association. His edited collection, *Media Queered*, was a Lambda Literary Award finalist. He has written for the *Christian Science Monitor*, *Chicago Tribune*, *Commentary*, *American Scholar*, and other magazines and press syndicates. He lives with his partner, Richard, a scholar of environmental communication, and has three sons living in Bangkok, Reading, UK, and Salem, Mass., and one granddaughter so far.

The University of Illinois Press
is a founding member of the
Association of American University Presses.

———————————————

Composed in 10.25/13 Marat Pro
by Kirsten Dennison
at the University of Illinois Press
Manufactured by Cushing-Malloy, Inc.

University of Illinois Press
1325 South Oak Street
Champaign, IL 61820-6903
www.press.uillinois.edu